THE DERVISHES OF THE NORTH

Rumi, Whirling, and the Making of Sufism in Canada

The thirteenth-century Muslim mystic and poet Jalal al-Din Rumi (1207–1273) is a popular spiritual icon. His legacy is sustained within the mystical and religious practice of Sufism, particularly through renditions of his poetry, music, and the meditation practice of whirling. In Canada, practices associated with Rumi have become ubiquitous in public spaces, such as museums, art galleries, and theatre halls, just as they continue to inform sacred ritual among Sufi communities.

The Dervishes of the North explores what practices associated with Rumi in public and private spaces tell us about Sufism and spirituality, including sacred, cultural, and artistic expressions in the Canadian context. Using Rumi and contemporary expressions of poetry and whirling associated with him, the book captures the lived reality of Sufism through an ethnographic study of communities in Toronto, Montreal, and Vancouver.

Drawing from conversations with Sufi leaders, whirling dervishes, and poets, Merin Shobhana Xavier explores how Sufism is constructed in Canada, particularly at the nexus of Islamic mysticism, Muslim diaspora, spiritual commodity, popular culture, and universal spirituality. Inviting readers with an interest in religion and spirituality, *The Dervishes of the North* illuminates how non-European Christian traditions, like Islam and Sufism, have informed the religious and spiritual terrain of Canada.

MERIN SHOBHANA XAVIER is an assistant professor of religion and diaspora at Queen's University.

The Dervishes of the North

*Rumi, Whirling, and the Making
of Sufism in Canada*

MERIN SHOBHANA XAVIER

UNIVERSITY OF TORONTO PRESS
Toronto Buffalo London

© University of Toronto Press 2023
Toronto Buffalo London
utorontopress.com
Printed in the U.S.A.

ISBN 978-1-4875-4541-3 (cloth)   ISBN 978-1-4875-4546-8 (EPUB)
ISBN 978-1-4875-4545-1 (paper)   ISBN 978-1-4875-4547-5 (PDF)

Library and Archives Canada Cataloguing in Publication

Title: The dervishes of the north : Rumi, whirling, and the making of Sufism in Canada / Merin Shobhana Xavier.
Names: Xavier, Merin Shobhana, author.
Description: Includes bibliographical references and index.
Identifiers: Canadiana (print) 20220480974 | Canadiana (ebook) 20220480990 | ISBN 9781487545413 (cloth) | ISBN 9781487545451 (paper) | ISBN 9781487545475 (PDF) | ISBN 9781487545468 (EPUB)
Subjects: LCSH: Jalāl al-Dīn Rūmī, Maulana, 1207–1273 – Appreciation – Canada. | LCSH: Sufism – Ontario – Toronto. | LCSH: Sufism – Québec (Province) – Montréal. | LCSH: Sufism – British Columbia – Vancouver.
Classification: LCC BP188.8.C3 X38 2023 | DDC 297.40971–dc23

We wish to acknowledge the land on which the University of Toronto Press operates. This land is the traditional territory of the Wendat, the Anishnaabeg, the Haudenosaunee, the Métis, and the Mississaugas of the Credit First Nation.

This book has been published with the help of a grant from the Federation for the Humanities and Social Sciences, through the Awards to Scholarly Publications Program, using funds provided by the Social Sciences and Humanities Research Council of Canada.

University of Toronto Press acknowledges the financial support of the Government of Canada, the Canada Council for the Arts, and the Ontario Arts Council, an agency of the Government of Ontario, for its publishing activities.

To Suganthy Ramkumar (Mami),
May it be love.

Contents

Acknowledgments ix
Note on Transliteration xv

Introduction 3
1 Situating the Study of Sufism in Canada 18
2 Early Sufi Communities in Canada 45
3 *Sama, Shab-i arus,* and Rituals of Remembrance 86
4 The Politics of Consuming Rumi 133
5 Gender Dynamics in Sufi Rituals, Praxis, and Authority 182
Epilogue 223

Notes 235
Bibliography 251
Index 267

Acknowledgments

During the completion of this book I lived, worked, and breathed in Katarokwi (Kingston) and Tkaronto (Toronto). I continue to learn about the traditions, ancestors, and keepers of these lands, especially of the Haudenosaunee and Anishinaabek peoples. As a settler of colour, I recognize that my presence here furthers the displacement of Indigenous peoples who have been and are the protectors of these lands, waters, air, and creatures. As someone who was displaced from the civil war in Sri Lanka, the irony of my presence on Turtle Island is not lost on me: the costs of colonialism, imperialism, and nationalism continue to result in settler-colonial violence and displacement on Turtle Island and around the globe. My solidarity remains with Indigenous communities and their sovereignty, and with all communities suffering oppression and occupation.

The opening for this book would not have been possible without my friend Shams al Haqq Farzad AttarJafari. Farzad and I connected over a decade ago, and even though we have tried collectively to dig through our memories we still can't figure out when our first meeting was. I do remember seeing him turn for the first time in 2009, when I was taken to my first *sama* at the Jerrahi Order in Toronto. I could not have imagined then that this book would be part of my future. Since then, he has become a dear friend and teacher to me, and has even come to spend time with my students, be it in Ithaca, New York, or Kingston, Ontario. He has also welcomed me to collaborate with him on his projects. When I first mentioned this book idea to him and I asked for help getting in touch with Sufis and *samazen*s, especially in Vancouver, he did not miss a beat. If it was not for his phone calls and WhatsApp messages, I would not have been able to connect with most of the dervishes in this book. Farzad (Shams), my deepest gratitude and love to you, Ya Hu!

With the help of Farzad, I connected with John Brozak, who has been gracious with his time, his insights, and his personal archives. John replied to all my questions and detailed queries via emails and texts, welcomed me to

Vancouver gatherings, and put me in touch with various other Sufis across the country. There were many Sufis who spoke with me about their tradition and practice and welcomed me into their spaces. I especially want to thank Ayeda Husain, Seemi Ghazi, and Tawhida Tanya Evanson. I remain grateful for the opportunity to know and learn from strong Sufi women leaders, and I value our friendship. As well, many Sufi teachers welcomed me into their communities and took time to speak with me: Raqib Brian Burke and Linda Burke (thank you, Linda, for helping me pin down Raqib!), Murat Coskun (Baba), Tevfik Aydöner (Baba), Peter Amir O'Loughlin, Majid Buell, Dale Genge, Zainb Paula Ford, Carol Sill, and Nurjan Mirahmadi. Thank you to my dear poet friends and favourite heretics, Sheniz Janmohamed and Zain Bandali, for sharing your voices for this project. My gratitude also goes to the members of the various Sufi communities, especially the Rifai Order, the Jerrahi Order, the Vancouver Rumi Society, Rumi Canada, and Sema Space. Many thanks also to Sara Abdel-Latif for reading portions of this manuscript.

This book has been published with the help of a grant from the Federation for the Humanities and Social Sciences, through the Awards to Scholarly Publications Program, using funds provided by the Social Sciences and Humanities Research Council of Canada. This research was also supported by funds from the Individual Research Grant provided by the American Academy of Religion (AAR) and by research funds from Queen's University. My thanks to my colleagues in the School of Religion for their continued support, especially Adnan Husain, the department chair. And thanks also to all my students, especially those at Ithaca College, where I started thinking about and researching this book, and the students at Queen's University, where I have been very lucky to teach courses on Islam in Canada and Religion and Popular Culture, which provided me the intellectual space to think through some of the ideas I discuss in this book.

I can't thank Len Husband at the University of Toronto Press enough. Len took such good care of this project from start to finish. Thank you to the two anonymous reviewers of the manuscript for your supportive and generous feedback. My dear friend Sheniz Janmohamed provided the stunning cover art for this book (you can find more of her work via Instagram @shenizpoetics). I am grateful to her for sharing her art and to the marketing and design team at the University of Toronto Press for creating a beautiful cover. Thank you also to Christine Robertson, the associate managing editor, and Matthew Kudelka for the meticulous copy editing and Stephen Ullstrom for his work on the index. My thanks to Sarah Morgan for her help in transcribing interviews over the years and to Jacqueline Giesbrecht, my PhD student, for all her help with this project.

As much as writing is a solitary process, I could not have done it without my communities. Thanks to colleagues and friends in Kingston, especially Courtney Szto, Carolyn Prouse, Thashika Pillai, and Crystal Woloshyn. Thanks also to my auntie-vention crew (aka Tamil Aunties) Nedra Rodrigo and Kaitlin Emmanuel. Kaitlin provided me with loving hospitality (with her famous pancakes for breakfast) and took care of me when I needed it the most. Our sessions together full of Tamil food and gossip always came at the right time.

I am particularly grateful to my three Zoom writing partners, without whom this book would never have been written. To Natasha Bissonauth and her cat, Blu (d. 2022). Their faces on my desktop held me accountable during our writing time, and Tash's brilliance continues to push me to think carefully and refine my discourse. I am grateful to Shehnaz Haqqani, a friend and colleague whom I first met during our time at Ithaca College. Our regular writing sessions and check-ins were necessary not only for the completion of this book but also for my mental health during the pandemic.

William Rory Dickson has continued to be a vital soundboard (often without much choice!). When I initially was thinking about writing a book on Sufism in Canada, we began collaborating on it together, but for various reasons I continued the project without him and despite this he still generously read drafts of this manuscript. Of course, I can't thank the Laurier/Waterloo WhatsApp crew enough for the daily dose of laughs and encouragements: Rachel Brown, Jason Ellesworth, Adam Stewart, Zabeen Khamisa, Amar Amarasingam, Rory, and Sahir Dewji (who we are pretty sure has this ridiculous group chat muted). Thank you especially to Zabeen for being such a generous support system during my hardest of days and celebrating me on the best of them. My love to Maxie, Shane, Atlas, and Will for adopting me into the Bai-Martin clan. I still smile when I think about our South Korean trip with absolute joy. To my high school friends Mary Punzalan and Herta Siarkiewicz (Bolgar), it has been such an honour growing up together; and to Bella Zacharioudakis, who rescued me in England and has stuck around since. Finally, my gratitude remains with Vanessa D'Souza for helping me up gently every time I fall.

The final revisions for this book were completed at the Cini Foundation in Isola di San Giorgio Maggiore, Venice, Italy. This has been my third time at the Cini Foundation, and it has all been possible because of the director, Francesco Piraino. I remain ever grateful to Francesco for the opening he provided by welcoming me to such a beautiful place to rest, reflect, and work while having access to the best pastries and gelato (if anyone needs gelato recommendations in Venice, please don't hesitate to be in touch!). Through Francesco I was lucky enough to connect with Feyza Burak-Adli and spend time in Venice together "working." Thank you to you both for your continued friendship, colleagiality, great meals, and laughter.

During COVID-19 a group of scholars who work on Sufism in North America started a monthly Zoom session to build community and engage in conversations around contemporary Sufism. I am very grateful to these wonderful scholars for the opportunity to informally chat and learn from one another about our respective research interests. This group included Marcia Hermansen, Rory, Meena Sharify-Funk, Jason Sparkes, Juliane Hazen, Besnik Sinani, Emily Hanlon, Rose Deighton, Rasul Miller, Megan Sijapati, Geneviève Mercier-Dalphond, and Elliot Bazzano. It is great to be in the company of such a wonderful community of scholars with shared interests and dedication to the field.

It has been a pleasure to be a co-host of the New Books in Islamic Studies podcast with the wonderful crew of Kristian Petersen, SherAli Tareen, and Shehnaz Haqqani. Reading books both in and out of my field and speaking with authors about their projects has been an intellectually transformative experience. I've learned to write better, read better, and ask better questions because of this platform. I remain grateful for the hard work of all the hosts of the channels. Thank you to all the authors who sat down with me for a conversation over the years for your generosity of time. I continue to be inspired by your work and believe that such connections are the best of what the academy can be when we support and learn from one another from a place of intellectual and personal curiosity.

I want to also remember colleagues who have passed on, especially Dr Sue-Je Gage, who was such a beautiful ray of light and joy during my short time at Ithaca College, and the late Dr Priscilla Uppal of York University, one of the foremost literary scholars and Canadian poets. I had the honour of being her graduate assistant during my Master's at York University. Writing on Sufism's literary influence in Canada made me want to reach out to her several times and pick her brilliant mind. I thought of them often during the writing process, especially as women of colour who cultivated academia in their own brilliant reflection against all odds. I am grateful that our paths connected momentarily. I hope you are resting in peace and power.

I am as ever most grateful to Dr Meena Sharify-Funk, my PhD supervisor at Wilfrid Laurier University. She has taught me everything about Sufism, from theory to practice (*adab*). The more time I spend in the academy, the more appreciative I am for having had such a generous and loving supervisor who took care of me holistically. Without Dr Sharify-Funk, I would not be able to think and write about Sufism the way I do or be the teacher I am today.

I want to thank all the front-line workers and health professionals who sacrificed so much during COVID-19 and helped all of us. I hope this global moment shifts us to better ways of living in care and compassion with and for one another, and that we tend to those who are most vulnerable, always. I dedicate this book to my aunt Suganthy Ramkumar (Mami), who lost her battle with cancer in June 2022. She was not a dervish in name but I have always known that she was one of those rare human beings who embodied the essence of the dervish nature: completely selfless, loving, beautiful, and jovial. It is hard enough to live a life dedicated to one's faith. To die in that faith in a state of complete peace and grace as cancer took over seemed entirely impossible, yet she did it without faltering. I know you are resting in love, though I miss you, Mami.

In the end my gratitude remains with everyone, named and unnamed, for all their love and support. However, any errors in what follows are a result of my own limitations, so please forgive me.

Merin Shobhana Xavier

Cini Foundation
Isola di San Giorgio Maggiore
Venice, Italy

Note on Transliteration

I italicize Arabic and Turkish transliteration throughout the study but do not use diacritical markings in my transliterations. In instances where I am quoting from other scholars or texts, I keep their diacritical markings and transliteration practices. Though this book uses both Arabic and Turkish references, I maintain Arabic transliteration practices when I am writing, such as using "a" for instance *sama* instead of *sema* and Mawlana instead of Mevlana, for the sake of consistency.

THE DERVISHES OF THE NORTH

Introduction

Nuit Blanche is an annual all-night festival that hosts various artistic and creative installations throughout the City of Toronto. On 30 September 2017 one of the festival's final events was held at the Aga Khan Museum and Ismaili Centre in Toronto, coinciding with the birthday of the thirteenth-century Muslim Sufi *shaykh* and poet Jalaluddin Rumi (d. 1273).[1] In honour of Rumi's birthday, whirling dervishes (*samazen*s) and musicians participated in an all-night event, which included the recitation of *zikr* (prayer of remembrance) and *sama* (sacred audition). The event attracted many art enthusiasts who were roaming the Nuit Blanche festival, many of whom were likely drawn to Rumi and the whirling dervishes through their exposure to him via popular culture. The audience was also well attended by members of various Sufi and Muslim communities in Toronto, who were there to partake in the spiritual and religious experience; for them, this gathering was a sacred ritual. This part of the audience included members and leaders from the Inayati and Nimatullahi orders as well as various Ismailis – that is, Shia Muslims whose leader is the Aga Khan. But the main event of the evening, *zikr*, was led by the Canadian Institute of Sufi Studies (Rifai Order), whose *shaykh* Murat Coskun, along with his wife Talar, and his dervishes (disciples), led *zikr* for everyone present with live music that included Turkish *ilahi*s (ritual songs). As *zikr* unfolded, members of Rumi Canada presented *sama* or turning. This public event, which brought together the many Sufi communities in Toronto in ritual collaboration at the Ismaili Centre (a religious space) to celebrate the birth of a thirteenth-century Sufi poet, captured the depth and breadth of Sufism as it is experienced in Toronto and more broadly in today's Canada.

In many ways, this was hardly a unique event – similar ones have become common across Toronto and in various other cities, like Vancouver and Montreal. A similar Nuit Blanche event for Rumi was held again in 2018, 2019, and 2022 at the Ismaili Centre (after a hiatus due to COVID-19). Festivals that focus on Rumi and the tradition of turning are often held at cultural centres and music venues in many Canadian cities. For instance, the Tirgan Festival, held at Toronto's Harbourfront from 27 to 30 July 2017, opened with a presentation by members of Rumi Canada and its affiliates, who included *samazens* like Raqib Brian Burke, the *samazen* master (*samazenbashi*), Mira Hunter Burke, Shams al Haqq Farzad AttarJafari, and Farima Berenji. They were accompanied by the musical group Regard Persian. This event, which honoured the Iranian community's contributions to Toronto, was opened by Canada's immigration minister at the time, the Somali Canadian Ahmed Hussen, who spoke proudly about how the Persian diaspora had contributed its culture to cities like Toronto, helping transform it into a more vibrant city and Canada into a more vibrant country. Hussen also underscored how Sufism and Rumi's teachings of tolerance and inclusion upheld the ideal of Canadian multiculturalism. My attendance at these Rumi events and countless others ignited many questions for me about Sufism in Toronto and in Canada, a subject that has been little explored in Canada by scholars of religion, Islam, and spirituality.

Rumi and his legacy were at the centre of many of the events I attended. Rumi, a Muslim scholar, poet, and mystic, is one of the best-known poets in the global west and arguably the most misrepresented. His relationship with a wandering dervish known as Shams of Tabriz radically transformed both his religious path and his mode of expression, which continue to inspire many nearly one thousand years later, though his popularity is not without some controversy. Among spiritual seekers and some in the Muslim community, Rumi's status as a cultural icon has generated its own politics, especially around his transmission and reception, and this requires some unpacking. Who *was* Rumi, and who has the right to claim him? Those contending for his legacy include Muslims, who cringe at the erasure of his Islamic ethos; contesting their hold on him are non-Muslim spiritual seekers, New Age enthusiasts, and Sufis (Muslims and non-Muslims) who see Rumi as their spiritual sage, master, and model of spirituality. This contention includes questions about translations and mistranslations of his poetry; the transmission of his poetry, especially on social media platforms like Twitter, Facebook, and Instagram; and the commodification of his name by social media influencers, yoga studios, cafés, restaurants, designers, poets, and much more. All of this has resulted in cries of cultural and "religious" appropriation (Bucar 2022). As a scholar of contemporary Sufism in North America, I am interested in the popularization of Rumi and the varying threads of these politics, which are the product of colonial legacies and the contemporary capitalistic consumption of popular spirituality. I have written about some of these dynamics with colleagues and have thought through these issues in varying iterations of my own scholarship, and I continue to ruminate on these topics with my undergraduate students in courses such as Religion and Popular Culture at Queen's University. In light of my intellectual curiosity, I began to think about the lived reality of Rumi and his legacy, not just in the popular spiritual marketplace or on the Sufi "New Age market" scene but also among Sufi communities themselves in Canada (Sorgenfrei 2013: 75). This line of inquiry has led to the book you are holding now, which aims to understand Sufism in Canada, especially in Toronto, Montreal, and Vancouver, through the prism of Rumi and his legacy among Sufi communities, especially in their performance of *sama* in public and ritual spaces. I begin by contextualizing Sufi and popular traditions within the history of some of the earliest Sufi communities in Canada. Then I trace how Rumi-based Sufi communities understand the ritual practice of turning while engaging with or responding to issues of gender dynamics and practices of popular consumption, as they maintain, preserve, and transform the tradition of Rumi and Sufism writ large in Canada and beyond.

This is the first monograph study of Sufism in Canada. That said, I must qualify what this book is *not* before I go on to discuss what it is. This book is not, unfortunately, a comprehensive history of Sufism in Canada. When I first started thinking about this project with my colleague William Rory Dickson, we envisioned it as more of a historical project that would map the development of Sufism from the east coast of Canada to the west. This ambitious goal was, in hindsight, likely impractical due to the sheer diversity of Sufism in Canada. Even so, after three failed SSHRC applications, I decided to go ahead with our initial project on my own and on a smaller scale.[2] So I began with what I knew – Sufism in Toronto, where I grew up and have known Sufi communities for more than a decade. As I started completing semi-structured interviews with poets, practitioners, and teachers in Toronto, they mentioned their institutional connections with individuals and branches in Vancouver and Montreal, and this drew me to those cities and their Sufi centres. Even with these initial linkages, the project was becoming unruly, for there were too many different Sufi communities in various Canadian cities for me to capture and there was no way I was going to be able to document and attend to the stories and lived realities of all of them properly, at least not in one book. So I had to refine my focus again. During my fieldwork, I noticed that I often kept coming back to Rumi through my encounters with Sufi communities in Toronto; meanwhile, social media (especially Twitter) were discussing and at times fighting over issues of cultural and religious appropriation. I became more and more interested in how Rumi was being taken up by Sufi communities themselves, for this was fuelling the popularization of Rumi, and some found this problematic. As I observed various Facebook and Twitter discussions around who Rumi was and who gets to claim him today, I realized that the Sufi communities I was exploring claimed and engaged Rumi in various ways, in ritual private spaces as well as public popular ones. I wanted to understand this process. Thus, it seemed that I had found my focus for this first book about Sufism in Canada, which documents Rumi-affiliated

Sufi communities in Toronto, Montreal, and Vancouver and their complex lived relationships with him through ritual praxis, namely *sama*, *zikr*, and poetry. This approach would serve as a stepping stone to understand how Sufism in Canada developed in the twentieth and twenty-first centuries. I am not suggesting that Rumi-based expressions or communities are the only forms of Sufism in Canada; rather, these are just one thread of the many textured realities of Sufism in Canada. Still, the popularity of whirling dervishes, especially in presentations to the Canadian public, cultural, and artistic spheres, is dominant, more so than in the United States and western Europe, at least as I have seen it. It behoves us, then, to ask why this particular expression of Sufism has taken a front seat in Canada. Perhaps the myth of Canadian multiculturalism that celebrates culture tokenistically and pluralism superficially, together with the prevalence of systemic Islamophobia, has informed the popularity of turning in Canada as an expression of culture and art, one that is not religious or Islamic. For these reasons – religious, spiritual, cultural, social, political – this focus on Rumi is a generative one, in that it productively captures how Sufism in the global west, including Canada, exists at a complex nexus. Finally, this particular case study on Sufism (via Rumi) challenges us to consider the discourses that inform, albeit implicitly, the study of Sufism in the west and the ways in which topics such as popular culture and consumption and gender dynamics are digested in the academic literature and how such discourses then inform the reductive approaches we take to the study of contemporary Sufism.

Conceptually, I am interested in locating the "Canadian" landscape of North American religions, popular spirituality, Islam, and Sufism. My scholarship to date has engaged Sufism both in its global forms and in its local North American and South Asian varieties. Still, even in my own scholarship on Sufism in North America, North America has not subsumed any nuances of Canadian-ness. I do not say this because I am invested in national borders forged by colonial and postcolonial states, and I am not devoted to maintaining these violent colonial geographies. Instead, I am interested in untethering "Canada" from the label of "North American" religions in order to understand whether such national and bordered histories and socialities have affected the development of Sufism in Canada, and if so, how. In this way, I hope this study will be of interest to scholars of Canadian religious studies. Has the development of Sufism in Canada followed similar or different trajectories or even logics of Sufism as it has developed elsewhere in the west, in the United States, Britain, Germany, and so forth? To answer that question, this book brings together various subfields of Canadian religious studies as they intersect with Sufism. These various subfields include popular spirituality in Canada and Islam in Canada, as well as studies of Sufism in the global west. I situate these fields of study as my conceptual framework in chapter 1.

I am not interested in staking a claim in the debates over translations of Rumi (or, for that matter, the Persian poet Hafiz [d. 1390]), for I am not a literary critic or translation scholar. Important threads on Twitter, such as the one maintained by the scholar Omid Safi, have highlighted these histories and problematics, though these issues have been the focus of the academic discussion about Rumi and Persian poetry for much longer (Lewis 2000; Sedarat 2019). What does concern me is the living legacy of Rumi among Sufi communities themselves in Canada, especially as produced by communities of varying religious, cultural, and spiritual locations and orientations that are engaging with Rumi's poetry, rituals (turning), music, and more, just as Rumi continues to be a global icon of popular spirituality. As an ethnographer I am drawn to the lived and embodied realities of Sufism and Sufi praxis. Following some of my previous co-authored scholarship on the popularization of Rumi (Sharify-Funk et al. 2017), as well as the work of scholars such as Sophia Rose Arjana (2020) and Franklin Lewis (2000), who have highlighted the commodification of Rumi, I shift the narrative here to explore how Canadian Sufi communities are adding to this broader process and what their responses are to the types of commodification that are unfolding around them. Mapping these latter processes will help us grasp how practitioners define Sufism in Canada as a religious, spiritual, and universal practice through affiliation with Rumi. As such, this book is not attentive solely to the establishment of Rumi and his teachings in Canada; it also examines what these constellations of practices and communities that orbit Rumi say about the making of Sufism in Canada and beyond.

Methodology

In May 2022 I attended SamaKhaneh, a three-day retreat in Whistler, British Columbia, at a Buddhist retreat centre, which was organized by Shams al Haqq Farzad AttarJafari, a *samazen* and Sufi teacher. Only a small group attended this in-person gathering held at the centre since it was the first such gathering since the COVID-19 pandemic began. We shared meals together and conducted nature meditations and all-night *sama*. Throughout the weekend, I participated in *sama* and meditation in various capacities, though often I tried to stay off to the side during ritual moments to observe and participate quietly. On the second day, during a conversation with one of the *samazen*s in the kitchen, she gently reminded me that I was not there simply as a witness, though I could be if I preferred. She encouraged me to participate by turning or perhaps by picking up a *daf* (drum) and providing voice and music to help hold the *sama* space. I was struck by this gentle invitation – I was being *called in to* the *sama* space – especially as I was struggling to navigate my role at the retreat: I was a researcher, but I was also someone with a personal interest in Sufism. That evening, during the intense late-night *zikr*, without having thought through how I should respond to the invitation, I picked up a *daf* for the first time ever and played it.

I begin my methodological reflections for this book with the above vignette in order to be transparent about my position in the field and my relationships with my interlocutors, many of whom I now consider friends. At the most basic level, my data for this project are based on an ethnography of Sufi communities in Toronto, Montreal, and Vancouver. That ethnography was generated by semi-structured interviews with various members and institutional leaders of Sufi communities in those cities. Ethnography has informed all of my research on Sufism in North America and Sri Lanka to date, for I find value in documenting the everyday experiences – especially of ritual and social contexts – that inform Sufism as an expressed reality and not merely a historical or textual one. In addition to my fieldwork, I completed twenty-one interviews, and those voices will be central to the discussions in the following chapters. Many of those chapters contain extensive quotes from my interviews. I wanted to catalogue and archive the voices of my interlocutors as key actors in the making of Sufism in Canada, especially those of women and racialized and/or queer Sufis.

Many of my interviews were completed in person in Toronto and Vancouver; however, as the COVID-19 pandemic unfolded beginning in March 2020, I also started conducting interviews via Zoom and participating in Sufi gatherings online. Those virtual gatherings later informed the digital ethnographic portion of my fieldwork. Between March to May 2022, as in-person activities began to reopen, I started fieldwork again. These activities included gatherings at Sema Space in Montreal and a weekend retreat in Whistler. Interviews are one way in which the voices of my interlocutors are centred in this study; however, not all conversations were recorded. Some of the most insightful moments in the field happened during car rides, while washing dishes and cleaning up after events, or during informal conversations with Sufis over tea and cookies. Omar Kasmani, in his ethnographic study of Qalandars in Sehwan, writes about these informal moments:

> Hanging out with fakirs [Sufi ascetics] while being skillfully observant demanded more than just being present in a given context or situation (Geertz 1998, 69). As I moved from interviews to conversations, from inquiry to sharing space and time, from recording devices to reflexive processes, I was able to gain a sense of how fakirs pulled together their orientation to extraordinary realms in continuity with the mundane and the everyday. I was equally exposed to moments of tension and enjoyment, privy to everyday gossip and pranks. (2022: 29)

As my relationships with dervishes deepened, and the lines of researcher and interlocutor were blurred, conversations and informal moments defined much of my fieldwork, as did my participation in ritual practices. Over time, my research became more and more focused on the ritual of *sama*, one that is based on the tradition of deep listening as sacred practice. The latter ritual teaching and practice then began to inform the type of *ethnographic listening* (or deep listening) that I adopted during rituals and when gathering data in formal and informal conversations. This project was primed by my engagement with Sufi communities in Toronto for nearly a decade, but most of my sustained fieldwork, especially in Montreal and Vancouver, including the interviews, was conducted between 2018 and 2022. I grew up in Toronto and have been involved in Sufi communities and events since my graduate student days (2009), especially while completing my dissertation on the Bawa Muhaiyaddeen Fellowship (BMF), which focused on its Toronto branch. I have not been initiated into any Sufi order, nor am I an official member of a Sufi community. Regardless, I do have connections to Sufism that span and extend beyond the intellectual and the academic world, and this has created some interesting insider and outsider challenges. Many of my interlocuters are community members and individuals whom I have come to regard as friends and fellow practitioners of Sufism; similarly, my ethnography of ritual practices encompasses my own participation in *zikr*s and prayers. Also, I participated in events such as Rumi commemorations at the Ismaili Centre in 2018, 2019, and 2022 where the organizers asked me to give an introduction both because of my academic study of Sufism and because of my own personal connections with their communities.

In their ethnographic projects about lived religions, scholars such as Thomas Tweed (2006), Robert Orsi (2006), and Amanda J. Lucia (2014, 2020) have alluded to the complex realities of fieldwork: insider/outsider dynamics are never entirely compartmentalized; the two bleed into each other and implicate every scholarly project in intricate ways. These complexities are accentuated because insider/outsider status is not solely a matter of religious identity; also implicated are gender, sexuality, race, ethnicity, culture, class, ableism, and much more.[3] In many ways, my involvement, even peripherally and noninstitutionally, with Sufi communities in Toronto provided me with access, for I was not just a scholar who showed up on the Sufi scene to start asking questions; most communities already knew me. I found it easier to access interviews and participate in rituals in Toronto. Montreal and Vancouver were uncharted territories for me; socially, I was an outsider, so in those cities I relied more heavily on personal introductions to access communities and members. My contacts in Toronto did a great deal to enable this access. In particular, AttarJafari made phone calls on my behalf, connecting me with Sufis on the west coast via WhatsApp and introducing me to individuals to speak with, especially in Vancouver. All of this is to say that my personal relationships with Sufi leaders, artists, and members in Toronto was vital for the success of this project.

As the COVID-19 pandemic reverberated around the globe, Sufi communities responded in diverse ways. Some of the Sufi communities I discuss in this book easily transitioned to hosting weekly, biweekly, and monthly *zikr* sessions online; others even Zoomed *sama* with whirling dervishes for Rumi's *urs* in December 2020. In the unprecedented circumstances, Sufi communities responded in innovative ways, and all the while, rituals continued to unfold through various online platforms. When these gatherings were open to the wider public, I joined in on Zoom sessions, *zikr*, and *sama* gatherings or listened to *sobhet*s (discourses) given by Sufi teachers. Some of these were posted live to Facebook. Cyber-Sufism is not a new phenomenon, and it has been well-documented, for example, by Robert Rozehnal (2019). So has the use of internet and cell phone applications for ritual practices (Sijapati 2019; Piraino 2016). These online meetings and gatherings in which I participated throughout the pandemic added another dimension to my fieldwork and inform my discussion in the chapters to follow. The ethics of online or virtual fieldwork are complex, especially as the field is new and ever-evolving, so I made sure that the social media, Facebook, Twitter, and Instagram accounts I followed were public and not private (Wheeler 2018). I attended virtual gatherings that were public (i.e., open to everyone) or where the Sufi teacher was aware of my academic work. Overall, then, my research for this book has involved multiple methodologies, though it has been defined in large part by ethnography, in addition to some archival research (e.g., digital and personal archives of Sufi leaders and students, and explorations of Canadian material culture, such as church newspapers and yoga magazines). My interviews and conversations, as well as ethnographic data, both in-person and digital, have helped me map the landscape of Sufism in Canada in the pages that follow.

Outline of the Book

This book situates the various threads of the lived legacies of Rumi in Canada as one example of the type of Sufism that has emerged in this country. Each chapter engages with specific expressions of embodied Sufism, be they ritual (chapter 3) or performative and cultural (chapter 4). In my discussion of these features of Sufi practice in Canada, I also embed the lived reality of Sufism in broader tensions that have emerged in the study of Sufism in premodern contexts and in its transmission to new geographies, such as Canada, the United States, and western Europe. These contested dynamics include questions about proper ritual contexts for the practice of *sama* (chapter 3), concerns about the transmission, appropriation, and commodification of Rumi (chapter 4), and anxieties around the role of women in ritual spaces and positions of authority (chapter 5). Overall, these individual chapters engage not only some of the lived expressions of Sufism in the contemporary Canadian context, but also how these manifestations of Sufism continue to be informed implicitly and explicitly by questions of Sufism's authenticity and proper practice as it has taken root in non-Muslim geographies.

Chapter 1 situates the study of Sufism in the global west, specifically in the context of (1) Islam and Muslims in Canada and (2) popular spirituality. Since I am trying to locate a specific (sub)field of Sufism in Canada, this chapter serves to position this (sub)field across numerous literatures, namely Islam in Canada, diaspora studies, Sufi studies, and popular spirituality. Collectively, these fields of study help frame this particular project and showcase how it can inform these respective literatures, such as those that attempt to unpack how Sufism is implicated in the study of Islam or popular spirituality in Canada. The chapter begins the story of Islam in Canada with conjectures about the first Muslims in Canada – the enslaved and formerly enslaved peoples who were forced across the Atlantic Ocean. I begin here because these narratives are likely the stories of the first Sufis in Canada. I take the reader through some archival possibilities as modelled by Black studies scholars, who challenge us to engage creatively with the Black Canadian archive (McKittrick 2006). I then turn to studies of Islam and Muslims in Canada, highlighting that Sufism, an important field of study, has been largely neglected in this country. I situate the study of spirituality in Canadian religious studies, underscoring how that field continues to be informed by a Euro-Christian-centred approach to spirituality that neglects how traditions such as Sufism, and people like Muslims, have been contributing to the popular spiritual marketplace and the spiritual but not religious demographic. The chapter concludes with a look at the academic literature on Sufism in the global west, examining how the formulation of Sufism in colonial and postcolonial times has informed how we approach contemporary Sufism and its diverse expressions. Having raised this backcloth about Islam and Muslims in Canada, popular spirituality in Canada, and the study of contemporary Sufism in the global west, I begin to map Sufism in Canada.

Chapter 2 uses interviews with Sufi students and teachers to tell the story of some of the first Sufi communities in Canada. The earliest Sufi institutions and communities included Muslims who arrived in the 1930s and the members of Gurdjieff societies in Toronto and Halifax. The chapter then turns to the communities of Inayat Khan (d. 1927) and the various branches that arose in Canada starting in the 1970s, especially through the leadership of Inayat Khan's sons (Vilayat and Hidayat Inayat Khan) and his student (Samuel Lewis or Sufi Sam [d. 1971]). I locate these communities of Inayat Khan in Toronto, Edmonton, Calgary, and Vancouver. I then shift my attention to another tradition of Sufism that began to emerge – Turkish Sufism, which includes the practice of *sama* (turning) that materialized with the arrival of Reshad Feild (d. 2016) in Vancouver in 1973. I provide a history of Feild's Vancouver years, of his teacher the Turkish Mawlawi Suleyman Loras (d. 1985), and of Murat Yagan (d. 2013). Yagan was initially Loras's translator during his stays in western Canada and

America; over time, he emerged as a Sufi teacher in his own right. These figures form the environment for the start of the Vancouver Turning Society, later known as the Vancouver Rumi Society. These early groups framed their Sufism in a far more universal language and often focused on the poetry of Rumi or the practice of turning. This latter community and its affiliates are a central focus of this study, for they remain the only groups focused specifically on the practice and teaching of turning (*sama*).

Around the time these early Rumi communities were establishing themselves, the arrival of larger numbers of diasporic Muslims in cities like Vancouver, Toronto, and Montreal further enriched Sufism in Canada. I discuss the founding of these diasporic Sufi communities, such as the Jerrahi Order in Toronto, by drawing from the oral histories I gathered from community members and leaders. In emphasizing these different layers, I signal to two broad trends in the development of Sufism in Canada. First, a far more universally oriented form of Sufism (i.e., not defined by Islamic law) was cultivated by Sufi teachers, both Muslim and non-Muslim, who arrived in Canada and appointed Canadian students to develop centres. This wave of Sufism can be located in the 1970s, during the broader countercultural era of spiritual seeking. Second, a diasporic Sufism began to emerge, especially after the 1990s, in various Muslim diasporic communities such as the South Asian, Turkish, and Persian. This chapter concludes by emphasizing that both these trends in Sufism have defined the current Canadian Sufi topography, which includes communities such as the Rifai Order in Toronto, Sema Space in Montreal, and Rumi Canada in Toronto. As such, Sufism in Canada has both universal and Islamic tendencies, while being defined by cultural and ethnic diversity and embedded in a global and transnational landscape with linkages to American, Turkish, and other regional contexts. For example, travel between California and Washington State among Sufi communities influenced the development of Sufism in Vancouver, and much the same happened between Toronto/Montreal and New York. Meanwhile, diasporic Muslim communities have played a significant role in the development of Sufism in Toronto (Turks, Iranians, and Pakistanis) and Montreal (Algerians). Despite the various ways in which these different forms of Sufism have emerged in Canada, some Muslim communities have branded universal Sufism as illegitimate. The chapter ends by gesturing to the roots of this criticism, asking whether the real matter at hand is racial or ethnic authenticity. Must a Sufi be "Brown" (code for Muslim)? If Sufism is not transmitted through Islam, can it be *real* Sufism? To explore these questions, in the two chapters that follow I analyse in depth a single ritual practice that I found present during my fieldwork – *sama*, or sacred audition. I use this ritual practice as a case study to explore what is at the heart of the sacred Sufi practice and why the popularization of this practice, especially as it is associated with Rumi, and the poetic and musical tradition it hinges on, has resulted in criticisms. These reproaches vary but they often swirl around disapprovals of cultural and religious appropriation and commodification.

Chapter 3 focuses specifically on the tradition of *sama* as a ritual practice among some Rumi-based Sufi communities. I contend that this practice is the dominant ritual unfolding on the Canadian landscape and a defining feature of Sufism in Canada in various spheres, in part because this practice is presented as a cultural or artistic expression (see chapter 4), one that fits nicely into the Canadian myth of multiculturalism. This chapter begins by detailing the development of *sama* and *zikr* in early classical Sufi textual traditions, drawing from the discussions and writings of premodern figures such as the Sunni theologian Abu Hamid al-Ghazali (d. 1111) and Rumi, who described *sama* as a tool for actualizing unity with Allah, which is the ultimate goal of Sufism. I then highlight how the practice of *sama* was transformed during the Ottoman period and finally banned during the rise of the Turkish secular republic at the start of the twentieth century. That state policy would help shift the development of *sama* outside of Turkey. After situating some of the premodern and modern histories and practices of *sama* in a Sufi as well as a Turkish context, I trace this ritual expression in Canada in the second half of this chapter.

In Canada, this practice was initiated by Reshad Feild and then solidified with visits from Suleyman Loras. Feild's and then Loras's students in Vancouver, especially Raqib Brian Burke, have been instrumental in training a second generation of whirling dervishes (*samazen*s), including Tawhida Tanya Evanson, Mira Hunter Burke, and Shams al Haqq Farzad AttarJafari, who have come to be leaders and teachers in their own right and are training a third generation of turners. In my discussion of *sama* in Canada I draw from my conversations with Raqib Brian Burke, Evanson, and AttarJafari and their understanding of this practice while drawing parallels to the treatment of *sama* among the classical Sufi figures introduced at the start of this chapter. I complement this discussion with ethnographic data to add nuance to this lived practice of turning as it is unfolding in Vancouver (Rumi Society), Toronto (Rumi Canada), and Montreal (Sema Space). In describing *sama* rituals in Canada, I provide details of the demographics of Sufi communities where I observed and participated in *sama* while specifying the technical features of the practice of turning and comportment, which are all aimed at the remembrance of God.

This chapter concludes by providing ethnographic reflections about another vital annual ritual I encountered during my fieldwork – the death anniversary of Rumi or the *shab-i arus*, which is celebrated in December. The last part of this chapter maps four *shab-i arus* gatherings that were held in Toronto and Montreal in 2019 and in Vancouver in 2020 (on Zoom). I do this in order to highlight how this practice has become tied to a Canadian Sufi landscape among diasporic and non-diasporic and Muslim and non-Muslim Sufi communities in Toronto, Montreal, and Vancouver. Overall, this chapter shows how

Rumi's legacy is maintained through the ritual practices of *sama* and *shab-i arus* in Canada, a custom that dates back to the classical period of Sufism. I note some of the transformations of this ritual in the Canadian context, such as those pertaining to gender, while stressing that some transformations will continue to unfold, especially now that this ritual expression has shifted to online platforms since the COVID-19 pandemic. Despite these changes to the ritual as it has developed in Canada, those who hold and lead *sama* and *shab-i arus* recognize the essence of these practices as sacred and timeless rituals that honour Rumi and his teacher Shams. They locate their rituals in traditional Sufism that is Islamic, notwithstanding interlopers keen to frame them as not real Sufis.

Chapter 4 shifts the discussion to the other facet of *sama*, namely poetry that has become a legacy of Rumi in public, cultural, and "secular" spaces. I locate popular expressions of *sama* and poetry in cities like Toronto and Vancouver to focus on the crux of one of the core public and critical conversations surrounding the popularization of Rumi today – the commodification and consumption of his legacy. Many Sufis and even academics have claimed that these processes have resulted in the *dilution* of Rumi and Sufism in the west. So this chapter begins by tracing how Rumi's legacy was popularized through literary translation and cross-cultural networks as a result of colonial encounters with the Muslim world. I argue that these colonial processes were a significant precursor to the creation of contemporary Rumi renditions, such as the works produced by the American poet Coleman Barks, as well as their reception. Then I theorize about the various arguments over Barks's renditions of Rumi's poetry, the main one being that they are meant for popular consumption and reflect cultural and religious appropriation. I parse out what the politics of cultural appropriation entail, especially for the spiritual marketplace in which Rumi and his legacy are embedded. Against this backdrop, in the rest of the chapter I provide a different perspective of this thorny discussion through the use of various case studies.

Here again, I return to my interlocutors – Sufis who are leaders, *samazens*, and poets, many of whom are Muslim, who centre Rumi in their cultural, aesthetic, and economic expressions in public spaces. I ask them how they understand cultural appropriation. I trace two main practices here: the expressions of Rumi's poems and the presentations of *sama*. In my analysis of the popularization of Sufi poetry in Canada, I consider the Zavieh Society in Vancouver, an organization that straddles a secular not-for-profit institutional framework yet is focused on teaching Rumi's works. It has been active for decades in Vancouver as a place where students gathered weekly under the direction of Dr Parviz Sahabi (d. 2022) to study the *mathnawi* (Arabic) (or Persian *masnawi*), Rumi's poems, in Persian. Recently, they added weekly English classes on the *mathnawi* as well. In light of conversations about translation politics of Rumi, I consider how the Zavieh Society has played a role in teaching Rumi's poetry in Persian and English to non-Persians and to anyone who is interested in the diaspora.

I then consider the practices of turning, which was discussed in its ritual contexts in chapter 3. Here I showcase how this practice is unfolding in cultural, performative, and aesthetic venues. These spaces include the Aga Khan Museum and Ismaili Centre and smaller performance venues like Small World Music, all in Toronto. In my examination of the programming at these cultural spaces, I centre the voices of the *samazen*s who participate in the presentation of *sama* as public performance to understand whether they distinguish between artistic and cultural venues when presenting *sama*. All of them said they did not; instead, they stressed that their presentations of *sama* to the public were in the name of Rumi, whom they were honouring. What mattered most for them was their intention (*niyya*), which was set in their heart (*qalb*).

The final example I consider in this chapter is of Naqshbandi Haqqani Kabbani Rumi Rose Garden in Vancouver. Parsing my interview with the current *shaykh* of the order, Nurjan Mirahmadi, I reflect on how the Naqshbandi Haqqani Kabbani frames the Rumi teas it sells not as a commodity but as a curative spiritual object, one that has been transformed by the ritual of *zikr* completed by the Sufi community in the storefront space. Thus, the philosophy of the alchemical transformation through the energy released during prayer is central to the Naqshbandi-Haqqani Sufi philosophy and theology, and not a matter of simple commodification, as it might first seem. In the final sections, the chapter turns to the voices of my interlocutors again to hear from them about why they think Rumi has become so popular in the twenty-first century and the complexities of this popularity in which they are embedded. This chapter ultimately complicates how Rumi, his poetry, and the tradition of turning exist in cultural and commodified spaces, especially as employed by practising Sufis, who do not view their participation in these non-ritual spheres as problematic or as eroding Rumi. They understand it as principally a work of service – they are sharing Rumi with a wider audience, even through the spiritual marketplace.

The final substantive chapter shifts in tone and approach. So far, the chapters have focused on contextualizing Sufi communities and mapping the central legacy of Rumi, specifically through the traditions of turning, music, and poetry, which I have argued inform one thread of contemporary Sufism in Canada. However, these ritual, cultural, and poetic expressions of Rumi's legacy miss other significant features and dynamics of Sufism in Canada, such as gender dynamics in ritual contexts, especially gendered authority. Conversations and debates about Sufi women have long tended to focus on their ritual involvement in Sufi practices and the nature of their authority. This chapter traces some of the realities of gender dynamics in classical and medieval Sufism. I mark two central trends in the discussion of Sufi women in textual and classical traditions as highlighted by scholars who study these materials. First, Islam has tended to glorify the feminine as a state of being, one that was developed by classical Sufi thinkers and masters like Ibn Arabi (d. 1240). That state of being also emerged in metaphorical tropes used by Sufi figures like Rumi. Yet this metaphysical idealization of the feminine did not readily translate into the veneration of Sufi women as social and/or biological beings; rather, it informed the disparagement of Sufi women generally, and led to the minimizing of women's roles in literary sources such as hagiographies. I then consider various anthropological examples of Sufi women's presence in ritual praxis or sacred spaces across some Muslim majority contexts; for example, I find leadership positions that are dependent on a familial patriarchal authority, such as a father or a husband. In my analysis of these examples, I showcase how women's bodies are employed as a vector for determining the legitimacy of Sufism as Islamic. That is, a true (authentic) Muslim community would indeed practise gender segregation and limit women's presence in authoritative roles. After considering some of these gendered patterns and politics in historical Sufism and its scholarship, I turn again to the Canadian Sufi milieu to reflect on how gender and women's roles have been informing Sufism in Canada; I also consider how women are employed as a vector for determining whether a Sufi community is New Age or Islamic. To that end, first, I reflect on the role of women's ritual involvement in *zikr* among the Rifai Order in Toronto and hear directly from *shaykh* Murat Coskun about his teachings, which have inspired the gender-egalitarian norms he cultivates in his community. Gender-egalitarian practices hinge on the realization of metaphysical approaches to Sufism, which ascribe no biological gender. Similarly, teachers like the Rifai Marufi Sherif Baba Çatalkaya understand the egalitarian practices of inclusion of women, both in Turkey and in North America, as the true tradition of Sufism and not as an innovation, as many claim it to be. It is such metaphysics, as outlined in the chapter's introduction, that informs mixed-gender turning. Even so, *sama*'s development as a mixed-gender practice has led to some negotiations and tensions in the Canadian context. I examine these gender dynamics as a factor in some of the transformations in turning that I noted in chapter 3, especially under the leadership of Feild, Loras, and Burke (a student of *shaykh* Çatalkaya), which ensured that gender was never a limitation in the practice of turning for *samazen*s.

The chapter concludes by focusing on two Sufi women teachers in Canada: Seemi Bushra Ghazi, based in Vancouver, and Ayeda Husain, based near Toronto. In my discussion of these two Sufi women teachers or *shaykha*s, I position their authority in the broader Sufi tradition of *shaykha*s and the legacy of Rumi, from whom they themselves glean their authority. These two teachers speak about how they conceptualize Sufism as a universal tradition that is deeply Islamic (both are Muslim). During such moments one comes to recognize how our notions of *Islamic* require revision, as Sufi Muslims themselves root their practice and authority within a framework of Islam they know to be universal, one that many interlopers miscategorize as New Age or popular spirituality and thus as a dilution brought about by the west. My discussion throughout these chapters challenges scholars to move beyond limited categories of Sufism's relationship to Islam, the problematics of Rumi's translation and commodification, and what constitutes real Sufism, so that they will understand how Sufis, especially Muslim Sufis in Canada, are utilizing Sufi identity in gender-egalitarian ways to transform how they enact Islam in Canada. The voices captured in this chapter indicate that many *shaykh*s, *shaykha*s, and *samazen*s are drawing from traditions of Sufism and do not see themselves as innovating for a western (Canadian) context when it comes to gender practices and authority, as some may suggest, but instead are returning to the essence of Sufism and Islam.

The book ends with a reflection on the current terrain of Sufi communities in Canada in the form of an epilogue. Also, since this is the first book on Sufism in Canada, a formal conclusion felt rather presumptuous to write. In the 1970s and 1980s, in an era of civil rights, feminist, and antiwar movements, Sufi communities emerged in the global west as seekers turned toward an eastern spirituality that was experiential and anti-institutional. The current moment is charged in other social and political ways. Many young people, especially from second- and third-generation Muslim diasporic families, are heavily involved in social justice work, be it gender, sexual, or racial justice (i.e., against Islamophobia), while also responding to climate catastrophe through social mobilization, civic engagement, and/or advocacy and policy work at grassroots levels. Meanwhile, social media and digital technologies have drastically altered how activists go about their work. All of this is subverting and shifting the current boundaries of Sufism, which scholars up till now have reductively approached as white Sufism, diasporic Sufism, and/or Sufism "for popular consumption" (though these are all intermingled, as this book will show). I point to examples of how some of the Sufi communities discussed in this book are responding to Black Lives Matter movements and fighting against ongoing state violence against Black, Indigenous, Muslim, and racialized bodies in Canada. The current sociopolitical moment, then, is potent but also latent, and the Sufi communities that are gaining traction among a new young generation of interested seekers are the ones that are engaging in these difficult questions. This has led to a socially engaged Sufism. My Sufi Muslim interlocutors do not necessarily view these tendencies as new or even as innovative. Rather, Sufism, which emerged as an ascetic countercultural antinomian movement before it became institutionalized in the medieval period, along with Rumi and Shams' legacy of radical subversive love, is today a fitting decolonial discursive platform and reservoir for social engagement, justice, and activism. Located at the intersection of Canadian Islam and popular spirituality, Sufism in Canada is ripe for this powerful moment, which will define new traditional iterations of Sufism, not just in Canada but in the global west writ large.

Chapter One

Situating the Study of Sufism in Canada

This chapter situates the fields of scholarship that inform my approach to the study of Sufism in Canada. First, I locate the study of Sufism in Canada within the field of Islam and Muslims in Canada. Any project that thinks and writes about Islam in Canada must start with an account of the first Muslims in Canada, who were enslaved or formerly enslaved Black peoples who had been forced from their African homeland by the transatlantic slave trade. Some of these first Black Muslims in Canada would likely have been the first Sufis. The following discussion is speculative and not the focus of this project; even so, it is vital to begin this account of Sufism and Islam in Canada by acknowledging this history, given that religious studies in Canada is too often framed as Eurocentric. Shifting the focus of the stories we tell is the first step in decolonizing the study of religion in Canada. I then examine how Islam and Muslims are viewed in Canada and locate the study of Sufism within these scholarly literatures (hint: it barely exists). I then explore other areas of study – diaspora, migration, and spirituality – as domains with which the field of Sufism intersects. These various discursive terrains will help locate this present case study, not only in the specific field of Sufism in Canada, which I think of as a subfield that crosses these various literatures, but also in popular spirituality, Islamic studies, and diaspora studies.

This chapter then positions the study of Sufism in the global west, drawing from writings about Sufism in North America and western Europe. I examine how scholars have framed Sufism either capaciously or restrictively in their discourses and how this has informed approaches to categorizing various Sufi communities and their practices. Some of these frameworks resort to coded language to label contemporary Sufi communities. The scholarship on contemporary western Sufism overlaps with studies of Islam and Muslim societies and with non-Islamic traditions and popular spirituality. This scholarship ranges from Neoplatonic thought to perennialism and traditionalism, as forms of universalism, while conceptually restrictive studies of Sufism frame it only within the Islamic tradition. In this chapter and throughout this book, I use a capaciously informed approach to my understanding of Sufism, drawing from the work of scholars like Shahab Ahmed (2016) and Alexander Knysh (1999, 2017, 2019), who for instance think of Sufism as containing a "discursive fertility" and "epistemological instability" (Knysh 2017: 57, 122). Furthermore, as Francesco Piraino explains, "in order to describe Sufism, we need several categories, such as mysticism, asceticism, esotericism, spirituality and more, and at the same time we need also to focus on the social dimensions of Sufi orders, which have contributed to shaping Islamic history" (2020: 2). This fluid conceptual approach to Sufism informs the lived reality I document via ethnographic data in this book.

Islam in Canada

Conversations about Islam in Canada often come under the umbrella of Muslim diaspora and immigration and address questions of integration and accommodation in the new host-nation. Yet Muslim diasporic communities are immensely diverse, as scholarship on Islam in Canada has consistently noted. The story of Muslim Canada usually begins with an account of early Arab fur traders, such as Peter Baker, and then moves on to the Arab and then South Asian Muslims who arrived here (especially male labourers). These earliest Muslims, who were likely from the Ottoman Empire, moved to the northwest frontier to trade (Hussain and Scott 2012: 182–3). Yet little is said about the role of Black Atlantic Canada and its intersections with Islam.

"Black Muslims" is a diverse category, one that includes cultural, racial, and ethnic contexts in relation to continental Africa, the Caribbean, and the Americas (Jackson-Best 2019). The scholarship on Islam in Canada often looks no earlier than the 1960s and 1970s and thus does not account for Islam's much earlier presence among enslaved and formerly enslaved peoples, especially Africans who came to Upper Canada or the Maritimes and the Islamic religious and cultural practices they may have maintained. An example is the early Black settlers in what is now Nova Scotia (Wigmore 2011). Scholars have noted that Muslims were present in Americas even before the arrival of enslaved Muslims. The first Muslims in the Americas were likely Moriscos, or those who were "enslaved from the Iberian and North African Moors on Spanish missions of exploration and conquest to the Americas," who probably did not leave descendants (Khan 2020: 36).[1] These historical legacies of early Islam in the Americas have been well-documented, as has the role of Sufism among these communities. As an example, the autobiography of Omar Ibn Said (d. 1864) makes references to Sufi literature (Diouf 2013; Khan 2020).[2]

Yet in Canada, much of this story is paid little attention. The history of slavery in Canada spans more than two centuries, dating back to 1629, when the first documented child (six or seven years old) was transported to New France from either Madagascar or Guinea (Wright 2022: ix). Slavery was practised in British North America until it was outlawed in 1833 (Wright 2022: ix). Scholars of Islam and Muslims in Canada need to start their story at this important juncture and engage with the scholarship on Black history in Canada. The archives here are a challenge but not impossible. As Donald Wright expresses in his foreword to Whitfield's *Biographical Dictionary of Enslaved Black People in the Maritimes* (2022), "archives are by definition capricious, sometimes generous and sometimes parsimonious, even cruel. They are especially unkind to historians researching the lives of enslaved people" (xiv). That is precisely why Whitfield's biographical dictionary, which contains the names of 1,465 enslaved Black people, is so necessary to engage with: in starting with the names of Black people in the Maritimes, we can begin to see markers of some of the first Muslims in Canada, some of whom arrived here from Africa, the West Indies, the Carolinas, Chesapeake Bay, and the northern states. Others were born in the Maritimes (xxii). As Whitfield goes on to explain:

> This book also helps us recognize that these enslaved Black people in the Maritimes had likes, dislikes, good traits, bad ones, and various levels of physical, spiritual and intellectual talent. We must affirm that notion that all of these slaves were unique individuals, despite the efforts of their owners and the wider British Atlantic world to dehumanize them. They were people – and their actions to keep their families together and fight for their dignity are poignantly told in many of the biographies in this book. Regardless of the lack of available primary sources, their stories deserve sustained investigation. (xxiii)

These archives are full of traces of stories that scholars of Islam in Canada need to hear. For instance, the story of Black migration on Canada's east coast is immensely diverse:

> Black migration is one of the hallmarks of the history of the Maritimes. These migrations – coerced and voluntary – connected the Maritimes to the United States, Africa, the Caribbean and Europe. Between 1605 and 1820, several thousand Black people settled in the Maritimes. These migrants included 3,000 Black Loyalists, possibly 1,500 to 2,000 Loyalists slaves, 550 Jamaican Maroons (from 1796 to 1800), several hundred slaves in Île Royale [Cape Breton], an unknown number of New England Planter slaves (possibly up to 200), a small number of slaves brought up from the coastal slave trade, and about 3,200 Black refugees from the War of 1812. We must understand the history of slavery within this larger context of migration throughout the British Empire, the Black Atlantic and the African Diaspora (xxv)

In Whitfield's dictionary one finds names that are proximate to Arabic, and thus potentially Muslim, such as Hagar (ca. 1788), "the daughter of Bathsheba and enslaved to Mr. Hecht, Hagar was baptized in 1788" (18). Record 1221 is of an unnamed person (ca. 1732):

> This unnamed Black person was enslaved to merchant, businessman, and large-scale slaveholder Jean Pierre Roma. Roma had planned to set up a settlement with slaves in Prince Edward Island, but he went to Louisbourg in 1732. Roma owned 12 slaves. In 1732, he imported four slaves worth 3000 livres. Roma noted that he had "2 negroes prime slaves and 2 negresses prime slaves, of the ardan nation [from the coast of Ouidah in Benin]." (201)

The names in these biographic records, and the regions from which they came, allow us to begin to speculate that these enslaved and formerly enslaved Black people in the Maritimes could well have had been Muslim. To truly understand Islamic history in Canada, we need to focus on these archives and the possibilities they unlock. For instance, we know that Mahommah Gardo Baquaqua was born in what is now Djougou, Benin (referenced as town of Zoogoo in his biography), around 1830. He was sold to Europeans and eventually was traded to Pernambuco, Brazil, where he was enslaved to various people before escaping in New York and returning to Haiti, where he converted to Christianity. He returned to New York for college and stayed in Canada, where he wrote his biography, titled *Biography of Mahommah G. Baquaqua, A Native of Zoogoo, in the Interior of Africa* (1854). There is no record of him after 1857. Questions surround the authorship of this book and the role played by its editor (Samuel Moore); even so, it captures some important details that help expand our knowledge of some of the first Black Muslims in Canada, even if their stay was temporary and they had already converted to Christianity. For instance, Baquaqua in his book confirms his religion as "Mahomedanism":

> My father ... rose every morning at four o'clock for prayers, after which he returned to bed, at sunrise he performed his second devotional exercises, at noon he worshipped again, and again at sunset. Once a year a great fast is held, which lasts a month, during this time nothing is eaten during the day, but in the evening after some ceremonies are performed, eating is allowed; after eating, worship is permitted in their own homes, and then assemblies for public worship are held. The place of worship was a large and pleasant yard belonging to my grandfather, my uncle was the officiating priest. The oldest people arrange themselves in rows, the priest standing in front, the oldest people next to him, and so on, arranging themselves in order according to age. (Baquaqua 1854: 9–10)

He goes on to describe *salat* and the communal gatherings of prayers during Ramadan, which culminated in the celebration of eid (10–11). He studied to be a Muslim cleric, despite his dislike of his teacher, his older brother, who was proficient in Arabic (27). He does little in his book to explain why he converted to Christianity, though he refers throughout it to the "light" of Christianity (Diouf 2013; Law and Lovejoy 2007; Austin 1984). The biography includes vivid and important details about his experience of enslavement, including on the slave ship: "Its horrors, ah! Who can describe? None can truly depict its horrors as the poor unfortunate, miserable wretch that has been confined within its portals. Oh! Friends of humanity, pity the poor African" (42). He writes about his arrival in the north:

> After this I returned to McGrawville for a short time, when, having a desire to see the manners and customs of people living under the Government of Queen Victoria, of whom I had hoard [sic] so much, induced me to go to Canada, where I remained a short time, and being so well pleased with the reception I there met with, I at once determined to become a subject of her Majesty, for which purpose I attended at the proper office, and gave the oath of allegiance, and procured my papers of naturalization without any difficulty. (64)

Numerous other autobiographical and biographical accounts of Muslims or former Muslims are available to us, such as that of Nicolas Said (1836–1882), a Sudanese Muslim, who in his *Autobiography of Nicolas Said, A Native of Bournou, Eastern Soudan, Central Africa* (1873) writes about arriving in Ottawa and being stuck without money until a pastor helped him:

> Rev. D. T. Johnston, a pastor of that parish, who loaned me ten dollars and told me I had better go to Detroit, Michigan or Buffalo, New York, where there were a great number of colored people; and where I could get into employment easier than to remain in Canada, where the cold was so intense. (200)

Other accounts include Benjamin Drew's *A North-Side View of Slavery. The Refugee: or the Narratives of Fugitive Slaves in Canada. Related by Themselves, with an Account of the History and Condition of the Coloured Population of Upper Canada* (1856). These numerous accounts need more focused study and attention to widen our sense of the earliest instances of Islam in Canada.[3] Yet even this brief foray into writings by some of the first Black Muslims in Canada tells us they were present in Upper and Lower Canada and practised Islam here as part of their cultural identity, whether or not they later converted to Christianity. For instance, scholarship on West African Islam – for example, by Ariela Marcus-Sells in *Sorcery or Science? Contesting Knowledge and Practice in West African Sufi Texts* (2022) – highlights the significant influence of Sufism in the practice of Islam – a strong indicator that many enslaved people from West Africa were likely steeped in this expression of Islam, which they tried to preserve through personal piety, as we see in the case of Omar Ibn Said.

So far, much of the documentation of Muslims in nineteenth-century Canada has focused on Muslims from the Middle East (the Ottoman Empire) and on the sacred spaces they established. There are records indicating that before Confederation, there were "Mahometans" from European and American nations in Ontario; the 1871 federal census records thirteen Muslims (Hussain and Scott 2012: 182). Canada's first mosque, Al Rashid, was established in 1938, in Edmonton (Hussain and Scott 2012: 183). Early developments can also be seen in the Maritimes (Nova Scotia) and in cities like Montreal, Ottawa, London, Thunder Bay, and Calgary, which by then had large communities of Lebanese and Syrian Muslims, refugees from the collapsing Ottoman Empire (183).

The early history of Black Muslims in Canada has received little scholarly attention. More has been paid to Canadian diasporic Muslim experiences, especially after the mid-twentieth century (Zine 2012, 2022; Selby, Barras, and Beaman 2018; Barras, Selby, and Adrian 2021). Much of the broad demographic shift was a result of Canada's new immigration policy of 1971, which opened the Canadian border to Egyptian, Eritrean, Ethiopian, Iraqi, Moroccan, Palestinian, Somali, and Sudanese newcomers. Up to this point, the Canadian immigration system had privileged educated migrants through a racist point system. In terms of the experiences of Black and/or African Muslim Canadians, much work has been completed on first- and second-generation Somali Canadians in cities like Toronto, Ottawa, and Edmonton, with a focused engagement on questions of the immigrant and refugee experience. Thereafter, various global political events, such as the expulsion of Asians from Uganda by Idi Amin (d. 2003) in 1972, led to an influx of Ismailis from East Africa (in Toronto, Calgary, and Vancouver). Various crises in the Middle East, such as the Iran–Iraq War (1980–8), the Gulf War (1990–1), and the plight of the Palestinians, led to growing Arab Muslim populations in Ontario (Ottawa, Windsor, London, Hamilton) and Quebec (Hussain and Scott 2012: 184–5). Most of the Muslim migration to Canada – around 70 per cent – took place in the 1990s and 2000s (Frishkopf 2011).

The 1970s also saw the arrival of Eastern European Muslims, including Turks, Albanians, Albanian Kosovars, and Bosnians, especially in Ontario, and this has had an impact on the Sufi communities examined in this book. South Asian Muslims began arriving as early as the 1960s and 1970s, and they would form an important diasporic community, especially in the Toronto region. They are a diverse diasporic community, consisting of people from India, Pakistan, Sri Lanka, and the Caribbean (Hussain and Scott 2012). The development of Islam in cities like Vancouver, Toronto, and Montreal followed localized trends and demographic realities. Toronto's Muslim community has historically been larger and more diverse (racially, culturally, ethnically, and religiously) than the ones in Vancouver and Montreal. Overall, Ontario has the largest Muslim population in Canada; other provinces have fairly large populations as well.

Recent controversies regarding Canadian Muslims related to accommodation, Islamophobia, and concerns over radicalization have drawn attention to Muslim communities and impacted how they are being studied (Zine 2022; Alvi, Hoodfar et al 2003; Bakht 2009; Kazemipur 2014; Selby, Barras, and Beaman 2018). Yet the role of Sufis in fostering constructive Muslim responses to these issues has been largely overlooked by the media and political commentators, as well as by academics. For instance, some scholars have contended that "Canadian Islam seems, on the whole (and myriad exceptions notwithstanding), to have lost its connection to the human world a world that is localized, affective, and rooted in human relationships, having been reoriented instead to address social problems inherent in putatively multicultural society" (Frishkopf 2011: 143).

The discussion that unfolds in this book suggests the opposite, at least for Sufi communities, some of which identify as Muslims. Some studies have captured that some Muslim communities, such as Sunni communities, have been broadly averse to Shia and Sufi practices and communities, often suggesting that Sufism is not Islam (Frishkopf 2009: 49). The framing of Sufism as a non-Islamic tradition has bifurcated and silenced Sufi Muslim experiences, thus placing them in the realm of New Age and popular spiritual studies (Sedgwick 2012). Simultaneous with the development of Islam in Canada through migration and the transplanting of an immensely diverse diaspora of Muslims has been the emergence of popular spirituality, which has developed in tandem with the migration trends noted above. This has coalesced and intersected with the development of Sufism in the twenty-first century.

Popular Spirituality in Canada

A Pew Research Center study of religion in Canada published in July 2019 found that about 55 per cent of Canadians broadly identified as Christian (Protestant and Catholic) and about 29 per cent as having no religious affiliation. Many Canadians – around 8 per cent – identify with the religious traditions of Islam, Hinduism, Sikhism, Judaism, and Buddhism as a reflection of their migration status (Lipka 2019).[4] The Pew study's findings also suggest that Canadians are more religious (29%) than the French (12%) and the British (21%) (Lipka 2019). The 2021 census data reported that 35 per cent of Canadians identified with no religion and that 5 per cent of Canadian respondents identified with Islam. Other sociologists of religion have suggested that a "cleavage" or "polarization" is growing between religious and non-religious populations in Canada (Wilkins-Laflamme 2017: 167). A recently coined term that has been used to capture the religious and spiritual landscape of the global west – one that has gained much utility in the study of Canadian religions and spirituality – is "spiritual but not religious" (SBNR) (Chandler 2011). Joel Thiessen and Sarah Wilkins-Laflamme's (2020) study provides quantitative and qualitative analysis of the growing population of non-religious identity (religious "nones") in Canada and the US. Overall, they found a "decline of organized religion" in both the US and Canada. This did not mean that religion and spirituality were disappearing; rather, there had emerged "a diversity of spiritual beliefs and practices along with nonbelief and secular attitudes" that are constantly "evolving" (5). Recent studies of spirituality and secularism in Canada note that spiritual practices have transitioned away from traditional (Christian) forms of religiosity toward secular and "new secular spiritual movement[s]," especially among the younger generation (Wilkins-Laflamme 2017; Mosurinjohn and Funnell-Kononuk 2017; Chandler 2011).[5]

Furthermore, the ebb and flow of religiosity in Canada reflects regional and provincial historical trends and histories. For instance, religion/Christianity is reported to have declined in Atlantic Canada and Quebec, while in BC there seem to be more spiritually oriented practices – a trend reflected in my study as well (Wilkins-Laflamme 2017: 167). BC is following similar trends as in Seattle and Oregon, rather than those in Ontario and Quebec (Bramadat, Killen, and Wilkins-Laflamme 2022). Thiessen and Wilkins-Laflamme include five different categories of "nones," two of those categories being "non-religious" and "spiritual but not religious," a demographic that is more representative of BC than of Ontario and Quebec. In their project on spirituality and secularity in the Pacific Northwest, Paul Bramadat and colleagues write that 49 per cent of their participants in BC said they had no religious affiliation (2022:13). Also, BC has been far more heavily influenced by Asian migration, whereas Ontario (among other regions) has drawn South Asians, Middle Easterners, and continental Africans and Quebec has attracted various French-speaking migrants, especially from continental Africa. In this study I do not presuppose a uniform trend in Sufi praxis and demographics across Canada; instead I set out to capture Sufism in Toronto, Montreal, and Vancouver, while attending to regional developments and transprovincial connections. For instance, there are trends that are evident across the cosmopolitan cities, and trends that render them very different, as will be noted with regard to factors such as age and ethnic/racial identity. I hope that future scholars who pick up this work will be attentive to provincial and regional histories of religion and spirituality when thinking about Sufism and Islam, especially as it is developing in BC.

Like many other studies that have examined diverse religious and spiritual ways of being, this book unsettles the notion that the practitioners of these forms of spirituality and/or secularity are only Christian/white individuals, even though that has historically tended to be the case. For instance, Muslims also dabble in popular spirituality. This study of Sufism in Canada complicates these trends by also locating racialized members' experiences of Sufism, especially Muslim practices, that may be identified in the sphere of popular culture or the practice of spirituality. For instance, in her book about the history of metaphysical religions in America, Catherine Albanese (2008) writes that the metaphysical demographic is "mostly white, more female than male, often middle-age, sometimes young and frequently urban dwellers ... middle class and upwardly mobile, better educated than average and not especially alienated from society" (509–10). Amanda Lucia (2014, 2020) in her studies of the female Hindu guru Amma and transformational yoga festivals found that "in general, the hippie movement, its later incarnation as the new age movement, and its most recent incarnation as the metaphysical spirituality of the twenty-first century have struggled to diversify their audiences beyond white middle and upper-middle classes" (2014: 155). The 1960s and 1970s were formative in defining the popular spiritual movements of Canada as predominately a white experience (see below).

The metaphysical culture that has proven to be a representative demographic thread of spirituality in American religious history has also influenced the development of spirituality in Canada. In Canada we see a similar early development of popular spirituality drawing from "Eastern" traditions, linked to Swami Vivekananda (d. 1902), whom many scholars of religion connect in turn to the introduction of Hinduism to an American audience at the Parliament of World Religions (1893) in Chicago. His journey from Bombay to Chicago in 1893 took him through China, Japan, and Canada. He arrived in Vancouver on 25 July 1893, where he met Jamsetji Nusserwanji Tata (d. 1904), an Indian businessman, who was on route to Chicago for the Parliament, and whom he joined. His train journey from Vancouver to Chicago took him through BC and across the Canadian Prairies, over the course of which he engaged with some interested seekers ("Swami Vivekananda in Canada"). Even before Vivekananda's arrival in Vancouver, scholars noted how trends in Spiritualism and Theosophy, which began in America, had already made their way into Canada. For instance, Spiritualism, which originated in nineteenth-century New York, arrived in Canada a few years later and spread coast to coast (Choquette 2004: 271), as had influential movements like the Theosophical Society (1875), founded by Henry Steele Olcott (d. 1907) and Helena Blavatsky (d. 1891). The first Canadian branch of the Theosophical Society was founded in Toronto in 1891, and subsequent branches opened in Victoria (Kshanti Branch) and Montreal (Mount Royal Branch), under the oversight of the Theosophical Society in New York ("Theosophy Canada").[6]

Decades later, similar spiritual cultures and communities expanded into Canada, aligned with various developments during the heyday of the American counterculture in the 1960s and 1970s. In an interview, Zainb Paula Ford, who connected to Sufism through Vilayat Inayat Khan (d. 2004), explained that in 1976, the Yogi Bhajan group (3HO Society or "Happy, Health, Holy") organized a World Symposium on Humanity in Vancouver.[7] The event included speakers such as Yogi Bhajan of the 3HO, Buckminster Fuller, Rolling Thunder, Swami Kriyananda, and Vilayat Khan.[8] It was at this event that Ford first encountered Vilayat Khan:

> I went to this thing, and it was pretty wonderful all together [in] ... 1976. I was what? Thirty? ... Seems like a pretty long time ago. Anyway ... I was very impressed with Pir Vilayat. He ... still had some dark colour in his hair at that point. And I remember ... he had incredible energy, an energy that I didn't understand. But I didn't know what Sufism was. And ... nobody said anything about initiation or anything like that. And I wouldn't know what it was anyway. But there was ... an event, there ... he gave a talk. And then on another occasion ... at that same event ... you're familiar with what's called Sufi dancing ... And they were all in these concentric circles in the ballroom of the Hyatt Regency downtown [Vancouver]. And the whole event was there. And ... one or two of his students [Pir Vilayat] had just done a Universal Worship ... he used to do these things called "cosmic celebration," which was the Universal Worship, which are you familiar with that? Yeah. So ... I remember that somebody, it was either him or somebody else was standing on a table in the middle of the room, because you couldn't see him otherwise. And ... they were leading these dances. And with like, I don't know, there must have been five or six circles of people in this huge, huge room ... and all dancing together. And then, at some point that ... part ended ... [and] Shlomo Carlebach came in. And he ... was in the middle, and he started playing guitar and singing, and everybody just kept on dancing. And ... it was like, some kind of initiation, it was quite amazing.[9]

Carlebach (d. 1994), known as "the singing rabbi," was involved in the spiritual scene in the United States and Canada, having lived in Toronto for a brief time.[10] Various conferences, bookstores (such as Banyan Books and Sounds in Vancouver), and magazines became important venues for the spreading of Sufism as well as sites of encounters for many seekers, such as Ford. For instance, *Yoga Journal*, a magazine focused on yoga practices and events, founded in California in 1975, is one source that reflects some of the popular spiritual and yogic practices unfolding across Canada at this time. That journal captured various speaking events and workshops, including events in Toronto, Vancouver, and Montreal in the late 1970s, 1980s and 1990s. For instance, the January–February 1992 issue of the journal has Babaji's Kriya Yoga initiations with M. Govindan with stops in Toronto (1–3 May). He was based in Montreal (117). Many in the community, such as senior members of the Inayati Order (then the Sufi Order International), were introduced to Sufism through their own spiritual journeys of seeking, which included yoga. A common trend in seekers' journeys toward Sufism was the introduction to "Eastern" spirituality via Ram

Dass (Richard Alphert) (d. 2019), especially through his classic *Be Here Now*, first published in 1971. The text makes a reference to Sufis, especially to breathing meditations, and compares this to other traditions, such as Hinduism (Dass 1971: 78). A classic on spirituality and yoga among American seekers, *Be Here Now* catalysed the seeker's quest and eventually led to the practice of Sufism for some of the Sufis I spoke to throughout this study. The Lama Foundation in San Cristóbal, New Mexico, which published *Be Here Now* (1971), also published *Toward the One* (1974) by Vilayat Inayat Khan, another pivotal text for many of the early Canadian spiritual seekers who eventually turned to focus on Sufism. During this period, then, it was traditions of Hinduism (especially yoga) and Buddhism that became formative spiritual paths for many seekers, though they were viewed separately from "ethnic" religious traditions in Canada, according to practitioners and scholars.

In their edited volume *Wild Geese: Buddhism in Canada*, John S. Harding, Victory Sōgen Hori, and Alexander Duncan Soucy (2010) describe the early development of Buddhism in Canada as comprising two waves. The first was before 1967, when Buddhism was defined mainly by Japanese migrants to Canada's west, including Vancouver, where the first Buddhist temple was built in 1906. The second wave began in the 1960s, when changes in Canada's immigration laws led to the arrival of Buddhists and their traditions from China, Vietnam, Sri Lanka, Korea, Thailand, Laos, Cambodia, and many other countries (4). During this second phase, another significant dynamic was broader countercultural change and the social movements it stimulated – women's liberation, Civil Rights, Black Power, as well as a burgeoning interest in Eastern spiritual traditions. This second stage saw the rise of figures like D.T. Suzuki (d. 1966) and Alan Watts (d. 1973) (4). Harding and colleagues explain: "The 1971 policy of multiculturalism in Canada and how the new social openness to alternative forms of spirituality have contributed to the increasing religious diversity, and hence to the surge of the Buddhist population. But one cannot escape history. In fact, it was the hostile attitude toward Japanese Canadians that first dispersed Buddhism across the continent" (5).

In the United States, changes in immigration laws in 1965 had a significant impact, opening the doors for various spiritual teachers, including Sufi teachers from Senegal, Sri Lanka, Turkey, and elsewhere. By the time they arrived, the cultural landscape was ready to receive their ideas: many Americans were turning against their inherited religious identities (especially Christian and Jewish ones) for social and political reasons and seeking new modes of meaning-making. These seekers turned to Eastern spiritualities such as Hinduism, Buddhism, and Sufism, thus perpetuating the binaries that had been created in the colonial contexts. Scholars of Hinduism and Buddhism in America have examined the racial and ethnic demographics of these communities. For instance, Amanda J. Lucia in *Reflections of Amma: Devotees in a Global Embrace* (2014) contends that simply discussing the binaries of Indian Hindus and white devotees serves little purpose, especially in light of Amma's (the hugging guru's) global traction as both a Hindu movement and a spiritual one.[11] Buddhism in Canada as it has developed has a number of parallels with Sufism in Canada and can help with understanding the arc of Sufism's development in Canada.

All of this led to problematic labelling of non-Christian religious communities, especially those that were deemed ethnically oriented. Early sociologists of religion, such as Rodney Stark and William Bainbridge (1982), sometimes referred to these communities as "cults" or "ethnic churches." Writing before such terms became taboo in religious studies, they described "cults" as part of a "deviant religious tradition" (1982; Dawson 1998). They viewed Asian religions in America as cults, but only when the adherents were mostly white. By contrast, when Asian immigrants formed religious groups in America, these were "ethnic churches" (see Lucia 2014: 195). The negative connotations of the term "cult" have largely led to its abandonment today; that said, many scholars still distinguish between religious communities of "inheritors" (ethnic insiders) and "adopters" (ethnic outsiders) (Lucia 2014). Lucia writes that "ethnic churches strive to support traditional culture, ethnicity and religion, whereas adopters' congregations display a countercultural and non-traditional initiative" (196). Cults and somewhat similar groups are often categorized today more broadly as New Age groups or spiritual organizations. Kathryn Lofton (2011) writes that "what unifies New Age beliefs is an optimistic view of the future, a rejection of any form of authoritarian doctrine or hierarchy, an ethic of self-empowerment, an eclecticism of beliefs and practices, and a press to use science for spiritual ends" (79).

Popular spirituality in the west is also tethered to commodities and consumption practices, albeit not limited to these. Scholars have shown how this is the case for "metaphysicals," who engage in commodifying and consuming various transnational spiritual (Asian/South Asian based) movements in the west. Lofton has highlighted similar tendencies, as a consequence of late modern capitalism in America, in her study on Oprah (2011) and her more recent study of popular culture and consumption (2017), as have others (Lucia 2014, 2020; Arjana 2020). This tendency to consume is tied to particular demographics, such as those of the New Age circuit. Aldred (2000) estimated that circuit at between 10 and 20 million and mostly "white, middle-aged, and college educated, with a middle to upper-middle-class income" (330):

> The New Age is thus not a strictly defined community headed by formally recognized leaders with an articulated dogma. Rather, it is a term that is applied to a heterogenous collection of philosophies and practices. There is a wide and burgeoning number of practices associated with the New Age, including interests in shamanism, goddess worship, Eastern religions, crystals, pagan rituals,

extraterrestrials, and channeling spirit beings, "Native American spirituality" is among the most popular interests. (330)

The commodification, consumption, and popularization of religious and spiritual communities is woven throughout my discussion of Sufism in Canada. I take it up specifically in chapter 4 when discussing the popular consumption of Rumi in the Canadian spiritual marketplace through literary, cultural, and performative expressions. The consumption of Rumi today, and of Sufism more broadly, raises productive questions, including how scholars should study and engage diverse expressions of Sufism. In a spiritual landscape in which consumption influences some expressions of Sufism, the place of Rumi and Sufism is one indicator of how Sufism is unfolding. It is fascinating that Sufism in the instance of Rumi Café (see chapter 4), which sells teas and various food items, is part of the Naqshbandi Haqqani Kabbani Rumi Rose Garden in Vancouver. Members of this Sufi community are diasporic Muslims as well as white converts to Islam. The café also has an online presence (Facebook and Instagram). The philosophy behind the selling of the Rumi teas and food items remains deeply tethered to Sufi philosophical and metaphysical practices held by the Naqshbandi Haqqani Kabbani community. So where one might initially have dismissed the Rumi Rose Garden café as another problematic example of popular commodification (thus, dilution) of Rumi, chapter 4 showcases that the landscape on which this café exists is far more complicated, especially when Canadian Sufis themselves are active producers of a commodity.

So it is important here to take stock of the geography of popular spirituality in Canada. This study makes the simple but seemingly basic claim that Islam and Sufism are an important thread of popular spirituality in Canada. Overall, the shifts in Canada's religious and spiritual topography have been influenced both by the declining practice of Christianity and by the rise in secular and/or non-religious (Christian) spiritual affiliations, as well as an increase in the involvement of non-Christian traditions, especially through post-1960s immigration (Bramadat and Seljak 2005; Wilkins-Laflamme 2017; Hussain and Scott 2012). As scholars continue to document the multitude of spiritual and religious expressions and modes of being in Canada, studies must also account for how non-Christian (e.g., Muslim) expressions of Islam are contributing to the landscape of popular spirituality in Canada, not only as a contemporary reality but as part of a broader historical process. We should not assume that Sufism in Canada exists solely as a diasporic expression. Furthermore, Sufi communities in Canada share "overlapping social circles" with other religious communities, including Muslim communities (Lucia 2014: 156). Despite this reality, Sufi communities in Canada have been framed as non-Islamic popular spirituality and at times as New Age. Here, then, we arrive at an ongoing conversation in studies of contemporary Sufism, especially in North America and western Europe, one that this book addresses: Is the expression of Sufism Islamic, spiritual, neo-Sufi, New Age, or much more than these? At the heart of this classification project is the broader issue of the legitimacy of Sufism, especially Sufism in North America and western Europe (Bazzano and Hermansen 2020; Knysh 2017; Sedgwick 2012, 2016; Taji-Farouki 2007; Xavier and Dickson 2020; Dickson 2015; Sorgenfrei 2013; Hazen 2017; Piraino 2020).[12]

The Emergence of Sufism in the West

The term Sufism, which is usually presented reductively as Islamic mysticism, was generated by eighteenth-century European scholars who were employed in various capacities by imperial institutions, such as the East India Company (Uždavinys 2005; Ernst 1997). These early interlocutors felt an affinity with Sufism, which they understood as originating in Persia but which they also comprehended as a perennial tradition that was not restricted to Islam and whose origins could also be located in other traditions, such as Hinduism and Buddhism. This disassociation with Islam was based primarily on their perception that Islam's core text, the Quran (in Arabic), was dry, literal, and legalistic, as well as couched in the tribalism of uncivilized Arabs (Masuzawa 2005:26). These tropes were strengthened by their commonly held perception that the Prophet Muhammad was the Antichrist – a perception that had taken hold since the early crusades and has continued even to this day in various neocolonial contexts. As William Rory Dickson (2022) explains, "many European scholars at this time understood genuine mysticism and philosophy to be products of the 'Aryan mind,' in contrast to Islam, which was understood to be a quintessential Semitic legalism" (3). So Sufism, with its poetry evoking themes of love and ecstasy and its "exoticized" wandering mendicants and whirling dervishes, did not fit the picture of Islam that European colonialists had imagined or constructed. Sufi tradition was integral to Islam across the Muslim world, yet European colonialists saw it as a non-Islamic Aryan, Persian, and perennial tradition and perpetuated it as such in their direct and indirect projects of transmission.[13]

Sufism, as we now refer to it, emerged out of colonial encounters between European and Muslim societies. These led to cultural and literary exchanges, especially among Orientalist scholars such as William Jones (d. 1794), the British philologist who served as a judge in Bengal for the East India Company. His interest in Indo-European languages drew him to study Persian and Sanskrit, which drew him in turn to read Sufi literary works, such as those of the Persian Muslim poet Hafiz. As many scholarly studies have noted, this was an early instance of Persian Sufi philosophies and traditions circulating within a complex colonial network. That circulation would soon influence the European Romantics, including Johann Wolfgang von Goethe (d. 1832) as well as the Transcendentalists in America, such as Ralph Waldo Emerson (1882) (Einboden 2014; Sedarat 2019; Sharify-Funk et al. 2017). The same era saw a multitude of travellers' accounts about regions such as Egypt (by the British translator Edward Lane [d. 1876]) that added significantly to the allure of Sufis as peculiar and antinomian figures. Among those accounts were many from the Ottoman Empire that documented the musical traditions of the dervishes, specifically the whirling dervishes, and their skirts (*tennure*) (see chapter 4) (Ernst 1997; Sedgwick 2016; Knysh 2017). Overall, these early accounts by non-Muslims of Sufi cultural, religious, and literary traditions presented Sufism as a non-Islamic and non-Arabic universal tradition; indeed, Sufism was sometimes perceived as rooted in Hinduism and Buddhism. The notion that Sufism is a non-Islamic universal tradition circulated during an era of imperial and colonial conquest, at a time when Muslims were viewed by Europeans as violent barbarians. This construction of Sufism had an appeal for various spiritual movements that were emerging in America, namely those affiliated with groups such as the Theosophical Society and the Transcendentalists.

Even while Sufism was being extracted, transmitted, and transformed for a non-Muslim audience, some Muslims themselves, from Turkey (Ottoman Empire) to Indonesia (Southeast Asia), were experiencing their own anxieties about Sufism in relation to Islam. Sufism was central to the eastward expansion of Islam from Arabia and had given birth to political and social forms of Islam in the medieval period through *tariqa*s (orders), yet there was ongoing tension about the proper form and expression of Sufism and its relationship with Islamic law and practice, as espoused by medieval scholars such as Taqi al-Din ibn Taymiyyah (d. 1328), who himself was an initiated Sufi. A backlash against Sufism and the development of anti-Sufism began to align with increased contact with Europeans and the ongoing violence of imperialism and colonialism (Sirriyeh 1999). During this era of collapse, as Muslims looked back on their glory years, some began to cultivate theological projects that viewed traditions like Sufism and Shia Islam as blemishes in the supposedly pure monotheistic and monolithic Islam of an imagined golden past. The positioning of Sufism against these projects exacerbated these rather entangled historical dynamics that were all subsumed under Islam (Ahmed 2016). All of this led to cleavages in discussions of Sufism and anti-Sufism. As Brannon Ingram has indicated, many groups, such as the Deobandi (who are mistakenly understood as anti-Sufis), "see[] Sufism as inseparable from Islamic legal norms. These, in turn, are inseparable from Islamic ethics and politics, broadly conceived" (3). Many groups that have an affinity for some aspects of Sufism are easily framed as "fundamentalists" and "Wahhabis," and this has led to further polarization in discussions of Sufism (Formichi 2020: 100). Often, as was the case with Ibn Taymiyyah, it was the "excessive" ritual practices associated with localized cultural customs (i.e., pilgrimages to saint's tombs) that were deemed problematic;

often, though, these criticisms did not amount to calls for tossing Sufism aside entirely. Sufism entailed more than ritual practices: it informed Islamic law, theology, and philosophy. The complete rejection of Sufism is not typical of most reformists' theologies (100): "The phenomenon of systematic Sufi contestation by legal scholars can thus be identified as a modern one. In fact, several scholars of Sufism agree that until the eighteenth century 'there has never been any clear and uniform pattern of enmity between the jurists and the mystics' and that 'Sufism was largely taken for granted as part of the fabric of daily life across Muslim societies from the Maghrib to Java'" (Formichi 2020: 85).

Even so, the "conversation and convergence between 'the law' and 'the soul' of Islam has been a consistent thread in the development of Sufism" (Formichi 2020: 85; Dickson 2022). The emergence of Sufism in the west (via Orientalism) was also closely linked to the silencing and at times purging of Sufism in some Muslim societies for political and theological purposes (e.g., Salafis), on the basis that *Sufism was indeed not Islamic*. Just as interest in Sufism was being planted into the spiritual and metaphysical landscape of western Europe and America (and the west more broadly), one figure began to emerge as the living face of this universal tradition of Sufism.

The Genesis of Living Sufism in the West

Inayat Khan arrived in New York via India with his cousins and brother as part of a musical troupe. Upon his arrival he found the racial and religious discrimination against Muslims and the general hostility toward them to be overwhelming, and this negative perception of Islam likely impeded acceptance of his teachings. These early experiences propelled his universal approaches to Sufism, at least when it came to the general public. Before departing for Europe, Khan married an American woman named Ora Ray Baker (Ameena Begum) (d. 1949), a cousin of Mary Baker Eddy, the founder of the Christian Science Church. Inayat Khan initially tried to frame Sufism for his American and then European audiences within Islamic practices, such as *salat*, and emphasized the legacy of the Prophet Muhammad and the Quran. At his centre in London, he even hosted *eid* celebrations and co-founded, with Ikbal Ali Shah (d. 1969), the Muslim–Christian organization Anjuman Islam. Despite these efforts, he found that his western non-Muslim audience had little interest in Islam (Dickson and Xavier 2019; Inayat-Khan 2006). Khan and his family moved to France in 1920; in 1923, they established a centre for his movement in Geneva, forming the Sufi Order, later renamed the Sufi Movement (Jironet 2009). Almost all of its members were non-Muslims interested in spirituality and esotericism. In 1921 Khan launched the Universal Worship Service, which remains central to the movement to this day. This ritual practice includes lighting candles in honour of various religious traditions of the world and reading passages selected from their respective sacred texts.[14] This negotiation and adaptation of universal and Islamic presentations of Sufism is found to this day in many other groups discussed in this book.

After Inayat Khan founded his Sufi Order, there was an interim period before more Muslim teachers began arriving in America and western Europe to spread Sufi teachings. There were also regional developments of Sufism, especially among African American communities in the United States. Due to growing internationalism, and especially as a result of Black nationalist movements and contact with continental African Islam, such as through the Nation of Islam (NOI) and the Moorish Science Temple (MST), Sufism formed a unique thread among the African American communities. Sufism was practised in some African American communities in the 1930s and 1950s; these communities were influenced by broader connections to the Muslim world, some of which are captured by Michael Muhammad Knight in his book *Metaphysical Africa: Truth and Blackness in the Ansaru Allah Community* (2020). Rasul Miller has documented these realities among leaders such as the Grenadian *shaykh* Daoud Faisal; he joined the Shadhili Order and went on to become a *muqaddam* (representative) of the Shadhili Order, receiving "authorization" from the Moroccan Sufi *shaykh* Ahmed al 'Alawi (Miller 2020a). *Shaykh* Daoud and his wife Mother Khadijah founded the Islamic Mission of America in Brooklyn in 1939 (Miller 2020a). Imam Al-Hajj Wali Akram was affiliated with the Chishti Order. He founded the First Cleveland Mosque in 1937. He held *zikr*, and according to Miller "this likely marks the first public Sufi gatherings convened by Black American Muslims in a mosque during the 20th century" (Miller 2020a).

Counterculturalism of the 1960s and Increasing Globalization

As discussed earlier, the counterculturalism of the 1960s and its aftermath saw a proliferation of Sufi activities and communities in the United States, Canada, and western Europe, especially in America and Britain. This was accelerated by growing immigration. These spiritual and social-political movements also influenced the Canadian spiritual and seeker landscape. In America, scholars have noted the formation of influential groups such as the Tamil Sufi teacher M.R. Bawa Muhaiyaddeen's (d. 1986) Fellowship (Xavier 2018) and Muzaffer Ozak's (d. 1985) Halveti-Jerrahi Order. The Fellowship would establish a branch in Toronto in the 1970s. As global immigration unfolded, more immigrants from Muslim-majority areas arrived in the west, "transplanting" Sufi communities from immigrants' homelands to their new host countries (Hermansen 1997). Such transplantation is evident with groups like the West African Sufis of the Muridi Sufi Brotherhood (Ahmadu Bamba, d. 1927), the Senegalese Sufis in West Harlem, and the Tijaniyya in Brooklyn, as well as the Barelvi-oriented Sufis from Pakistan. Clearly, the state of New York has been an important site for the development of Sufism in America; from there, it would seep into Canada through cities like Toronto and Montreal (an example being the Jerrahi Order, discussed in chapter 2). The Alami *tariqa* in Waterport, New York, dates back to the late 1970s, when a Bosnian teacher, Asaf Durakovic (d. 2020), arrived in the US, though he spent some time in southern Ontario (Canada) before then. The Alami *tariqa* is a Khalwati-Hayati group whose members are white and African American, South Asian, and Eastern European (Hazen 2017). This group requires its members to eventually adopt Islam and practice *sharia* in order to fully participate.

The development of Sufism in the western Europe follows patterns similar to those noted earlier while encompassing some key differences. For instance, Ron Geaves frames the development of Sufism in Britain as "transcultural and transnational" in that Sufism in Britain, in contrast to America, was experienced largely by the Muslim diaspora (especially various South Asian Muslims). Still, British Sufi groups also transcended singular cultural and ethnic community socialities, and thus included people from Turkey, Malaysia, and North and sub-Saharan Africa (Geaves 2000, 2009; Geaves and Gabriel 2013: 1).[15] Despite the immigrant and ethnic-based development of Sufism in Britain, there have been parallel forms of localized Sufism there as well. Irina Tweedie (d. 1999), a Russian-British teacher of the Naqshbandiyya-Mujaddidiyya, is a representative example. In 1961 she became a student of Radha Mohan Lal (d. 1966) in India, who was part of a Hindu-Sufi family. Tweedie's books about her spiritual journey, such as *Chasm of Fire: A Woman's Experience of Liberation through the Teachings of a Sufi Master* (1979), sold widely and led to an extensive lecture tour in North America and Europe. After Lal's death, Tweedie returned to England and began to host intimate meditation groups. During one such session in 1973, she met Llewellyn Vaughan-Lee, her successor, who established the Golden Sufi Center in California in 1992 (Dickson 2020). The Golden Sufi Center is a transnational community with followers in Australia, South Africa, Canada, the US, and Chile; Vaughan-Lee has become a formative Sufi teacher globally. He teaches, writes, and lectures particularly on Sufism, dreams, and Jungian psychology.[16] Vaughan-Lee visited Vancouver in 1992 to give a lecture on Sufism and dreams for the Vancouver Jung Society; this led to the founding of an informal group. A group affiliated with this community is now based on Salt Spring Island, where they meet in the home of Dale Genge. Vaughan-Lee has since designated his son Emmanuel Vaughan-Lee as the teacher of the community. Though Vaughan-Lee identifies his group as non-Islamic, the Golden Sufi Center in California does have roots in the Naqshbandiyya-Mujaddidiyya in India (Dickson 2022: 10).

Other teachers from Muslim homelands who travelled to England and established Sufi centres include Javad Nurbakhsh (d. 2008) and Muhammad Nazim al-Haqqani (d. 2014). There are branches of both these communities in Canada, and is discussed throughout this study. The former travelled extensively between the US and the UK before finally settling in England in 1986 (Milani et al. 2017). Nurbakhsh inspired the development of more than thirty-five active Nimatuallhi centres globally, including in England, France, the Netherlands, Germany, Spain, Sweden, Mexico, Mali, Senegal, and Canada (Toronto).[17] He authored several books on psychology and Sufism (he was a practising psychiatrist), which have been translated into English, French, Spanish, and Italian (Küçük 2008: 314).[18] The order publishes the semi-annual *Sufi: Journal of Mystical Philosophy and Practice*, now edited by Alireza Nurbakhsh, the son of Javad Nurbakhsh as well as his successor. Milad Milani (2017) has discussed how Javad Nurbakhsh reformulated Sufism, particularly Iranian Sufism, in ways that that reaffirm Orientalists' definitions of Sufism (Persian tradition) for a contemporary New Age and western audience. In so doing, Milani raises the issue of whether such framing of Sufism can be referred to as Sufism at all anymore.

The Cypriot Naqshbandi leader Nazim al-Haqqani travelled to Britain in 1974 and established a centre in London, after the death of his teacher Abd Allah Dagestani (d. 1973) in Damascus, forming the Naqshbandi-Haqqani Order. He succeeded in attracting followers from both convert and traditional Muslim backgrounds, not only in western countries but also in Turkey, Syria, Sri Lanka, and Malaysia. In 1990, Nazim's student and son-in-law Hisham Kabbani moved to the United States, where he founded branches; these include mosques, centres, and a retreat centre on a farm in Fenton, Michigan. Kabbani has been a rather polarizing figure in America's Muslim community, for he has praised leaders like George W. Bush and Tony Blair for fighting terrorism. He supported these political leaders because he was a fervent critic of "Wahhabi" Islam, but his essentializing rhetoric was denounced by many Muslims, who viewed him as contributing to Islamophobia, especially as a "native" expert (Dickson 2014). Chapter 4 will discuss in more depth the affiliate Naqshbandi Haqqani Kabbani group located in Vancouver. Centres for this community also exist in Montreal and Toronto, but this study does not engage with them.

Many of the trends noted in the development of Sufism in western Europe and North America are also evident in the development of Sufism in South America. Scholars like Mark Sedgwick highlight that diasporic Sufism has had the least impact on that continent, as migration to the global west did not include the same level of mass migration to Latin American countries (Sedgwick 2018). In this regard, conversion to Sufism, either due to historic genealogies traceable back to Muslim ancestors in Spain/Al-Andalus (with parallels to what occurred in African American communities) and/or through interest in mysticism or esoteric traditions and Islam more broadly, have prompted the spread of Sufism in South America (Gallardo 2016; Chitwood 2021). However, the study of Sufism in South America requires more attention to ascertain the nuances of its development in the diverse regions; scholars like Marta Domínguez Díaz (2021) and Lucícia Cirianni-Salazar (2021) have taken up this work.

Traditionalism and the Making of Western Sufism

Since the turn of the twentieth century, traditionalism has become important to the development of Sufism in Europe and North America. This trend has been influenced by the travels of European seekers to Muslim regions and their acquaintance with Islam and Sufism. French esotericist Réne Guénon (d. 1951) was a significant figure in the emergence of modern traditionalism. He was initiated into Sufism by Ivan Aguéli (d. 1917), a Swedish painter and anarchist, who connected Guénon with the Shadhiliyya, which prompted Guénon's eventual move to Cairo in the 1930s, where he acquired his new name, Abd al-Wahid Yahya.[19] Frithjof Schuon (d. 1998), also known as Isa Nur al-Din, was a Swiss Sufi author who was influenced by Guénon's thoughts on traditionalism and became linked to the Alwaiyya Shadhiliyya, an Algerian Sufi order of Ahmad al-Alawi (d. 1934). Shaykh al-Alawi became known in Europe and America because of Martin Lings's (d. 2005) book about him titled *A Sufi Saint of the Twentieth Century* (1961). Schuon wrote about different religious traditions, highlighting the philosophy of perennial wisdom (*sophia perennis*) "at the heart of human religious history" (Dickson 2015; Sedgwick 2016). Schuon established a branch of the Shadhili-Alawiyya. In his teachings he emphasized *zikr* more than other Islamic practices, though he often oriented his understanding of Sufism toward the Hindu philosophy of Advaita Vedanta (an understanding on non-duality). The latter highlights the differing approaches of Guénon and Schuon: the former emphasized Islamic "tradition" while the latter moved beyond it. For instance, Schuon's interest in Native American spirituality led to his initiation into the Sioux nation and his incorporation of rituals such as the sweat lodge. In 1965, a mystical vision of the Virgin Mary altered the course of Schuon's Alawiyya branch and led to the group being renamed the Maryamiyya (see Sedgwick 2004, 2016). As a result of his connections with Victor Danner, a professor of religious studies in Bloomington, Indiana, the Maryamiyya Center was established in Bloomington in 1967; Schuon moved to Indiana in 1981. Schuon and the practices of the Maryamiyya have recently generated many controversies, especially regarding Schuon's alleged sexual indiscretions with underage youth in ritual contexts.

Today, the Professor Emeritus of Islamic Studies at George Washington University, Seyyed Hossein Nasr, leads the Maryamiyya. Nasr, originally from Tehran, was exiled during the Iranian Revolution in 1979 due to his close ties to the imperial court of Shah Pahlavi. During his studies at MIT, he encountered traditionalism through the writings of Schuon and eventually met him in 1957. With the passing of Schuon in 1998, Nasr "re-asserted the order's Islamic nature and emphasized Schuon's role as a traditional Muslim Sufi *shaykh*" (Dickson 2012: 132). Some of Schuon's students still feel that Schuon was a "primordial" sage who taught a pure esotericism ultimately beyond any single tradition. For them, Islam is not central to his teachings but merely a useful framework for esoteric knowledge. The Maryamiyya has several followers affiliated with the western academy. These member-scholars publish on Sufism for both academic and non-academic audiences and influence academic and public opinions on Sufism.

Some of the above dynamics – the transmission of Sufism through literary and cultural exchanges that influenced Transcendentalism, the arrival of Inayat Khan, the role of Sufism among some African American Muslim communities in the mid-twentieth century, and the arrival of the many Sufi teachers beginning in the 1960s – capture the "polygenetic" roots of Sufism in the west (Xavier and Dickson 2020: 2). These various roots are also informed by larger social processes of globalization and the resulting migrations of various diasporic communities. Throughout this process, Sufi practices and poetry have been a popular spiritual commodity. Still, there have been other trends as well. For instance, Sufism has been employed and distilled as part of Sunni Islamic ethos among various popular Muslim preachers in the west. An example here is the American Muslim convert and leader Hamza Yusuf, the founder of Zaytuna College. Yusuf frames Sufi ethics, values, and philosophies as broad Islamic spirituality within Sunni and legalistic (*fiqh*) traditions. Another example is the American Islamic scholar and Sufi Nuh Ha Mim Keller, a *shaykh* in the Shadhili Order (Grewal 2013; Hermansen 2020).[20] These figures inform another trend in the transmission of Sufism into the west, especially among younger Muslims, within the paradigm of Sunni legalism and spiritual comportment (*adab*). Still, as has been evident since Inayat Khan first arrived in America, expressions of Sufism here are highly diverse; it is an Islamic and/ or universal/perennial movement that is also New Age and pluralistic. This book will attend to this observation throughout its discussion of Sufism in Canada.

Sufism in Canada

In Canada, every account of Sufism must begin with Sufi practices by early enslaved Black Muslims in Canada. The earliest historical presence of Sufism in the Americas was among slaves who had been forcibly imported to the Americas from west Africa. The Atlantic world was defined by Black spirituality and religions, which included expressions of Sufi Islam, as documented by historians such as Sylviane Diouf in her book *Servants of Allah: African Muslims Enslaved in the Americas* (2013). Many free Black men and women ("twice as many") "emigrated" to Canada from the Americas, as noted earlier. Many scholars, such as Katherine McKittrick (2006), have highlighted the deep legacies of Black history in Canada – legacies that are often glossed over. This is of particular interest for those who are documenting the story of Sufism in Canada. Black Canadian history included Muslims and likely comprised those with ties with Sufism. Omar Ibn Said, who was born in Futa Toro, Senegal, and died in Bladen County, North Carolina, is an example of this important legacy. Said's famous autobiography makes key references to Sufi literature (Holub-Moorman and Stasio 2020). Marion Wilson Starling's *The Slave Narrative: Its Place in American History* (1988) provides some early accounts of runaways to Canada but makes no specific mention of Sufism. More research in their vein is needed in Canada.

Murray Hogben's *Minarets on the Horizon: Muslim Pioneers in Canada* (2021) provides some insightful accounts of Muslim settlers, especially in the North and on the Prairies. For instance, he recounts the life of Saleem Ganam in Regina; his father Sied Ganam (Sied Ameen Ganam Kadri) was from modern-day Lebanon and arrived in New York City in 1901 before making his way to London, Ontario, and eventually to Manitoba (42–5). In his recollection of his family story, Saleem mentions: "You see, our family is descended directly from Shaikh Abdul Qadir Gilani, the Persian Sufi saint of the eleventh century Baghdad, so we belong to the Qadiriyya sect" (qtd in Hogben 2021: 49). The stories of these early Lebanese and Arab Muslims are stories of "pioneers" who crossed the Canadian frontier and started working as pedlars, farmers, and entrepreneurs. Scholarship on Islam in Canada has made passing references to Sufism. For instance, in her study of Muslim communities in Quebec, Sheila McDonough concluded that Sufism, and Sufis, could provide an alternative picture of Muslim identity in Canada to counter the "demonization of Islam" pervasive in western media after 9/11 (2005: 134). That demonization is a common trope that often problematically positions Sufism as "good" Islam to remedy supposed "bad" Islam. McDonough discusses how in the early 2000s a number of Muslim Canadian immigrants turned to Sufism to "find sources for a spiritual dimension in their lives to counter the confusion created by the challenges of a life in a new and demanding culture" (133). Other studies, such as by Michael Frishkopf of Muslim communities in Edmonton, have expressed that there are "no Sufi groups operating openly, and in my experience Sufism has never been the subject of weekly sermons or mosque lectures and study groups," in contrast to cities like Montreal and Toronto, where there are more active Sufi communities (2009: 50). Frishkopf goes on to explain that Sufism "itself, spiritual source and practical scene of so much of the Muslim soundworld, does not easily take root in Canada; Sufi activities in larger, more diverse cities (especially Toronto and Montreal) are constantly threatened by more powerful reformist ideology eyeing their activities as un-Islamic, and seeking to unify the Umma on a more 'rational' basis" (64).

Regula Qureshi has mapped the origins of one of the first South Asian Sufi communities in Toronto, the Sufi Study Circle, which formed around the University of Toronto Islamic Studies professor Dr M. Qadeer Shah Baig (d. 1988), and which remains active under his successor Syed Mumtaz Ali (2003) (see chapter 2). Her study begins to capture some of the sonic ritual practices of this particular South Asian community. There have been allusions to some of the ways in which Sufism has influenced contemporary Canadian poets, such as Serge Patrice Thibodeau (Talbot 2006), and artists and musicians, such as R. Murray Schafer (Sharify-Funk and Dickson 2017), who have been influenced by traditions of Sufism, especially poetically and musically (see chapter 4). At the same time, there has been some mention of the lived realities of Sufism in cities such as Montréal (Mercier-Dalphond 2021; LeBlanc 2013; Haddad 2008) and Toronto (Xavier 2018). Meena Sharify-Funk and Jason Idries Sparkes's contribution to the edited volume on *Producing Islam(s)* (Barras et al. 2021) remains the first chapter to provide a general overview of Sufism in Canada.

It was not until the post-1971 changes in immigration policy that a more sustained presence of a diasporic Sufism emerged in Canada, largely among new immigrant communities, who had brought with them their practices of regional Sufi Islam. Academic studies have documented this development as the genesis of Sufism in Canada. Early scholarship on Islam, such as Mohamed Nimer's *The North American Resource Guide: Muslim Community in the United States and Canada* (2002) and Sheila McDonough's chapter on "The Muslims of Canada" (2000), mentions Sufi communities, especially in cities in Ontario. Regula Qureshi, in her chapter contribution to Barbara Metcalf's study of Muslims in North America and Europe (1996), examined Sufi practices among South Asian Muslims in Canada, especially through ritual performances of *zikr*. These early important surveys of the different forms of Islam in Canada were only beginning to gesture toward Sufism in Canada. Also, these studies presented Sufism as emerging only through migration. As this book captures, that is only half the story of how Sufism took root in Canada.

The Sufi communities documented in this study include groups with diasporic Muslim members as well as western Sufi communities that take universal approaches. Diasporic Sufi communities themselves vary culturally; they include Turkish (Eastern European), Iranian, and South Asian Sufi groups. As indicated in my discussion in the first half of this chapter, the use of generalizing labels to frame Sufi communities in the United States and western Europe can be limiting, and I do not want to reproduce such labels here. I simply do not see them as productive when engaging with ethnographic data. What I *will* try to do is map Sufism as it is developing in Canada so as to illuminate the role played by Sufism in Islam and popular spirituality. I do not hold that one form of Sufism (i.e., as practised within the strictures of Islamic law) is more legitimate or authentic than another; rather, as an ethnographer, I find it necessary to centre the voices of my interlocutors who are defining, contouring, and curating Sufism in Canada and informing global Sufism. Hence, the voices of my interlocutors will occupy much of the space in the chapters that follow. This book contends that Sufism in Canada exists across various intersections of religious (Islamic) and spiritual practices and practitioners. It sets out to challenge notions of a pure or pristine religious and spiritual practice of Sufism. Of course, I don't think that private/public and secular/sacred are easy binaries, but I will be using these terms to gesture toward some of the practices I am documenting and the fluid spheres in which they are unfolding.

The possibility of an unadulterated religious tradition has been seriously questioned by scholars of Sufism such as Carl Ernst, who have highlighted the limitations of theoretical notions of "syncretism." Such labels assume there was a pure culture or religion that existed for mixing to unfold in the first place (Formichi 2020: 45). Similar intermingling between local cultural tendencies and newly imported cultures and religions has been the basis of discussions of Islam in other regions, for instance in Asia and South Asia, where conceptual frameworks such as "mystic synthesis" and "trans-culturation" have also been employed (46). For instance, as Ernst notes, the idea of "syncretism" emerged as a "derogatory description of misguided attempts to reunite Catholics and Protestants" who were deemed "irrevocably separate" (2005:17). He explains that

> syncretism, by proposing that religions can be mixed, also assumes that religions exist in a pure unadulterated state. Where shall we find this historically untouched religion? Is there any religious tradition untouched by other religious cultures? Has any religion sprung into existence fully formed, without reference to any previously existing religion? If pure and irreducible religions cannot be found, a logical problem follows; syncretism becomes a meaningless term as everything is syncretistic. (17)

Taking Ernst's problematization of syncretic religions for granted, much of this book will be treating Sufism as a fluid commingling of popular spirituality and Islamic diasporic tradition – as often negotiated and constructed by people who identify with Sufism and are involved in its practice, especially through praxes such as of *zikr* and *sama*. It is these lived realities of Sufism that will shed light on complex social, economic, legal, and political influences across the expanse of Muslim-majority geographies. As Formichi (2020) writes in her discussion of Sufism in *Islam and Asia*, "in the fourteenth to sixteenth centuries Sufi orders took shape as more structured institutions of devotion, learning and obedience. On the other hand, the use of vernacular languages, connections to structures of power, and visionary elements caused both the further propagation of Sufism among the masses and the emergence of outright condemnation from the jurists who were losing ground, echoing some of ibn Taymiyyah's thoughts on

Sufism" (84). She notes that in regions such as South and Southeast Asia, shrine visitations, intercessions, and the veneration of Sufi teachers were perceived as (pejorative) vernacular or localized manifestations of Islam and Sufism. This dynamic of a globally constant Sufism with local manifestations of vernacular and cultural Sufi particularities has long been resorted to in studies of Sufism. There is often a tendency to negate the local as less authentic because it has taken on the hue of the geographic culture into which it has been transmitted; yet this suggests there was a pure or transcendent Sufism to start with. There was not.

Regarding the framing of Sufism in the west as less authentic *because* it is western (at times code for white), I am not interested in establishing the legitimacy of Sufism in Canada relative to Muslim contexts. I move away from the categories of New Age and New Religious Movements (NRMs) and use the term "popular spirituality," albeit loosely, for I understand that the meanings and expressions of Sufism are diverse for my interlocutors. They do not see themselves as practitioners of New Age spirtuality or an NRM. Rather, they identify as Sufi or with Sufism. Sociologists like Francesco Piraino have pointed out that terminologies such as New Age are of limited utility, especially when analysing Sufism. Piraino also distinguishes between "esoteric" traditions and differences within the categories of "perennialism/universalism" and traditionalism (2020), for often these labels and identities mean different things to different practitioners. At the other end of the spectrum, Dickson suggests that "shifting the focus from Sufism's relationship to Islam, to considering Sufi approaches to shariʿa, or Islamic law (*fiqh*)" may be a more productive way to frame these discussions (2022: 2). He adds that "since very few would have questioned Sufism's Islamic nature prior to the modern period, this analytical shift has the advantage of contextualizing contemporary Sufism within the much more extensive history of intra-Islamic difference over Sufism and shariʿa" (2). Inspired by these scholars' interventions, I think about Sufism capaciously, especially in its contemporary global manifestations. As such, I take an expansive and inclusive approach to studying Sufism in all its variations. Casting a broad net leads me to the worlds of New Age spirituality, NRMs, contemporary Islam, diasporic communities, digital religions, and much more. Wading into these worlds of diverse expressions, embodiments, and material/digital cultures allows me to critically engage with *what people do* and how they define what they do even while I probe how identities such as race, gender, class, and culture implicate how we think about religion. Though I problematize the hegemonic and colonial realities that impinge on how Sufism is consumed in our modern world, I am far more invested in situating the ways in which Sufism has been deeply transformed by both non-Islamic and Islamic cultural and religious traditions, in other words, its rich "entangled" history (Saif 2019).[21] In *The Venture of Islam*, Marshall Hodgson summons an approach to the study of the "Islamicate" world that includes both Muslim and non-Muslim influences on the formation of Islam. His study invites scholars to move beyond textual and legalistic worlds to consider how trade, travel, culture, economics, and much more defined the formation of Islam (1974); meanwhile, scholars like Bruce Lawrence have framed this idea through the lens of an "Islamicate Cosmopolitian Spirit" (2022). At the same time, Shahab Ahmed's monumental study *What Is Islam?: The Importance of Being Islamic* (2016) invites us to consider the "pre-text" (text here being Quran or revelation) that has informed what we think of as Islamic as much as the text itself. In speaking specifically to Sufism, Knysh (2019) theorizes that "'Sufism' serves as a meeting place of discourses and imaginations, both Muslim and western, namely 'internal' and 'external' to Islam as a devotional tradition," and it is at these "meeting places" that ideas of Sufism are "being (re-)negotiated, (re-) adjusted and (re)articulated" by differently located peoples (58). Like Knysh, Ahmed, and others, I contend that it is far more useful to move beyond questions of *dilution* and *authenticity* of an unspoiled Sufi tradition, and shift to dwelling in the in-between spaces and lived realities of Sufism in all its contexts and variations, be it institutional to non-institutional Sufism. In this regard, Rumi specifically, and ritual praxis and/or popular culture more broadly, serve as productive analytical tools for us to process the reception of Sufism today in light of Sufism's complex history and the overlapping spheres within which it exists.

Conclusions

This chapter has developed the conceptual frameworks I will be using to reflect on and process Sufism in Canada. It started by locating the history of Islam in Canada in the stories of the first Black peoples. This historical orientation is an essential decolonial move, for it places Canadian Islamic history in the context of the violence against non-white peoples, first Indigenous, then Black, and other racialized peoples. The lack of focus on Black and African Muslim history amounts to a deep erasure of the history of Canada broadly and Islamic history specifically. Though this book is not about Black Muslim history, I hope that placing my discussion of Sufism in this broader context will encourage scholars of Islam and Muslims in Canada to do the necessary work of starting the story we tell of Islam in Canada with Black history, and also encourage scholars to boldly enter into the archives and radically reimagine the stories we tell about the first Muslims in Canada. This chapter gestures to that possibility as a first step toward unsettling the whiteness in which Sufism is Canada is often centred.

The chapter then situated the fields of Islam and Muslims in Canada and highlighted the limited attention given to the study of Sufism within this particular body of academic work. This book on Sufism in Canada begins to fill this lacuna so as to engage with the diversity of Muslim expressions of piety. Many practitioners of Sufism in this country are non-Muslims, and this is hardly unique to Canada: many international studies have documented the same thing. For this reason, I have oriented the reader to some of the literature on New Age spirituality, NRMs, and popular spirituality in Canada, as this remains an overlapping site where Sufism in Canada has established itself. As a result of this coexistence of diverse expressions of Sufism that span Muslim and non-Muslim practitioners, I then addressed the problematics related to discourses of authenticity or orthodoxy in how contemporary Sufism is practised, especially in relation to Islamic law. Reflecting these complex expressions of Sufism in both historical and contemporary iterations, scholars often either propose a capacious or restrictive approach to the study of Sufism in the contemporary west. In this study, I take a capacious approach to Sufism; as I explained earlier, this is because I am attentive to rituals and practices of my interlocutors in the field who inform my analysis, and less so to textual or legalistic conceptualizations of Sufism. Regardless, the controversy over Sufism's legitimacy, especially in relation to Islamic law or lack thereof, hovers over the practices I document. So I return to these contestations throughout my discussion in the chapters that follow. This chapter introduced some of the Sufi movements in North America and western Europe; the next chapter focuses on Sufi communities in Toronto, Montreal, and Vancouver. It provides a history of Sufism in Canada through particular institutions and communities.

Chapter Two

Early Sufi Communities in Canada

The Sufi Order International (now Inayati Order) is one of the oldest Sufi communities in the west. At the turn of the twentieth century, Inayat Khan founded communities in western Europe and initiated students in America, who would continue his legacy. Little has been written about the Sufi Order International (now Inayati Order) and other organizations with Canadian branches, like the International Sufi Movement. Inayat Khan never visited Canada (from what we know); it is through his sons and their students' visits that his teachings reached Canada. This was just the beginning: many other Sufi teachers later established centres and communities in Canada. This country presented a significant opportunity for Sufi teachers, who viewed its vast hinterlands as fertile ground for Sufism and spirituality. This chapter maps the history of some early Sufi communities in Vancouver, Toronto, and Montreal. The history and practices of some early Sufi communities in Canada, such as the Inayati Order, are presented here for the first time. The history I chart is based on data collected from semi-structured interviews with community members and leaders (*shaykhs*/*shaykha*s) of various Sufi groups; this is complemented by archival research as well as references to memoirs, especially of Sufi leaders in the US who were tied to the same Sufi teachers, such as Suleyman Loras (d. 1985). This chapter is not meant to be a comprehensive historical survey of Sufi communities and movements in any one city or in Canada. Rather, it presents some initial institutional patterns of Sufism in some Canadian cities as a means to frame the discussion of the complex legacies and praxis that surround Rumi in Canada, which later chapters will explore closely.

My discussion of Sufi communities in Canada here is framed around two broad trends. First, these communities arose from a predominately North American base, established by teachers from Muslim or Sufi lineages who wanted to found Sufi and spiritual centres in Canada. This trajectory was key to Sufism's growth on Canada's west coast, as evident in the development of the Vancouver Rumi Society. Second, the Sufi communities which emerged in the

1990s and early 2000s was defined by a diasporic contingent, an example of this being the Turkish Jerrahi Order of Canada. These latter groups have since diversified ethnically and culturally as more diasporic Muslim Sufi communities have established themselves in Canada. However, I do not presume that these two kinds of Sufism took form in mutually exclusive ways; indeed, they overlapped quite intimately. Sufi communities in Canada today include groups that are variously (1) diasporic and Muslim, (2) non-Muslim spiritual seekers who are predominately white, and (3) a blend of both. Below, I will also highlight how ritual practice that included music and the meditative movement, or dance, was a common thread among many early Muslim and non-Muslim Sufi communities, such as the Gurdjieff Society of Canada, the Sufi Islamia Ruhaniat Society, the Sufi Study Circle in Toronto, and the Vancouver Rumi Society.

It will become clear in this chapter that the institutionalization of Sufism in Canada has been tied to regional developments of Sufism in the United States and western Europe. For example, transregional and transnational ebbs and flows will become apparent when we examine Sufi communities in the Cascadia region, which includes Vancouver. Travel between California and Washington states among Sufi communities led directly to the growth of Sufism in Vancouver, while in cities like Toronto and Montreal, movement between New York and southern Ontario was vital to Sufism's development in the east. These transregional ebbs and flows reflected broader global trends, especially globalization through migration. That said, the diversification of Sufi communities over the past few decades has hinged on particular migrational trajectories unique to cities in Canada. For instance, the arrival of diasporic communities from Muslim-majority regions such as Iran, Turkey, Senegal, and Pakistan significantly expanded and transformed Sufism in Toronto and Montreal. By contrast, Vancouver has been defined mostly by Asian diasporic communities and has a far more religiously unaffiliated and spiritually driven demographic of practitioners of Sufism. Even so, a Persian diasporic presence has informed Sufism in Vancouver, as we see with the Vancouver Rumi Society. Sufism in Canada, then, has been defined by an interest in broader popular spirituality; at the same time, trends in Muslim immigration have further diversified the regional variations of Sufi communities. In sum, Sufism in Canada is global, transnational, and transregional (between the United States and Canada), and across these various Sufi communities, Sufism's relationship to Islam and Islamic practice is constantly being questioned, especially in terms of the legitimacy of different Sufi communities – are they Islamic or New Age? (See chapter 1.)

Early Sufi Communities in Canada

For most of the nineteenth century, Sufism was as an abstract concept that made sporadic appearances in print media, especially in church periodicals and mission reports (as chapter 4 highlights). Before then, it was likely that Sufi practices were embodied by early enslaved or formerly enslaved peoples (see chapter 1). Sufi practices among some of the first Muslim "pioneer" families have been noted (Hogben 2021). It was not until after the loosening of immigration policy in 1971 that Muslims began to arrive in Canada in appreciable numbers. It is at this point that one begins to encounter more records of Sufi communities in small pockets of early Muslim communities across Canada, especially in cities like Toronto. Amir Hussain (2001) in his meticulously researched dissertation on Islam in Canada writes that "due to the 'interorization' of practices by certain Sufis, it is difficult to say with certainty when Sufism 'began' in Canada" (74). Some hold that Maulana Muhammad 'Abdul 'Aleem Siddiqui, (or al-Qadiri) was the first known Sufi in Canada (174). The Indian-born Siddiqui travelled to Canada in 1939, speaking, for instance, at the al-Rashid Mosque in Edmonton, and later in Toronto as well (174; Waugh 2018).

The Gurdjieff Society of Canada

By the early twentieth century, itinerant Muslim preachers were infusing their sermons with Sufi teachings in newly developing mosques in Canada. In the mid-1900s, non-Muslim forms of Sufism were beginning to develop, based in particular on the teachings of Georges Ivanovich Gurdjieff (d. 1949). Gurdjieff was born in Armenia and had travelled widely in Central Asia and Tibet. He was a rather elusive figure with a murky history. He emerged as a spiritual teacher and philosopher who established a teaching known as the "Fourth Way." He was recognized for incorporating music into his spiritual practices, and his various publications were of interest for seekers of spirituality and Sufism.[1] The Gurdjieff Foundation: Society for Traditional Studies, founded in 1954, was the first Gurdjieff institution in Canada.[2] A student of Gurdjieff, Louise Welch, and her husband William visited Halifax from New York in the summer of 1970 at the request of some students in Nova Scotia. That visit led to the formation of the Gurdjieff Society of Atlantic Canada, which was sustained under their leadership ("About Us", *Gurdjieff Society of Atlantic Canada*).[3] That community has continued to gather and hosts group meetings that entail communal practices (cooking together), meditation, and the practice of movements ("the Work") and music. All of these are central to Gurdjieff's teaching. Explaining "the Work," Mark Sedgwick writes:

> Gurdjieff was also a pioneer in the development of a new practice to accompany his theology – or, perhaps "psychology" would be a better term. The "parallel series of physical, mental, and emotional exercises" that became known as "the Work" make up the practice of the Gurdjieff movement … The most distinctive exercises were physical, initially known as "quick yoga" or "sacred gymnastics" and later

known as "the Movements." The mature form of these exercises was partly inspired by the *sema* of the Mevlevi *tariqa*, as unusual form of *dhikr* that involves turning (known as "whirling"). There was also exhausting manual labor sometimes called "super-effort," and emotional exercises that had no name which will be referred to in this book as "discomfiture." (2016: 178–9)

Thus, the earliest Sufi community to emerge in Canada was based on Gurdjieff's teachings and involved music and movements inspired by the turning of the whirling dervishes. Turning and meditative movements were already emerging as a ritual among non-Muslim Sufis. The Toronto Gurdjieff community, at times in collaboration with the Halifax community, hosted various public events and talks that featured lectures by Ravi Ravindra, the current leader of the Atlantic group, who is a Professor Emeritus at Dalhousie University in both comparative religion and physics. Ravindra lectured on yoga and Gurdjieff.[4] Other events hosted by this society included musical presentations based on Gurdjieff's teachings, which included "temple music, hymns, dervish chants, Sayyids and Asian songs."[5]

The Sufi Study Circle in Toronto

Not until the late twentieth century did Canada see the systematic development of Sufi communities, at least of a diasporic origin. The Sufi Study Circle of the University of Toronto was founded by the Indian Muslim Dr Mirza Qadeer Baig Gudri Shah Baba (1931–1988), who came to Toronto in the 1950s as a professor of Islamic Studies at the University of Toronto (Hussain 2001: 110). He was one of the first South Asian scholars to join the University of Toronto (Qureshi 2003: 71). Baig was from Ajmer, India, where he had been initiated into a branch of the Chishti community known as the Gudri Shah branch. He began to teach Sufism (both academically and informally) and founded the Chishti Sufi Study Circle in Toronto (Hussain 2001: 113; Qureshi 2003: 71). Regula Qureshi in her study of this group writes:

> Dr Qadeer Baig taught Sufism in his introductory course on Islam, and then invited interested students to discuss Sufi texts in an informal seminar on Sufism. This seminar was held on Wednesday evenings in the University's International Centre where many foreign students used to eat their dinner. Called the Sufi Study Circle, the meetings were open to everyone and were well attended by students from Pakistan as well as Canada. Interest in these meetings was especially high in the early years of Mirza Qadeer Baig's Sufi work during the 1960s. (2003: 71)

Baig also held gatherings, such as *zikr*, in his apartment on Thursday evenings. Over time, these meetings came to include *sama* (sacred audition) with *qawwali*

(Sufi devotional) singers (71). Baig had "non-Muslim Anglo-Canadian students," whom he took to Ajmer to initiate into Sufism (71). Though he would become the successor of his Sufi lineage (Gudri Shah lineage) after the death of his own teacher, it seems that this was not a role he publicly shared, according to Qureshi; instead he leaned more into his status as a professor (71). The Sufi Study Circle was registered with Ontario as a corporation with the title Society for Understanding the Finite and the Infinite (SUFI) (Hussain 2001: 175). Baig taught at the University of Toronto until his death in 1988. Before his death, a former student, Syed Mumtaz Ali, was named the successor of his Sufi order. This community continues to gather on Wednesday nights for teachings; on Thursday evenings, there is *zikr* in Ali's apartment. The teachings of this community are based on the practice of Islam; "the effort here was also to keep Canadian disciples within the rules of Islam and away from what Shaykh Syed Mumtaz Ali calls a western-style 'Pseudo Sufism' that considers itself above the laws of Islam (shari'a)" (Qureshi 2003: 74). Qureshi explains that this policy was likely a response to Toronto's growing South Asian Muslim population, especially Muslims from Pakistan, some of whom were "neo-conservative" and wanted to ensure that any Sufi practice conformed to Islamic rules (74).[6] Even early on, because Toronto's South Asian Sufi community was growing and non-Muslim students were showing increased interest, the community was concerned about being branded "pseudo-Sufi" by South Asian Muslim diasporic communities in Toronto (see chapter 1). This question of what constitutes legitimate Sufism, especially in terms of Sufism's relationship with Islam and Islamic law, has also arisen in studies of Sufi communities in the US and western Europe.

Between 1939 and the founding of the Gurdjieff societies and the Sufi Study Circle in Toronto, another important thread emerged in Sufism in Canada. Just as in the US and western Europe, Sufism was being established by teachers who travelled to Canada to teach a predominately non-Muslim audience. This led to the Sufi Order of Inayat Khan, which established a South Asian universal form of Sufism that would continue to be taught by Khan's sons and students. It would be followed by the Turkish-infused Sufism as represented by Reshad Feild and Suleyman Loras in Vancouver.

Sufi Order International and Its Affiliated Groups

Vancouver, with its Pacific breezes and soaring mountain backdrop, has always been a point of entry for those coming to Canada from South and East Asia. The Canadian west coast's idyllic landscape has attracted many spiritual seekers, especially given that it is so close to US cities like Seattle and the state of California, which were then and still are anchors for spiritual and esoteric communities. It is no surprise, then, that Vancouver has played a unique and important role in the development of Sufism in Canada.

One of the west's oldest Sufi orders is that of Inayat Khan, who established the Sufi movement in western Europe. It was his sons, however, Hidayat and Vilayat, who along with his students would help spread his teachings throughout the US and Canada and deeper into western Europe. Inayat Khan's students and family members established communities in his name across Canada, from Vancouver and Calgary to Toronto. Vilayat visited Vancouver, Toronto, Montreal, and Edmonton in the 1970s and 1980s. Samuel L. Lewis's (aka Ahmed Murad Chishti, or Sufi Sam) (d. 1971) students would also play an important role in Canada. Lewis's relationship with Sufism is often framed as eclectic and even New Age, a label that he in fact ascribed to himself. Upon his death, his students published a series of lectures titled *This Is the New Age, In Person* (1972). Lewis founded the Sufi Islamia Ruhaniat Society in 1970 (renamed Ruhaniat International in 2002), which had a branch in Nelson, BC.

An early organizer of Inayat Khan's community in Canada was Carol Sill, who was a student of Shamcher Bryn Beorse (1896–1980) a Norwegian engineer and spy during the Second World War who had met Inayat Khan in the Netherlands when he was asked to serve as his translator.[7] Sill came to Sufism through books, first *The Sufis* (Shah 1964) and then one of Inayat Khan's books, which were available from the Lucis Trust Library, a lending library in New York City that specialized in Theosophical works.[8] She connected with Shamcher through correspondence, which she works to archive today through email newsletters and digital archives.[9] Sill held meetings in Edmonton starting in 1975; these led to meetings in Banff and Calgary and eventually to retreats at Lake O'Hara, west of Calgary, attended by Hidayat Inayat Khan (d. 2016). At the time, Hidayat was the head of the International Sufi Movement founded by his father. The lectures given at the retreat by Hidayat were compiled by his Canadian students in a book titled *Sufi Teachings: Lectures from Lake O'Hara* (1994), published by Ekstasis Editions in Victoria.[10]

Vilayat, the other son of Inayat Khan, who would eventually lead the Sufi Order International, visited Vancouver around three times, first in the 1970s, then in 1980s and 1990s. In chapter 1, Zainb Paula Ford described meeting him during a spiritual conference in Vancouver. Inayat Khan's diverse communities, through his two sons and now his grandson, Zia Inayat-Khan, remain a central thread of Sufism in Canada today. Currently Zia, the son of Vilayat, is the spiritual leader (*pir*) of the Inayati Order (formerly the Sufi Order International). The Inayati Order has active centres in Toronto (and Oakville since 2017), Vancouver, Calgary, Montreal, Ottawa, and Kingston. In some of these cities, such as Kingston, the members are mainly of the Ruhaniat Order, whose practices focus on dances of Universal Peace as developed by Sufi Sam. Below I map some of these early branches of Inayat Khan's communities in Vancouver and Toronto.

VANCOUVER

According to some of its leaders, the Inayati Order (the Caravan of the Heart) is one of Vancouver's oldest Sufi groups, if not its first "organized" Sufi community. In the early 1970s, there were some Sufi gatherings around the Mawlawis (see below). The Sufi Order's meetings were held in Vancouver for more than four decades. Amir Peter O'Loughlin, originally from Hamilton, Ontario, moved to Vancouver and has been serving for more that thirty-five years as the National Representative in Canada, along with Zainb Paula Ford, another leader of this particular branch, who has been a teacher of the Inayati Order in Vancouver for more than three decades. Though initiated mainly into the Inayati Order (through Vilayat when it was the Sufi Order International), O'Loughlin, like many other Sufis in Vancouver we encounter in this chapter, has also been initiated into the Rifai Marufi (via Çatalkaya), a Turkish Sufi order (see below). O'Loughlin's first encounter with Sufism was when he was travelling in India in 1973 with a group of educators. At the time, he was interested in yoga, Buddhism, and Hinduism but had not heard of Sufism:

> O'LOUGHLIN: The day I got there, a friend of mine couldn't sleep, I couldn't sleep, we were too excited. We went out at dawn into the winding alleys and through this, what I later found out was the *dargah* [shrine] of Nizamuddin Awliya[11]... have you been to the *dargah*?
>
> XAVIER: Yeah.
>
> O'LOUGHLIN: Anyway, we found ourselves underneath this wall, this big white wall listening to divine singing and we were just both transported into this *hal* [spiritual state], this is like 5:30 in the morning, it was so beautiful. I didn't know what it was, went back, had our tour. Later on, she met Mansur Johnson and Shahabuddin, got connected to the Inayati world, I sort of started getting connected. We pieced together about two years after that when we started to learn more about it that [it] was the *dargah* of Hazrat Inayat Khan.
>
> XAVIER: So, you didn't make it to the *dargah*?
>
> O'LOUGHLIN: I was under the wall.
>
> XAVIER: Okay.
>
> O'LOUGHLIN: But that was an initiation.

O'Loughlin understood this moment as an initiation into the path of Sufism. He started meeting teachers through his friends, and this led him to connections with Shahabuddin David Less, who had studied with Vilayat, Lewis (Sufi Sam), Joe Miller (d. 1992) (of the Sufi Ruhaniat International), and Swami Sundaranand (*yogi* from India).

Since then, O'Loughlin has been holding gatherings at his home on a biweekly basis. The gatherings consist of singing and studying the teachings of Inayat and Vilayat Khan. The reading is often emailed prior to Thursday evening, and members arrive ready to discuss it and ask questions. These weekly gatherings average ten to twelve people. When I attended one such gathering in February 2020, there were around ten. O'Loughlin and Ford led the discussion; O'Loughlin, who is a musician and performer, also provided music.[12] He estimates the regular membership of the entire Vancouver group to be 100 to 150:

> You know what you saw last night, twelve people come to Thursday group, we used to have larger public gatherings. We used to have spiritual dances that would be forty or fifty people. I used to do inter-spiritual *kirtan* or music evenings. I haven't done those for a couple of years but they used to attract a lot of other people. So, the broader community obviously there's probably a hundred or a hundred and fifty. The people who come regularly for study is much smaller and a few young people are coming but mostly it's an older demographic and we don't advertise, you know, we have a website … It's not a proselytizing … I mean we have a presence in social media, there's a Facebook page, actually not a local one but a national one. But you know … I always believe that the people, who are meant to find us, find us … It was never our agenda to have, like a big group, in a separate building, that kind of stuff. So just not our style. We're different than other groups.[13]

This community tends to be a bit older and mainly white, from the generation of Vilayat Inayat Khan and his students (over fifty). In this, it resembles the Toronto community (see below). This group is apprehensive about advertising too widely, for it might attract the wrong audience – a stance that was shared by various Sufi leaders I spoke to throughout my fieldwork: those who are meant to come, will come.

The Vancouver branch of the Inayati Order hosts gatherings that include *zikr*s and *urs* (death anniversary) celebrations for Inayat Khan, as well as dances of Universal Peace. O'Loughlin collaborates often with Persian musicians in Vancouver for numerous Sufi events. He has studied Farsi to ensure the proper use of Rumi and Hafiz in his presentations and performances. This music tradition is central to the legacy of Inayat Khan and the Inayati Order to this day, as Inayat Khan was first and foremost a musician. During our conversation, O'Loughlin explained that, setting aside the Mawlawi connections that were forming with some early leaders of what is now the Vancouver Rumi Society (see below), Inayat Khan's community was the earliest Sufi group in Vancouver:

> There was a very small study group here when I first moved here, there was a smattering of Mawlawis like Majid who were connected to the Mawlawi tradition and then later on the Rifai Marufis which kind of blended the whole Turkish Sufi world kind of just went out as a big blend so people like … Seemi and Majid, Raqib, they're all connected to the Mawlawi-Rifai world and I've taken hand in the Rifai Marufi, Sherif Baba is one of my teachers. So, I kind of straddle both

worlds that way, although the Inayati initiation is my primary initiation. But we were certainly the, you know, early organized Sufi group here, as organized as Sufi groups ever get.[14]

One trend noted not only in Vancouver but also in my interactions with some of the Rumi-based Sufi communities in Toronto is that they have tended to have multiple formal or informal affiliations with Sufi leaders and communities. This tendency is not shared by other groups, such as diasporic Sufi communities and the Canadian Institute of Sufi Studies group (another branch of the Rifai Order) in Toronto, who maintain strict initiatic allegiance. In reflecting on the Sufi scene in Vancouver, O'Loughlin noted some of the changes that have unfolded throughout his time, mainly having to do with the diversification of immigration to the region, which has resulted in some interesting and at times difficult dynamics vis-à-vis other Sufi communities, which question his community's authenticity:

> O'LOUGHLIN: It's changed so much ... I think the biggest change has been that the early groups were very I would say inter-spiritually oriented cause you know the Inayati Order was in its essence inter-spiritual. It's definitely not an Islamic Sufi group ... Have you been to a Universal Worship of the Inayati Order?
> XAVIER: No, I haven't.
> O'LOUGHLIN: So, there's rituals around recognizing the absolute equality of all religions and representations of God that way. And certainly, the Rumi Society being focused on Rumi, well Rumi was also, as much as he was Muslim and many of his references are Quranic, you know he ... transcended any form of religion. So then in the late nineties, I want to say the late nineties, maybe mid nineties there arose like two or three groups that are more ... I don't know what the word would be, conventional, a bit orthodox kind of if you're not a Muslim, "you're not a Sufi kind" of groups. A couple of Persian groups that have arose, so much more traditional eastern groups started to arise. Naqshbandi group, a couple of Naqshbandi groups, one Persian group ... So that was the main thing that happened. We ... started this unity *zikr* back in the late nineties, Sherif Baba's inspiration was all the groups should come together and do various *zikr* and that was an interesting encounter because our groups, the ones who had been there for a while ... there was nothing to proselytize because we weren't really representing something that we were in a missionary position. But these other groups started to come and kind of started to proselytize and ... it actually didn't work out in the end because as much as we would say you can't go cherry picking other, you know, *murids* [students] of other paths, like this is not what this is about, and you're not here to proselytize a religion, but they just wouldn't stop. So, we actually had to just say no, that's not what it's about, this is not about converting you know a bunch of white people to Islam. Anyway, yeah so ... it was a difficult time. And really there hasn't been a lot of cross-pollination with those

groups since then because I don't think they see us as Sufis, frankly, which is a shame.

In the 1990s, the arrival of diasporic Muslim (Sufi) communities to Vancouver led to the diversification of Sufi communities and some moments of tension, especially as some Muslim Sufi communities attempted to convert non-Muslim white Sufis to Islam, in order to ensure what they felt was the proper expression of Sufi practice. Similarly, Baig's group wanted to affirm that his students practised Islam – otherwise, they would not be seen as real Sufis. For members of the Inayati Order and for O'Loughlin, who continue to see Sufism and the Inayati Order through the lens of "inter-spiritual" philosophy and practice, such moments created some disappointment and "shame," in that the authenticity of their expression of Sufism was being challenged. Many of the students who are senior members of the Inayati Order in Vancouver and Toronto had come to the Sufi Order through Vilayat, who was not a practising Muslim. Zia, though, is a practising Muslim. He has explained that Inayat Khan's own Muslim and Sufi background informed his mystical teachings, especially his roots in South Asia's Chishti tradition. Accordingly, Khan's movement presents a continuity of Sufism from South Asia to the west rather than a radical departure (Inayat-Khan 2006). Zia is presently the leader of the Inayati Order, which is currently headquartered in Richmond, Virginia, though he was formerly based in New Lebanon, New York. The order is transnational and has ties to several countries, including Canada, Britain, Switzerland, Australia, and India.[15] His move to Virginia in 2017 was due in some part to the travel accessibility it offered; in particular, it allowed easier movement between South Asia and North America, where Zia has been building more connections. Another likely reason for the move was to disentangle from his father's orientation and approach, which had been developed at the Abode of the Message. These broader generational and theological shifts and outlooks of Sufism within the Inayati Order from Inayat, to Vilayat, to Zia are perhaps best captured in the change of the movement's name from the Sufi Order to the Inayati Order. Again, such institutional rebranding points to a reframing of the movement more as a Sufi *ṭarīqa*, which Zia understands is in keeping with his grandfather's legacy. However, not all the students who are part of this community agree with these changes (Dickson and Xavier 2020). This issue is ongoing for some members of the Inayati Order, such as O'Loughlin or Ford, that is, those who came to the Sufi Order International through a far more universal practice of Sufism, which in the present day seems more Islamic than in the past, even though one need not be a Muslim to participate in the Inayati Order. Thus, the question of how to properly engage and practise Sufism isn't uniformly agreed upon even within individual Sufi groups or orders.

TORONTO

The Toronto branch of the Inayati Order has no formal centre; as in Vancouver, gatherings are held in members' homes. The Toronto community has its origins in the early 1970s. Hafiz, who leads one of the centres of the Inayati Order in Toronto, explained that he first encountered the Sufi Order International in California when he was living in Oregon.[16] When he moved to Canada, he learned there was a group in Toronto, which had formed during a visit by Wali Ali Meyer, a teacher (*murshid*) in the Sufi Ruhaniat International (SIRS). He had come to Toronto from San Francisco to present a workshop that led to the formalization of a group.[17] Hafiz was a leader of that group (when the Sufi Order had a system of leaders) until he went on sabbatical from that position from 1983 to 2003, during which time another member of the branch led it. Hafiz explained that the positions that can be held in the Inayati Order are "representative" and "coordinator," adding that representatives "can initiate people into the order and give spiritual guidance."[18] The group has between forty or fifty initiated members and around thirty "active" members (who attend regular events).[19] Despite having changed its name from Sufi Order International (or Sufi Order of the West) to the Inayati Order, it continues to refer to itself as the Sufi Order in Toronto because the steps have not yet been taken to legally change that incorporated name in Canada (at least at the time of our conversation in late 2018).

The Inayati Order offers various rituals and practices. In Toronto these include monthly *zikr*, quarterly retreats, and Universal Worship, in addition to special events like a New Year's Eve celebration called the Festival of Lights. There are also dance circles, along with smaller esoteric schools and workshops for initiated students, led by Hafiz. In Oakville, Nizam un-Nisa or Ayeda Husain offers biweekly *zikr* (see chapter 5). Hafiz, who was born into a Jewish family, has been with the order since the 1970s. He does not necessarily collaborate with other Sufi communities in Toronto (as similarly noted by O'Loughlin in Vancouver), though he has sometimes worked with groups like the Threshold Society and the Rifai Sufi Order in Toronto. Ayeda Husain takes a different approach. She comes from a South Asian Muslim background and has made efforts to collaborate with various Sufi communities in Toronto (see chapter 5). These varying approaches, both at the institutional level of the Inayati Order and more broadly, have led to shifting dynamics between some members and leaders of the Sufi communities in Toronto and Vancouver. There is more dialogue now even within the Inayati Order about the relationship between Sufism and Islam. In our conversation, Hafiz explained that "the Inayati Order and other orders that may be under the … label 'universal Sufism' … I know occasionally on our website you know … we'll get comments, oh they're not real Sufis cause they're not Muslims … So there is, as I said, sometimes spoken, sometimes unspoken … questions that people have about our authenticity … Yeah, so sometimes that's a barrier."[20]

The universalistic tendencies of the Inayati Order have meant that many of its members are located within other religious traditions even while practising Sufism. There have been noteworthy precedents for this tendency, which is not merely a modern development. For instance, one sees such fluidity of religious and spiritual practices among Jewish Sufis: Rabbi Zalman Schachter-Shalomi, for example, was initiated by Vilayat Inayat Khan.[21] Schachter-Shalomi's connections to Canada are strong: he taught at the University of Manitoba in Winnipeg for nearly two decades. He has also been involved, for example, in Trappist spirituality (Catholic). In an interview, he explained that "it began in the sixties and a resensitizing where we are. And then later on, more intuitive stuff, and gestalt and psychology moved from behaviourism to Freud and then to humanistic psychology to transpersonal psychology, all of which is in order to fill that need, that hunger that people have for the intuitive and the emotional" (qtd in *Religion and Ethics News Weekly*, 30 September 2005).[22]

Schachter-Shalomi was eventually initiated into the Sufi Order in 1975 in California, and founded the Desert Fellowship of the Message, often described as a "Sufi-Hasidic" group. The tradition of Schachter-Shalomi is alive and well in the order known as the Inayati-Maimuni Order (referring here to the classical Jewish philosopher Maimonides) and led by a student of Schachter-Shalomi, Netanel Miles-Yépez, who is of Mexican heritage.[23] The connection with Schachter-Shalomi would be significant for figures like John Brozak (see below) of the Vancouver Rumi Society. The historical connections between Jewish and Islamic mysticism, especially because of shared philosophical and theological traditions via Neoplatonism, have been discussed by scholars such as Mark Sedgwick (2016). Sufism intrigued Jewish thinkers like Rabbi Abraham Maimonides (d. 1237), the son of Maimonides; others have noted how mystical traditions of Judaism (Kabbalah), Christianity, and Islam have historically influenced one another because of their extensive contacts in the Middle East. Many non-Muslim Sufis in communities such as the Inayati Order, and in Rumi-based societies in Vancouver, come from Jewish communities. The ease with which Sufism blends traditions such as Judaism, Christianity, Hinduism, and much more, in cities like Toronto, Montreal, and Vancouver captures a historical reality and not necessarily an innovative New Age one (which is the label assigned to the Inayati Order by many Muslims and academics; see chapter 1).

Despite not being a Mawlawi Order or having any Turkish roots, the Inayati Order is fairly active in sharing the tradition of Rumi in its various locales. For instance, Zia regularly hosts retreats and commemorations for Sufi figures, such as Rumi and also his own grandfather. These events are held sometimes in Virginia and other times at the *dargah* of his grandfather and father, Vilayat, in New Delhi, India. These gatherings have also shifted to a collaborative platform and include Sufi teachers from different orders. For instance, to commemorate the 812th birthday of Rumi, in September 2019 a weekend retreat was held that included Nur Artiran, a Sufi teacher from Turkey, *shaykha* Fariha al-Jerrahi of the Nur Ashki Jerrahi Order in New York City, and teachers from the Mouridiyya Order (from Senegal), along with whirling dervishes from Toronto and Montreal, musicians, and academics, such as Dr Carl Ernst of the University of North Carolina. This focus on Rumi is evident among the Inayati leaders in Canada, especially O'Loughlin, who regularly presents *sama* with members of Vancouver Rumi Society (see chapter 3). Also, *shaykha*s like Ayeda Husain focus on Rumi and his poems in biweekly *zikr* sessions (see chapter 5).

The Sufi Order International, then, is one of the earliest Sufi communities to have been established in Canada. Parallel to the development of Sufism in Canada among diasporic Sufi communities, which include the South Asian Sufism of Baig in Toronto, there was also then a South Asian flavour of universal Sufism emerging among the Inayati Order, especially through Sufi Order International and the International Sufi Movement among Canadians. Due in large part to teachers like Vilayat, Hidayat, and Sufi Sam and their respective students who held retreats and workshops in Canada, this led to the emergence of branches. While the Sufi Order was established in cities like Vancouver, Edmonton, and Calgary by the 1970s, another important thread of Sufism was flourishing, one tied to the traditions of Rumi and Turkish Sufism.

The Vancouver Rumi Society

The story of the Vancouver Rumi Society centres on several figures and their separate journeys that brought them together. The story of Turkish Mawlawi (Mevlevi) Sufi *shaykh* Suleyman Loras (Dede) in America is captured in Simon Sorgenfrei's doctoral dissertation *American Dervish: Making Mevlevism in the United States of America* (2013). However, the following sections describe the development of the Vancouver Rumi Society specifically, which was initially entangled with the Mevlevi Order of America but has since become a separate body.[24]

JOHN BROZAK

In early 1969, when Brozak was an undergraduate student at the University of British Columbia, he attended a performance by the San Francisco Mime Troupe. Brozak was fascinated by one of the performers, George Mathews, who was playing a beggar. After the show, he approached the actor and asked what he had been doing on stage. As this conversation unfolded, Mathews, who would become a close friend, mentioned his guru, Sufi Sam, and the Sufi Ruhaniat International. Over the next few years, Brozak made repeated visits to Marin County, California, where he attended *zikr* gatherings; while there, he also visited the House of Love and Prayer in San Francisco, a spiritual community space organized by rabbis Schachter-Shalomi and Schlomo Carlebach.[25] Brozak recounted that these were the years before the explosion of spiritual communities in the 1970s. He remembers that even in Vancouver, only one bookstore, called Yoga Vedanta, had a few books by Inayat Khan; he purchased these but did not relate to them at the time. That was about the extent of his exposure to Sufism until his encounter with Mathews at UBC. Such moments capture the broader seeker culture of the 1970s, especially in the Cascadia region, that encompassed the dances of Universal Peace led by Sufi Sam as well as various other spiritual communities like that of Jewish-Sufi spirituality in California.

In the early 1970s, Brozak was initiated into a Sufi order in Seattle under the teacher Atiya (Charlotte) Brautlacht. During a weekend retreat at Brautlacht's home, he met Reshad (Richard Timothy) Feild (d. 2016), a Sufi teacher based in the UK. Brozak took the Greyhound bus from Vancouver to Seattle to attend one of his gatherings. After meeting him at this retreat, he stayed in touch with him through letters and other encounters, such as Sufi dancing in Marin County in California:

> So, there was a good connection that weekend, it wasn't [till] then on the Monday, I think that ... he was holding an outdoor workshop in a town called Bellingham, at the university, which is just halfway between Seattle and Vancouver. So, I got there before he did and so I was already in the field where the workshop was going to take place. So, I was walking down the hill to meet him, and he and the other people who were with him were walking up the hill and when [he] got about ten feet away from me ... there was just this huge sort of opening experience that I had. So that sort of really hooked me.[26]

Brozak was also among a group of students who were studying the works of E.J. Gold (b. 1947), a spiritual leader in the human potential movement on the west coast; he was connected to the Gurdjieff movement described earlier (Petsche 2014).[27]

Back in the UK, Feild was assigned the task of establishing spiritual centres in the Americas under the direction of his Sufi teacher, Bülent Rauf (d. 1987). Vancouver was of particular interest to them. Rauf was a Turkish teacher who traced his lineage back to the Andalusian Sufi master Muhiyddin Ibn Arabi (d. 1240). He had an antique shop in London, where Feild also owned a shop, and this led to their connection. The teachings of Ibn Arabi are central to the Beshara Centre at Swyre Farm in England, which would become the home for Rauf's teachings (Taji-Farouki 2007; Miller 2018).[28] Feild would write about his experiences with Rauf in *The Last Barrier: A Journey into the Essence of Sufi Teachings* (1976). He lived an eclectic and turbulent life of spiritual seeking, especially in the pursuit of healing (Miller 2018). He had started out as a member of the British folk group The Springfields (which split up just as the Beatles were rising to fame) and went on to study Tibetan Buddhism (in Scotland under Chögyam Trungpa). Soon after, he met Vilayat in London. It was only years later that he met Rauf and began pursuing Sufism, which brought him to Turkey. In the preface to the second edition of *The Last Barrier* (2002), Feild explains that Rauf was represented in the character of Hamid. That edition includes a preface by Coleman Barks, as well as the 1973 letter from Rauf that assigned Feild the task of going to Vancouver to set up a centre:

> Like all perfect victories should be, it will then be beneficial to Him, to you, and to Vancouver. Tell the people of Vancouver and Canada that man, who is the complete image of God, is eternally linked to Him whose image they are in consciousness of this fact, and they were not invented to be a lot of footloose and fancy-free robots, unguided, irresponsible, and left to be tossed about by waves of a fate brought about as a consequence to their own action, the control which has slipped from their hands. Ralph Waldo Emerson says, "Woe unto him who suffers himself to be betrayed by fate." (Rauf qtd in Feild 2002)

Around this time, Brozak's name came up as the potential leader of the venture in western Canada, as Brozak explained to me:

> I guess I had his address in England so I would write him these long twelve-page letters you know ... In January of 1973 [he had written] saying that his teacher had given him the job of coming to North America and ideally South America, and opening up I think it was seven spiritual centres which by that time people were starting to do. And one of them was in Vancouver and he was I think told, anyway, so apparently ... he was sending out sort of one of his students out here, to do it and when they were sitting around he had this school already in England called Beshara. And so they were sitting around and his teacher Bülent had given him this assignment. He said well I only know one guy in Vancouver, this sort of crazy guy, I don't know if he said crazy, but this guy here writes me these long, long letters. And in those days they would have all been handwritten. So, he said I only know one guy there and his name is John Brozak and the guy sitting next to him almost had a heart attack because that guy was the George [the performer he met at UBC] who had first introduced me to Sufism.[29]

Brozak went to Grass Valley, California, to meet Fattah Tremoureux, another student of Feild's, who was to help set up the Vancouver Centre. They drove back to Vancouver together and rented a small house at 27th and Dunbar. Brozak and Tremoureux booked a room at the YMCA in downtown Vancouver to host a talk by Feild on 31 October 1973 titled "The Straight Way of Love and Knowledge" (see figure 2.1). The talk was attended by two people (one who happened to be the man who had hitchhiked with them on their drive back to Vancouver). Shortly after this first talk, a group of interested seekers started a

2.1. Poster of talk during Reshad Feild's first visit to Vancouver in October 1973. Poster courtesy of John Brozak, who organized the event.

forty-day reading group on the *Twenty-Nine Pages: Introduction to Ibn 'Arabi's Metaphysics of Unity* by A.E. Affifi (1938), which had been compiled by Rauf for the Beshara community to study in England. The forty-day study group included students from E.J. Gold's community as well as students from Bellingham in Washington state.

After the course ended in December 1973, Feild returned to England and Tremoureux returned to California, leaving Brozak the leader of the new

Vancouver centre. Enough interest grew in the small Sufi community that they began renting a house on 7th Avenue near Oak and Granville. Feild returned the following year to visit this house. In the early days Feild travelled between England and North America. He began to teach turning (*sama*) and *zikr* to anyone who was interested (women and men). This early iteration of the group was known as the Vancouver Turning Society. Brozak reflected on this early practice and how they adapted to the lack of proper ritual attire. Sometime in late (summer) 1974 or 1975 they presented their first public presentation of *sama* at the Vancouver Playhouse to a sold-out audience of close to 600 people:

> So Reshad, one of the ways he worked was always to have a project. Always good to keep people busy. So I know we started working on this *sama* and they had some instructions from Reshad so he was teaching people how to turn and they had some very basic drawings or something so you know the *sekke* is the hat, symbolizes the tombstone. Well ... they're usually made from felt, [there's] like a couple of felt makers in Konya and Istanbul who will make them ... Because we didn't have access to felt makers, [people] made their hats from cardboard. So, the first *sikkes* that were used here were cardboard ... I heard from somebody that he still has his cardboard *sikke*. Anyway, so ... we rented what was called Vancouver Playhouse, which is about a 600-seat theatre. We actually sold it out. We turned people away ... So we did a *sama* there.[30]

By the mid-1970s, then, Feild's students had begun to focus on *sama* as their regular practice, even seeking out the appropriate ritual attire. Sorgenfrei (2013) notes many of the same initial challenges in the development of the Mevlevi Order in America, especially around the lack of proper ritual attire for the whirling dervish outfits. With limited resources, they managed to organize public presentations of *sama*, selling out large auditoriums. Brozak tried the turning practice once but did not feel that it was for him. He saw his role as organizing the community and the events that were brewing around Feild in Vancouver.

This early tradition of turning that started with Feild would be solidified in the late 1970s and early 1980s by another Turkish teacher, Suleyman Loras. In the late 1970s, Loras would visit Vancouver. Loras had an authoritative (albeit ambiguous, according to some) relationship to the Mawlawi tradition in Konya. He was born in 1908 and grew up next to Rumi's mausoleum (or the Mawlawi *tekke*). He started his training when he was fifteen years old. By the time he was initiated into the order, the *tekke* had been closed, Sufism having been banned in Turkey (see chapter 3) (Sorgenfrei 2013: 111). Some understand him to have been a *shaykh* from Konya; others understand that he had been asked to be a representative and did not necessarily have the authority to initiate other teachers (*shaykh*s) (111). Many of his American and Canadian Sufi students believed he was the *shaykh* of Konya (by way of Celaleddin Bakir Celebi) and followed the Mawlawi tradition. Regardless, he was known to be a devoted disciple of Rumi, having spent decades helping in the Mawlawi lodge and kitchen in Konya before it was shut down, and that he taught and initiated students and practised *sama* (Sorgenfrei 2020: 124–5, 2013: 112).[31] He was also a tailor, famous for his impeccable three-piece suits, in which he was often photographed.

Loras visited Los Angeles on 19 April 1976 to see Feild and his students at the recently founded Institute for Conscious Life. Feild had met Loras in Konya when Bülent sent him to visit Rumi and Shams's tomb, as he explains in his novel. This relationship led to Loras visiting Feild and his students and to the establishment of the Mawlawi tradition, especially of the practice of turning taught by Feild. This practice of turning was later solidified through Loras's son, Jelaleddin. Feild's students were impressed that he included women in the teaching of *sama*. Loras visited Vancouver several times in the 1970s (1976, 1978, 1979); because he did not speak English, a translator was hired from the Canadian Turkish Society to translate his *sohbet*s or talks.[32] This first translator did a poor job, so he was not asked back. When Loras returned to Konya, he mailed mimeographed instructions on how to perform *sama*, which had been written in Ottoman Turkish. Brozak needed to get this document translated. At the time, he was working at a warehouse in Gastown and knew a couple of Turks who also worked there. So he approached them about getting this instruction translated. This would lead to his connection with Murat Yagan (see below).

Brozak eventually split with Feild, largely over his struggles with alcohol, which made his behaviour unpredictable. Brozak's own path to Sufism was through the Vancouver Rumi Society, though it included connections with other Sufi teachers he encountered along the way, such as Irina Tweedie and her successor Llewellyn Vaughan-Lee, who heads the Naqshbandiyya-Mujaddidiyya.[33] Brozak stepped away from Sufism for a few decades, but after attending a Rumi poetry reading held by Coleman Barks at UBC, he started gathering again with some of the early students in this community. The early, loosely organized group of Sufis who were friends invited other Sufi teachers, such as Kabir Helminski, to visit and give talks, but there was no immediate connection with some of the visiting Sufi teachers. At this time, the small group of students gathered regularly, reading Ibn Arabi and Rumi and completing *zikr* at their respective homes. Soon they also started gathering for *sama*, and on 17 December for the *shab-i arus* (the death anniversary commemoration) for Rumi at UBC's Asian Centre.

Feild and Loras eventually parted ways. Bruce Miller recounted much of this history in his autobiography *Rumi Comes to America: How a Poet of Mystical*

Love Arrived on Our Shores (2018). He suggests that Loras was not impressed by Feild's drinking, unstable behaviour, and attitude toward his students. The split between Feild and Loras led the latter to appoint his son to take over the Mawlawi *tekke* that had emerged since his initial visit. Loras's son, Jelaleddin, had studied the Halveti and Mawlawi traditions in Turkey and later had gone to New York, where he spent time with Vilayat before moving to the west coast and connecting with Lewis's students and the Islamia Ruhaniat Society. In 1981, Jelaleddin formed the Mevlevi Order of America (Sorgenfrei 2020: 127; 2013). Thus the Vancouver Rumi Society traces its lineage back to Loras and Feild. Loras visited Vancouver regularly in the later 1970s, initiating four teachers to continue the practice of turning in that city; he also taught Raqib Brian Burke the tradition of *sama*.

RAQIB BRIAN BURKE

Burke had been raised as a Catholic but had explored various religious traditions and been exposed to spiritual experiments through his father, a renowned Canadian journalist. When he was twenty-three and beginning to explore on his own, he encountered Sufism for the first time. He saw a poster for a talk by Reshad Feild, which did not mention Sufism. Burke recounted to me:

> And ... my initiator was Reshad Feild and I just saw [a] poster on a telephone pole ... You know, evening talk at this address and it didn't mention Sufism, but it just talked about sort of unity of religions, some sort of general way. And that sounded intriguing. And ... so at the end of that talk, Reshad just said to the audience, "um, okay, don't go home. We are home." And no one knew [how] to handle that ... but essentially ... his initiatory group was sort of born at that moment because enough of those people decided they weren't gonna leave. They ... were just gonna stay. Right.[34]

This encounter began Burke's journey toward Sufism. It was through Feild, then, that the practice of turning during *zikr* gradually became central, as Burke described:

> He would stand up in a ... *zikr* circle that would be not bigger than this room, just a few people. And ... everyone would be saying Allah, Allah ... He would sort of go like this [demonstrates turning]. And then in the middle of it, he would say, "I don't really know how to do this, but ... it's like this" and then he would get down again, we'd continue ... the *zikr* ... so ... that was my first introduction.[35]

Around this time, many of those who were interested in this practice, in both Los Angeles and Vancouver, often taught themselves. They even began sewing their own Konya dervish outfits and presenting the practice in public – for example, at a UN conference in Vancouver in 1976, where Feild spoke. Feild was at this time travelling between Canada, the US, England, and Turkey, and he would take some of his students to Konya to observe *sama* as it was practised there. Turning became further entrenched in this group after a visit by Loras:

> When [Dede] arrived for his first visit in Vancouver, he started walking around the living room and we rented the house room out in the university and, he started doing something and ... basically saying ... "Okay, just everybody get up and just follow me. And you follow me." And he'd bow then just, and, "follow me" and I remember joining the line and going, what is he doing? Don't ask, just follow, follow? ... And Dede had this incredible quality and he couldn't speak English but he would expect us to understand his Turkish. So, he would be ... explaining and ... he'd have this big smile and ... be very so excited. And ..."now we do this and now we do this" ... and it would still be a complete mystery. But it was presumably ... you could tell he was talking about something absolutely wonderful.[36]

At this time, Feild explained to his students that they were going to focus on this practice for forty days and nights, as was his tendency. So the students sewed the clothes for the ceremony and worked on figuring out how to perform it by examining photographs from Shems Friedlander's photography book titled *Rumi and the Whirling Dervishes* (1975), which contained photographs of the dervishes turning in Konya. As Burke explained, "we literally used that book to try to figure out how this ceremony worked and so we got it mostly wrong, but enough to make people believe that we were doing it."[37] There had been various presentations of this practice in smaller spaces, as noted earlier by Brozak, but Feild decided to host a ceremony at a large theatre in Vancouver. Burke had not been part of the original six students who were turning. For this presentation, Feild wanted twelve dervishes. Burke was selected as one of them and was asked to teach the others:

> BURKE: So I got to watch the original six. Yeah. And then more or less at random, you know, Reshad sort of chose I guess another six. And then the thought was like, okay, well now we have to train these ... people. And ... who's gonna train ... even the people of the original six felt like they didn't know how to do this. But now Reshad wanted to train the new people. He didn't know. Right. So somehow more or less at random like, "well, well Raqib ... why don't you train everyone?" ... But we all sort of understood that no one knew what they were doing, but we were supposed to figure it out. So, so then we poured over ... every photograph [in the Friedlander book].
>
> XAVIER: Wow.
>
> BURKE: And would say, look, his ... right foot is sticking out. See that ... his right foot is sticking out and ... it's not his left foot. So ... it has to start with your right

foot. And ... then later on you go, yeah. But look at this one, he's got his hand on his heart not up in the air. You're supposed to change like first you put it in the air then you're supposed to put your heart and no ... I look at this photograph over here. Like this part is, see which direction he's face. Look, the *shaykh* is, must be over there. So, look, he's looking at the *shaykh*.[38]

This moment began the process whereby Burke slowly learned turning through the transmission provided by Feild and Loras and began teaching it to others. When Loras died, his son Jelaleddin (d. 2021) took over the Mevlevi Order of America. Burke felt no allegiance to him, and this led to some tension and eventually to some separation between the Mevlevi Order of America and the group in Vancouver, though students moved between these groups. Like other Sufi students in Vancouver, Burke eventually took hand with Sherif Baba Çatalkaya. On the basis of Loras's authority and training, Burke has come to be known as the *samazenbashi*. Sorgenfrei explains that the *samazenbashi* are "experienced sheikhs who are chosen by the Postneshin ["skin sitter" or sheikh who sits at the head of *sema* ritual] to help him conduct the *sema*, direct *semazens* and control the pace of the ritual" (2013: 143). Burke holds the turning classes in Vancouver. He has dedicated his practice to learning and teaching this meditation and has trained a second generation of *samazen*s, including his daughter Mira Burke, and students Shams al Haqq Farzad AttarJafari and Tawhida Tanya Evanson (see the following chapters). One of the teachers whom Loras initiated is Majid Buell, who to this day holds the post or authority of this tradition in Vancouver, which has allowed members of the Vancouver Rumi Society to host rituals without the presence of Jelaleddin Loras.

MAJID BUELL AND MURAT YAGAN

Another significant figure in the Vancouver Rumi Society is Majid Buell. Initially from the United States, Buell worked in the military with high-security clearance (NORAD). He left the military when he learned that his life was under threat because of his antiwar stance. He decided to move to Montreal because of a Leonard Cohen song, but when he got there he had a near-death (or death) experience – his heart stopped for a couple of hours. That episode radically transformed his life and led to him seeking his true purpose. His quest brought him to Ram Dass's *Be Here Now* (1971). He learned that one of Dass's students lived in an *ashram* in Thunder Bay, Ontario, so he went to see her. He stayed with the community in Thunder Bay for about a week. He felt that the community was not for him and continued on to Vancouver, where he began exploring various spiritual communities and centres. Though Vancouver had a Sufi Order by then, he was more interested in Hindu traditions at that point. He studied with a meditation master for two years. In 1976, while working as a United Way agent, he ended up at a conference where he encountered Feild's whirling dervish students. This was the first time he had ever heard of whirling dervishes, and something about them enticed him. So he joined the group.

By then, Feild's group was renting a house in North Vancouver. Buell remembers Vancouver being part of a broader spiritual landscape in the 1970s: travelling teachers from Los Angeles or Asian countries would stop over in Vancouver en route to other destinations. Groups such as the 3HO (Happy Healthy Holy) Sikhs had a storefront on 4th Avenue in downtown Vancouver that hosted packed daily lectures (up to sixty-five regular attendees). Buell and his group would advertise their Sufi gatherings at their talks, drawing in people to their Sufi community. Buell's ex-wife, who is Jewish, also practised Sufism (they were married by Loras). So they spent time with Carlebach's group. Buell recollects that during the early days of the Sufi house, sometimes more than sixty people came to the meetings. He remembers this vividly because he was the cook who would get phone calls about how many people to prepare meals for.

Around 1977–8, when Feild and his students were starting their group, Murat Yagan (d. 2013) also started teaching Sufi classes. Yagan writes in his autobiography *I Come from Behind Kaf Mountain* (1984) that he founded the Kebzeh Foundation and the Essentialist Church of Christ and held classes on Sufism, during which time he developed his philosophy of Ahmsta Kebzeh or "knowledge of the art of living" (Bram and Hatina 2014: 67). Yagan located his philosophy within New Age spirituality, "aimed at purifying the human body and soul and nurturing qualities of love" (69). Yagan's background was eclectic as well. He was a Circassian-Abkhazian from Turkey, and his mother had been initiated into a Naqshbandi Order. Yagan himself had once been a Bektashi dervish. During his three-year *chillah* (retreat) he experienced a vision of Jesus, which his *shaykh* told him was to be his path. So he eventually converted to Christianity. He moved to Canada with his family on 25 November 1963, migrating between Vancouver, Mission, Vernon, and Prince Rupert, BC, the first few years. He writes that during his time in Canada, "I was becoming very disturbed with Christianity" and began to retreat from Christian practices and community, which only made him feel further isolated (Johnston and McIntyre 1997: 138). He worked as a carpenter and owned various businesses over time, including a restaurant and small café; he even took up real estate. His encounter with Brozak, who approached him for help with translating Ottoman Turkish, transformed his path. He began attending *zikr* held by Brozak and Buell and became intrigued by Suleyman Loras, whom he met in 1978, when he flew to Boulder, Colorado, to serve as his translator:

> I flew down to Boulder in June to have my first meeting with him. I found Dede Effendi a small and frail person, also very soft-spoken. He had undoubtedly been raised in a fine Ottoman Mevlevi tradition and spoke very refined Ottoman Turkish. I immediately switched my Turkish to meet with his. We hugged each other in

a traditional Mevlevi way, kissing each other's hands crossways simultaneously. At that time, he was seventy-six years old. We had a very nice, full, and enlightening meeting in which I told him my story and he told me that, no matter what I told him, he had made up his mind already that he had accepted me. In his opinion, he said, I had the light of Christ and that he knew that I have received my initiation from *Meclis-i Ezel*, or Original Creation. (153)

Yagan became the principle translator during Loras's visits to Vancouver, as they both spoke Ottoman Turkish. Brozak explained that the relationship between Loras and Yagan was very natural, which helped in the translation process between the two:

Well, he studied at a Bektashi *tekke* in Istanbul, which is still there and I visited it. And ... around the same time that Suleyman Dede was studying at the Mawlawi *tekke* in Konya. So, the next time that Suleyman Dede came back here, you know, we had Murat, who could translate. That was like this marriage made in heaven, right ... They sort of adored each other, as it were. You know, because they both came from that Ottoman period, they both had ... a similar cultural background, so Murat could just you know he could just do spot on translation ... Murat tells this sort of story, you know, there's an expression from I think Mevlana ... The Sufi is the son of the moment. So you have to be prepared for anything when you're on a Sufi path or whatever. And Dede was in Boulder, and this probably would have been like late '70s, early '80s and Reshad just phoned Murat and said we need a translator here, this isn't working. So, Murat told the story, he put his toothpaste, toothbrush [and went].[39]

Yagan writes that on 19 June 1978, Loras visited Vancouver and stayed with him at his house on Point Grey Road for three days before visiting the North Vancouver Mawlawi *tekke* (of Brozak and Buell). He adds "while he was staying at my place, he called me to a special meeting with him and initiated me directly as a *Mevlevi* Sheikh, putting me directly under the Sikke of the light of *Mevlana*, 'God help you,'" he said (154). Loras wanted the *tekke* in Vancouver to have a *shaykh*, so a vote was held. Four *shaykh*s were appointed as teachers in training; two of them would be Buell and Yagan. Around this time the group began to split apart: the different *shaykh*s, including Yagan and the other two, went their own way, starting smaller groups in Campbell River and on Gabriola Island. Buell remained in the house in North Vancouver with a smaller group of students, where they continued the practice of *zikr* and studying. During our conversation in his home in North Vancouver, Buell shared with me how he often wondered where the manual was to be appointed as a *shaykh* in training, since he felt he had no idea what he was doing at the time.

Buell got married and travelled to Israel, England, and eventually Turkey in 1979, where he met Loras. During his time in Turkey, Buell was fully exposed to Turkish Sufism. He had encounters with students of Muzzafer Efendi and Rifai *zikr* and turning (in Istanbul), long before meeting Sherif Baba Çatalkaya in Vancouver and taking hand with him to become a Rifai Sufi. He travelled to Konya, where he visited the tomb of Mawlana. He later recounted that little was happening with his Vancouver group in the 1980s, though much more was taking place in the US, especially with Feild's own group. By then, Feild had returned from the UK, landing in Boulder, Colorado. He started a centre there (after the Institute for Conscious Life was disbanded owing to issues with the property they were renting), even though Loras wanted to start one in Los Angeles. This group established by Feild grew for a while, but after Brozak's separation from Feild and Feild's new ventures in various other cities, the Vancouver group slowly waned. In the early 1990s, Coleman Barks held a workshop at UBC about the poetry of Rumi. At that workshop, Buell ran into his "old Sufi buddies," who began gathering again informally at one another's homes. Seemi Bushra Ghazi attended one of these gatherings, which reignited the group.

SEEMI BUSHRA GHAZI AND SHERIF BABA ÇATALKAYA

Seemi Bushra Ghazi is a lecturer in Arabic at UBC. She traces her family's religious roots to the Chishtis and Sabri Chishtis in India. She draws her lineage from her inherited traditions of Sufism in South Asia and her own academic and intellectual journey in North America, which has informed her expression and practice of Sufism. Ghazi is known for her stunning Quran recitation, which has been included in Michael Sell's *Approaching the Qur'an: The Early Revelations* (2007), as well as the PBS documentary, *Islam: Empire of Faith* (Gardner 2000).[40] She was a graduate student at Duke University in a cohort that included the scholar and public intellectual Omid Safi; she was also a student there at the same time as Zia Inayat-Khan.[41] She is involved in various Muslim women's spirituality organizations, such as the Women's Islamic Initiative in Spirituality and Equality. Ghazi is a student of the Rifai Marufi Sufi tradition (through Çatalkaya) and has taken hand with Zia of the Inayati Order. Today she is a Sufi teacher and *shaykha* in her own right (see chapter 5). She is a founding member of the Vancouver Rumi Society with Brozak, Buell, and Raqib Brian Burke. It was during a chance meeting with Ghazi, Burke, and Brozak, at a weekly house *zikr*, that they came up with the idea of hosting the Rumi Festival in Vancouver in 1998 (see chapter 4); after that, they formed the Vancouver Rumi Society. On its webpage, the group describes itself as follows:

> Starting in the 1970's with Reshad Feild and Suleyman Loras Dede it has been involved in education and charity work. It has put on Zikr (chanting) and Whirling (Sema) Ceremonies on an almost continuous basis and has public speakers who

give talks on Sufism on request. We have been involved with many other mystical and religious denominations in the spirit of cooperation and cultural exchange. The overall purpose of the society is to promote the understanding of the spiritual unity underlying all religious truths. We organize spiritual gatherings open to people of all faiths. We encourage the study of all spiritual writings, focusing on the poetry and works of Moulana Jelaluddin Rumi, a mystic who lived and wrote during the thirteenth century (C.E.).[42]

Çatalkaya is the final thread in the development of the Vancouver Rumi Society. Çatalkaya was born in Istanbul and was trained in classical traditions of the Quran. He came to the teachings of Sufism in his mid-thirties. This led him to explore and connect with various Sufi orders, including the Rifai-Marufi, Halveti, Qadiri, Bektashi, and Naqshbandi. Trained as a religious scholar, he encountered in Istanbul the sermons of Muzaffer Ozak al-Jerrahi al-Halveti (d.1985), who was an imam at a local mosque.[43] This further attracted him to Sufism. In 1991, one of Ozak's American students, Nur al-Jerrahi (aka Lex Hixon) (d. 1995) invited Çatalkaya to New York to the Masjid al-Farah, the centre of the Nur Askhi Jerrahi lineage of Ozak's order in the United States. Çatalkaya served as the imam for some time there, attracting a small following. It was there that he met the Turkish-American Cem Aydogdu, who invited him to North Carolina, where he lived.[44] His community here was connected with Ghazi. Ghazi then invited Çatalkaya to speak at the Rumi Festival in Vancouver in 1998. There, a small group of students formed around Çatalkaya. Like other teachers before him, Çatalkaya travelled back and forth between Turkey and America. Eventually this small group disbanded (around 2008). Most of its members moved to Seattle, where Çatalkaya's US branch is still based. They continue to hold the annual Rumi Fest there, which first started in Vancouver. They collaborate with Hare Krishna and Christian communities. Çatalkaya's visit led to the rebranding of the Vancouver Rumi Society (formerly the Vancouver Turning Society) and the institutionalization of the Unity *Zikr*, a monthly practice that continues to this day. Unity *Zikr* is held on the last Friday of every month at the Quaker Hall in Vancouver (during COVID-19, it moved to Zoom). When it was held in person, the gathering also included turning classes. The practice of this *zikr* draws from various Sufi orders and traditions but has roots in Turkish Sufism. It attracts Muslims and non-Muslims.[45] The turning instruction is given by Burke or his trained students.

Buell, like many others in Vancouver affiliated with the Rumi Society, met Çatalkaya in 1998, when he came to give a talk at the Rumi Festival organized by Ghazi, Brozak, and Burke. Buell spoke about his initiation with Çatalkaya after the passing of Loras in 1985. Buell had not given hand (i.e., become initiated, *baya*) to another living *shaykh*:

So, I joined with … Sherif Baba [Çatalkaya], and the one thing I liked about him was finally, after all of those years, I finally got to get … real *sohbet* [discussions]. I finally got to get that you know, that dialogue, which I mean the last time I was in that kind of dialogue was with Murat in '78 and so we had that dialogue again. So that was good and what I find is with … Sherif Baba, you tune in and then the mind goes, no matter what he's talking about, you just go … And the more you go with him, the more energy gets downloaded into you. So, it keeps working on you interiorally [sic], and this is a different tradition than say the Jerrahi where they have a fixed system of you know, you do this step, you do this step, you do this step and then you go to the *shaykh*, the *shaykh* interprets your dreams and then you go to this step and you know and so on. That kind of path is a very formal, almost like a school path. Now not that I don't think that Sherif Baba had that path, I mean I think originally, he had that path, but he realized in North America, North America is not going to be able to do it that way. And so he's become very eclectic and universal, but he's also a trained imam.[46]

Çatalkaya travels regularly between the US (Seattle), Canada (Vancouver), and southern Turkey. He has been a formative thread of Turkish Sufi tradition in Vancouver and has built on the foundation laid by Feild and Loras. For many Sufis in Vancouver affiliated with the Rumi Society, Çatalkaya helped solidify their Sufi path, as well as their relationship with Rumi. Buell's experience with a living Sufi teacher in the figure of Çatalkaya was vital for his conceptualization of Sufism. This connection helped him make sense of the role and relationship of Rumi and Shams that is formative for his spiritual practice of Sufism:

So, my version … of Sufism is the more you submit, the more you surrender, the more you surrender, the more the source comes, the more the source comes, the more *ashk* [ishq/Love] comes, the more *ashk* [ishq] comes the more you can embrace the enemies. That's it and it's not that hard. The trouble is it's all overlaid with intellect. Everywhere, everything is intellect … If you can get the mind out of the way, which is not that easy, you know … you'll reveal yourself. It's as simple as that … I mean, I've tapped into this over twenty, thirty, forty years but it's taken me this long to actually formulate it enough to be able to recognize that … Sherif Baba has this thing, he looks into someone's eye and he says you don't exist and then I don't exist, you exist, I don't exist, or something and goes back and forth and somewhere in that middle point, between you don't exist and I don't exist or whatever, is existence. So … If anybody can get out of the way of … trying to understand the meaning of something, and yet going beyond that to understand how it is, in reality, then they can grasp what Rumi grasped because Rumi got it from Shams.[47]

Rumi's legacy of turning has been foundational to Canadian Sufi communities. Many who were involved with Feild were non-Muslims, as were the students of

Inayat, Vilayat, and Hidayat Khan across Canada. Some, like O'Loughlin, Ford, and Hafiz, expressed that they were often challenged about their practice of a universal Sufism, though members of the Rumi Society did not express similar challenges in Vancouver. Both the Inayati Order and the Vancouver Rumi Society are universal expressions of Sufism in that their practices of Sufism are not predicated on the practice or adoption of Islamic law. This is not unique to Canada; indeed, some of these groups are branches of centres in the US and western Europe. Still, what is noteworthy is that by the 1990s, *sama* was emerging as a significant Sufi practice and would continue to expand beyond Vancouver to Toronto and Montreal into the 2000s. The tradition of turning, especially through the Turkish Sufism of teachers like Feild, Loras, and Çatalkaya would continue to grow in Vancouver. However, in cities like Toronto, the arrival of Muslim diasporic communities, especially from Turkey and South Asia, would add another layer to Sufi traditions on the Canadian landscape.

Diasporic Development of Sufi Communities in Canada

Immigration to Canada in the 1980s and 1990s fostered a proliferation of Sufi communities in Canada tied to diasporic and ethnic communities of Muslims, for example, Shadhili, Naqshbandis, and Chishtis, and Senegalese Sufis in Montreal (Haddad 2008; LeBlanc 2013). Persian-affiliated groups, such as the Nimatullahis, began to grow in the 1980s and 1990s, especially after the 1979 Iranian Revolution, which drove an increase in Iranian immigration to cities like Toronto and Vancouver.[48] A similar diasporic change in Canada driven by world events was the 1990s influx of Ismaili Muslims fleeing Uganda. These communities have formed their own sub-group but have also tended to connect with Sufi ritual practices and expressions, especially in the public sphere. Below, I map some of the Sufi communities that emerged in the 1970s in Canada as branches founded by Sufi teachers in the US. Some of these new Sufi orders in Canada, such as the Jerrahi Sufi Order, have drawn heavily on Turkish and eastern European diasporic communities in cities like Toronto. I will be focusing specifically on Sufi communities with Rumi affiliation, such as the Jerrahi Order and the Rifai Order, because of their influence on the spread of Rumi and Rumi poetry and their ritual expressions of turning. In doing so, I highlight how the entrenchment of Sufism in Canada can be tied to a growing Muslim diasporic presence in cities like Toronto, Vancouver, and Montreal.

Jerrahi Order of Canada

The Jerrahi Order in west-end Toronto is a Turkish community. At the core of this diasporic community is Tevfik Aydöner, the *shaykh* of the Jerrahi Order in this country. Aydöner came to Canada from Turkey as a young man, after some time in Germany. In the 1980s, while living in Mississauga, he began to take note of some of the cultural attitudes of the Canadians he was working with at Carlton Cards, where he worked as an import and export assistant manager. As a young man with a growing family, he was looking for a way to give back to his new country, which he felt had given him so much in terms of hospitality, a career, and a safe place to raise his children. He also began to notice other people's lack of appreciation for Canada's hospitality and opportunity. This led him to think about how he could give something tangible – perhaps a community for the next generation, especially now that he had children of his own.

He met Dr Ahmet Fuad Sahin (d. 2019), who had come to Canada from Turkey in 1958 and settled in the Niagara region, west of Toronto. Before he died, Sahin had been appointed to the Order of Canada for his leadership and service in Canada's Muslim community. He helped create the Islamic Foundation of Toronto, the Islamic Society of Niagara Peninsula, and the Canadian Turkish Muslim Association. He was also the founder and former president of the International Development and Relief Foundation.[49] Aydöner had been involved in the founding of the Canadian Turkish Islamic Heritage Association, but he felt it was not exactly what he was looking for. By chance in 1983, he had an opportunity to travel to Turkey for a week (as a gift); while there, he connected with some of his friends from his earlier career in the hotel business. Through a series of curious events, which Aydöner interpreted as mystical, he was introduced to Tosun Bayrak (d. 2018), an New York artist. Bayrak had been appointed the *shaykh* of the mosque community in Spring Valley, New York, by *shaykh* Muzaffer Ozak, who had come to the US from Istanbul. Ozak had initiated several students, and this led to different branches of his Jerrahi Order in the US (such as Nur al-Jerrahi's Nur Ashki Jerrahi in New York City).[50]

At the time, Aydöner was hesitant about connecting with Sufism. All he really knew about it was from some poems by Rumi and the Turkish Sufi poet Yunnus Emre (b. 1238). Still, his meeting with Bayrak in Turkey left an impression on him, so in 1984 he travelled to Spring Valley to meet him. Most of those he met there were non-Turks and non-Muslims. For instance, Bayrak had attracted Rabia Terri Harris, an academic and convert to Islam, to the movement. This second encounter with Bayrak at his community in New York left a lasting impression on him:

> They [were] all showing respect to this fellow ... he didn't put like all of this, you know how they put the *shalwar* and this and that. They want to look like somebody ... They're like no, this guy has a simple way, he says okay. Any questions you know come here. I said cool. Good. Anyway, then I say why did you come this way? ... This is the club I want to import to Canada. Music is here and ... motivation to education, sports and well-being ... and then giving them Islamic tradition but also

same thing as Judaism and Christianity, the same faith ... and ... it's beautiful. So, this way I can ... bring in their heart and their understanding of Hazrat Mevlana Jalaluddin Rumi or Yunnus Emre or Hafiz or you know Ghazali's teachings and ... all of this stuff. So, they can come to balance life, they can respect their parents, they don't swear at their grandparents.[51]

Bayrak encouraged Aydöner to become a "servant." Aydöner was very interested in "importing" this model of Sufism to Canada but hesitated to take on the formal role of *shaykh*, feeling he was not trained to be any kind of authority at that level. So in 1984, he started hosting gatherings in his basement. At first, ten or so people attended these gatherings. For around two decades, a small group about fifteen met in temporary spaces, such as member's homes, a mosque, or a church space they had rented for the night. Around 2005, a church in Etobicoke (New Covenant Pentecostal Church) was listed for sale, and they purchased it. They meet there to this day.

Aydöner estimates that the Jerrahi community in Toronto has about eighty-five families. He adds that members of this community must make some effort to follow the basic tenets of Sunni Islam, such as daily prayers and saying the rosary (*tasbih*), as well as make a commitment to controlling their desires: "They say in Sufism, hands and your personal parts. Whatever comes out of these, if you promise you are going to control them as much as you can, then you can become a member. That's the requirements."[52] There are no monthly membership fees, though regular attendees are encouraged to donate for use of the space and the meals and tea the community offers. The weekly gatherings are open to all. One does not have to be initiated to participate in Saturday evening gatherings, which consist of *sohbet*s (discussions) led by Aydöner, *isha* (evening *salat* prayers), and *zikr*, which often includes live music and sometimes *samazen*s (usually on special occasions). The Jerrahi community separates men and women for much of the gathering. Women are required to practise veiling and sit in the balcony; the men sit in the main part of the *dargah* and in the circle with Aydöner during *zikr*. This division has led some people to separate from the Jerrahi Order, for they perceive the gender norms as too traditional and conservative. One of them is Murat Coskun, the leader of the Rifai Sufi Order (see below and chapter 5). Notwithstanding these gender dynamics, the *daragh* is open to all faiths, and both men and women are welcome. Aydöner's *dargah* regularly participates in open houses in Toronto, and inter-faith evenings, and it hosts *iftar*s for the public during Ramadan. They try to engage Sufism with the broader community, social justice work, and even politics (see this book's epilogue). This latter focus aligns with Aydöner's original intention to cultivate a community that gives back to Canada, but one rooted in the traditions of his heritage and religion – a socially engaged Islamic-Sufism.

Aydöner reflects on some of the things that make Sufism – in his experience – different in Canada than in Turkey, the fount of his cultural tradition.[53] He explains that some of the ritual practices he follows, such as cycles of prayers, have changed in Toronto but that this has been more a function of time, as they gather communally only once a week, whereas in Turkey there may be daily gatherings in a *tekke*. He notes some broader cultural tendencies that are distinctive in the Canadian context, tendencies grounded in the cultural and ethnic demographic diversity within the Jerrahi Order itself:

> In Turkey you talk more about national problems, and what's happening here and there and you talk about Muslims ... and Turkish Muslims, Sunni Muslims, and the teachings of Mevlana ... [and what] others said but according to our customs and descendants. Here, I have a dozen different customs. Where I have Christians and Jews and Hindus and ... so I have to try to, well I ask ... my almighty to help me so I can get my language to their language. It's not only my broken English, that's already a problem, and besides that Amy [as an example] comes from a family of maybe from Montreal or maybe from somewhere else ... You come from maybe you are born here but the parents came from I don't know where. So Chinese and Japanese people you see here and this and that.[54]

Put another way, the diverse ethnic, cultural, and racial composition of the Jerrahi Order requires that Aydöner be accessible to his varied *murids* (students) and their experiences and cultural backgrounds. The Turkish context may have focused more on the political realities of Turkey and various intra-Muslim dynamics; in Toronto, he has students from Turkey, eastern Europe, and South Asia, as well as Canadian converts, and he must somehow tend to all their needs while speaking to them in ways that are relevant and comprehensible. Even so, the Jerrahi Order understands itself as a "traditional Sufi Order," as its website notes ("Jerrahi Order of Canada").[55] While Aydöner understands Sufism through a cultural universalism and welcomes all to the centre, to take initiation with him one must practice Islam, which is different from what we have seen with other Sufi communities such as the Inayati Order and the Vancouver Rumi Society. Another group that once overlapped somewhat with the Jerrahi Order but has since formed a separate community is the Rifai Order in Toronto.

The Rifai Order: The Canadian Institute of Sufi Studies

At the heart of the Rifai Order is *shaykh* Murat Coskun. He grew up in the Middle East in a Christian household and came to Canada when he was around sixteen. In Toronto, he did not identify with his religious upbringing. The loss of his father while he was at university led him to question his life and purpose. In his twenties he began to search. As he explained, he "avoided any major religions whether Christianity or Islam, I started to go after Buddhism, Yogaism [sic], all eastern religions."[56] Coskun now began looking for a teacher. At the time, he was part of a Gurdjieff reading group. A friend invited him to attend a talk by the Turkish Sufi teacher Cemil Aksoy (d. 2018), the grandson of Kenan Rifai, in Toronto:[57]

> Then one of my friends one day said that a dervish is coming to talk to people if I'm interested. I said no, like I'm staying away from Islam and all kinds of things [laughing]. And … he said but … there's not enough people to listen to him; it will be appreciated if there are some faces. So, I just took my face there, I met my teacher there that night. He was the grandson of a great Sufi master who lived in Istanbul in the 1920s and he was educated by him, he came to Canada in the sixties.[58]

Coskun traces his order's lineage via Cemil Aksoy through to his grandfather, Kenan Rifai. The order's website explains:

> Murat Baba was taught on this path by Cemil Aksoy (d. 2018), may God preserve his secret, who learned this path at the feet of his grandfather the great shaykh of the 20th century, Kenan Rifai. We trace this path from Kenan Rifai through the years to our Pir, Ahmed er-Rifai, through to our beloved light of guidance, Muhammad, God bless him to the Angel Gabriel who brought this teaching from the Divine Source of all knowledge, God.[59]

Upon meeting Aksoy, Coskun became more interested in Sufism, especially when he learned that his Gurdjieff group's teacher knew Aksoy as well. This connection helped him realize that Sufism and Gurdjieff were linked. So Coskun, along with a handful of other Turkish men, continued to study informally with Aksoy once a week at a friend's house. Coskun seemed to be the only student there who was truly interested in the teachings. Aksoy suggested that they meet one on one, but Coskun, confessing his shyness, insisted that more students come. At this point, Aksoy told him he did not have *ijaza* (authorization) to initiate dervishes, and directed Coskun to Tosun Bayrak, who could.

Initially, Coskun's group met in the basement of his home outside Toronto. He did not advertise this group. Eventually, Atique, today an executive member of the Rifai, heard about these small gatherings and visited with another friend. He described that experience: "The most important thing is when we did come the first day, we felt we were at home. Like the heart felt it was not something you can like read in a book or anything. A feeling that comes from right inside you, very powerful. So, Alhamdulillah, we're still here."[60]

A unique reality of the Rifai Order is Coskun's own story of his journey of Sufism, especially as an Armenian Orthodox Christian. He explained:

I'm an Armenian, Armenians traditionally they hate Turks [laughing]. And ... because of their history and Turks happened to be Muslim and ... Armenians are Christians. So of course, like even within my own family still now half of my family are Christians ... I could ... be harsh, force my way and turn people off or I could be ... me and let them see the change in me. And that way ... I love Jesus so why should I reject him from my life ... Although I wasn't a practicing Christian I always loved Jesus as a human being ... So to me, a sincere Christian is going the same direction as I am ... so there is no difference in the religions as long as they are properly guided.[61]

Coskun's own journey is thus one of the things that attracts students and seekers to his community. His group has been meeting in Toronto's west end for a decade in a rented space. In the early days they met upstairs in a church, but over the past few years they have shifted to the main floor, which also serves as a yoga studio. The community meets biweekly. They have begun building a more permanent *dargah* space on property Coskun owns outside the city. The construction work is being done entirely by volunteers from among Coskun's dervishes (or *murid*s). At their biweekly gatherings, they recite *zikr* (which is not segregated by gender), with music; at times, some *semazans* of their order conduct a turning. The same gatherings include mixed-gender *salat* and breaking of fast during Ramadan. Coskun's son, David, is a trained whirling dervish. This community also hosts annual death anniversary celebration (*urs*) for Rumi (see chapter 3).

The biweekly gatherings in Toronto are open to everyone and attract a diverse crowd, racially, ethnically, religiously, and in terms of gender and sexual orientation. Coskun's order has drawn together the youngest and most diverse group of individuals I have come across in my fieldwork. One reason for this diversity is his accessibility; another is the location of the meetings in Toronto's downtown west end. Many of the dervishes and regular attendees are academics, university students, and activists. Unlike the Jerrahi Order, which Coskun and his wife used to belong to, the Rifai Order does not separate in terms of gender. Furthermore, just as with the Jerrahi Order, people of all faiths and cultures are welcome. Coskun, though, understands Sufism through Islam and the practice of ritual aspects of Sunni Islam (i.e., five-times prayers and fasting). I will be returning to Coskun and his community regularly throughout this book but especially in chapter 5 when I discuss gender.

Toronto's Nimatullahi Community

Another Sufi group is the Nimatullahi in the west end of Toronto. This predominately Persian community is based on the teachings of Javad Nurbakhsh.[62] The order is led today by Javad Nurbakhsh's son Alireza. The Nimatullahi Sufi

Order also has a Vancouver centre or *khanqah*, which, like the Toronto centre, is predominantly Persian. It also has a centre in Montreal.

The Toronto community meets weekly for *zikr*. The centre is a beautiful space; when you walk in, you feel as if you have stepped into a *khanqah* or Sufi lodge in Iran. The house is filled with religious paintings and prints, mostly of works/quotes attributed to Nurbakhsh, and is lit by candles during Sunday gatherings. The floor is covered with Persian rugs. The dominant symbols throughout (especially curtains) are the *kashkal* (begging bowl) and two axes, which symbolize the cutting of wood (for livelihood) and the cutting of one's ego. During my visit in December 2019, I noticed that most of those present were Persian,[63] but some white people were also present (these likely were converts), as well as one Black man. On this cold December night, between thirty and forty people were present for *zikr*. There were also young children, who did not stay in the main gathering room when those in attendance were completing *zikr*, but rather came in afterwards for tea and Persian sweets, which were distributed by some disciples with the greeting "Ya Haqq" (the Truth, a name of God).

There was no gender segregation at this gathering. The only separation was between the initiated, who sat in the inner room, and the uninitiated, who sat in the library. In the library there were books in Persian and in English, mainly by the Nurbakhsh. There was also the *Sufi Journal* (all the collections in English and Persian), a magazine published by this order. The Nimatullahi Order in Toronto meets on Thursdays and Sundays for *zikr*, which starts promptly at 8 p.m., when the lights are turned off (one sits in darkness) and a discourse is given by Nurbakhsh, first in Persian, then translated into English by his son, Alireza. *Zikr* also includes recitation of the names of God through music. It is Persian music that has come to define the experience of *zikr* for this community. Events such as those at the Aga Khan Museum, though framed mostly as public and secular, draw from the Persian Sufi musical tradition (see chapter 4). Some of the musicians who participate in performative presentations of *zikr* in public spaces are members of orders like the Nimatullahi.

The Nimatullahi Order has branches in several Canadian cities, just as the Naqshbandi-Haqqani Order has branches in Vancouver and Montreal. I will say more about the Naqshbandi-Haqqani Order in Vancouver in chapter 4, when I discuss their Rumi Café and storefront. Though the Jerrahi Order, the Rifais, and the Nimatullahi Order do not capture all the examples of the diverse Sufi groups that have formed in cities like Toronto, Montreal, and Vancouver, they do begin to capture some of the historical contexts and waves (increase in Muslim diasporic populations) that led to the founding of Sufi communities in the late twentieth century in Canadian urban centres. By the 2000s, most Sufi communities in Canada were branches or extensions of Sufi communities in the US or western Europe. This was the case in the 1960s and 1970s in Vancouver. Or they have grown from diasporas of Iranian, Turkish, and South Asian

Muslims. Two other communities trace their lineage back to Feild, Burke, and Loras in Montreal and Toronto (started by the second generation of Canadian whirling dervishes), and these would help drive the further spread of the Rumi's legacy in Canada.

Rumi Canada

The story of Rumi Canada, which began in Toronto, is also the story of Shams al Haqq Farzad AttarJafari. AttarJafari is an Iranian Canadian *samazen*. He was exposed to Sufism as a child in Iran, but it was not until he came to Canada that he began to pay more attention to his father's practice of Sufism. The death of his father in 2005 led him to take a renewed interest in the tradition of his ancestors. Around that time, while he was living in Vancouver, AttarJafari began studying Rumi's *Mathnawi* at the Zavieh Mystical Society (see chapter 4). Those studies ignited his curiosity about the lived practice of Rumi's teachings. This in turn drew him to Raqib Brian Burke of the Vancouver Rumi Society, who would become his *sama* teacher:

> I started learning with Raqib, I was exposed initially to Naqshbandi tradition, then … Mawlawiyya. I got initiated as a Mawlawi dervish and then as the *samazen* a few years after Raqib Baba helped me a lot in that process. *Shaykh* Kabir [Helminski] helped me a lot in that process but the main teacher who kind of what you see comes out of me and Rumi Canada … [and] what manifests on this stage is Raqib, his influence I think is very strong on me.[64]

After studying with Burke in Vancouver, AttarJafari moved to Toronto for various reasons. Finding himself alone in Toronto after having spent so much time with a vibrant Sufi community in Vancouver, he started thinking about creating a community that would focus on the teachings of Rumi and his legacy through poetry, music, and turning:

> I asked myself … oh Allah, [why] I'm here? Nothing's a coincidence. And then I realized yeah, we all can change and serve the universe and … life by our actions. For me it was to spread … that attention to the beauty of love because when this practice of *sama* happens, if somebody really dives into it they will feel better, whether it is watching, sitting, or they're practising it. So, I decided to be of service to that and I said Ya Hazrati Mawlana [Rumi], if it's supposed to be done wherever, just use me, I'll put it in practice. So, to organize it I have operation management and … productions … skill[s] so Rumi Canada came to exist … slowly as an idea. Logo came first, everybody was working with me, so excited and all and then you see the one thing that I always decided to ask the friends is that first is the … mystical message from Hazrat Mawlana so you're not drawing this set and that set and the

direct message cause we are familiar with it. So, when you want to do something, whether it's music, meditation, practice, a teacher who comes, you can always ask, is it Rumi talking to them through somebody? And let me serve it and whatever the music you've seen coming out of Rumi Canada, that was the intention to become the tongue for others and Hazrat Mawlana and Shah Nimatullahi. All of the Sufi mystics, that's just them ... yeah so that whole thing came to existence, honestly, it's beautiful to see it grow.[65]

Though registered as a not-for-profit organization in 2017, Rumi Canada has been active as an unofficial group since 2012. Members of the group include dervishes (*samazens*), who may be initiated into other Sufi *tariqa*s and have taken hand with other *shaykh*s, as well as those who practise Buddhism, yoga, Shamanism, Indigenous spiritualities, and other religious and spiritual traditions. AttarJafari welcomes everyone who is interested in learning about the teachings of Rumi and Hafiz and is especially interested in the practice of turning and sacred audition.

AttarJafari, who has travelled and practised Sufism in Iran, Turkey, the US, and Canada, has found that the Canadian landscape has allowed him to cultivate a community like Rumi Canada with minimal judgment, though he is aware that criticism exists of some of the work Rumi Canada does, especially as it further popularizes Rumi (see chapter 4). He has also found that the Canadian landscape offers a porous arena for turning inward and focusing on inner cultivation. He recognizes that his identity and homeland connect him to Rumi and Hafiz in very intimate ways (i.e., he speaks the native languages), he is also very clear that Rumi does not belong to him: "He doesn't just belong to a Muslim boy who's from his region, he's universal and I need to respect it and actually if you look around you'll notice that."[66] I will be discussing AttarJafari and Rumi Canada in more depth in the next two chapters, especially as it sheds light on the practices of turning and the ritual of *sama* and its emergence in Canada, which form the substantive discussion of this book.

Montreal Sema Space

Tawhida Tanya Evanson is one of whirlers who is regularly seen with AttarJafari. She is an Antiguan Canadian *samazen* based in Montreal. She is also a poet, performer, and arts educator and director of the Banff Centre Spoken Word Program in Vancouver. She is the author of *Book of Wings* (2021), a novel that traces her spiritual journey. She studied for fifteen years under Rifai Marufi Sherif Baba Çatalkaya and Raqib Brian Burke, her *samazenbashi*. She has turned in public events in Europe, Turkey, Japan, India, and Kazakhstan with the Vancouver Rumi Society and Rumi Canada, as well as with the Turkish Canadian disc jockey, composer, and producer Mercan Dede and the Iranian

American music group Niyaz (see figure 2.2). Evanson holds regular turning workshops and meditations in Montreal (see chapter 3).

The Sema Space started in Montreal at the request of an interested seeker, who reached out to Evanson after attending one of her presentations of turning. Evanson moved back to Montreal in 2013, and by February 2014 the group had started formerly under her leadership. Evanson went on to explain: "So one workshop became a monthly gathering that's been going on for five to six years now. And so it's kind of something that replaces the Unity Zikr in Vancouver that I came from."[67] Montreal is home to various other Sufi communities, including the Naqshbandis (Centre Soufi Naqshbandi), Masjid al-Iman, the Nimatullahi Sufi Order (La Maison des Soufis), and Muridiyya. Some of the ritual practices, such as those of the Naqshbandi communities, enforce gender segregation, not only in Montreal but also in Vancouver and elsewhere. Sema Space was created in part to address that circumstance. The tradition of turning is central to the Sema Space that Evanson has created in Montreal. That space differs from other Sufi communities that presently exist, many of which are diasporic Sufi communities, particularly with French African connections. Sema Space is modelled on the Unity *Zikr* gatherings in Vancouver. Evanson at first hesitated to profile the space and community on social media, as the Vancouver Rumi Society has little social media or Web presence (beyond its homepage); those who are interested often come through word of mouth or join the group's email listserv. Similar sentiments were expressed by O'Loughlin in relation to the Inayati Order. Evanson eventually did create a Facebook page called Sema Space; it was named that as a means to curate and protect the space and keep it focused for those who are very deliberate about the practice of turning. Her monthly gatherings attract Muslims and non-Muslims who have interest in *tasawwuf* (Sufism):

> I would say most people don't really have experience of *tasawwuf*, but they are coming from an experience of Islam that may have been positive or negative. It might have been negative and they're seeking to remedy that or it might be positive and they want a deeper experience of it ...And that tends to be women as well. Others are just seekers and they might only come once and never come again and some keep returning.[68]

Evanson's group attracts a strong contingent of women. This demographic trend reflects Evanson's role as one of the few woman *samazen*s, not just in Montreal but across Canada, with authority to lead a community and teach. Sema Space is also unique because it is located in Montreal and is a bilingual space (French and English). Generally, little speaking is involved during *zikr*, aside from the recitation of the litanies, which are in Arabic, and the songs (*ilahi*s), which are are sung in Turkish. The introduction and housekeeping rules that precede the practice are in both French and English:

2.2. Evanson turning with the music group Niyaz, who she regularly tours with. This was the Fourth Light Project at the Flato Markham Theatre in Ontario on 7 March 2020. Photograph by author.

> We do the same thing at Sema Space, where we always start, kind of at zero, unless you're in the advanced class and we're doing other things that are more specific, but otherwise we start the same way and it actually starts with some poetry, and then some explanation that is bilingual English/French, and then a spontaneous readings of Mawlana or Hafiz or Attar or Abu Said, you know something like that. And then a warm-up, like we actually do a physical warm-up so people don't hurt themselves … and then you know, introduction to *sama* and the musician comes and then it's like who knows, who knows, Hu [Him] knows what's going to happen [laughter].[69]

Evanson also notes that there is freedom to "dress comfortably," for "there is no dress code" for participants.[70] Evanson believes in cultivating and hosting a space that is truly open to everyone:

> The idea is to be yourself … Everyone is welcome and that's also [my] understanding of *tasawwuf* is that all are welcome no one should ever be turned away and

so that's why it's also by donation. If you have money great and if you don't have money great – there's always enough money to kind of keep it going, and that's the most beautiful thing.[71]

The structure of the monthly gatherings follows some of the Turkish traditions of Sufism, which have influenced Evanson's approach:

Some people are interested and some people are not interested in going deeper into that practice and that's okay because they take what they need and they bring that into their lives and their families and their communities so that's enough too. But yeah, the advanced class, that's when we study more Mawlawi techniques to do the traditional Mawlawi ceremony, but then we also do some other practices like singing *ilahi*s, just have *sohbet*s as it emerges and, yeah, so it means that once a month we meet for like six hours or so like a long day. The advanced class and the Sema Space ... is open to the whole community.[72]

Sema Space positions itself in the Mawlawi practice of Sufism, because of Evanson's training with Burke, who traces his lineage back to Loras and the Mawlawi tradition of Rumi. AttarJafari, mentioned earlier, also traces his lineage through Burke and the Mawlawis but includes the Persian Nimatullahi Order (through his Persian identity) and other American Sufi teachers, such as the Kabir Helminski, who also traces his lineage through the Mawlawi tradition in Turkey. So there is a notable trend for many dervishes to maintain multiple Sufi lineages, a tendency that can be found in some historical and classical practices of Sufism.

Reflecting on Sufism in Canada and the US, Evanson notes that the two countries have much in common but in some ways are notably different. For her, it seems that in the US there are many more organized Sufi groups, such as the Inayati Order, that have existed for well over a century. At the same time, she feels that some of the cultural/political realities of Sufism have been migrating into Canada. This has especially been her experience with Turkish Sufism, the politics of which are far more tied to Sufi expressions in diasporic contexts.[73] Many who do not come from Turkey and enter Sufi communities that are Turkish-based are often unaware of the political landscape they have entered. Another notable trend Evanson has noticed while holding Sema Space in Montreal for nearly two decades is that many people (though not all) come first to Sufism and then come to see Islam as a religious expression of Sufism. However, she noted that the cultural traditions or perhaps *adab* (etiquette) that inform some of the central practices of Sufism are at times far more difficult to transmit than religious ones:

EVANSON: It's quite vast in that way ... One thing I observed in the east is that first you are Muslim then you can become a student of *tasawwuf* [Sufism] or dervish. Normally you shouldn't really say I'm a Sufi because then I would have disappeared already [laughter] so I'm just a student here, or dervish or like *murid* you know, something like that. So there first you are a Muslim, then you are dervish, and here it's the opposite. Here a lot of people will be exposed to *tasawwuf* and they'll start to sit with the teacher and start practices and then, sometimes, that leads them to becoming Muslim. So that's kind of what I've seen here. And sometimes it doesn't lead people to become Muslim, but the interesting thing is that lots of people regardless can study *tasawwuf* in the west without out any repercussions. So, you can be Jewish, or atheist, or agnostic, and study *tasawwuf* or be a student of *tasawwuf* in the west. Whereas that's more rare in the east, you know, where there's kind of more of a formula of first Islam and then *tasawwuf*.

XAVIER: Right. Yeah.

EVANSON: So that's what I kind of see as the major difference between east and west and otherwise it's also culture realities and things like you know an industrialized country versus a developing country, you know, taking luxury for granted …
It's just a different way of interacting with people and interacting with guests. For example, the notion of the guest is a gift from God, that is a very kind of eastern and also African notion. But it's not one that's very popular or very kind of known in westernized cultures. Yeah, it might be practised slightly and if you come from a family that is from another country, like if you're first-generation immigrant, then you might still have those practices, but I think all of those elements, all of those aspects of culture are all part of this. And if you don't have any experience of at least one year in another culture, you'll never have any notion of probably 85 per cent of what informs *tasawwuf* in many ways.[74]

As with other Sufi teachers and students introduced in this chapter, Evanson's approach to Sufism, as expressed in her Sema Space in Montreal, maintains a framing of Sufism that is universal but informed by cultural practices, especially Turkish culture. Sufism is not confined to Islamic ritual practices, though expressions of Sufi rituals, especially of turning, are located in them. One need not be a Muslim to encounter or engage with these rituals. The dynamic between Sufism and Islam is a thread the remainder of this study will take up. From Evanson's point of view, it is *adab* or etiquette that informs many Sufi practices. For some Sufis, the essence of Sufism is *adab* or "beautiful behavior" (Rozehnal 2019).

Communities and spaces that are cultivated by AttarJafari and Evanson, through their lineage back to Burke and Loras, solidify the tradition of Sufism in Canada in its varying expressions, especially in form, be it a universal Sufism as one sees with the Inayati Order and Rumi societies in Vancouver, Toronto, and Montreal, or a diasporic form of Sufism with groups such as the Jerrahi Order in Toronto. However, one specific form of expression that has defined Sufism in Canada is the practice of turning or *sama*. The next two chapters dive deeply into this practice. The classical era of Sufism is discussed in chapter 3. Then chapter 4 considers how this practice has emerged as a popular and performative expression, along with poetry.

Conclusions

This chapter has captured the polygenetic development of Sufism in Canada. Early Sufi movements were evident in this country in the form of Gurdjieff societies at a time when there were only nascent Muslim communities in Canada. The later development of Sufism in Canada seems to have been an after-effect of the countercultural period of spiritual seeking that defined the 1970s and 1980s. Those decades saw the founding of various branches of Inayat Khan's group through his sons Vilayat and Hidayat in Toronto, Edmonton, Calgary, and Vancouver, as well as Sufi Sam's community, the Ruhaniat International. While the universal Sufism of Inayat Khan was being planted firmly across Canada, Reshad Feild arrived in Vancouver in 1973 and set in motion another trajectory of universal Sufism, this one linked to Bülent and Loras. The lineage of Feild and Loras informed the early development of Sufism on the west coast. While these early western Sufi orders with universal inclinations were taking root, the 1990s saw the arrival of diasporic Muslims, who began to affiliate with growing Sufi communities such as the Jerrahi Order. Thus, the development of Sufism in Canada is tied to two concurrent and intersecting processes: (1) the countercultural era of the 1960s and 1970s and (2) changes in immigration patterns beginning in the 1990s.

The emergence of Sufi communities in Canada was also tied to developments in Sufism in the United States. As groups forming around Inayat Khan, Sufi Sam, Feild, and Loras were establishing American centres, they set their sights on Canada as a place to expand; at the same time, Canadian students of these teachers began opening centres in Canada. Sufism in Canada today is a blend of these parallel and related trends. In terms of demographics, Sufism in Canada has attracted both Muslim and non-Muslim spiritual seekers. Many Sufis maintain fluid religious and spiritual identities; others have been initiated into specific orders, such as the Rifai or Jerrahi traditions. There is no single or dominant way to be a Sufi. That said, the transmission of Sufism to Canada required some adaptations to a new social and cultural milieu. In this chapter, some Sufi teachers pointed this out; in Toronto, for example, Aydöner of the Jerrahi Order mentioned how he caters his teachings to a highly diverse cultural and religious audience and how this makes Sufism in Canada a different experience from Sufism as historically practised in Turkey, his birthplace. Others, such as Evanson, make clear that more than culture and religion, it is the *adab* or proper etiquette that many hold as the entirety of Sufism. At times this is difficult to transmit to Canadian students of Sufism who do not come from a Muslim cultural heritage.

This chapter has described various threads of cultural Sufism, namely South Asian and Turkish. In my interview with Hafiz, a member of the Sufi Order International in Toronto, he explained that the Sufi Order in Toronto (established in 1973) and Sufi Studies led by the University of Toronto's Professor Baig were two of the earliest Sufi communities in Toronto. Sufi Order International, through Inayat Khan, traced its lineage to Chishti Sufism, as did Professor Baig and Sufi Studies. Another thread of cultural Sufism has been the Turkish Sufism of the Mawlawis, noted in the discussion of the development of Sufism in Vancouver; yet another is the Persian Sufism of the Nimatullahi. These various forms of cultural Sufism (via diasporic communities) and the western Sufi communities such as Inayati Order thus form the complex geography of Sufism in Canada. Some adherents approached Sufism through a universal lens (i.e., one does not need to be a Muslim to practise Sufism), while others linked the tradition intimately with Islam, in particular through practices of Islamic law.

Ahmet T. Karamustafa in his study notes that in the Mawlawi Order, which developed after Rumi's death, two tendencies were established simultaneously. The first was the "arm of Veled" (Rumi's son), which focused on "legally acceptable channels" to "Rumi's ecstatic piety"; the second entailed a "refusal to exercise any control over ecstatic spiritual experience," known as the "the arm of Shams" (Karamustafa 1994: 82; Sorgenfrei 2020, 2013: 108–9). Clearly then, this debate about the proper format for experiencing Sufism, even among the followers of Rumi, has been ongoing. Even so, some Sufi Muslims have criticized those Sufi communities that are western and universal for not really being Sufi. Questions about what is authentic, especially when aimed at western-based Sufi communities, have stimulated an ongoing debate both among academics (see chapter 1) and within Sufi and Muslim communities themselves. This debate, which is hardly recent, in turn raises questions about what constitutes legitimate transmission and expression of Sufism in the global west. Are there other metrics in play here for assessing Sufism? Does racialization play a part in such assessments (i.e., white Sufis)? Or is the debate really about adherence to Islamic law? These questions are hardly unique to Canada; indeed, they are being raised in studies of American Sufism and in Sufism in the west more generally. Yet these analytical questions may not always be productive, for they hinge on shaky assumptions about Sufism. The following chapters shift focus to the performative dimensions of the practice of *sama* among the interlocutors I have introduced in this chapter. This reframing of the study from discourse to praxis may help us refine our analysis of Sufi expressions in contemporary contexts, such as that of Canada. Sufism has been firmly established as a spiritual, religious, and Islamic practice in Canada today. *Sama* constitutes one thread of popular Sufism that has emerged as a ubiquitous ritual and aesthetic performative reality in an era of rapid globalization, technologization, and mass commodification. Instead of avoiding or dismissing these complex expressions and processes, the next two substantive chapters tackle them head on.

Chapter Three

Sama, Shab-i arus, and Rituals of Remembrance

The tradition of whirling or turning associated with the Mawlawi Order of Rumi in Turkey has seeped into contemporary western popular culture. Early European travellers in the Ottoman Empire noted the alluring practice of turning and the *tennure* (white skirt) of the dervishes. One of the first travel accounts to focus on Sufi traditions was by Georgius de Hungaria (c. 1422–1502) (Lewis 2000; Sedgwick 2016). Georgius was captured by the Turks and held as a slave in Ottoman lands. During this time, he began to question his Christian beliefs and became attracted to Islam and Sufism. In his account he writes about the dervishes he encountered, "who sway their entire body in a regular and well-measured manner, with a decorous, dignified, and very chaste movement of their limbs, matching the rhythmic modulations of the musical instruments, creating finally a whirl of dizzying velocity, a rotation and revolution, in which the power of these performances consist" (qtd in Lewis 2000: 500).

The tradition of turning to the music or *sama* (sacred audition) drew the attention of many European Orientalists and non-Muslims for centuries. In the late twentieth century, Reshad Feild and Suleyman Loras, a Mawlawi *shaykh* from Konya, began teaching men and women to turn in Canada (Vancouver) and the US (Los Angeles). The *samazens*' tradition of turning has also been transmitted through other Sufi orders with connections to Turkish Sufism – for example, through Kabir and Camille Helminski of the Threshold Society, a branch of the Mawlawi Sufi Order, headquartered in Louisville, Kentucky,[1] and through *shaykha* Fariha al-Jerrahi of the Halveti-Jerrahi Sufi group in New York City. Both these orders trace their lineage to their Turkish teacher Muzaffer Ozak. The transmission of turning has not been solely about spreading the teachings of Rumi; it is also about preserving the ritual of *sama* in the contemporary world, given that it has been outlawed in Turkey since the early twentieth century and is still outlawed and now exists as a cultural expression both in and beyond the Turkish world.

A close look at the practice of turning in Canada highlights the central role this ritual plays for some Turkish and Rumi-affiliated Canadian Sufi communities. In this chapter I suggest that the practice of turning has been and still is central to the development of Sufism in Canada. When considered in tandem with the discussion in chapter 4, it seems clear that the practice of turning has been well received in Canada as a cultural expression; however, this is in the context of tokenistic discourses of Canadian multiculturalism as well as growing Islamophobia, which casts this practice less as religious (Islamic) and more as cultural. Yet turning has a longer history in Canada than this would suggest, going back more than fifty years to the 1970s, as we saw in chapter 1. Some of the earliest iterations of Sufism in Canada involved turning (i.e., through Gurdjieff and Sufi Sam). In Vancouver, for instance, the transmission of authority passed on to Majid Buell and Raqib Brian Burke from Loras, during his visit in 1976, which informed the preservation of this practice. This resulted in the tradition of *sama* evolving into a distinct feature of Sufi praxis in Vancouver.

In this chapter, then, I begin by situating the practice of *sama*, with a specific focus on the Turkish historical context as this influenced the development of *sama* in Canada. I then discuss the music and the practice of turning, as the musical dimension of *sama* is significant with regard to how Sufism has permeated public and secular spaces, such as the Aga Khan Museum and smaller venues such as Small World Music in Toronto (see chapter 4). I then turn to early accounts about the practice of *sama* in Vancouver, emphasizing the oral narratives offered by Buell and Burke as well as two students of Burke's, Shams al Haqq Farzad AttarJafari and Tawhida Tanya Evanson. Sufi groups, including the Jerrahi Order in Toronto and the Canadian Society of Sufi Studies (Rifai), also incorporate turning in their *zikr* and hold *sama*, especially during commemorative events like Rumi's death anniversary and *shab-i arus* (in December). In the second half of this chapter, I draw from my field journal to reflect on the *shab-i arus* commemorations held by the Jerrahi Order and Rifai Order in Toronto, Sema Space in Montreal, and the Vancouver Rumi Society. I provide detailed ethnographic reflections to capture the rich traditions of *sama* and *zikr* that inform the lived practices of Sufism in Canadian cities, while mapping how *sama* has maintained its classical features in Canada even while changing to reflect its new landscape. In short, this chapter situates the tradition of *sama* as it is unfolding in Canada as part of a longer historical tradition and sets up the discussion to follow in the next chapter, which explores the cultural and aesethetic performative expressions of *sama*. First, though, I need to explain how *sama* emerged as a sacred ritual.

Sama

Sama is a practice of *zikr* (remembrance of God) and is understood by Sufis to be bidden in the Quran, which asks the reader to remember God constantly (Avery 2004: 3). Historically, "aural stimulation" was used to "induce altered states," especially through "music, poetry and recitation of the Qur'ān," both in ritual and social contexts, which over time became more public and known as *sama* (2). *Sama*, then, is active listening (or sacred audition) with the "ear of the heart". It is "an attitude of reverently listening to music and/or singing of mystical poetry with the intent of increasing awareness and understanding of the divine object described; it is a type of meditation focusing on musical melody, by use of instruments, mystical songs or combining both" (Lewisohn 1997: 4).

Music and dance were central to the development of some of the earliest Sufi movements and communities, even before the thirteenth century, when scholars began to note the formalization of Sufi ritual musical practices. Annemarie Schimmel reports that "musical sessions" were held in the second half of the ninth century in Baghdad and that *sama-khanas* (*sama* halls) were dedicated to the presentation of this music at this time (1992:196). The use of music generated sweeping theological and legal polemics on the permissibility (*halal*) of music in Islam (Lewisohn 1997; Michon 2006).[2] The Hanbali jurist Ibn al-Jawzi (d. 1200) wrote in *Talbis Iblis* (*The Dissimulation of the Devil*) about the distractions of *sama*:

> Music makes man forget moderation and it troubles his mind. This implies that man, when he is excited, commits things which he judges reprehensible in others when he is in his normal state. He makes movements with his head, claps his hands, strikes the ground with his feet, and commits acts similar to those of the insane. Music leads one to this; its action appears to be like that of wine, because it clouds the mind. This is why it is necessary to prohibit it. (quoted in 157)

Groups such as the Brethren of Purity (Ikhwan as-Safa), who collected vast texts of philosophy, science, and art in the tenth century, wrote extensively on music in relation to philosophy. In one such epistle, they expressed how the "rhythm produced by the motion of the musician evokes for certain souls residing in the world of generation and corruption the felicity of the world of the spheres, in the same way that the rhythms produced by the motion of the spheres and the stars evoke for souls who are there the beatitude of the world of the spirit" (qtd 154).

The Brethren of Purity were likely influenced by Greek Neoplatonic philosophy of music, which tied the expression of music to the full grasping of the ideals of beauty and harmony. They added that the critique of music was not aimed at music as permitted by the prophets; rather, it was aimed at music "for the purpose of diversion, for sport, for the incitation to enjoy the pleasures of the lower world" (155).[3] Other early Sufis, like Dhu'l Nun the Egyptian (d. 859), expressed that "listening (as-*sama*') is a divine influence which stirs the heart to see Allah; those who listen to it spiritually attain Allah, and those who listen to it sensually fall into heresy" (qtd 155). The debates over whether the use of music was permissible were thus tied to issues of morality, which were not the concern of Sufis, who found a ritual utility for their own spiritual practice and ultimate goal of achieving unity with the divine (Michon 2006; Avery 2004).

Early Developments of Sama in Sufism

Historical archives bring to light earlier times when dervishes "carried long clubs, bugle-horns and percussion instruments, such as tambourines and drums, to the accompaniment of which he would dance in imitation of the movements of apes and bears, emitting animal sounds as he went." These were efforts to "induce ecstasy" (Kuehn 2018: 262). These practices are documented in early western Iran – in Transoxiana, Khurasan, and Asia Minor – and from North Africa to India. Many of the dervishes I spoke to located their practice of turning within these regions and practices, emphasizing that the ritual of turning and the sacred practice of listening to music may be traced back far earlier than the Ottoman and Turkish tradition of turning in which they were classically trained. These raw practices of dance and music, often imitating sounds of animals and nature, were at times "radical socio-religious critiques" of formalized religious norms (262). In early mystical traditions in Turkey and other regions, one also finds communities such as the Alevis (Bektashis), who at times mingled Sufi traditions with indigenous shamanism of Central Asia. This fluid ritual sharing of traditions and practices is evident with the Dance of Forty as well as the Dance of Cranes, which models "the transformation of shamans into birds which take flight" (Markoff 1995: 158–9). Some orders, such as the Rifais, are noteworthy for their unique poetry and its expression in movement. Writing about his encounter with a group of Rifai dervishes of Wasit in their lodge during his travels, the North African Ibn Battuta (d. 1368 or 1377) described their *zikr* and its music:

> They had prepared loads of fire-wood which they kindled into a flame and went into the midst of it dancing; some of them rolled in the fire, and others ate it in their mouths, until finally they extinguished it entirely. This is their regular custom and it is a peculiar characteristic of their corporation of the Ahmadī brethren. Some of them will take a large snake and bite its head with their teeth until they bite it clean through. (qtd in Khuen 2018: 268)

Many European Orientalists were fascinated by the practice of ritual snake handling in *zikr*, as seen in Edward Lanes's travelogues (Sharify-Funk et al. 2017). In Turkey, groups from the Halveti (Khalwatiyya) and Rifai place ritual music at the centre of their Sufi practices, especially of *zikr*. The Ottoman Mawlawi *sama* (as an institutional experience) is the most commonly evoked example of this, but the tradition of combining *zikr* with music and contemplative movement dates back to even before Ottoman Turkey, to ancient Iran (Persia) and South Asia. At the heart of *sama* practice, then, is the remembrance of Allah through the recitation of *zikr*.

Zikr

Sama is a ritual form of *zikr*, which itself is the contemplative remembrance of Allah, usually through the recitation of the ninety-nine names of God (*asma ul-husna*). It is a core ritual in most if not all Sufi communities. In *zikr*, one aims to control and focus one's breath in an effort to return to one's primordial state, in which one's true essence (the soul or *ruh*) dwells in union with God. Jean During notes the following three features of *zikr*: (1) a repetitive formula; (2) a pulsed or rhythmic articulation; and (3) a specific vocal utterance (accentuated breathing, sound produced while breathing, non-articulated sounds, etc.) (2018: 281).

The practice of *zikr* reflects the central theological call of Sufism, which is to remember one's essence and transcend one's ego or self (*nafs*) – put another way, it is to die before one's physical death, as was attributed to a *hadith* of the Prophet Muhammad. *Zikr* can unfold through silence, or recitation (without music), or it can be expressed through music, especially the sacred concert of *sama*. Sufis such as the Sunni theologian Abu Hamid al-Ghazali (d. 1111), who is often associated with a sober (as opposed to ecstatic) form of Sufism, writes about the role of the spiritual concert (*sama*) in *The Revival of the Sciences of Religion* (*Ihya Ulum ad-Din*):

> Hearts and inmost thoughts, song and ecstasy, are treasuries of secrets and mines of jewels. Infolded in them are their jewels like as fire infolded in iron and stone, and concealed like as water is concealed under dust and loam. There is no way to the extracting of their hidden things save by the flint and steel of listening to music and singing, and there is no entrance to the heart save by the antechamber of the ears. So musical tones, measured and pleasing, bring forth what is in it and make evident its beauties and defects it contains like as a vessel drips only what is in it. And listening to music and singing is for the heart a true touchstone and a speaking standard; whenever the soul of the music and singing reaches the heart, then there stirs in the heart that which in it preponderates (qtd in Michon 2006: 162)

Having first emerged as a form of free expression, *sama* developed over time a particular structure. According to Al-Ghazali, *sama* depended on "proper time, place and brethren" (qtd in Lewisohn 1997: 8). Regarding the right time, Muhammad al-Tusi in his book on *sama* wrote that the "proper time is when their [the Sufis] hearts enjoy purity so that they desire to concentrate their aspiration in seeking their Beloved's goodwill" (qtd 8). Here time refers not to the "temporal realm" but rather to the mystical and spiritual one (9). For al-Ghazali, Tusi, and others, the right place for *sama* was in a Sufi lodge (*zawiya* or *khanqah*) or mosque, though the former was to be "preferred over other spots, since the mosque was founded for sake of the bodily devotion and the heart created for the sake of divine gnosis and the theophany therein" (Tusi, qtd in 9). Here again, however, temporality does not refer to the proper space to gather and perform the *sama*; rather, the *sama* must unfold in the "no-space," or space of the metaphysical heart, the seat of the throne of the Divine that Sufis seek (Lewisohn 1997). Still, it is important to have an ideal physical space to host the metaphysical realities that may unfold therein.

Finally, with regard to right company, *sama* was conducted in spaces for members who had been initiated and were part of a Sufi order. Al-Ghazali and many Sufi masters held that novices and the non-initiated should not participate in *sama*, for they might not have the capacity to endure the "taste" (*dhawq*); thus, their time would be better spent in other ritual training, such as *zikr* or service. Other Sufi masters did not agree: Abu Said Ibn Abi l-Khayr (d.1048) held that there was value in beginners tasting *sama* (10).[4] In the end, though, the practice was centred above all on accessing the Divine. "Despite the difference in opinions concerning permissibility of music audition for beginners, it is evident that the Sacred preludes, preconditions, encompasses and ultimately, defines the ambience of the Sufi's tradition"; thus; without Sacred (God/Divine) "there is no Sama'." So expressed figures like Ghazali (12). Speaking to this, Rumi writes:

> Not every man attains the *sama'* true and pure,
> Nor every bird may feed on figs (qtd 9).

Mir Husayn Harawi (d. 1318), similarly adds:

> For Sama''s not for one who's bound by nature's urges,
> wound up in greed and passion. Unless you cast aside
> all this, how should it be fit for you?
> Not all who languish merit such aperitif.
> Only the burning heart
> is cut out for it.
> When all who tread this way hazard all away,
> lose their stakes for the sake of God, this is no place
> for vain men to try their luck, or arrant folk to joke about. (qtd 12)

Poetic Recitations and Musical Ambiance

Another core feature of *sama* is the use of poetry to access the Divine and achieve a state of union. Al-Ghazali explains that "a strange verse of poetry will rouse the heart with more fervour than recitation of the Koran" (qtd 21). Lewisohn adds: "Music constitutes the poem's emotional body of water; the poem-fish is born and swims in the ocean of *sama* for without music, the vertical dimension of *sama*, the poem expires on the dry land of literal and horizontal meaning" (15). The significance of the synthesis of these elements and of poetry is captured in Tusi's treatise on *sama*:

> The audition of this group [*al-ta'ifa*, i.e., the Sufis] consists in mystical deliberation over (*mulahazat*) the hidden mysteries [concealed] within the highly refined poetry (*al-ash'ar al-raqiqa*) which are sung by the cantor (*qawwāl*) when touched by ecstasy (*wajd*) realized by the assiduous heart of the gnostic and the perfect disciple. Such audition induces them to set aside resistance and through being drawn to the Unique Almighty Being to become aware of the spiritual subtleties and mysteries. In order to remove these veils, on most occasions after the performance of obligatory religious duties, they have chosen [the practice of] audition (*Sama'*) to beautiful voices since human nature is inherently inclined to the voice in order to procure by means of it what is beneficial and repulse what is harmful. (qtd 15)

Here, again, the invitation is to listen to the words of the poetry (audition) just as one would to the music to help transcend form and achieve ecstatic union with the Divine. As the Persian Sufi poet Mahmud Shabistari (d. 1337) writes:

> The soul's *sama'* is not compacted
> Alone of words and consonants.
> No, in every pitch and strain
> there's another enigma contained. (qtd 16)

Thus, words and consonants signal the truths of the relationship between the Divine and the human being, which is the focus of Sufism. Poetry, then, is set to music, which further amplifies the themes evoked by the poetic language, be it longing, separation, love, or union with the Beloved.

According to Sufi masters, each musical aspect of *sama* has "sacred ambience." For instance, the *daf* (tambourine) symbolizes "the cycle of all created beings," the *ney* (flute) is meant to reflect the "divine light penetrating the seed of man's essence," and the singer's voice reflects the "divine life which descends from the inner most arcana to the levels of the spirits, the hearts, and the consciences" (13). As the Persian poet Maghribi (d. 1408) writes in his *ghazal*, the point of it all is to focus on the unity of the Divine:

> Sure, in a painting,
> or in a drawing
> there is nothing but a painting and a drawing

> Yet Mani
> is hidden deep beneath
> in all the art of Manicheaism
>
> See nothing in all the songs and tunes and rhythms and lines
> But the Rhythm-maker, the Musician, though
> Tones, scales, vibrations, emanations
> be thousands. (qtd 14)

In the end, "to listen to music is therefore ... to open oneself to an influence, to a vibration of suprahuman origin 'made sound' in order to awaken in us the echoes of a primordial state and to arouse in the heart a longing for union with its own Essence" (Michon 2006: 163). All these elements, place, time, poetry, and music, are vital components of *sama*, and experiencing them can induce, movement, or dance in the listener.

Meditative Movement

Ahmad al-Ghazali (d. 1126), writing nearly a century before Rumi, explains the symbolic significance of every instrument for the voice of the singer and concludes by saying the following of the dance in *sama*:

> And the dancing is a reference to the circling of the spirit round the circle of existing things in order to receive the effects of the unveilings and revelations; and this is the state of the gnostic. The whirling is a reference to the spirit's standing with Allāh in its inner nature (*sirr*) and being (*wujūd*), the circling of it looks and thought, and its penetrating the ranks of existing things; and this is the state of the seeker of Truth. And his leaping up is a reference to his being drawn from the human station to the unitive station and to existing things acquiring from him spiritual effects and illuminative aids. (qtd 167)[5]

Figures like Tusi and Ahmad al-Ghazali reflect on the role of dance in *sama*. Abu Hamid al-Ghazali, for instance, writes that one should remain composed and be as still as possible, but "if ecstasy overcome and move one without any self-volition, will one be absolved and not blamed because of it. But whenever one's volition returns, then [the rule is to] to return to stillness and response" (qtd in Lewisohn 1997: 27). As Lewisohn reminds us yet again, "at this advanced degree, the *Samāʿ* ceremony reaches such a climax within the mystic's heart that both immobile meditation and rapturous dance appear as incidental. The mystic's inner absorption is so total that music, prayer, and dance dissolve in the ineffability of the musical experience itself" (28). In his *Awarif al-maʿarif*, a Sufi manual, Abu Hafs Umar Suhrawardi (d. 1234) writes about the need for silence and control during *sama*:

The aspiring disciple, yearning aspirant, sincere wayfarer and seeker inspired by divine love must invest himself with the robes of pious vigilance (*taqwa*), which inspire him with steadfastness and grant him hidden powers of will, and which bear the fruit of high spiritual rank and salvation in the hereafter. In this fashion, the flames of divine yearning within him will be rekindled every moment and freshly renewed so that God's grace – the bounty of this world, will bless all of his days, such that in *sama'* he will be able to control his movements, except when he is unable to keep his peace – like a person who must sneeze, no matter how much he wishes not to. (qtd 8)

The harmony of these different elements of *sama*, the music, poetry, and movement, defines the practice. In the words of Tusi: "Hence, while the ear hearkens to the subtleties of the harmonies of the Infinite, the eye apprehends the harmonies of movement, the heart the subtleties of ideas, and reason (*'aql*) knows rapture of the harmonies of the Infinite" (qtd 21). The purpose of *sama* is to induce *wajd*, or ecstasy, which leads to a consciousness of "selflessness"; in this way union with the Divine is made possible at the height of the ritual (22). Shibli (d. 945) expresses this state by writing: "When I suppose that I have lost it, I find it and whenever I imagine that I have found it, I lose it" (qtd 22–3). Thus, in the state of *wajd*, one is not losing oneself so much as finding (*wajada*) the Divine, which is the ultimate end goal of *sama*. As Kenneth S. Avery (2004) writes in his *Psychology of Early Sufi Sama'*, the goal is "heightening of spiritual awareness culminating in various types of ecstasy, alterations of the psyche, and spontaneous physical reactions. The physical and psychological impact of chanting and recitation, especially with the accompaniment of music, was powerfully effective, far beyond the semantic force of the words being heard" (3).

Not all Sufi communities practise the same form or litany of *zikr*, especially with accompanying music. The version of *zikr* (silent, loud, use of music and movement, etc.) reflects each Sufi group's distinct lineage, region, and culture. *Zikr* practices among Sufi groups like the Jalalis (in India), who follow the saint Jalal al-Din Husayn al-Bukhari (d. 1384), included ritual elements such as handling live snakes and scorpions; other communities practised bloodletting and self-flagellation (Kuehn 2018: 268). Dance and music, then, have been a formative praxis for many Sufi communities. A good example here are the Chishtis in South Asia, who have developed unique Qawwali music and dance meditations (often ecstatic and trance-inducing). This practice is common at Sufi shrines on Thursday evenings, such as in Ajmer Sharif. The Mawlawi Order is the one Sufi order that has formalized turning or whirling (movement) and music; they have practised these since Ottoman times.

The Mawlawi Order and Sama

The tradition of the Mawlawi Order and the practice of turning one sees today were not founded by Rumi himself. That was likely done by Rumi's eldest son Sultan Walad (Velad) (d. 1312) after his father's death. There is some debate about the extent to which Walad formalized *sama* – scholars such as Hülya Küçük (2010) have suggested that it was likely even later, under the leadership of Ulu Arif Celebi (d. 1320), or perhaps even after with Adil Celebi (d. 1460), that the "final shape" of *sama* took place (64).[6] Walad was significant for the Mawlawi Order in helping formalize some key aspects of practice, including the institutionalization of *chelebis* (or *chalabis*: descendants of Rumi, *shaykhs*), in addition to parts of *sama* practice (Küçük 2012a). Still, the essence of *sama* and its significance for the Mawlawi Order can be traced to Rumi and to his experiences after the passing of his teacher, Shams of Tabriz. In his *ghazal*, Rumi writes:

> At the time of samāʿ, the Sufis hear another sound from God's throne.
> You go ahead and listen to the form of the samāʿ; they have another ear.
> The samāʿ of my ear is Thy name, the samāʿ of my intelligence is
>   Thy cup. So build me anew, for by Thy Spirit, I am ruined!
> When you have left clay, you will quickly enter the garden of the heart.
>   Then on that side, what is there but samāʿ and pure wine?
> When you come into the samāʿ, you are outside of the two worlds.
>   The world of samāʿ is outside of this world and that.
> Although the roof of the seventh heaven is high, the ladder of the
>   samāʿ passes beyond the roof.
> Dance everything other than Him under your feet! The samāʿ
>   belongs to you and you belong to it!
> No one dances until he sees Thy Gentleness—
>   Thy Gentleness makes infants dance in the womb.
> What is so special about dancing in the womb or in nonexistence?
>   Thy Light makes bones dance in the grave!
> We have danced much over the veils of this world— become
>   nimble, oh friends, for the sake of the dance of that other world!
>   (qtd in Chittick 1983: 328)

Scholars such as Annemarie Schimmel (1992) express how *sama* was the "axis" of Rumi's poetry (200). There is a popular folk tale associated to Rumi, in which one of his disciples was reading the *Futuhat al-makkiyya* (*The Meccan Openings*) of the great Sufi master Ibn Arabi. After listening for a bit, one of the *rabab* players began to play. Smiling, Rumi replied, "Are not the *futūhāt* [openings] of

Abu Bakr-i *rabābī* better than the *Futūhāt al-makkiyya*?" (qtd 200). In this tale, the ecstasy induced by music is far more raw for Rumi than what he felt hearing the magnum opus of the metaphysician Ibn Arabi. Interestingly, Ibn Arabi was highly critical of *sama*, considering it "the worst kind of *bid'a*" (Knysh 1999: 257). On the other hand, for Rumi, as William Chittick (1983) writes, "music and dancing are primarily inward states, and only secondarily phenomena in the outward world," and thus in his poetry the "minstrel" also takes on the role of inner states, such as that of the "saki in winedrinking" (325). Music and contemplative movement became formative for Rumi's practice of remembrance of Shams and the Divine (which were not necessarily separate). The *sama* of inward states was often evoked by my interlocutors, including Raqib Brian Burke (see below).

With the rise of the Ottoman Empire after the fall of the Seljuk Sultanate (well after the death of Rumi), the Mawlawi Order forged strong ties with the Ottomans, receiving strong state and financial support, though the state also maintained ties to other orders, such as the Bektashi, Halveti, and Naqshbandi (Saglam 2017: 417). Under the Ottomans, the Mawlawi Order became known for its musical and literary traditions:

> The intense music that the Mevlevis inherited from their master Jalāuddin has inspired many classical musicians and composers in the Ottoman Empire. In fact, the best pieces of Turkish classical music, such as those by 'Itrī (17th century), were composed by artists who were either members of, or at least loosely connected with, the order. (Schimmel 1975: 325)

Irene Markoff (1995) describes some of the segments of an Ottoman *sama* as she encountered them during her fieldwork:

> The introduction segment of the ritual includes a poem in praise of the prophet known as *naat* and composed by Itri (1640–1712) that is sung unaccompanied, a *taksim* generally performed on the important end-blown flute (*ney*), and a *pesrev* (prelude or composed piece) for instrumental ensemble in fixed meter that uses a specific melodic mode (*makam*) and a metric mode (*usūl*) comprising a "great" circle of 28 primary beats that are repeated twice. It is at this point that the dervishes walk in procession around the ceremonial space and engage in ritual bowing. (158)

The turning increases its pace over time, usually in the third *salam* or section, and then slows down again in the fourth *salam* (158). Here the Turkish and Ottoman cultural backdrop is reflected in the various instruments used, such as the *ney* (end-blown flute), but also the *kanun* (plucked zither), *tanbur* (long-necked plucked lute), *ud* (short-necked, plucked lute), and *kudüm* (a pair of small kettledrums) (158).[7] Schimmel (1992) reflects on the *sama*:

One can also see in the *samā'* the movement of the spheres around the pole, the heavenly dance that permeates all of creation from the angels down to the least minerals. But one can also interpret it as a dance of death and resurrection: the dervishes, solemn in their long black cloaks, walk thrice around the *meydan*, the place where the master stands, to kiss his hands. Then, as the character of the music changes, they cast off their black cloaks, symbol of the perishable earthly body, the transfigured person at the time of resurrection. Next, they whirl around the spiritual center, moths dancing around the candle; the *samā'* is a symbol of death and resurrection in Love, an ever-newly enacted return to the Fountain of Life. Beginning with the hymn in honor of the Prophet, whose closest confidant Shams-i Tabriz, it ends with a long, sonorous prayer and the deep call Hū! ("He!") acknowledgment that He is the One who gives life and death; who is the Living from whom everything comes to whom everything will return. (203)

As mentioned in the above introduction, it was precisely this meditative ritual of the white-dressed Mawlawi dervishes that so intrigued many travellers in the Ottoman Empire, who then painted and wrote about it (Barber 1986). For instance, Julia Pardoe (d. 1862) wrote about her visit to Turkey and her encounter with this practice in *The City of the Sultan: and the Domestic Manners of the Turks* (1837). I quote at length from it here, largely for the sake of comparing it to Schimmel's earlier description:

One by one, the Dervishes entered the chapel, bowing profoundly at the little gate of the enclosure, took their places on the mat, and, bending down, reverently kissed the ground; and then, folding their arms meekly on their breasts, remained buried in prayer, with their eyes closed, and their bodies swinging slowly to and fro. They were all enveloped in wide cloaks of dark coloured cloth with pendent sleeves; and wore their geulafs [genlaf, Dervish hat], which they retained during the whole of the service.

I confess that the impression produced on my mind by the idea of Dancing Dervishes was the very reverse of solemn; and I was, in consequence, quite unprepared for the effect that the exhibition of their religious rites cannot fail to exert on all those who are not predetermined to find food for mirth in every sectarian peculiarity. The deep stillness, broken only by the breath of prayer, or the melancholy wailing of the muffled instruments, which seemed to send forth their voice of sadness from behind a cloud in subdued sorrowing, like the melodious plaint of angels over fallen mortality – the concentrated and pious self-forgetfulness of the community, who never once cast their eyes over the crowds that thronged their chapel – the deep, rich chant of the choral brethren – even the very contrast afforded by the light and fairy-like temple in which they thus meekly ministered to their Maker, with their own calm and inspired appearance, heightened the effect of the scene; and tacitly rebuked the presumption and worldliness of spirit that would have sought a jest in the very sanctuary of religion.

The service commenced with an extemporaneous prayer from the chief priest, to which the attendant Dervishes listened with arms folded upon their breasts, and their eyes fixed on the ground. At its conclusion, all bowed their foreheads to the earth; and the orchestra struck into one of those peculiarly wild and melancholy Turkish airs which are unlike any other music that I ever heard. Instantly, the full voices of the brethren joined in chorus, and the effect was thrilling: now the sounds died away like the exhausted breath of a departing spirit, and suddenly they swelled once more into a deep and powerful diapason that seemed scarce earthly. A second stillness of about a minute succeeded, when the low, solemn music was resumed, and the Dervishes, slowly rising from the earth, followed their superior three times round the enclosure; bowing down twice under the shadow of the name of their Founder, suspended above the seat of the high priest. This reverence was performed without removing their folded arms from their breasts – the first time on the side by which they approached, and afterwards on that opposite, which they gained by slowly revolving on the right foot, in such a manner as to prevent their turning their backs towards the inscription. The procession was closed by a second prostration, after which, each Dervish having gained his place, cast off his cloak, and such as had walked in woollen slippers withdrew them, and, passing solemnly before the Chief Priest, they commenced their evolutions (44–5)

In Pardoe's description of the practice you sense her "impressions" of the entire ritual, which left her intrigued and curious. She found the "Dancing Dervishes" and their "evolutions" compelling. Similar published accounts of *sama* helped popularize the tradition, which led to paintings and photographs of it, such as a painting by the French Orientalist Jean-Léon Gérôme (d. 1904), "The Whirling Dervish" (ca. 1868–89).

The rise of Turkish *sama* practice in the west has been informed in part by the banning of Sufi groups and practices in Turkey after Mustafa Kemal Atatürk (d. 1938) rose to power and launched his secularization project (Sorgenfrei 2013). Sufi orders and lodges were outlawed in 1925, along with "traditional clothes and headgear … calligraphy and even music"; those who maintained these practices could now be charged with "corruption," political "disunity," and misleading people (Saglam 2017: 413, 417–18). After 1928, the Turkish constitution stopped recognizing Islam as Turkey's official religion. The country was now officially secular. After all of this, Sufism vanished from the public and political milieux (418). Laws like the following were now passed:

Article 1: All of the Sufi hospices in the Republic of Turkey, whether pious endowments, personal property of *shaykh*s … will be closed and the right ownership suspended … The graves of sultans and the shrines of dervishes are closed and the occupation of shrine custodian is voided. All persons who reopen closed-down Sufi hospices, hostels, or shrines, or those people who use mystical titles to attract followers or serve them, will be sentenced to at least three months in prison and a fine of 50 lira. (qtd in Aslan 2014: 6)

Even some Sufi *shaykh*s supported this modernizing project. The new republic's views on Sufism had by then – indeed, even before Ataturk's rise – captured the growing anti-Sufi sentiments of some Salafi and reformist Muslims, who viewed Sufis as "corrupt, superstitious, irrational, unscientific and a major cause of economic backwardness and laziness in the society" (Saglam 2017: 418). Curiously, many Orientalist scholars shared this perspective, viewing Sufism as a backward tradition (Sharify-Funk et al 2017). Scholars like Burcu Saglam argue that Turkey's modernization project still protected the "real" and "authentic" Sufis of the historical past, such as Rumi himself (419). For example, Rumi's mausoleum in Konya was transformed into a museum (the Konya Museum of Historical Works) in 1926. It was permitted to remain open, leading some to speculate that Atatürk harboured some goodwill toward Rumi (Saglam 2017). Indeed, some (perhaps Loras?) contended that Atatürk himself was a Mawlawi, and others have suggested that Atatürk saw Rumi as a "'reformist' who accommodated Islam" (Miller 2018; see also Saglam 2017: 419). All of this complicated the position of Sufis and Sufism in the new modernizing and secularizing state project: "Sufi orders were weakened and illegal but their visions and divisions of social world were still significant and enjoyed a relatively high level of legitimacy" (415). Moreover, the transformation of Rumi's tomb did not prevent visitors and pilgrims from visiting it (Aslan 2014; Nikolaisen 2004). The conversion of Rumi's grave in Konya into a museum and the banning of Sufism brought about a complex shift in the practice of turning as a Turkish cultural and heritage practice; no longer was it necessarily a ritually bound one. It is useful to keep this in mind as we consider shifts in *sama* in Canadian cultural spaces in the next chapter.

Sufism is still banned in Turkey. Yet one can still walk the streets of Istanbul and easily find a café presenting tourists with supposedly authentic whirling dervishes. And every 17 December, the *shab-i arus* (death anniversary) of Rumi is celebrated in Konya at Rumi's grave. The *urs* of Rumi attracts thousands of visitors, tourists, and pilgrims from around the globe. At the same time, Sufism among Sufi orders is still practised in secret. At a state level, then, the tradition is often presented as a cultural legacy of the Ottoman Empire and Turkish identity. The political reality of Sufism and Sufi practices, and even more so the cultural transformation of Rumi and whirling into a Turkish secular project, have gone hand in hand with the spread and popularization of this practice in the west (Aslan 2014). In his photo memoir *Rumi and the Whirling Dervishes* (2003), Shems Friedlander notes that UNESCO invited the Mawlawis to Paris in 1964 to present the practice of turning to a European audience (22). Selman Tuzon of Istanbul and Suleyman Loras of Konya, along with nine *samazen*s, shared the practice, and nearly a decade later the tradition was introduced to western Canada (22).

Whirling in Canada

One of the earliest references to whirling in Canada is found in *The Canadian Churchman* of 11 March 1915, in an article titled "Turkey and Islam" by a British Anglican missionary, the Rev. H.U. Weitbrecht (d. 1937). Writing about the Ottoman Empire, he described the religion of the Turks as follows:

> In religious belief the Turkish Molsems [sic] are mainly Sunnis that is to say, they belong to the great majority of Moslems who revere the first four khalifas and follow the sunnat or custom of Mohammed, embodied in the Traditions, as the complement of the Quran. The Sufi or mystic school is represented by the durvesh orders [sic]. These include those known as the "dancing" and the "howling" durveshes [sic], whose exercises are in reality less grotesque than their sobriquet seems to imply. The dancing is a form of ecstatic devotion not unlike that of David which called forth the disapproval of Michal. Among the nomad Tatars in the central highlands of Asia Minor, quasi-sacramental rites are observed which seem like remnants of former Christianity. The Druzes of the Lebanon and the Yazidis of the Mosul district represent heretical idolatrous departures from Islam accompanied by secret rites and teachings. (151)

In Canada, as in many other places, including the Americas and western Europe, the allure of the whirling dervishes was generated through print and literary culture well before the physical arrival of Sufis. These early references to dervishes and whirling in a Canadian publication signal its "less grotesque" elements dating back to the late nineteenth century. Here, we must also consider the tradition of music among Sufi communities – for example, as examined by Michael Frishkopf, who in his study of ritual music in Canada found a notable "silence" regarding musical traditions and even resistance to music in early diasporic Canadian Muslim communities (2011). Discussing the presence of reformist Muslim movements that found music problematic, Frishkopf writes: "But Canada provides a receptive environment for a particular brand of reformist thought, one that is necessarily tolerant of non-Muslims, but not at all tolerant of Muslim difference, and which consequently provides little space for ritual diversity and its aesthetic elaborations, including music ritual" (125).

Frishkopf wonders why "musical ritual [is] so scarce" in Canada. Yet as the previous two chapters showcased, it was precisely these music and meditative practices that took off among non-Muslim Sufi communities in Canada (2011: 125). For these early Sufi groups, music, meditative movement, and poetry were all at the heart of their encounter and experience of Sufism. At the same time, in the contemporary moment, the overt public presence of the tradition of turning should be placed in the context of multicultural discourses that essentialize cultural expressions, even while systemic Islamophobia is intensifying in a country where Muslim communities have been present for hundreds of years. These trends need not be mutually exclusive. As noted earlier, the sites and practices of *sama* have been manipulated in the past, such as by the nation-state project in Turkey. This signals how rituals transform over time as a result of social, religious, and political factors. Given this complex terrain, this chapter and the next capture these nuanced sonic, ritual, and aesthetic dimensions as they are unfolding in Canada.

Reshad Feild was the first Sufi teacher to teach turning in Vancouver, as early as 1973. Feild learned the practice of turning from his teacher Loras during a visit to Konya, which he describes in his memoir *The Last Barrier* (2002). Loras explains why turning is important:

> If you are quiet and in a state of prayer when you Turn, offering everything of yourself to God, then when your body is spinning, there is a completely still point in the center ... The heavens respond; and all the invisible kingdoms join the dance. But the world does not understand. They think we Turn in order to go into some sort of trance. It is true that sometimes we do go into that state you call ecstasy, but that is only when we know and experience at the same time. We do not Turn for ourselves. We turn around in the way we do so that the Light of God may descend upon the earth. As you act as a conduit in the Turn, the light comes through the right hand, and the left hand brings it into this world ... We turn for God and for the world, and it is this most beautiful thing you can imagine (Loras qtd in Reinhertz 2001: xv)

Feild shared the practice of turning with anyone who was interested, Muslim or non-Muslim, initiated Sufi or not, man or woman. Mixed-gender whirling broke with historical precedent, which often did not allow women to whirl, at least not publicly, though there are varying opinions on this history. Majid Buell, one of the first people authorized to hold *samakhane* in the Vancouver *tekke*, reflected on this early moment in 1973, when he and other interested Canadian Sufis started the practice of turning:

> BUELL: And there was about twelve regulars or whatever, maybe thirteen, maybe more. Around that same time ... It was decided that we should...all learn the turn, the whirling. So, it kind of wasn't really the most accurate version but we all got up at 4 a.m., there was a church over here, and people actually drove from

Bellingham [city in Washington state], which is right across the water like an hour and a half away and they went back to work.

XAVIER: So, they would come here, do the whirling, and then drive back?

Buell: Yeah, we did it for ninety days, nonstop. So that was the training because nobody knew what the training really was, so they made it up. And they thought the more intense it would be, the better it would be. Really, silly in the end but I mean it would give everybody a stop.

XAVIER: Who was teaching it? Or were you all just doing it like very?

BUELL: I'm not sure who actually started it but … Reshad Feild I think, had been told how to at least get a few of the positions right. And over the years, of course, you know, we got Jelaleddin Loras and all kinds of people, you know. But we got this bit right. At least and the right direction kind of things. Cause there's two directions you can go in.

XAVIER: Right, right, yeah. And with men and women, everybody just kind of whirling, there wasn't…

BUELL: No, there wasn't any separation and that was our thing. We weren't going to do that.[8]

Feild began the tradition of turning during his earliest visit in Vancouver, when Bülent sent him there to start a centre (see chapter 2's discussion of Brozak and Burke). It was around this time that Raqib Brian Burke also started turning. Speaking about the practice of learning to turn with Feild, Burke recounted:

But an ability that Reshad had was that when we were practising those times, when people actually stopped faking and … started relaxing and then something else was happening that they didn't understand, he would call out "That's it!! That, that's it!!" And I don't think he knew what it was. Right. And we certainly didn't know what it was. Right. But his voice calling out, I think, confirmed that, that beautiful feeling you were having at that moment … That's what we were after. And … if you could just stay in that feeling, then actually he didn't care about the details. If … this thing could create that, then he trusted. Okay. Just keep following that. And the details … you know, someone will come and correct all the details and … the details don't matter in that regard. But that is very much the opposite of the traditional training. The opposite is you get the details. Right. And we won't let you into the ceremony until we observe you to get all the details, right. A hundred percent all the way through. And now you've finally earned your … permission to take part in this ceremony.[9]

When Burke first started turning under the leadership of Feild, especially to present to the public in Vancouver, he never imagined he would still be doing the practice nearly fifty years later. He expressed in our conversation that as he turned, "it reinforced that experience of being home and not that I need to keep doing this the rest of my life but ... I wanna stay home ... And if this was the best way to do it ... yeah."[10] This tradition of focusing on the inner aspect of the practice of turning was emphasized by Suleyman Loras (Dede), as Burke explained: "Well ... the guidance that ... Suleyman Dede gave to us was the inner experience ... experience it from the inside first and then ... learn the outer part."[11]

In 1978, after Loras and Feild separated, Jelaleddin was sent to North America to take over the centres that had been founded by his father. Jelaleddin became a formative figure in the teaching of turning in the US (Sorgenfrei 2014). After learning from Feild, Buell and Burke were initiated by Loras to teach turning and hold *zikr* gatherings, which further institutionalized the practice of turning. Under Feild's direction, the practice of turning had not been formalized; it was through contact with Loras and Jelaleddin that the ceremony – especially Mawlawi turning – became more of the focus in Vancouver. While Feild's students – Buell, Burke, and others – were slowly teaching themselves aspects of turning, Loras's son Jelaleddin came to Vancouver to continue training the *samazen*s, especially in the ritual logistics of the ceremony as opposed to the private gatherings and public presentations that Feild had focused on with his first Vancouver students. The Ottoman mode of *sama* informed the *sama* tradition transmitted through Loras and Jelaleddin. It centred on music, the recitation of poetry, and turning, with various "set forms of movement that increase in speed and intensity" while including the four *salam*s mentioned earlier (Markoff 1995: 158).

With the passing of Suleyman Dede in 1986, the Vancouver group began to wane, except for the yearly gatherings held on the death anniversary of Rumi (*shab-i arus*) in December and occasional *zikr*s, held by Buell. Burke did not take hand with Jelaleddin; even so, he was involved with Jelaleddin's community. In the early 1990s, Burke went to Konya with Jelaleddin and some other North American students to turn in a private session outside Rumi's tomb. This was difficult to arrange, given that even local whirling dervishes could not get permission to turn in Konya. Though the formal Mawlawi practice still informs Burke's and his students' *sama* practice, especially in public presentations, as we will see in the next chapter, the inner experience that was stressed by Feild and Loras still influences much of Burke's approach to turning, which he has passed on now to the second generation of turners, including Tawhida Tanya Evanson, his daughter Mira, and Shams al Haqq Farzad AttarJafari.

The use of instruments in Canada has varied, depending on the availability of musicians who are able to perform live. In the early days, Persian musicians like Amir Koushkani, an ethnomusicologist, composer, and performer, as well as an instructor and player of Persian stringed instruments, especially the *tar* and *setar*, regularly performed at large public gatherings. Koushkani continues to be a key performer of Persian *sama* music in public and private presentations of *zikr*, especially in Toronto, where he is now based. Latif Bolat, a Turk who now lives in California, also regularly presented Sufi music for such gatherings. One also sees the use of *daf* in ritual contexts. In Canada, Sufi music has been inspired largely by Persian and Turkish instruments, reflecting the presence of Turkish and Persian diasporic communities in cities like Toronto, Vancouver, and Montreal.

Zikr, Sama, *and* Shab-i arus *in Vancouver*

In Vancouver, Unity *Zikr* (held on the last Friday of the month) is a monthly community gathering that is now almost three decades old. It started in 1998 as a collaborative effort by Seemi Ghazi, John Brozak, Majid Buell, and Raqib Brian Burke after their encounter with Çatalkaya. These gatherings have done much to preserve the tradition of turning that was introduced by Feild and solidified under Loras, then his son, and finally Çatalkaya. Their *sama* borrows from the Turkish traditions but has gradually transformed itself as more and more *samazen*s have brought their own cultural and ancestral flavours to the tradition of turning (see below). Ghazi explains the intention of the Unity *Zikr*s in Vancouver:

> So at least once a month we'll have *sama* gatherings and ... you know individual *samazen*s who are learning, there's a circle of people who are really giving them the kind of deep teaching, the energetic teaching and ... I think this is something that we all feel like it's new energy coming, there are younger people coming and a lot of that generation from the time of Reshad Feild or Suleyman Dede, who had this transmission, I mean Mira's [Burke] a part of it ... That shows you something about Raqib's transmission because transmitting something to our children is, in some ways, the hardest thing and his daughter is so beautiful and she's received this so fully, right.[12]

Burke taught and trained his daughter Mira, who has been featured in various documentaries, such as *Sufi Soul: Mystic Music of Islam* (2005), and has performed with the Canadian Turkish DJ Mercan Dede. She presents the practice at various *sama* events across Canada, both private and public. Mira began exploring the practice of turning in high school for a research project:

> I always wanted to whirl, but I did not have the inspiration until I started my thesis. I have childhood memories in the North Vancouver *tekke*, of whirling feet and the smell of rose incense, and chanting and candlelight and the hems of dervish skirts in motion. Suleyman Dede even held me as a baby, and my dad feels that Dede's transmission gave me the will to turn. (qtd in Miller 2018: 263).

Mira eventually moved to Istanbul, where she began to explore the tradition further along with other expressions of movement in which she had been steeped:

> At that point, I didn't understand the history of the practice nor the restraint in the tradition movement. But my Waldorf background in Eurythmy, Rudoph Steiner's approach to movement, had already pulled me toward expressive movement. Eurythmy is a movement that makes sound visible. I was learning Eurythmy and the Turn simultaneously, and the cross-pollination between these two forms felt like a natural progression. Today, my father continues to radicalize the turn in his own deeply unique way, and he acts as my greatest defender, especially when I'm dismissed as a tea house dervish. (qtd 264)

I return to some of the themes raised above by Mira and the critique of the "tea house dervish" in chapter 4's discussion of the popularization of Sufism. Still, it is helpful to recognize here that she traces her lineage back to Loras and also to Turkey.

The format of the *zikr* held by Vancouver Rumi Society for Unity *Zikr* thus follows mainly the Turkish tradition of Sufism they have inherited as part of their tradition through Feild and Loras. Along with turning, the Unity *Zikr* includes the recitation of *zikr*, which Ghazi explained:

> So, we have this general pattern. We usually start with a *gulbang*, do you know what the *gulbang* is? So *gulbang* in Turkish Sufism is the invocation ... You invoke the lineage, the prophet, the *awliya* [saints], it's kind of like the *rabata*, the connection and while it's being invoked people will say Allah, Allah, Allah, Allah, Allah, Allah, Allah and it ends with a *Hu* and then the *zikr* begins. So, we usually begin with that and ... *bismillah* [in the name of God, the merciful, the compassionate], *astaghfirullah* ["I seek forgiveness from Allah"] and *salawat*, blessings on the prophet ... Then go into the names and *la illah illallah* [There is no god but God]. At some point there without breaking the *zikr*, we all just stand up and then do various forms of *zikr*, you know, in the circle. I will recite Quran or I will recite over it. Other people also might recite something poetry, Arabic, Turkish, Urdu, over the *zikr*, during the *zikr* ... And afterwards we usually do a really kind of universal *dua*, praying for all of humanity starting kind of with our inner circle and moving out, humanity, the animals, the plants, every ecosystem, we pray for the savannah, we pray for the desert you know, we pray for the rainforest ... that's all improvised.[13]

The style and flavour of *zikr* thus has varied depending on who attends and what traditions and practices of Sufism the participants bring to the gathering. Ghazi explained this further:

But sometimes people come and it's their first time, right, and so there's turning for an hour and then after that we sing usually Turkish *ilahi*s and those are in Turkish, sometimes some of them are translated into English ... Then we do a *zikr* that's a sitting *zikr* which might last anywhere from well twenty minutes to an hour for a sitting *zikr* and then we do standing *zikr*, right. And ... in between there might be some *sohbet*s [conversation], some teaching, poetry, somebody might recite poetry. You never know who's going to come with instruments, with drums. I mean ... I remember one time ... all of these beautiful Persian women came, a whole group of them, and they were these amazing *daf* players but also, they were just really used to being in Qadiri *khanqah*s [Sufi lodges] in Iran. So, for them, they were just going into *hal* [ecstasy]. They were like dropping like flies going into *hal* [ecstasy] and then you've got like your people who've just come in off the internet, and it was like whoa ... I mean it was beautiful and it was very safe because I was grateful there was a sister there and who really knows how to ... go around and make sure everyone's okay and ground[ed]; that kind of thing because it needs more than one person if you're going to go to those kinds of ecstatic, really ecstatic places right. But ... so that can happen too, right, other times it's just very gentle, and as I said, it precedes by inspiration.[14]

*Ilahi*s have been central for most Turkish-based Sufi communities, especially those that are tied to Rumi in various ways. They are a popular form of poetry that is sung to music and are regularly used in ritual contexts, especially for ceremonies such as *zikr* and *sama*. Ghazi has been part of Unity *Zikr* since it started in Vancouver after the Rumi Festival. She has been present ever since and leads the *zikr* regularly with other key senior members (Brozak, Burke, and Buell). This tradition of turning has gone on to influence Burke's students Shams al Haqq Farzad AttarJafari in the creation of Rumi Canada in Toronto and Tawhida Tanya Evanson with her Sema Space in Montreal, as well as the rituals they have cultivated in their communities.

Samazen Shams al Haqq Farzad AttarJafari

Shams al Haqq Farzad AttarJafari, an Iranian Canadian based in Toronto (though he has since relocated to Vancouver), is the head of Rumi Canada. Chapter 1 provided the story of his Sufi organization, Rumi Canada, and of his own journey through Sufism both through his family's heritage and then after his relocation to Canada from Iran. His path has centred on Rumi, but he has studied with many teachers, including Dr Parviz Sahabi at the Zavieh Mystical Society (see chapter 4), Kabir Helminski of the Threshold Society, Zia Inayat-Khan of the Inayati Order, and of course Raqib Brian Burke. As the head of Rumi Canada, he organizes various events around the life and legacy of Rumi across Canada and collaborates in and performs at events around the globe. Since I have known him in Toronto, he has held *sama* sessions about once a month. Rumi Canada does not have an official space, so he often uses the Jerrahi Order's centre in west-end Toronto; recently, he has also been using a meeting room at the Ismaili Centre in north Toronto. These are attended by anywhere from ten to twenty people, though events focused on the *urs* or birthday of Rumi draw larger numbers (in the hundreds, depending on the venue). The monthly *zikr* sessions include live musicians, the recitation of sitting *zikr* (in a circle), and the opportunity to learn to turn. AttarJafari provides some basic instruction for first-time turners, including notes on how to position one's feet and hands, how to make small turns before attempting a full turn, and how to maintain the momentum of turning. Advanced students and *samazen*s of AttarJafari also attend and help newer students with the practice of turning. As the session begins, poetry of Rumi and Hafiz is shared, and the attendees are invited to share or read (a book of poetry is passed around and opened at random). The gatherings hosted by Rumi Canada focus on the practice of *zikr* and *sama*. They are open to anyone, and the attendees vary by age (young and old), gender, race, and religion (Muslim and non-Muslim). During our conversation in the Jerrahi Order centre before a *sama* session, I asked AttarJafari to explain the tradition of *sama* as well as its purpose:

> XAVIER: So what is *sama*? What is the whirling practice? How would you describe it? I know it's hard cause you're ... a master of it.
>
> ATTARJAFARI: Yeah, no ... I'm not actually, I'm a student of it, but *sama* is ... a very deep tuning to a certain frequency of what you may call life. The essence of life and the universe and ... some call it ... listening. And then ... I call it a very deep listening ... So that ... you're kind of tuning inward, you're ascending to your planes of humanity until you go get your *ruh*, you may translate it as soul. There's only one *ruh*, Sufi soul. So that's when you and I become one because there's no person in that stage. So, through this listening you ascend or some may turn inwards toward it. And ... then yes, it begins with the listening and *zikrullah* so you keep your mantra. (*models inhaling and exhaling*) Allah ... Allah ... Allah ... Allah ... Allah ... Allah ... Allah ... Allah Allah ... Allah ... Allah ... Allah ... Allah ... And then once you get to this beautiful space that's very still, that's right in the centre of your being and there ... it becomes very pleasant and then maybe that's what we call Divine ... or Rumi calls it. And once you taste that ecstasy it's very beautiful and ... we need it like oxygen actually. So, we're thirsty for that. So, we practise this. And literally we die, we dive into the energy of stillness with that and we try to stay very centred to it and not get distracted. So overall [it's] moving meditations. It's a form of a *zikr*. So, it's not that we just randomly turn until we get dizzy and go and kind of lose it and ... It's not about losing it, actually going and falling. It's actually a journey you're going through and it's very intentional what you're going through ... Then to be honest with

you, there's different forms of it. What a beautiful *sama* is the one that you're not too distracted because the intention is to go inwards. So ... you have least amount of movements and then you just allow the *nafas* (Persian for breath) or the breathing to take over and turn you counter clockwise and ... then you get to this beautiful space or place that everything is music. You're thirsty for that. So we do *sama*.

XAVIER: Yeah.

ATTARJAFARI: And we miss it. It could be done sitting or whirling, if you're distracted we do it whirling. That's what the *sama* is to me. I could go on a lot longer but it's a very deep topic but it's the ultimate stage of experience of *tasawwuf* [Sufism], *sama* and it exists among all Sufis in one form or another, some dance, some sit down, some do body movement, it's all called *sama* and it's the inner listening. And it's to achieve the state with the one, the union with one. That is the controversial part but ...

XAVIER: The achieving of the union?

ATTARJAFARI: Becoming one with the union.

XAVIER: Because it's heretical?

ATTARJAFARI: Right, yeah. So, we achieve that through *sama*, intentionally. We hope to achieve it, sometimes we don't achieve it, but if we do then *alhamdulillah* [thank God], you come back a different person, transformed every time this happens.[15]

Turning, AttarJafari explains, is a form of *zikr*, an act of remembrance, which is central to Sufism and found among almost all Sufi communities, though not all use music and movement for this contemplation of the Divine, as noted by Sufi masters such as Tusi and Abu Hamid al-Ghazali. Some Muslim communities and even some Sufi groups view the use of music and movement as problematic. For instance, some sub-branches of the Naqshbandi order do not use music and frown upon the use of movement. This ritual practice has generated theological debates and even protests. The inner goal of achieving absolute union with the Divine has raised serious concern among some anti-Sufis, who deem such practices heretical because they challenge notions of monotheism (*tawhid*).[16] Yet from the perspective of Sufis, it is that very same principle of absolute monotheism that has brought them to this practice. Sufis like AttarJafari hold that once one's lower self is transcended, only the Divine (the true essence of one's being) remains. Anti-Sufis often understand Sufi ritual expressions as *bida* or innovation, and some reformist groups associate Sufism's musical rituals with local cultural expressions (or popular Islam), despite such rituals' long historical place in early Islam and Sufism (Frishkopf 2011: 123; Michon 2006).

Still, AttarJafari's audience is not just Sufi communities. It includes those who visit public and cultural spaces, such as museums, performance halls, and festival stages, like the Aga Khan Museum in Toronto, and this popular exposure of Rumi has brought the tradition of whirling dervishes to a wider audience (see chapter 4). The diversity of audiences, especially in terms of Muslims and non-Muslims partaking in a central Sufi ritual, has led to some curious dynamics and responses from participants at monthly gatherings. Some have felt that the presentation of *sama* is too universal; others, that it is too Islamic, as AttarJafari explains:

> I get it from both sides. I get it from the people who thought we are too progressive and then some who thought we're religious because I'm saying *zikrullah* a lot and [it] has Islamic mantras in it. But then, I come from a rooted tradition that I learned from the *shaykh*s and the *pir*s of the Sufi *tariqat*s. And for us, because I attract religious and the non-religious ... There's a little bit of a misunderstanding around this practice and Hazrat Mawlana and Hafiz that they think they are nut bars and they did whatever they wanted to do. No, they had a structure. They had foundation; they did their *zikrullah*. They woke up and they did their *namaz* or they sat at dawn and that's all of us, what we do. Any dervish who [is] initiated, he does this daily practice, otherwise tries. So, you have to be connected to the source, to the *pir*, and then we do some sort of a daily repetition so you have routine. And you are constantly reminding yourself that it's not you ... in the control and it's safe and it's fun, you know?[17]

AttarJafari's understanding of the tradition of *sama* and the practice of turning is located deep within the tradition of Islam and the teachings of his *shaykh*s, namely Rumi (Mawlana) and Hafiz, which he traces back through his own cultural lineage to Iran. He explains that though many are attracted to the poetry and the universal legacy of Rumi, figures like Rumi and Hafiz were also deeply embedded in the practice of Islam, which included the performance of regular prayers (*salat*) and meditation that defined their contemplative practice of *zikr*. At the heart of some of the resistance AttarJafari describes are contestations over the legacies of figures like Hafiz and Rumi, who are often celebrated for their religious pluralism and universalism. Many who come to Sufism, especially turning in North America, often do not realize that these figures' universalism was defined by their understanding of and relationship to Islam. Franklin Lewis (2010) in his monumental book on Rumi captures this point succinctly:

> It will simply not do to extract quotations out of context and present Rumi as a prophet of the presumptions of an unchurched and syncretic spirituality. While Rumi does indeed demonstrate a tolerant and inclusive understanding of religion, he also, we must remember, trained as a preacher, like his father before him, and as a scholar of Islamic law. Rumi did not come to his theology of tolerance and inclusive spirituality by turning away from traditional Islam or organized religion, but through an immersion in it; his spiritual yearning stemmed from a radical desire to follow the example of the Prophet Mohammed and actualize his potential as a perfect Muslim. (10)

The practice of *sama* through the words and legacy of Rumi points to the ritual of *zikr*, which trains one's breathing but also focuses on recitation of the names of God (*asma ul-husna*) as found in the Quran. The practice that is unfolding in Canada can be traced back to the traditions of classical Sufis, who were preoccupied not only with the format of *sama* but fundamentally with the ultimate goal of *zikr*, one that is expressed here by AttarJafari. The practice is not about the self or moving meditation or music, yet those tools offer a possibility of returning to one's primordial state of being in which only the One (Allah) remains. Practices such as turning and *zikr* are only a means to this end, which is ultimate unity and oneness (*tawhid*). As these ritual practices are offered in various contexts by teachers such as AttarJafari, various forms of resistance emerge. For some, the practice of *sama* is too Islamic; for others, too universal. These responses capture the diverse participants who are drawn to the practice in cities like Toronto and Vancouver.

Samazen Tawhida Tanya Evanson

Tawhida Tanya Evanson is the most prominent woman *samazen* in Canada (see chapter 1). She locates her practice of turning and Sufism not only through her teachers Burke and Çatalkaya but also in her spiritual and personal connections to Turkey and her ancestral ties to Afro-Caribbean spirituality. The latter traditions and cultures continue to define her practice of *sama* and Sufism, which she has cultivated as her legacy, not only in Canada but on the global stage, on which she shares her turning practice. During our conversation, I asked her who a dervish is and how her own practice is unique:

> I mean, anyone can take hand with a *shaykh* at any time, if it's right, if it's *haqq* [truth] ... it happens. So, and then it's up to you if you continue with a group or if you continue just doing your own studies because there are some solo dervishes out there, but a whirling dervish requires more practice and technique if you're going to do the traditional Mawlawi whirling ceremony. So that was about four months of practice, of weekly kind of practice, in order to do that ceremony in the most beautiful way. So, it's kind of more classical training. And then the training continues, we still keep doing different practices connected to the Mawlawi whirling tradition, but we're also looking at ... where the Mawlawi whirling tradition comes from and where it exists in the world through different animist practices. So that's part of the studies that this one [I am] is doing and also my *samazenbashi* Raqib Brian Burke is doing those studies.[18]

Students of Burke like AttarJafari and Evanson have been studying the practice of *sama*, not only in its development in Ottoman and Turkish contexts or through the Mawlawi Order but also beyond these regions and traditions. Their aim is to trace the roots of this meditation back to shamanistic and Indigenous cultures around the world. Evanson has learned much about *sama* from that effort.

The Sema Space emerged when her teacher Çatalkaya gave Evanson permission to hold *sama* with live music and *zikr*. The monthly gatherings at Sema Space in Montreal follow an outline similar to that of the *zikr* practices noted by Ghazi during Unity *Zikr*:

> So our group is based in *sama* because the permission that was given to this one [me] is to ... have *sama* with live music and the *zikr* happens naturally. We do the same thing every time. We start in the same way, which most gatherings start with *fatiha* [Opening *Surah* of the Quran] and maybe poetry and maybe singing *ilahis*. So sometimes there's fifty people in the room, turning, some of them might do the *zikr* with me, but generally I'm holding the space so that they ... can do the *sama* and that's why it's Sema Space ... And ... some people have been coming since the beginning, and a couple of years ago we decided maybe we should present the ... ceremony for Mawlana in Montreal because no one else is doing that ... So, what was created was an advanced *sama* class in Montreal and so some people who had been doing it for a long time had joined that class and actually became *samazens*. So now there's whole group of *samazens*, maybe about seven, in Montreal who have all *tennure* (robes), they have their *mest* (shoes) and we've done the *urs* ceremony twice.[19]

Evanson ensures that everything is bilingual during the *sama*, and thus the gathering is conducted in French, English, and Turkish (such as in the singing of *ilahis*). A land acknowledgment or a statement of recognition of Indigenous territory in gratitude and solidarity is shared before the ritual begins. Following the model we saw earlier in Unity *Zikr* with the Vancouver Rumi Society and Rumi Canada led by AttarJafari, the practice of *zikr* and *sama* is central at Sema Space, which attracts a variety of people from different walks of life. Many women attend Evanson's monthly gatherings, for Evanson is one of the only *sama* teachers who is a woman. The attendees represent multiple generations – children, their parents, and their grandparents.

Sema Space is held in a rented space in the Little Portugal neighbourhood of downtown Montreal. The large dance studio is available for live local musicians, who usually are invited by Evanson. The musicians come from various cultural traditions, be they Persian or Turkish. Evanson provides a warm-up before the turning practice begins, as well as some direction for first-time turners. She encourages everyone to move as their body calls them and in whatever way they feel comfortable with, offering technical advice to individual practitioners. The flexibility and fluidity of the practice cultivated by Evanson is why many regular attendees keep returning. They include Muslims and non-Muslims, Sufi and non-Sufi. For Evanson the turning practice is not just about the method, ritual, and practice of turning; rather, the aim is to remember, as AttarJafari evoked earlier:

> Rather than telling people what to do, it's more about helping people remember ... how are things done in this space and everybody in the end does remember. And it's not only during our kind of more ancient version of the ceremony, but even afterwards, like clean-up time and everyone takes a job, and does it without being asked ... So those memories of how to be in community.[20]

Evanson's gatherings offer opportunities for people to be in community with one another. Tea is available in the small kitchenette outside the dance studio space. After the *sama*, everyone is invited to partake of food and snacks, which are brought by those in attendance (potluck style). Participation in this is also an act of remembrance, besides allowing everyone to converse together. All of this is connected to the broader practice that Evanson has created for her community in Montreal. Some of this also unfolds during AttarJafari's gathering, as the attendees gather informally. There is no formal sharing of a meal, though.

Evanson explained that the ethnic and cultural demographics of Montreal make the profile and reception of her students rather different than in a city like Toronto. She does not host many large-scale public events of the sort that AttarJafari has arranged in Toronto, in spaces like the Aga Khan Museum and Ismaili Centre (see chapter 4), although she presents *at* them. In Montreal the Iranian/Persian or Turkish diasporic presence is not as dominant as in Toronto, where many attendees are there to listen to live Iranian/Persian and/or Turkish music. Montreal, though, has a higher population of Arabic-speaking French (African) Muslims. Some of these Muslims have tended to gravitate toward traditional Sufi communities, such as the Naqshbandi-Haqqani Sufi Order (Haddad 2008; LeBlanc 2013). In holding gatherings at the Sema Space, she has often found that many do not know what a whirling dervish is; they may know who Rumi is, however. Many of her students are French Canadian women (European/white descent), but there are also women from Iran, Turkey, India, Pakistan, and Southeast Asia. She has found that whatever the cultural and religious background of those who come to Sema Space, "most of the people are interested in kind of doing it as a practice." Evanson hopes this will inform their lifestyle.[21] If they are interested in the origins of turning, they often pursue this knowledge by studying with Evanson. Evanson has thought carefully about the space she has created for her students. Interested seekers will find their way to her community for the real work of Sufism, which is healing and unifying:

> It's not called like Sufi whirling, you know? Because it's just Sema Space, you have to really look for us. So, the ones who come are the ones ... who are thirsty. So,

it's kind of again, like an open secret. We just try and navigate these waters so that the ones who are looking for us will find us. And ... yeah, so it kind of works that way ... But I just made it ... using language like *sama*, what's *sama*? If you don't know, well you have to really kind of look for it and read the description and what it is and what's happening and we're trying to encourage people to participate so that it's not just a free concert, this is about healing, this is about unity. So, there's some lines that we're navigating and also to remove perhaps the gaze of the other. When people are very vulnerable in doing *sama*, if people are just there watching them, then they become very vulnerable to that gaze and so we just try navigate the waters to make it a safe space for everyone ... so that everyone can be fully, you know, so that everyone can get along with their polishing work, you know? They're there to clean themselves, to polish themselves. And so, you want to make sure it's a safe place for people to do that, because also it is mostly women and also sometimes children.[22]

The idea of cultivating a safe space for participants is shared by Ghazi, AttarJafari, and Evanson across the three cities. All three locate the practice of turning within the classical practice of remembrance and achieving unity with the Divine, but all three are also very careful to cultivate a safe community for those who attend. Thus, though the ritual space is open to anyone regardless of their religious and spiritual beliefs, the goal is the same: a spiritual state of unity. It is not just to come to listen to the music.

Evanson's practice, teaching, and studies of turning have led her to realize that meditative movements are common in shamanistic cultures around the world. For her, part of this genealogy is based on her own ancestral lineage. Evanson's father is Antiguan and her mother is European. Growing up, she was exposed to Christian (Protestant and Catholic) traditions; today, she finds that the histories of Antigua and of the transatlantic slave trade, especially in regions like Ghana, are vital to her relationship to turning and to her story of being a Sufi:

A lot of the studies that this one [I am] is doing and also Raqib [Burke] the *samazenbashi* were looking at the experience of *tasawwuf* all over the world and my interest is of course in the African continent. Also, it basically all goes back to shamanic practices and sometimes the crescendo of traditional dances have *sama* in them, but there are also experiences of like pre-Islamic, I'm talking about pre-Islamic tradition in West Africa that have *sama*, like particularly the Zangbeto in Benin is exactly the *samazen*. I'll let you look into the Zangbeto of Benin, but the Korean shamans also whirl holding knives and then they lick the knives after. The Buddhists in Tibet turn both ways, very slowly, and some of the Tibetan practices, like exercise practices, include turning twelve times to the left, twelve times to the right, and monks turn also as part of their practices and also indigenous people here in the Americas have turning as part of their different dances, shawl dances, fancy dances, different things like that, and you can see it at powwows as well. So that's also a really beautiful thing to see, but I always wondered why am I here with these people [laughter] doing this. How did this happen? And I'm pretty sure it's not through the European on my mother side of the family and that is Catholic and coming from Normandy, but ... I mean my dad is from Antigua from the West Indies and so you don't know where you're from before that right? Because of the transatlantic slave trade there's no records, you could do some DNA testing, but it still will just tell you a few different African tribes that you might be from, including some other cultural groups as well, but there's some connection apparently in Antigua through the dialect that has emerged in Antigua, like the creole. There's a connection with a Hausa of Ghana and actually if you look at the Hausa ... people [in] Ghana they're all Muslim and many are Muslim and so when I look at also some of the history of Antigua there was a slave song that went *La Allah lala* and so I thought, oh, okay, well there you go, that's how it came [laughter]. It had just been dormant because a lot of Africans were brought as slaves to a lot of the West Indian islands. They became British or they became French and a lot of energy is still there in Antigua. There's still no store to buy musical instruments because drumming was illegal. So, a lot of these qualities that would allow shamanic practices to happen like having music instruments and being able to gather were all illegal and so it was squashed out, but if you look at the records, there is evidence that some of the Africans that came were Muslim and were also possibly Sufi. So, I'm just going to go from that and it's possibly true and it's possibly wishful thinking [laughter]. Yeah, otherwise, I'd like to think that anyone can be a student of *tasawwuf*, like anyone can be Christian, anyone can be Buddhist, and it shouldn't matter what the colour of your skin is, it's more about how far your memory can take you so that you can bring others into ancient memory as well. Because *zikr* just means remembering, right? So, and *sama* means listening. They're words from another language, but the translations are pretty clear.[23]

Evanson's study of the roots of the tradition and focus on remembrance as central aim of any meditative dance practice in Sufism remain vital for the work she cultivates in Sema Space. This is work she is doing with her teacher Burke and other *samazen*s, like AttarJafari. Evanson is also clear about tracing the tradition of *sama* not to fifteenth-century Turkey but before that to twelfth-century Rumi himself, during whose time whirling was a rawer "animistic" and "shamanic" practice, before it became formalized under the Mawlawi Order. A popular story has it that Rumi was walking through the bazaar one day, when upon hearing natural sounds around him, such as the clinking of metal as the metalsmith worked at his trade, he grabbed a pillar and slowly began to turn in ecstasy. Thus, teachers and practitioners like Evanson are invested in locating the genesis of turning beyond the formula of the Ottoman tradition.

The exploration of pre-Ottoman traditions of turning has led to collaborative presentations, such as with Indigenous dancers and presenters. An Indigenous student is studying with Evanson (see chapter 4). More importantly, Evanson personalizes the practice of turning by locating her own ancestral lineage through her father in Antigua to West Africa. She is attentive not only to the traditions of Islam but also to pre-Islamic expressions and cultures of the African continent that are tied to dance, music, and movement, such as Indigenous traditions of the Hausa of Ghana. She understands that these traditions, in essence, share practices evident in other cultural and religious contexts, such as Korean Buddhism and the Indigenous practices of the Americas. Schimmel (1992) similarly documents the historical breadth of these expressive meditative movements in other cultures:

> Most religious traditions have viewed dance as a way to relinquish one's earthbound gravity and become united with the spiritual world; whether one thinks of wild Dionysian revels or the harmonious Apollonian dance of classical antiquity, whether one considers the Native American sun and rain dances, or the cultic dances to honor the deities as was common in the tradition of India, dance is always something that leads us out of this world of matter. Maulana [Rumi] knew this well, and his love for the spiritual Sun Shamsuddin is aptly expressed in the language of dance. (202)

Evanson traces her ancestral lineage back to some of the first Muslims in the Atlantic world, who arrived here as slaves. This lineage traced by Evanson is part of her effort to recognize the true essence of *sama*, one that at its core is a practice of remembrance. As a ritual practice, it transcends any religion or particular form of Sufism. That practice is available to anyone who intends to work on unblocking their memory. *Sama* is a contemplative tool to help one return to one's primordial state through recovering one's first memories, as noted in the introduction of this chapter and as relayed again here by Jean-Louis Michon:

> The animating power of music comes, we have seen, from that which it is in essence, a manifestation of the Divine Word, a language that reminds man [humans] of the state in which, before creation, he was still united with the Universal Soul, radiated from the original light, which reminds him of that instant in pre-eternity when, according to a Quranic saying frequently cited by the Sufis (7:172) the Lord asked souls "Am I not your Lord?" They answered "Yea!" It is the memory of this primordial covenant (*al-mīthāq al-awwal*) and the nostalgia for it that music evokes in hearts entrapped in earthly attachments. (2006:166)

Evanson is clear that the intention of the practice goes beyond the labels of Sufism or even Islam; rather, what is central, especially with the practice of turning, is remembrance. The whole point of the practice is to remember, so Evanson is more interested in transmission:

> I think it happens naturally for a lot of people, but it doesn't also happen for some people and what's interesting is, that you can also be alone on this path and not have any group practice and still be a student and you're just doing your own studies and basically you're doing it through books or perhaps through some interaction with a teacher ... like this is about transmission. So, it's not about the body, it's about the transmission. That's the most important part, and that transmission is also connected to memory. You're almost like, sparking people to remember. That's part of the transmission. It's not telling you what to remember, it's like a catalyst for your own ancient memory.[24]

Transmission here can be understood as studying with a Sufi teacher who has an established lineage (*silsila*) that goes back to the Prophet Muhammad. However, transmission can also be tied to memory, as Evanson has explained. Sufis hold that they have always known the essence of the truth and reality (God) but that they have forgotten this truth. Thus, transmission of this truth exists within all human beings as a God-given gift, and one's role on the Sufi path is to remember this transmission. For Evanson the practice of *sama* unearths that memory. That is why she makes it clear that she is not a teacher; rather, she holds the Sema Space for those who are interested in turning to remember: "But I also don't call myself a teacher. I just hold the space. This one is *hiç* [nothing in Turkish], this one is *hiç*, right?"[25] She continues:

> So, the idea is that it also takes the onus off of me and it's also about everyone's experience and they'll have an inner and an outer experience because that's the cool thing also about these experiences is that you're in it, but you can also see everyone else's light, as you're having your own light experience. So, it's very powerful because of that ... It's your remembering that's going to happen and we all have the ability or I like to think that many of us have the ability to remember because we all have the blood of the first women [Eve].[26]

For Evanson, as for AttarJafari, Burke, and Ghazi (in Vancouver), *zikr* and *sama* centre on the core essence of remembrance, a sense of being home or returning. They are not worried about the inherited religious identities in which their students are located or in their cultural, racial, or gendered locations. For them, regardless of these outward forms, the call of *zikr* is simply to turn inward to remember, and as such it is a call that is available to anyone. They also understand that this practice offers people healing and relief. Indeed, this approach to *sama* was held by some early Sufis, like Tusi, who wrote:

> When [by means of music] the various limbs of the body become properly collected, hatred and aversion is removed and concord (*hukm al-tawāfuq*) appears. Discord and dissension (*al-tanāfur*) belong to darkness whereas concord comes from Light – so when darkness is dispersed and light shines forth, one's worldly affairs and spiritual realities become uncovered with a clarity which a thousand efforts could not have accomplished. (qtd in Lewisohn 1997: 24)

And of course, this sentiment of healing offered by the ritual is also evoked by the master himself, Rumi, in the fourth book of his *Mathnawi*:

> Samaʿ is food of lovers;
> The strands of dispersed imagination
> in it fain concentration.
> The fantasies of the inner psyche in music find strength;
> No, transcend strength, by the wail
> of the flute and horn, take form. (qtd 25)

The idea of *sama* as "food" for the inner heart has been evoked by various Sufis over time and in different places (25). In continuing to build on this discussion of expressions of turning in Canada, the final section turns to two other Turkish Sufi communities that maintain the practice of *sama* in their gatherings while focusing on another ritual celebration, the death anniversary of Rumi. The yearly gathering of the *shab-i arus* serves as a pinnacle ritual commemoration that honours the living legacy of Rumi for the communities in Vancouver, Toronto, and Montreal.[27]

Shab-i arus

Rumi died on 17 December 1273. In anticipating his own death, which many Sufi masters seemed to have had the foresight to do, Rumi evoked the following words:

> If wheat grows from my dust, and if it's baked
> as bread— intoxicated will increase.
> The dough: intoxicated! and the baker!
> The oven too will sing ecstatic hymns!
> When you come to my tomb to visit me
> Don't come without a drum to see my grave,
> For at God's banquet mourners have no place (qtd in Schimmel 1992: 30–1)

Rumi's funeral brought out Jewish, Christian, and Muslim mourners. Popular tales relay that his cat passed away a week after, saddened by the loss of his master (31). Historically, Rumi's day of passing has been commemorated with "drum" and music, just as he requested. Yet this classic ceremony was barred in Turkey after Sufism was banned. In 1942, in Konya, the Turkish Republic held the "first public and large-scale commemoration" of Rumi's death anniversary. It included the publication of Rumi's poems and narratives of his life and the Mawlawi Order in magazines and various print media (Saglam 2017: 419). Though it had been banned in Turkey, and Sufi lodges had been closed down across the country, Sufism continued to hold a precarious but invisibly popular presence there. Rumi's tomb in Konya (*Yesil Türbe* in Turkish), which is officially a museum, continues to attract busloads of pilgrims and tourists, and his death anniversary or *shab-i arus* on 17 December has drawn thousands from around the globe. It is a popular pilgrimage destination during the weeks of celebration, which include *sama* and presentations of turning (Nikolaisen 2004; Aslan 2014). Schimmel (1992) remembers visiting Turkey in December 1954, when she was invited to give a talk, and having the opportunity to visit Konya, which led to a surprise encounter:

> We stayed with an amiable and well-to-do family, and late in the evening we were brought to a large mansion in the center of the old town, in which two armchairs had been set out for the noble guests. With amazement we observed as a group of elderly gentlemen unwrapped mysterious parcels out of which emerged flutes, rebabs, tambourines, even dervish caps and gowns. What was going on? The Mevlevi ritual had been prohibited ever since Ataturk had closed the dervish lodges in 1925 – how could it be possible that all the implements were still in use? Hafiz Sabri, who taught the recitation of the Koran in our faculty, smiled: "You'll see, your dream will come true! – and he was right. For the first time in twenty-eight years the men began to perform the mystical dance together, and we listened to the music, the flutes, the drums, the powerful introductory praise song for the Prophet, and saw the men turning, whirling, their white gowns unfolding as though they were large white moths turning around a candle or atoms whirling around the sun, like the stars in cosmic harmony. (195–6)

Schimmel adds that the Mawlawis were allowed to perform the ritual at the tomb of Rumi the next day, as the event was being documented for a film (196). Since the 1950s, the practice of Mawlawi *sama* has been held in Konya at Rumi's tomb, unofficially.

The tomb of a Sufi saint is known as a *mazar* (shrine), though the name given to such a shrine may vary according to cultural location. For instance, tombs may be called a *dargah* (court or doorway) and may be part of a larger complex, such as a *zawiya* (Arabic) or *khanqah* (Persian) or *tekke* (Turkish). These sites usually contain the tomb of a holy figure or saint (*wali*), though they are not necessarily dependent on the physical presence of a holy figure's internment.

For example, the association with the saint's legacy or memory in another form, such as through a relic, may also define the shrine. The development of these sites as memorials for holy figures, either with connections to the Prophet Muhammad's family, such as his cousin and son-in-law Ali or his descendants, is common across Muslim societies (Arjana 2017). These nodes have wide appeal among their adherents primarily because of the belief that being in intimate proximity to these holy figures, both in life and in death, enables one to access their grace or charisma (*baraka*) due to the figures' own spiritual proximity to the Prophet Muhammad and/or Allah. This access, however, is especially porous upon the death of the saint. Death signals the union with the Divine, a state that a Sufi strives for in life yet fully actualizes only in death. This is why the death anniversary of the holy figure is a significant day of commemoration. *Urs* (literally meaning "marriage" or "spiritual nuptials" as translated by Schimmel) is a day of celebration, for it is the day the Sufi wedded (died in) the Divine. In India and Egypt, this festive and holy occasion is celebrated at the tomb or a shrine of a Sufi saint over several days; in other instances it may also be celebrated at the homes of practitioners, as evident in Sri Lanka and was likely the mode of commemoration for early diasporic Muslim communities in America (Bellamy 2011; Hoffman 2009). A central practice that has solidified in Sufism in the west, in the US, Canada, and western Europe, is the commemoration of the death anniversary of Rumi across various types of Sufi communities, whether of Islamic or universal tendencies.

For instance, in my conversation with Ghazi of the Vancouver Rumi Society, she explained that in addition to the monthly *zikr* gatherings that are held, the death anniversary of Rumi is celebrated every 17 December, and has been for years. The ability to host this annual commemoration of Rumi has been due in large part to the authority of Buell, who was initiated by Loras (see chapter 1). Though Suleyman Loras's son Jelaleddin was appointed the successor of the Mevlevi Order of America, in Canada the authority of Buell and the ability of Burke to hold *sama* allowed for the preservation of the practice of *urs*, which has continued to this day:

> So on December 17 we do ... the formal Mawlawi *sama*, usually the music is not the traditional Ottoman *sama* music ... We have beautiful Persian musicians who have worked with us and are very close with us and they now know just what is the energy of those four *salam*s ... So we'll have ... poems by Mawlana, other instrumental music, and we'll practice for the four *salam*s. This last time it didn't work to have them, so Amir O'Loughlin did it and he brought his music and ... I sang and there was flute and a harp actually. So, there were different instruments and it was completely different. And again, it was just like working with the energy of the *salam*s. So, we had some Turkish *ilahai*s, some of his [O'Loughlin's] original compositions.[28]

The gathering is usually held at the University of British Columbia and draws a diverse crowd. Like the practice of the *sama,* the *shab-i arus* takes its form from the Turkish and Ottoman context. In Canada, though, it has been transformed based on the availability of musicians who are able to present the music for the *samazens* to turn to. As Ghazi noted, during the last *shab-i arus,* O'Loughlin, who is a leader of the Inayati Order in Vancouver (see chapter 1) as well as a musician, presented the music. These annual events then bring together different Sufi orders in Vancouver to commemorate the death anniversary of Rumi.

When I was conducting fieldwork for this project, one of my goals was to attend the different *urs* gatherings for Rumi in the year 2019, which marked the 746th death anniversary of Rumi, to map how this practice is developing in Canada, in addition to the regular *sama* I have documented so far. Several Sufi communities in Toronto hosted the *urs* for Rumi: in Toronto, they were the Jerrahi Order, which tends to be a more diasporic-leaning Muslim Sufi community; and the Canadian Institute of Sufi Studies (Rifais), which tends to attract a more diverse Muslim and non-Muslim crowd (see chapter 1). Meanwhile, in Montreal, Evanson hosted *shab-i arus* for her regular community at Sema Space. Below, I draw from my field journal to describe some of the practices I documented during these *urs* and the spaces where they unfolded as a means to further contextualize the voices of Sufi teachers and *samazens* we have heard from already. I pay specific attention to the demographic composition of these gatherings and rituals to highlight the similarities in ritual practices of the *urs* among the variously orientated Sufi communities. The transformation and transmission of the *shab-i arus* is maintained not only through the diaspora, especially among Turkish Sufi communities, but also among Sufis with affiliation to Rumi-based movements, such as Rumi Canada and Sema Space. In the end, however, it is important to note that aside from the definitive coalescing of Sufi rituals of *sama,* the *shab-i arus* forms another central praxis of Sufism in Canada that cuts across diverse spectrum of practitioners and further affirms the legacy of Rumi.

8 December 2019: Shab-i urs *(The Wedding Night), Sema Space, Montreal*

The trendy and cosmopolitan city of Montreal is one that I have been getting to know better (though I had lived there as a child when I first came to Canada). I have been attending some of the monthly *sama* gatherings in Montreal for fieldwork, spending time with Evanson and her Sema Space community. For this community, 8 December 2019 was a very special occasion – the *urs* commemoration for Rumi. The event started at 4 p.m. The turnout for this *urs* of Rumi was the largest I had seen up until then. Many of those present were not part of the small circle of *samazens* who meet regularly for *sama* once a month. Some were students at various universities in Montreal, who brought their friends for the first time; others were regular attendees, who busied themselves setting up the food table and working in the small kitchenette. The crowd was a culturally and religiously diverse; there were more women than men. This gender composition is noteworthy: Evanson has noted that, being a woman teacher, the space she provides is attractive for women, who want a safe community. The event attracted many white people but also many racialized Muslims, such as East Asians, Persians, and North Africans. Montreal's ethnic and cultural demographic informs the type of Sufism that is unfolding there, which differs from that of Toronto and Vancouver. I noted throughout the night that I may have been the only South Asian person at the gathering, which would not have been the case had the event been in Toronto. About thirty people were present, not including the musicians and *samazen*s. A donation of $15 to $20 was suggested, though Evanson has long stressed that everyone is welcome, whether they are able to contribute or not.

As at most other events, the gathering started with all the attendees sitting in a circle around the perimeter of the dance studio space. There were five men musicians, holding various Persian and Turkish instruments, such as the *ney*, the *tar*, and the *santur*; I also saw a violin and a *djembe* (drum). Montreal is known for its lively music scene, so many of the musicians whom Evanson invites are part of her larger performance networks. The gathering hosted eight *samazens*. Burke, the *samazenbashi*, had come from Vancouver for this event. AttarJafari and his student had come from Toronto. The rest were Evanson's students, from Montreal and environs. The *samazens* were of mixed gender, and most were white; three were racialized; one was Métis.

The *sama* began with a land acknowledgment, followed by an explanation of the significance of the gathering, which was to commemorate the death anniversary of Rumi. It was intended to celebrate the wedding of Rumi to his beloved (Allah). Everything was explained in both French and English. Evanson and Burke together introduced what was about to unfold, telling the attendees who Rumi was and sharing one of his poems. Burke then explained what would happen during the longer ceremony (the second half of the gathering), which would be non-structured, that is, everyone present could turn, according to their levels of comfort and interest. They could continue into the night. To model the practice, he asked for three volunteers to come forward, demonstrating how they could turn and hold the space (by walking through the *sama* space). The first *sama* was formulaic and structured. This one closely followed the classical Ottoman practice that has been noted by writers such as Friedlander and Schimmel and had been introduced by figures like Loras and his son during their visits to Vancouver (Friedlander 2003; Schimmel 1992). Since no *shaykh* was present, that role was served by the *samazenbashi*, Burke. The dervishes walked in one by one and sat on the floor, each in front of a white sheepskin (representing their ego); Burke sat on a red sheepskin, which is meant to represent Shams in the ceremony. The gathering started with the sound of the *ney*, evoking the pain of separation, and the opening lines of Rumi's *Mathnawi*: "Oh hear the reed flute, how it does complain / and how it tells of separation's pain" (qtd in Schimmel 1992: 197).

After that, the dervishes slapped their hands on the floor, "indicating the day of Last Judgement" (Friedlander 2003: 87). Burke stepped forward, bowed his head, and began to walk three times around the perimeter of the space (usually the *samakhane*, here the dance studio), while each *samazen* followed behind him, stopping to take a bow at the post (the red sheepskin) before proceeding. Here Friedlander explains:

> As they bow they look between the eyebrows of the dervish opposite them and contemplate the divine manifestation within him ... This is known as the Mukabele (to return to action) and has become the name for the Mevlevi ceremony. This part of the sema is known as the Sultan Veled [Walad] Walk, in honor of Rumi's son, and symbolizes man's identity and his place within a circle. (87)

The first *sama* held by Burke and Evanson kept to many of the traditional elements of the *sama* noted in Mawlawi Ottoman contexts. This ritual formula and structure was not evident in the other two *shab-i arus* gatherings I will be describing. Burke held the space for most of the first *sama* session. Holding space usually means ensuring that those who are turning are tended to. Burke was dressed in a black shroud and walked in and around the other *samazen*s while directing the *samazen*s to certain positions. All the other *samazen*s were in white *tennure* (long white skirts) and *sikke* (dervish hats). Toward the climax, as the rhythm of the music and speed of the turning picked up, Burke joined in the turning. During this first, formulaic *sama*, the musicians mainly improvised (see figure 3.1).

After this first *sama*, there was a short break. Then the turning resumed again, and this time everyone was invited to take part. This second stage was less ritually formulaic, more fluid, and again honoured the practice of turning that Burke had been introduced to in his early encounters with this practice with Feild and Loras. Those who wished, picked up the *daf* (Persian drum) and provided music; others joined the *samazen*s, who had changed out of their *tennure* and *sikke* into their regular clothes to turn or to sit in silent meditation. Evanson and other *samazen*s took turns walking through the space among those who were turning, helping some of the turners with their form while reciting *zikr*. One participant started turning and lost her balance. The seasoned *samazen*s, especially Burke and Evanson, tended to her and made sure she was okay. She eventually sat back in her spot on the outside of the circle while Evanson and Burke cared for her. Others lay down on yoga mats on their backs or their sides and closed their eyes. Some left the event, others stayed on. At times,

3.1. *Shab-i arus* in Montreal. Photograph by author.

Burke modelled the types of hand and foot positions to follow. He also created a line (with everyone holding hands), which he led in movement of feet and hand coordination while reciting various *zikr* litanies, such as *Allah Allah Hayy* (God, God, the Living). Evanson also led *zikr* and sang Turkish *ilahis* – she had a book of these; some joined in while others turned at their own pace.[29] The turning and meditation continued until 11 p.m. (six hours of *sama*). Some of the attendees, including the musicians, left as they chose, while Burke and some *samazens* continued to turn into the late night.

The event had been organized as a potluck, and many had bought food to share – veggie samosas, rice, and curry, but also sweets, such as cookies. The sharing and eating of food took place in between the first and second *samas*. This gave the *samazens* time to breathe and reorganize. The sharing of food brought people together in conversation. In my conversations with some people throughout the night, I learned anecdotally how they came to hear about Sema Space. Many had come because of their interest in music and had heard about the event through their networks and social media (e.g., Facebook). Many were white non-Muslims, while others were of Muslim heritage. When I was leaving the gathering at the end of the evening, I started walking with one of the participants, an older white woman. She explained that she was a musician and played piano for the Montreal Ballet. Because of her inconsistent schedule, she was unable to regularly attend Evanson's monthly meetings. When I asked how she had learned about Sema Space, she said it was through her musician friends that she heard about this workshop. She was drawn to Evanson, especially because she is a woman, adding that she loved her energy. She had met Evanson through a mutual contact, the Turkish Canadian disc jockey Mercan Dede, whom Evanson had toured with for some time. So it appears that the music scene plays a significant role in attracting those who are interested in Sufism or spiritual seekers to Sufi spaces and communities like Evanson's. The same trend is evident in Toronto (see chapter 4).

Spaces like Sema Space offers a taste (*dhawq*) of Sufi ritual. This is formative for how seekers and Sufis, be they Muslims or not, come to turning as well as to Sufism more generally. There is an openness to experimentation at Sema Space, especially since Evanson offers a welcoming and fluid space that encourages those who attend to participate instead of just sitting and gazing. People wear what they are comfortable with, even the *samazen*s, who were all dressed in white shrouds (*tennure*) for the first part of the short *sama* changed into casual attire for the second, longer freestyle *sama*. Some took shawls that were available on the railing and covered themselves (their heads or faces); others just whirled as they were. Many picked up the *daf* and contributed musically. There was much fluidity and exploration. The informal turning manifested itself naturally. This particular *shab-i arus* was intimate and relaxed compared to the next two examples I encountered, and as such captures a particular lineage and tradition via Evanson to Burke, Loras, and Feild.

Shab-i arus: *14 December 2019, by Rifai Dargah in Toronto*

Roncesvalles is a trendy neighbourhood in west-end Toronto. It is here that the Canadian Institute of Sufi Studies (Rifais) gathers biweekly for their *zikr* sessions on Saturday evenings in a yoga studio (rental space). On this cold December evening a special community gathering was held for the *urs* of Rumi. The *urs* was advertised widely on Facebook and attracted a large crowd (more than fifty). Many were regular initiated members of the Rifai Sufi Order; others were friends and family, some visiting for the first time. Members of other Sufi communities in Toronto were also present. *Sama* was performed by members of the Rifai Order, which included three men *samazen*s and one woman. One of the men was the son of Coskun, the *shaykh* of the Sufi order. AttarJafari attended but did not participate in turning. The Rifai have their own community of Rifai-initiated dervishes who have turned in their *sama*, and individuals like AttarJafari and his students also turn with their community, especially at larger public events, for example, when presenting *zikr* at Noor Cultural Center in Toronto.

Just as at the Sema Space – and I would note much the same at practices in Vancouver – this Sufi community's *urs* ceremony included the singing of *ilahi*s by members of the Rifai Order, which formed the first part of the ritual commemoration. The second part of the event included *zikr* led by *shaykh* Coskun, who sat at the head of the circle. Here, the Rifais have an active *shaykh* present at the ritual presentation of the *urs*, whereas Burke embodied this role as the master *samazen* in Montreal and Majid Buell serves this role for the Vancouver Rumi Society. The Rifai Order has a core group of musicians who regularly practice and present *zikr* and *ilahi*s in Turkish, not only for private ritual gatherings but also for public events such as presentations at the Aga Khan Museum or the Noor Cultural Centre in Toronto. The gathering also included a *sohbet* (conversation) on Rumi given by Coskun. Like the one at Sema Space, this gathering included a shared meal organized by the dervishes of the order (as part of their service). A photographer took pictures of the event, which were later posted on Facebook. The attendees were asked to donate $20 to the community fund.

Zikr involved both sitting and standing *zikr*, with no gender separation. Today, with attendance growing steadily, there is less space for standing *zikr*, which involves moving in a circle while holding hands; this is still done if there is enough space to manage it. So in addition to the *samazen*s, who are not a regular feature of biweekly *zikr*, the *zikr* involves more active movement. The circle follows the tradition of the Rifai Order, whose gatherings tend to be more ecstatic, with a trance-like atmosphere. What is unique about the regular gatherings of this group is the ethnic diversity of those who attend. This is a function of the group's location in Toronto's downtown west side, given that many other Sufi communities are located farther out of the city. Accessibility, then, is a strength of this community space and the Rifai Order. Also, the Rifais attract younger Sufi practitioners, drawing heavily from twenty-to-forty demographic (as also seen in Montreal). Generally, the gatherings are open to all: initiated and non-initiated can attend. Many members of this order are academics and social justice activists, which captures an important feature of present-day Sufism in Canada (see the epilogue of this book). The gender-egalitarian practices (see chapter 5) and religious and ethnic diversity of this community render it a prime example of the type of Sufism that is developing in cities like Toronto. That type encompasses elements of Turkish Mawlawi, Jerrahi, and Rifai cultural and ritual practices and has transformed various gender norms for a Canadian (Toronto) context. Their commemoration of the death anniversary of Rumi is similar to Evanson's in Montreal (from two different Turkish traditions) in its intimacy and community focus. However, the Rifai *zikr* was less fluid than what we saw in Montreal, in that it involved only *zikr* and chanting. Neither the turning nor the music was open to everyone's full participation, as was the case in Montreal; only those who had been initiated into the Rifai

Order could serve as musicians and *samazens*. These two examples of the *shab-i arus* differ markedly from our final example.

Jerrahi Order Shab-i arus: *17 December 2019, University of Toronto*

The Jerrahi Order's *shab-i arus* was held on 17 December at Innis College at the University of Toronto. It was co-sponsored by the Canadian Society for the Advancement of Turkish Studies (CSATS), a Toronto-based not-for-profit organization that organizes academic and cultural work on Ottoman, Turkish, and ancient Anatolian history.[30] The auditorium at Innis was packed to the point that many people were turned away at the door. Those who did manage to enter the auditorium found space to sit down on the floor, on the stairs, and by the stage. Of the three *shab-i arus* discussed here, this one attracted the most attendees – close to 200 people. In the three examples provided here, one sees sharp differences in the ways that Rumi's death anniversary is commemorated, which is partly a function of venue size, though all three traditions trace their lineage back to Rumi (via Turkish traditions). The audience for the event at Innis was mainly Turkish and Muslim, probably because it was being co-sponsored by a Turkish organization and thus widely advertised in the city's Turkish diasporic community. There were some non-Muslims. It also felt more like a family gathering, in that many families attended together (including young children and grandparents).

Unlike the gatherings held at Sema Space and by the Rifais, there was no collaborative participation in *sama* or *zikr*. The programming had been pre-set and was hosted by a master of ceremonies. The venue at Innis was highly accessible due to its downtown location. The opening speaker framed the event as more a public lecture than a ritual *sama*. Professor Şerife Yalçınkaya of the Ege University in Izmir, Turkey, at the time a visiting scholar at the University of Toronto, delivered the opening presentation. Her lecture, titled "Rumi's Mystical and Literary Journey," focused on the history of Rumi, his poetry (including in original Persian and Turkish), and his legacy. She delivered the talk in English, and the audience, many of whom were Turkish families, seemed to lack interest in it, for it was quite academic for this sort of public gathering. She situated Rumi as a Muslim from Anatolia through meticulous use of maps, which would be of interest to a largely Turkish audience. After this opening lecture, there was a short break, which included light Turkish snacks and coffee and tea in the lobby. The space was overcrowded, and food and tea inevitably ran out.

After the break, the *sama* was held on the stage. It included live music from an all-men troupe of dervishes of the Jerrahi Order led by *shaykh* Tevfik Aydöner and many musicians, who were also part of the Jerrahi community. AttarJafari, his student (Emod), and the son (David) of Murat Coskun of the Rifai Order were the *samazens* who turned. The turning ceremony began with the *ney*, as is traditional (the other two gatherings started the same way). Here, members of different Sufi communities, especially *samazen*s, had gathered together. Those communities included Rumi Canada, the Rifai Order, and the Jerrahi Order. However, whereas the gatherings at Sema Space in Montreal and by the Rifai included mixed-gender turning and musicians, this one was led only by men and boys, with no women on stage. Women members of the order were sitting on the side of the stage taking photographs. When the Jerrahi Order presented this practice at the Ismaili Centre for the Nuit Blanche in 2019, again it consisted solely of men, either as musicians or as *samazen*s. Women had no active roles in these public presentations of *zikr* and *sama*. Aydöner explains that the Jerrahi Order understands Sufism as dependent on the practice of Islam. It is possible that the effort to maintain the Turkish tradition of Sufism and turning has led to gender-segregated piety in ritual contexts, not only during public presentations of *sama* but also in private weekly gatherings (see chapter 1).[31]

The packed auditorium likely paid little attention to these details; it seems that they were all there to see the *samazen*s. The minute the *samazen*s took to the stage, most of the audience took out their cell phones and began snapping photographs and recording videos. Many of the older *hijabi* Turkish women sitting beside me and in front of me were sending videos and photographs to their WhatsApp group chats, presumably to their friends and family, perhaps in Turkey as well. Clearly, many were there for the *samazen*s, though *zikr* was introduced as a sacred practice. The master of ceremonies and *shaykh* Aydöner asked everyone to remain silent while actively being present for meditation; however, the raised-high cellphones did not seem to reflect this religious moment (figure 3.2). Moments like these draw us back to the classical writings on *sama* that were introduced at the beginning of this chapter with regard to proper *adab* (etiquette) of the audience and participants during the ritual of *sama*. It would be interesting to reflect on whether al-Ghazali or Tusi would view such moments infused with mass-audience technology as following the requirements of "proper time, place and brethren," which al-Ghazali expressed were necessary for proper *sama*.

In reflecting on these three different *shab-i arus* gatherings held in 2019 in Toronto and Montreal, one notes many similarities across these variously located Sufi communities. Those similarities include the use of music, recitation or singing (*ilahi*s), and turning as ritual modes of expression for rememberance, and of course the focus on Rumi and his poems. These latter elements have continued to be core features of the tradition of *sama* and *zikr* as it has entered Canada. This is true not only of the *shab-i arus* I documented here but also of *zikr* and *sama* that I documented in Vancouver, Toronto, and Montreal. At the centre of it all has been the tradition of turning, a practice that can be traced back to the transmission that Burke inherited as a teacher (*samazenbashi*)

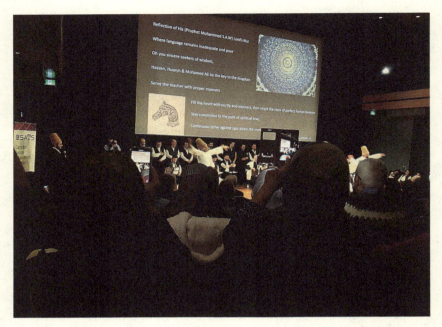

3.2. *Shab-i arus* held by Jerrahi Sufi Order at the University of Toronto in December 2019. Photograph by author.

through Feild and Suleyman Loras. In reflecting on these ritual practices that are unfolding among Sufi communities with Turkish roots and affiliation to the legacy of Rumi, it is clear that two of the central forms of Sufism that have solidified in Canada are the practice of *zikr* and, more specifically, the tradition of *sama*. The significance of *sama* as central to the development of Canadian Sufism was signalled by Ghazi of the Vancouver Rumi Society: "I think this is a real centre where the transmission of *sama* is taking place ... I mean Raqib [Burke] is just ... an extraordinary *samazen* and an extraordinary turner, dervish, soul, unique soul in the universe, completely. And then but he's even more an extraordinary teacher and if you look around ... if you look at Tanya [Evanson] right, if you look at Farzad [AttarJafari]."[32]

The practice of turning exists in groups like the Jerrahi and the Rifai Orders, and their lineage of turning is through their respective *silsila* that lead back to Turkey, specifically through the Jerrahi Order in America. Their current *shaykh*s are not active teachers of this practice. The focus on turning as a practice – which was passed on to Burke and subsequently to his students, who are now teaching a third generation of turners – has led to the concretization of the practice and tradition beyond their Sufi communities and to the creation of new Sufi spaces and communities across Canada, such as Rumi Canada and Sema Space. They continue to hold and preserve an ancient tradition that is central to Sufism, which they understand as extending back to Turkish and Persian classical periods, and even farther back than that. In gatherings at which Burke is present, he holds the circle by heading the ceremony of *sama*. At the beginning of *sama*, the *samazen*s bow to the teacher, be it a *shaykh* of a different order or Burke himself. Though a Sufi *shaykh* or *samazenbashi* (like Burke) is present to hold larger ritual gatherings of *sama*, in smaller private gatherings in Montreal or Toronto, *samazen*s like AttarJafari and Evanson hold these positions as the senior trained *samazen*s. In the end, all the *samazen*s are located within various lineages of Sufi orders, or *silsila*. This is a significant form of institutionalization of transmission in Sufism that leads back to the Prophet Muhammad. AttarJafari's lineage takes him back to Iran and his own ancestral heritage to Rumi. Evanson's lineage takes her back to her Afro-Caribbean ancestors and pre-Islamic traditions, as well as to her own teacher, Çatalkaya. Still, the Vancouver Rumi Society (Unity *Zikr*), Rumi Canada, and Sema Space all hold transmissions of Rumi, and this transmission continues to transform itself in Canada as *samazen*s bring their own unique legacy to the practice, which ties them to a deeply rooted classical Sufi tradition even while paving new paths forward, starting with figures like Raqib and Mira Burke, and Shams al Haqq Farzad AttarJafari, and Tawhida Tanya Evanson.

AttarJafari and Evanson are influential students of Burke and have become teachers in their own right, establishing communities such as Sema Space and Rumi Canada. Their students study the tradition of meditative movement to locate the essence of the practice. And just like their teachers, they share the tradition of turning when invited, especially by other Sufi teachers, as Aydöner and AttarJafari did during the *shab-i arus* in 2019 at the University of Toronto. Coskun's communities' *shab-i arus* included the *samazen*s from his own dervish community, some of whom trained with AttarJafari. A significant point of departure between most of the groups (Sema Space, Rumi Canada, the Rifai, and the Vancouver Rumi Society) and the Jerrahi Order relates to gender-segregated practices (see chapter 5). Except in the Jerrahi Order, mixed-gender turning is now the norm in Canada. One can also see it in the United States among Muzzaffer Ozak's students, such as *shaykha* Fariha in New York and Kabir and Camille Helminski's Threshold Society. Mixed-gender turning, then, is not unique to Canada but is part of a broader trend in the west, though it is not common (at least publicly) in Turkey.

It can be said that the tradition of *sama* has become embedded in Canada. This, at a time when Sufism in Turkey itself is on shaky ground. For the many Sufis who take part in it, the tradition of turning centres on remembrance. *Samazen*s like AttarJafari and Evanson share this tradition with all who come to them. For them, whatever the space and whatever instruments they use, the end goal is to cultivate an opening to remember the human being's primordial state, and one can only do this by recollecting the one source, Allah. The practice of turning is a unique tradition that solidified under the Mawlawi community and is now deeply rooted in the Canadian landscape of Islam, Sufism, and popular spirituality:

> Oh come, oh come! You are the soul
> of the soul of the soul of whirling!
> Oh come! You are the cypress tall
> in the blooming garden of whirling!
> Oh come! For there has never been
> and never will be one like you!
> Come, one like you have never seen
> the longing eyes of whirling!
> Oh come! The fountain of the sun
> is hidden under your shadow!
> You own a thousand Venus stars
> in the circling heavens of whirling!
> The whirling sings your praise and thanks
> with a hundred eloquent tongues:
> I'll try to say just one, two points
> translating the language of whirling.
> For when you enter in the dance
> you then leave both these worlds
> For outside these two worlds there lies
> the universe, endless, of whirling.
> The roof is high, the lofty roof
> that is on the seventh sphere,
> But far beyond this roof is raised
> the ladder, the ladder of whirling.
> Whatever there is, is only He,
> your foot steps there in dancing:
> The whirling, see, belongs to you,
> and you belong to the whirling.
> What can I do when Love appears
> and puts it claw round my neck?
> I grasp it, take it to my breast
> and drag it into the whirling!
> And when the bosom of the motes
> is filled with the glow of the sun,
> They enter all the dance, the dance
> and do not complain in the whirling!
> (Schimmel 1992: 203–4)

Conclusions

During the COVID-19 pandemic, many Sufi communities transitioned to online platforms for Sufi gatherings, *zikr*s, and *sohbet*s. In May 2020 the Inayati Order, which even before the pandemic had positioned itself well to use online platforms, began hosting weekly virtual *sama*. The first of these was led by the Vancouver branch of the Inayati Order and included music from Amir O'Loughlin, accompanied by AttarJafari turning. Throughout the hour and a half of the virtual gathering, there were more than seventy participants from all over the world, including members who logged in from Germany, Switzerland, and the US. Zia Inayat-Khan (also known as Sarafil Bawa among his students) led the opening and closing prayers. During such moments, it becomes evident that the tradition of turning that formed in Canada, starting in Vancouver, has taken a global stage, especially through Zoom *sama* gatherings, which have become the new ritual norm in this pandemic era. The practice of *sama* and the community of *samazen*s in Canada is now far-reaching. AttarJafari and Evanson have toured North America and the world, but in this time of virtual rituals, their training, which locates them within a very particular genealogy of the development of *sama* in Vancouver through Burke and his teachers, Feild (via Bülent), Loras, and his son Jelaleddin, has done much to establish and spread moving meditation beyond the Canadian milieu.

Though music has always been central to the Inayati Order with its South Asian roots –Inayat Khan, the founder, was himself was a musician – that order did not formalize meditative dance movement and turning as central ritual expressions until *samazen*s like AttarJafari, Evanson, and some of their students began to connect with Zia. Thus, Zoom *sama* captures not only the technological transformation of the ritual practice through a new digital platform but also the influence of *samazen*s on other Sufi orders, such as the Inayati Order. These shifts highlight the transformation of the ritual of *zikr* as the turning *sama* continues to be transmitted into new Sufi communities. With any ritual, there are bound to be transformations as a result of transmission processes, especially to address the needs of the new cultural milieux into which rituals have entered. These changes have included gender-egalitarian practices (other communities have not welcomed such shifts).

This chapter began with classical Sufi writers in the premodern period speculating about proper etiquette and expression of *sama* in their time. In Canada, the requirements are negotiated by individual *samazen*s and Sufi *shaykh*s for their communities. Even Sufi communities with similar cultural origins do not always agree on gender norms or on forms – thus, the *sama* and *shab-i arus* encountered in this chapter all locate the practice within Rumi's legacy and his call to remembrance, a call that is a common goal in all of Sufism, regardless of how it manifests itself. *Sama* in Canada continues to maintain a mainly

Ottoman and/or Turkish register and formula, although the tradition has led to many new Canadian *samazen*s uncovering the roots of this turning practice as central to the traditions of Persian, African, Indigenous, and shamanistic cultures. Where this practice is maintained in ritual contexts in *zikr* and commemorative sacred spaces, the practice of turning has also been staged in cultural, performative, and aesthetic spaces, and this has led to further notable transformations and moments of resistance. These instances raise questions about the commodification and cultural appropriation of Rumi and his legacy. Sufism, especially through the practice of turning, has been framed as a cultural practice that feeds neatly into the state apparatus of the discourse of multiculturalism as well as into the systemic Islamophobia that has led Sufism to differentiate itself from Islam. Yet this complex terrain does not limit the significance of *sama* presentations for *samazen*s and Sufi teachers, who share them beyond their communities, as we see in the next chapter.

Chapter Four

The Politics of Consuming Rumi

On 16 April 2020, on Facebook, while promoting Omid Safi's new online course "The Heart of Rumi's Poetry," Zia Inayat-Khan posted the following: "My grandfather said, 'Rumi's work is so great that if one has read and understood it one has learnt every philosophy there is.'" Safi has not been the only one to utilize online platforms to share Rumi's teachings. Baraka Blue, a musician and artist, offers similar classes at the Rumi Center for Spirituality and the Arts, including courses such as "The Ocean in a Drop: The Poetry and Philosophy of Rumi." On 8 February 2020, on Facebook, Baraka Blue posted the following, which I quote in its entirety because it succinctly lays out the politics of Rumi that I engage with in this chapter:

> How many times have you heard Rumi mentioned from the pulpit at Friday prayer? How many times has the Masnavi been taught at your local mosque? How many Muslim conferences have centered, or even acknowledged, the poetry and philosophy of the world's most influential mystical poet?
>
> I am the first to acknowledge that the pop culture version of Rumi is superficial and stripped of its deeper symbolic potency by virtue of being divorced from its metaphysical context. But, I would encourage my brothers and sisters in Deen [faith] to consider another perspective through which to view this situation: that of divinely gifted opportunity. The best-selling poet in America is our master Mawlana Rumi. He is beloved not only as a great poet but as one of the great spiritual teachers of human history. His words are everywhere we look. This is a great opportunity because it shows that while many of our fellow countrymen are unable to see the beauty, depth, and universal truth in our Deen, they have a great affinity for Sufism in general and Rumi in particular.
>
> Coleman Barks, (who was exposed to Rumi through his teacher Shaykh Bawa Muhiyadin [sic]) and other popularizers of Rumi, have done a great service to this Deen and may Allah reward them immensely. Sure, his versions are often 50% Rumi and 50% Barks (and it would do one well to keep that in mind when

reading them), but he must be commended for rendering Mawlana's timeless wisdom into beautiful and moving contemporary American post-Whitman free verse. Anyone who has tried to translate anything, especially poetry, into another language knows how great of an accomplishment this is. That is not to say that I don't personally have critique of some aspects of Barks' versions, nor that anyone else should not; but it is to say that, with all its imperfections, he has done a great service to this Deen and to the English-speaking world. We could simply complain that the bridge he has built is imperfect or we could express gratitude to God for giving us a head start and then get busy finishing the bridge!

Yes, often Barks downplays Islamic references in order to translate the meanings into references familiar to a general English-speaking audience who are unfamiliar with our tradition. To a greater or lesser extent, this is what all translators do when translating literature from one cultural context to the next.[1]

Critiques of the erasure of Islam from Rumi's popular English renditions by poet-translators like Coleman Barks – more about him below – should be considered in light of what Baraka Blue highlights as another pertinent issue for some, and that is the erasure of Rumi from Islam. That same assessment has been offered by scholars like Safi with regard not only to Rumi but also to the Persian poet Hafiz.[2] This is part of a broader translation and transmission history of Sufi literary traditions dating back to medieval times and extending, more systematically, into Europe's colonial encounters with Muslim cultures. That history continues to inform the expansion of Sufism into non-Muslim societies.

This chapter examines the voices and practices of various artists, *samazen*s, and Sufis on the Canadian artistic scene who are engaging with the traditions of Rumi in public spaces, be it through presentations of Rumi at festivals, performances of turning at venues like the Aga Khan Museum, or the commodification of Rumi – for example, the selling of Rumi teas by the Naqshbandi Haqqani Kabbani order in Vancouver. In exploring these examples, we will find that Sufis themselves are actively involved in various ways in the spreading of Rumi beyond their communities. Some of these practices can be viewed as commodifying, distributing, and/or popularizing Rumi. Nevertheless, for many of the communities and people involved in the examples that follow, the distribution of Rumi and his legacy is not just about commodification; rather, it is tied to service and ritual practices. For instance, for the Naqshbandi Haqqani Kabbani Order in Vancouver, the selling of Rumi teas is possible only because of the alchemical transformations these products have undergone during the practice of *zikr*. And the *samazen*s who take part in cultural festivals and the poets who share Rumi's legacies through *ghazal* and spoken word are offering a taste (*dhawq*) of Sufism and recentring of their cultural heritage at the same time. Various productions centred on Rumi-based commodities overlap with artistic and cultural expressions. This chapter begins by examining the colonial legacies of textual transmission that have helped popularize Sufi poetry; it then examines the Canadian context.

The Diffusion of Sufism through Transcultural Literary Networks

During their travels through the Muslim world in colonial times, and while serving as imperial agents, European non-Muslims became enamoured with the "exotic" Sufis and their literary tradition and began to translate and publish many of its poets, including the Persians Hafiz and Saadi Shirazi (d. 1291). Saadi's *Gulistan* was available to European audiences by the sixteenth century; Hafiz's *Divan* and Omar Khayyam's (d. 1131) *Rubaiyyat* were available in English translation by the end of the eighteenth (Aminrazavi 2014). These same texts were used to teach languages, such as Persian, to the employees of imperial institutions like the East India Company. One highly influential Orientalist scholar in this vein was the philologist William Jones (d. 1794). In a letter to Charles Reviczky (d. 1793), a Hungarian diplomat, he wrote: "Our Hafiz is most assuredly a poet worthy to sup with gods; every day I take pleasure in his work, which gives me more delight by its charm and attractive style" (Cannon 1970: 9).[3] From very early on, piecemeal translations of Sufi poetry were influencing writers far beyond the Muslim world, in Europe itself. Sufism's association with Persia (i.e., not the Arab world) reflected a broader belief that Indian and European languages were part of the "Aryan" or Indo-European linguistic family, which included Persian and Sanskrit, whereas languages like Hebrew and Arabic belonged to the family of Semitic languages. These linguistic categories were racialized when figures like Wilhelm von Humboldt (d. 1835) tied linguistics to a racio-religious order.[4] This informed how Orientalists like Jones engaged with Sufism. Thus, Jones saw Sufism as a "metaphysical theology, which has been professed immemorially by a numerous sect of *Persians* and *Hindus*, was carried into Greece, and prevails even now among the learned *Muselmans*, who sometimes avow it without reserve" (qtd in Sharify-Funk et al. 2017: 111). Orientalists' early encounters with Sufi poetry would affect European movements such as Romanticism (ca. 1780s-1830s). Sufi poetry influenced poets like William Blake (d. 1827) and Percy Bysshe Shelley (d. 1822). The German Johann Wolfgang Goethe's (d. 1832) long engagement with Hafiz led him to produce various "translations," some of which paralleled his own life to that of Hafiz's (Einboden 2014).

Literary Transmission of Sufism to America

Literature that engaged with Persian poetry and especially with Sufi poetic traditions influenced not only European movements like Romanticism but also the spiritual ethos brewing in America, which took the form of Transcendentalism, the Theosophical Society, esoteric thought, and perennialism (Albanese

2008; Sedgwick 2016; Saif 2019; Sedarat 2019). The growing influence of Sufi literary traditions is evident in the use of names such as Hafiz in American print culture. The first "popular" reference to Hafiz (Hafez) was in *The American Museum or Universal Magazine* in 1792. The *New York Magazine or Literary Repository* (1790) published a story titled "Tale of Hafez," based on two characters named "Hafez and Saadi" (Aminrazavi 2014: 4). These examples signal to the popularity of these names at the time, even though such stories did not offer any historical facts about these figures.

In the American milieu, at a time when spiritual and esoteric movements were taking root, Sufi poetic themes began to permeate the writings of Ralph Waldo Emerson (d. 1882), who had read Saadi, Hafiz, and Khayyam, as well as Walt Whitman (d. 1892), a student of Emerson, who employed the trope of love in much the same way as Hafiz (Sedarat 2019). Emerson wrote: "Hafiz praises wine, roses, maidens, boys, brides, mornings and music, to give vent to his immense hilarity and sympathy with every form of beauty and joy; and lays the emphasis on these to mark his scorn of sanctimony and base prudence" (1858:728). Some studies have noted similarities between Whitman's themes and imagery and those of Rumi (Ford 1987: Fayez 1980). For example, the "mystic relationship with the sea" is evident in the following two poems, by Rumi and Whitman respectively:

> Happy was I
> In the pearl's heart to lie;
> Till, lashed by life's hurricane
> Like a tossed wave I ran.
> The secret of the sea
> I uttered thunderously;
> Like a spent cloud on the shore
> I slept and stirred no more. (Rumi, qtd in Fayez 1980: 40)

> The seas all cross'd ... the voyage done,
> Surrounded, copest, frontest God, yieldest, the aim achiev'd,
> As fill'd with friend, love complete, the Elder Brother found,
> The Younger melting in fondness in his arms. (Whitman, qtd in Fayez 1980: 41)

But by the end of the nineteenth century it was Khayyam and Hafiz, not Rumi, who had gained traction among both Europeans and Americans. Khayyam's poetry was beginning to circulate widely, influencing figures like Mark Twain (d. 1910), F. Scott Fitzgerald (d. 1940), and T.S. Eliot (d. 1956). There were Omar Khayyam clubs in England and America, and Khayyam's name was being used to advertise chocolates, cigarettes, and tobacco (Sharify-Funk et al.

2017: 129). In many ways, the popularity of Khayyam and Hafiz foreshadowed Rumi's ascendance in the twentieth and twenty-first centuries: "Sufism became entrenched in the American literary and spiritual scenes in two ways; the scholarly in the late eighteenth and early nineteenth centuries and the popular in the twentieth century" (Aminrazavi 2014: 3). Rumi's popularity in North America would solidify through the efforts of Coleman Barks.

Coleman Barks and the Making of an American Rumi

In the early 1990s, at the insistence of Robert Bly, another American poet and popular translator, Barks began self-publishing his own versions of Rumi's poems. Barks had had a mystical dream about an elusive figure. Shortly after that, he had connected with a member of the Bawa Muhaiyaddeen Fellowship, who introduced him to M.R. Bawa Muhaiyaddeen (d. 1986), a Sufi teacher from Sri Lanka based in Philadelphia. When he saw Bawa, he knew he was the man in his dream. Bawa encouraged Barks to pursue his Rumi publication project. Barks has often said that the relationship between Bawa and himself paralleled that of Rumi and Shams, and he credits the possibility of completing his "translation" largely to Bawa. Since then, Barks has sold more than two million copies of his versions of Rumi's poetry – twenty-two volumes over three decades (Ciabattari 2014). Barks has been criticized over his "translations," especially as he does not speak Persian. However, he explicitly states that he is not "translating" but rather vernacularizing Rumi for an American audience. In his vernacularization process he employs translations of Rumi by scholars such as John Moyne, A.J. Arberry, and Reynold Nicholson. Arberry and Nicholson were early Orientalist scholars who widely influenced the reception of Islam and Sufism in the English-speaking academy (Sharify-Funk et al. 2017; Irwin 2019).

Other figures besides Barks have been part of this popularization process. Daniel Ladinsky has been heavily criticized for his "translations," which many have called forgeries rather than literal translations (Safi 2020; Sedarat 2019). Nevertheless, he claims to have had a dream in which Hafiz visited him: "About six months into this work I had an astounding dream in which I saw Hafiz as an Infinite Fountaining Sun (I saw him as God), who sang hundreds of lines of his poetry to me in English, asking me to give that message to 'artists and seekers'" (Ladinsky, qtd in Safi 2020). There is a long history of translators who do not speak the languages they are translating, such as Persian or Urdu, and have instead used Orientalists' translations as intermediary texts, which is what Barks did. Emerson did much the same, using Hammer-Purgstall's German translations as intermediary texts to access Hafiz (Sedarat 2019; Sharify-Funk et al. 2017).

Deepak Chopra, Andrew Harvey, and Robert Bly, as well as various academics (e.g., Omid Safi and Annemarie Schimmel), and American Sufi teachers like Kabir and Camille Helminski of the Threshold Society, have all published translations or renditions of Rumi's poems for popular audiences, but it is Barks's renditions of Rumi's poems that have received the strongest traction and generated record sales. Barks's Rumi has achieved a level of popularity that has influenced music videos and albums, such as "The Guest House" by the American band Coldplay.[5] The American pop culture icon Oprah Winfrey is a Rumi enthusiast. Her website maintains a list of "20 Books of Poetry Everyone Should Own," and on it she includes Barks's *The Essential Rumi by Rumi* (1995), alongside volumes by Maya Angelou, Emily Dickinson, and Robert Frost (Sharify-Funk et al. 2017).[6] Many literary and Islamic scholars have pointed to the political issues inevitably posed by translations. A key issue here is "privilege" – put another way, who has the authority, the capital, and the capacity to participate in "translation"? – and the impact that translations can have in this era of systemic Islamophobia, anti-Muslim violence, and racism (Daulatzai and Rana 2018; Kazi 2018).

Rumi and the Politics of Consumption, Commodification, and Cultural Appropriation

An issue at the heart of Barks's Rumi projects is the commodification they entail. In her books *Oprah: An Icon* (2011) and *Consuming Religion* (2017), religious studies scholar Kathryn Lofton (2017) discusses how religion generates socialities of consumption: "Consumption is loss. After consumption, something is gone: gone because of use, because of decay, or because it was destroyed. In economic terms, consumption describes the using up of goods or services having exchangeable value. In pathology, consumption describes the progressive wasting of the body" (1). However, she adds, consumption can be viewed from a different critical vantage point: "consumption describes something that is constantly happening ... We choose to consume some things rather than others, and there is a creative power attached to such selection" (2). For Lofton, then, "purchase is a social act": "consumer culture, like religion, could be merely another emblem of alienated self-consciousness. Or, it could incite the beginning of a new self-consciousness to liberate us from the very obsession it compels" (13). So, where in the previous chapter it was easy to view the ritual practices of *sama* and *shab-i arus* in the context of the sacred (because they unfolded in ritual spaces, which seems to clearly suggest holiness), some scholars often take issue with notions of the sacred when popular culture and consumption are involved, because our neat categories are thereby blurred. This chapter explores that liminal space, as "commodity deserves sacred regard" (Lofton 2011: 199).[7] One may feel that consumption and commodification are secular matters, but "the secular is not an absence of religion; rather, the secular is religion's kaleidoscopic buffet" (209). For my analysis of Rumi in this chapter, I am inspired by Lofton's work on Oprah and her iconic status. To quote from her at more length:

> I am studying what we're watching and what it consistently conveys. For the field of religious studies, such critical attention is one way we sidestep the pieties of our objects in order to discern patterns in those traditions, sects, scriptures, and rites that correlate to other cultural objects. I conduct this particular scrutiny because it tells us about how religious forms are configured by and through the modern moment. From this investigation, I have found that whatever distinguishing marks we make between commodities and religion, they are, for all practical purposes, arbitrary. Our consumption and our religiosity can be described only in their infectious, ritual commingling, both in their distribution and in their consumption. (212)

Popular spirituality in the west is tethered to consumption and capitalism as a result of postcolonial legacies. Scholars like Amanda Lucia, who has studied the global Hindu movement of Amma (2014) as well as transformational yoga festivals (2020), have showcased how this is the case with "metaphysicals" and with the spiritual but not religious (SBNR) demographic; in the west, both engage in the consumption and commodification of transnational spiritual (Asian/South Asian based) movements. Lucia (2014) explains: "The metaphysical market is ripe with saleable products and services. In fact, one of the primary critiques of metaphysical spirituality asserts that the metaphysicals have rampantly commodified and corporatized religion. Not only have they propagated the consumeristic self-as-commodity mentality, but also 'inner spirituality has been put to work for the purposes of outer prosperity'" (203).

Similarly, Lisa Aldred (2000) writes about how those involved in the New Age scene appropriate and consume Indigenous spiritualities:

> In the so-called postmodern culture of late consumer capitalism, a significant number of white affluent suburban and urban middle-aged baby-boomers complain of feeling uprooted from cultural traditions, community belonging, and spiritual meaning. The New Age movement is one such response to these feelings. New Agers romanticize an "authentic" and "traditional" Native American culture whose spirituality can save them from their own sense of malaise. However, as products of the very consumer culture they seek to escape, these New Agers pursue spiritual meaning and cultural identification through acts of purchase. (329)

Whether it involves yoga, mindfulness, or Indigenous spirituality, New Age and popular spiritual practices are tied to purchase (Jain 2015; Aldred 2000; Wilson 2014; Arjana 2020). Thus, the consumption of Rumi generates questions about the fluid state in which Sufism exists today in Canada and the west due to its "ritual commingling" of consumption and religiosity and the challenges this generates for our notions of "pieties" (Lofton 2011: 212). Still, some of the resistance to thinking about Rumi through a consumerist lens is due in part to restrictive perceptions of Islamic consumption and popular culture.

Islamic Consumption and Popular Culture

We must rethink the notion that consumption is foreign to Islam if we are to discuss the consumption politics of Rumi, not just in the west's spiritual marketplace but also in Muslim societies. As the previous chapter indicated, pilgrimages to Rumi's burial shrine are a popular commodity in Turkey, where tour packages are available for the ultimate Rumi travel experience. Similarly, pilgrimage to Mecca, the Muslim Holy City, has long been commodified in Saudi Arabia. When we begin to look past Sufi-related commodities in the Muslim world, we notice many other forms of what Chiara Formichi (2020) calls "pious consumption" in the *halal* market:

> Global expenditures in religious sub-markets reflect the impact of "pious consumption": the global *halal* food market is valued at about US$630 billion, about as much as the Islamic fashion industry is estimated to be worth in 2020; by then, *halal* tourism is expected to reach US$220 billion, between 10 and 15 percent of the global market. (243)

Discussions of Islamic consumption often begin with the Muslim practice of consuming *halal* products, especially food and drinks. However, the *halal* market has become very expansive and "lucrative" in late modern contexts (Nasir 2016: 157). From Muslim fashion to food consumption and *halal* tourism, marketplaces of consumption are hardly foreign to the Muslim world (Shirazi 2016; Bucar 2017). Consumption is not defined just by goods Muslims may purchase; it is also defined by the cultures and media that are consumed. Here, popular culture is an important site of analysis, not only because it has capital and is lucrative but also because popular culture is a site of political and social resistance across the Muslim world, especially in terms of media such as theatre, art, and performance (Nieuwkerk, Levine, and Stokes 2016; Arjana and Fox 2018).

Studies of Islam and popular culture remain at times reductive partly because of the common perception that Islam does not interact with popular culture, which is simply false. That perception is in part a result of Islamic tenets that have restricted particular aesthetic representations for theological reasons (e.g., no images or icons). In fact, contemporary trends in popular culture capture the ways in which Muslim expressions of piety and devotion are at the heart of the production, distribution, and consumption of music, television shows (as evident in the globally popular Turkish series *Resurrection Ertugrul*), movies, comic books (*Ms. Marvel*, now also a television series), art, theatre, fashion, and much more.[8] A notable example is the resort to various musical genres as a form of creative resistance against Islamists and oppressive nation-states, including their political and theological beliefs (Nieuwkerk 2011). These involve the use of hip hop and rap, especially since the rise of Black Muslim movements in America like the Nation of Islam and the Nation of Gods and Earths. These have spread beyond the American milieu, carrying with them a globally influential form of religious "rebel" music (Khabeer 2016; Aidi 2014; Gray 2015). Other artist collectives have been informed by Afro-futurist thought, which has led to Muslim futurist collectives producing art, music, and fashion in America.[9] Remember, then, that though popular culture is at times deeply tied to capitalism, consumption, and commodification practices that place it within the realm of neoliberalism and market consumption, popular culture has also provided agentic sites of resistance. So "popular culture not only works against or with power structures, but power works through and within popular art itself" (Nieuwkerk, Levine, and Stokes 2016: 2). The unsettling of power is visible in studies of Black popular culture movements and productions, such as jazz, blues, and rap (Gilroy 1995; McKittrick 2020). If popular cultural expressions of Islam are not the pertinent issue here, then it seems that discussions of Rumi, commodification, and consumption gesture implicitly to the main (unnamed) concern at the heart of this discussion – cultural appropriation.

Rumi and the Problematics of Cultural Appropriation

In their article "What Is (the Wrong of) Cultural Appropriation?," Patti Tamara Lenard and Peter Balint (2020) conceptualize cultural appropriation as "an act knowingly conducted by an appropriator, i.e., it is the deliberate use of a cultural practice or symbol from others and adopting it as one's own, where this use is contested, and where one *knows* that the practice or symbol is central to the culture of others" (342).[10] Their framing of cultural appropriation as "normative" rather than "descriptive" is intentional: they are attempting to locate the "moral" culpability that deems certain "cultural engagements" as appropriative while highlighting that the degree of "wrong" attached to cultural appropriative behaviour is also contextual. For them, at the heart of this act or exchange is the extraction of a "symbol" that is "taken and used" but not "exhausted" (338–9). It follows that the "thing being taken needs to be of value to those it is taken from, and this value needs to be claimed in some way" (339). Here, Lenard and Balint offer five criteria for determining this value: (1) the thing appropriated must be "ordinarily central to the culture's collective life in some way," (2) it must be "ordinarily recognizable as such by its members, or a large number of its members," (3) it must have "value to a significant number of it members," (4) it must involve consideration of those who are most affected by the practice and likely have the least power (versus those who have the most power), and (5) the historical or contemporary status of the symbol or practice must be considered (339–40). Another factor that informs cultural appropriation for these authors is the *landscape* of a multicultural society, in the sense that migrants' "symbol or practice being used needs to be claimed and its use contested by those from whom it is being appropriated" (340). Here, "contestation" by the community matters and indeed is necessary to mark the practice as culturally appropriative. In this regard, however, the authors do not count a "twitter storm" as sufficient (341). Sometimes "consent" may even be a way to avoid cultural appropriation, but who is at liberty to give that consent is not easily discernable and raises further questions (341).

In the end, for these authors, the factor that definitively marks behaviour as culturally appropriative is "power structures": those who are appropriating the cultural artefact of value are in a socially and perhaps economically privileged position relative to those they are appropriating *from*, especially when profit is involved (343). Here, we get to the heart of the heated responses we often see when cultural appropriation has occurred: "often anger about cultural appropriation is, rather, anger about power inequalities, or persistent historical injustices, or the personal profit that people gain at the apparent expense of others' cultural practices" (347). The notion of profit is especially pertinent here: we live in a postcolonial (or neocolonial) world in which xenophobia and other forms of cultural, racial, and religious bigotry inform many of the political, social, and economic structures we inhabit. Many of the criticisms of inadequate translations of figures like Rumi and Hafiz, and many of the issues surrounding their commodification, are tied to the broader spoken (but at times unspoken) realities of cultural appropriation. As Lucia (2014) explains: "The politics of cultural appropriation and adoption frequently develops into an intense debate and defensive postures among participants. The vehement discourses surrounding such issues signify a great deal of latent anxiety about cultural and intellectual property, identity, and the historical reality of exploitation through colonialism and orientalism" (212).

Lucia's reflections resonate with the realities of Sufism in the west. In the early development of western Sufism, there was a correlation between the practice of Sufism among white non-Muslim westerners and the fomenting of colonial violence against Muslims and their societies. The practice of Sufism by non-Muslims (white people) brought about the cultural appropriation of Sufism and the erasure of its Islamic roots. As a result, white Sufis who take part in such exchanges have been perceived as part of the problem even while they benefit economically from the popularization of Rumi (e.g., Barks). This circumstance is worsened because of the colonial legacies that preceded these moments of appropriation:

> Thus the appropriation of these "possessions" by others outside of a national, ethnic or cultural community becomes tantamount to stealing (a view often represented in the contemporary controversies concerning museum collections); such actions should be critiqued, shamed and punished. When representatives of the

dominant imperialistic power appropriate cultural commodities from previously colonized minorities, the sting of cultural exploitation amplifies intensely. (213)

Rumi's popularity amounts to a standard-bearer for historical colonialism as well as for today's racist portrayals of Islam and Muslims in popular culture, for burgeoning neo-Orientalism, blatant Islamophobia, and anti-Muslim violence. Muslim cultures and societies, and individual Muslims (especially women), experience racism, violence, and bigotry. They are reduced to one-dimensional people without agency, voice, or even nuance. Against this specific backdrop of Islamophobia and anti-Muslim hostility, the acceptance of Rumi as a universal spiritual master rid of any Islamic particularity only exacerbates the imbalance of power. As these prejudices continue to unfold, Rumi's name and his spiritual legacy have been folded into the consumerist realities of the spiritual marketplace (Roof 1999; Lofton 2017; Arjana 2020). People who are socio-economically and racially privileged benefit from the selling of Rumi, whose name has cachet, be it in Hollywood or in cafés and bookstores around the world. Yet the figures involved in the production, distribution, and consumption of Rumi commodities are various, and as Lenard and Balint explain, in such instances context matters. How, then, are we to untangle these complex identity politics? For example, "whiteness" is not a productive litmus test for Sufi-ness or Muslimness, as figures like Barks place his spiritual lineage and identity within Sufism. Thus, vetting what constitutes appropriative behaviour when it comes to Rumi soon becomes a fickle exercise. Perhaps some examples are easier to vet (or sanction) than others; still, who has authority to gatekeep? Hence, a different set of questions is needed here, ones that require actual engagement with the popularization of Rumi. Conversely, how do the poets, performers, and the dervishes we have encountered in this book distribute and curate Rumi for a public audience? What do they think about how Rumi is presented by others? What types of public and artistic spaces are dervishes cultivating beyond their ritual contexts (see chapter 3)? How are cultural venues such as the Aga Khan Museum curating their programming and contributing to the popularization of Rumi? The rest of the chapter addresses all this.

The Early Sufi Literary Scene in Canada

Various historical references to Sufism in print culture begin to tell a story of Sufism's emerging popularity in Canada, especially through literary traditions, as documented earlier for America and western Europe. One example is found in Canadian church newspapers like the *Church Guardian of Montreal*, published in Halifax between 1879 and 1895, which provided both national and world news. It was largely a Church of England publication that also printed articles about Christian life and religion. In its edition of 30 June 1886, there is mention of Sufism, specifically within a discussion of Sikhism. In a section titled "Mission Field," which includes notes from China, Japan, New Zealand, and East Africa, under "India" there are updates on missionary developments, followed by reports about the religious scene in India. Here we find the following discussion of Sikhism and Sufism:

> The religion of the Sikhs – founded by Nanak in 1504 – has been too little considered though the qualities of its professors might well have stimulated curiosity. Dr. Trumpp, indeed, transalated [sic] the *Adi Granth*, its scriptures; but Mr. Pincott, who has now come forward with the results of profound research, joins issue with the former scholar as to the origin and character of Sikhism. He holds it to be based on Parsian [sic] Sufism, and as intended to be a compromise (however unsuccessful of late) between Mohammedanism and Hinduism. (12)

In continuing this discussion of the links among Sikhism, "Mohammedanism," and Hinduism, the writer draws some comparisons between the sayings of Guru Nanak and Hafiz, a Persian poet who by then was well-known among European Romantics and American Transcendentalists:

> The saying of Nanak, There is no Hindu and there is no Mussulman he regards as pointing to a system designed to efface the distinctions separating those two religions in India. While remaining nominally Hindu, Nanak abolished caste; he adopted the pantheistic theories of Sufism in much the same form as Hafiz sang them: he hold up the final absorption of the soul in the Divine essence as the end of life; and retained the dogma of the transmigration of souls as the mode of overcoming the even influence of Maya. (12)

This particular article and its engagement of Sufism, Sikhism, and Islam (Muhammedanism) captures the early presence in the news media of some notions of Sufism in Canada. This transmission of Sufi ideas, through Hafiz's philosophy (even if misunderstood) into the west, was first noted through literary transmission and translations, as discussed earlier, which would go on to draw interest among various spiritual seekers.

By the early twentieth century, Canadian presses such as I. Beling Tetens (in Toronto) were printing books that engaged with eastern spirituality, including Hinduism and Persian Sufism. This is noted in the publication *The Dabistàn or School of Manners The Religious beliefs, observances, Philosophic Opinions and Social Customs of the nations of the East* (ca. 1901) by David Shea and Anthony Troyer, who were members of the Royal Asiatic Society. The English poet Henry Newbolt's (d. 1938) *The Sailing of the Long-Ships and Other Poems* (1902), published by George N. Morang & Company in Toronto, included the poem "The Sufi in the City," which evokes Omar (likely Khayyam) in its last stanzas: "O Sons of Omar, what shall be close Seek not to know, for no man living knows: But while within your hands the Wine is Set Drink ye – to Omar and the Dreaming Rose!" (56–7). Flora Annie Steel (d. 1929), the English author of many books based on her two decades in India, wrote *The Mistress of Men* (1917), a novel centred on Nur Jahan (d. 1645), the wife of the Mughal emperor Jahangir (d. 1627). That novel, printed in Toronto by S.B. Gundy in 1918, is full of South Asian Sufi references, for example, to poets such as Amir Khusrau (d. 1325), dervishes, and the Sufi master Nizamuddin Awliya (d. 1325) (137). These select examples capture how Toronto printing presses published works at the turn of the twentieth century on Islam and Sufism. The *ghazal*, a Persian and Urdu poetic form, one that is most popularly associated with the poetry of Hafiz and Rumi, has a clear lineage in Canada. Thus, poetry was one path along which Sufism made its presence known in Canada's literary, cultural, and spiritual topography.[11]

The Canadian Ghazal Tradition

Since these early instantiations of Sufism in literary print culture, some Canadian poets have adopted the tradition of Sufism in the form of *ghazal* poetry. One such poet is John Thompson (d. 1976), who was born in England and moved to Sackville, New Brunswick, to teach at Mount Allison University. He is often regarded as the first poet in Canada to adopt *ghazal*. His works were published posthumously in a collection titled *I Dream Myself into Being: Collected Poems* (1991). The "free-verse *ghazal*" took hold in Canada in the 1970s, mainly through figures like Thompson, whose poetry collection *Stilt Jack* (1978) would influence other Canadian poets, such as Phyllis Webb in *Water and Light: Ghazals and Anti Ghazals* (1984) (Winger 2009). Thompson was influenced by classical figures such as the Urdu *ghazal* poet Mir Taqi Mir (d. 1810) and W.B. Yeats (d. 1939), among others (12). The *ghazal* tradition taken up by Thompson fostered a unique Canadian style of free verse that included Ahmad's *Ghazals of Ghalib* and the *ghazals* of Adrienne Rich (13–15). In his foreword to Thompson's *Stilt Jack*, Winger explains:

> Part of *Stilt Jack*'s complexity has to do with other poets in different cultural geographies. But the book's declared form – the ghazal – is not the traditional ghazal of Rumi or Ghalib or Hafez or the practitioner Thompson seems to have admired most deeply, Mir Taqi Mir. As the great American ghazal poet Agha Shahid Ali noted, after all, some counter-cultural English-language poets writing ghazals in the 1960s sometimes did not seem to know the form's original precepts, rhythms, or rules. Instead, they tended to pick what they liked – an illogical disjuncture between couplets, a simultaneous address to higher and lower powers, a complex

focus on grief and loss and love, a shared system of symbols, a direct naming of one's teachers – And to abandon the rest, ignoring the form's fundamental stringencies, metrical structures, and cultural roots. What was left, a form many of us now call "the free-verse ghazal," is not the same form as the traditional one, whose English-language version, I should add, continues to evolve in a parallel lineage alongside the version Thompson initiated in Canada. Ali referred to those written in the traditional form as "real ghazals in English"; the ones in *Stilt Jack*, for him, I'd bet, were part of a vast complex of appropriations. "For those brought up in Islamic literary traditions, especially Persian and Urdu ghazal," Ali explains, referring to the explosion of the English-language free-verse ghazal in American poetry since the 1960s, "to have many of these arbitrary near-surrealistic exercises in free verse pass for ghazals was – is – at best amusing." (n.a.)

In his own poems, such as in *Stilt Jack*, Thompson replaces what would be the Divine in Muslim tradition with the Anglican Divine and his cultural and physical terrain with that of his New Brunswick landscape (Winger 2019). In his introductory notes to *Stilt Jack*, Thompson highlights that the *ghazal* originated in Persia – more specifically, in the "great master of the ghazal in Persia" Hafiz and, hundreds of years later, in the Urdu poet Ghalib (Thompson 2019, n.a). These Persian and Urdu traditions were then transposed onto the Canadian context, having been scrubbed of their particular cultural and religious modalities. It seems it was the structure of the *ghazal* and the themes it explored that attracted so many early poets, who drew from those structures rather than the cultures and traditions of the original *ghazal* poets.

Sufi poetic traditions have influenced many Canadian writers. For instance, Sufi traditions are visible in *The Handmaid's Tale* (1985) by Margaret Atwood, who includes the following "Sufi proverb" at the beginning of her book: "In the desert there is no sign that says, / Thou shalt not eat stones." Atwood's use of this "Sufi proverb" has led some scholars to examine her story and its characters for traces of Sufism (Workman 1989). Other twentieth-century Canadian poets were inspired by the themes and messages of Sufi poetry and philosophy – for example, the Acadian poet Serge Patrice Thibodeau, especially in his *Le quatuor de l'errance* and *La traverse du désert*, both published in *Dans le Cité* (1995). These collections engage with the poetic traditions of Rumi, Ibn Arabi, and Inayat Khan (Talbot 2006: 160). Like the Sufi poets he cites, Thibodeau credits his inspiration to a higher source, the Divine ("au creature, à Dieu") (qtd in 161). Talbot has pointed out to how "Sufi discourse allows [Thibodeau] to discover significant new resources in his quest for an encounter with the divine, and shapes his conception of self, transcendence, and sensuality" (162).

Poetry has always been central to the expression of Sufism and its transmission around the world, and in its travels, that poetry has been transformed by the new cultural registers it has encountered. That transformation is continuing today, tied to broader trends of popularization and commodification in various literary spheres, especially non-Muslim ones. Echoing Baraka Blue's comments earlier in this chapter, Safi adds:

> There is one last element: It is indeed an act of violence to take the Islam of Rumi and Hafez, as Ladinsky has done. It is another thing to take Rumi and Hafez out of Islam. That is a separate matter, and a mandate for Muslims to reimagine a faith that is steeped in the world of poetry, nuance, mercy, love, spirit, and beauty. Far from merely being content to criticise those who appropriate Muslim sages and erase Muslims' own presence in their legacy, it is also up to us to reimagine Islam where figures like Rumi and Hafez are central voices. (2020)

The voices I capture in the remainder of this chapter understand their relationship to Sufism and Islam through the legacy of Rumi, which they bring into the various artistic, cultural, and spiritual spaces in which they work. However, such spaces are complicated precisely because they exist at the nexus of commodification, consumption, and (sometimes) cultural appropriation. In foregrounding these voices and embodied realities, I further nuance our conversation around the popularity of Rumi and his role in the spiritual marketplace. I begin by discussing the Rumi Festival held in Vancouver in 1998, whose model has become the norm on the Canadian landscape.

Rumi Festival Vancouver

Rumi's poetry began to spread in Vancouver in the 1970s, when Feild arrived there. Since then, Feild's students have been using Nicholson's and Arberry's translations of Rumi in their gatherings, along with the Persian originals, as some of them are Persian speakers. Majid Buell notes that they did not use Barks's versions because they did not become available and popular until the 1990s. John Brozak or Buell never thought that Rumi would explode onto the scene the way he has.

The Rumi Festival developed rather spontaneously when Seemi Ghazi connected with John Brozak and Raqib Brian Burke during a *zikr* gathering in Vancouver (Figure 4.1).[12] In my conversation with Raqib Brian Burke about the organizing of the Rumi Festival, he was clear that this was not meant to be a formal *sama*; rather, it was inspired by some of the early presentations Feild had put together in Vancouver in the 1970s.[13] The organizers had to secure a venue for the festival – it would be a Jewish community centre – and then bring together musicians who could capture both the Turkish and Persian traditions and legacies of Rumi (they found Amir Koushkani and Latif Bolat). The festival included a concert on Friday night, followed by a full-day workshop on Sufi teachings. Ghazi expressed that they worried

4.1. Poster of Rumi Festival. Courtesy of John Brozak.

initially about ticket sales, because the event was being held on a May weekend in Vancouver (a time when people would prefer to be outside). To the organizers' surprise, turnout was better than they expected. At the end of the festival on Sunday, they held a *zikr*, "facilitated" by Zuleikha Story Dancer, a student of Vilayat Khan and teacher in the Inayati Order. She was also a trained dancer, who had studied *kathak* in Afghanistan as well as classical Hindustani music.[14] The event included Mercan Dede (Arkin Allen), a Turkish Canadian composer, *ney* (flute) and *bendir* (drum) player, DJ, and producer.[15] Ghazi spoke about how the event came together, with everyone's involvement:

> [Zuleikha] came up and then she led this incredibly beautiful *zikr* on Sunday. I just remember ... the light was just pouring through the window and she has this beautiful voice and her harmonium, she's just like so gifted. So that was amazing, and Mercan Dede, I don't know if you know Mercan Dede ... came out just to support us [from Montreal], he had brought all of th[is] beautiful *ebru* work that he'd done and paintings. And he was selling them and just donating all of the money to the thing. He was amazing. So, all of these people came together and it kind of created [and] coalesced [into] a community. And the community is I mean definitely ... here to Seattle to Portland and to Bellingham in between ... this kind of North West ... community.[16]

Ghazi notes the significance of this transborder reality: this early Rumi Festival in Vancouver attracted attendees from Seattle and Portland. This was the only time the festival was ever held in Vancouver (indeed, in Canada) since it started in 1998. Subsequently, it was held in North Carolina, where Çatalkaya was based. It is now held in Seattle, where Çatalkaya's group moved in 2008, in September in honour of Rumi's birthday. Also notable about this first festival was the collaborative effort it entailed among the various Sufi communities and those with an interest in Rumi. Ghazi explained:

> I think it served this function of bringing people together. Some of them were these Reshad Feild people, there were Suleyman Dede people, there were Inayati people, there were Ruhaniat people, there were people who just came in who had experience from other orders. They had been to Qadiriyya in Iran or their families had been something in India or they were just like seekers from wherever ... you know, heard Rumi, had read Coleman Barks so this really diverse kind of group of people. And what's remarkable to me, is actually so many of the people and those kinds of coalescences have continued, like people still are kind of flowing in and out and kind of working with each other in different formulations and formations over all these years.[17]

This sort of collaboration has been maintained over the decades of public events focused on Sufism and Rumi, not only in Vancouver but also in cities like Toronto, where such festivals have become the norm (see below). Many who participate, whether as organizers or attendees, come with a broad spectrum of experiences and connections to Sufism and, at times, to Rumi. Thus, one draw of such festivals has been Rumi and specifically his poetry. Poetry, then, is one way in which Rumi continues to be popularized in Canada today.

Poetic Legacies of Rumi

Tawhida Tanya Evanson's journey in Sufism was catalysed through Sufi poetry. Besides being a *samazen,* she is a poet, performer, and producer, as well as the arts education director of the Banff Centre Spoken Word program.[18] So where turning is part of her spiritual practice, it also informs her work as a poet and performer in other spaces and other artistic projects. She has been performing for more than twenty years at poetry festivals around the world and has published two collections, titled *Bothism* (2017) and *Nouveau Griot* (2018), as well as a novel, *Book of Wings* (2020). During our conversation she explained that it was during her time in Vancouver in 2000, when poets came up for a week and presented their work, that she first encountered Sufism beyond the poetry of Rumi and Hafiz. That introduction led to a connection with a friend and poet who was a practising Sufi. In 2001, that friend took her to a Sufi retreat, where she met Çatalkaya, who had come up to Vancouver from North Carolina. Evanson would participate in the monthly Unity *Zikr*s and regularly join Çatalkaya. Çatalkaya returned to Istanbul, where he is still based. A year later, in 2001, Evanson took hand with Çatalkaya in Vancouver, first as a dervish and then as a *samazen* (see chapter 3). Her journeys through Sufism and turning are intimately tied to her work as a poet, writer, performer, and arts educator. Evanson shared some of the ways in which Rumi and his poetry are central to her work, especially at the Banff Centre, where she directs residencies and workshops:

> I like to definitely pass on Rumi and I work at the Banff Centre for the arts and lead a residency for spoken word artists and I make them turn because I believe that if you give a workshop it should be that you're sharing a part of your practice whether it's your art practice or spiritual practice, for me it's all one thing. And so, because my practice and life are so connected to Mawlana, I always share. We use Mawlana as a guide for writing exercises and then at the end we do introduction to *sama*. And that's always a great thing for people, especially Indigenous people, people of colour who perhaps have always [had] a thirst but they didn't know … [W]hat should I be drinking to satisfy this thirst[?]. And I think that has to do with kind of not having access to shamanic practices, and even Sufism is something that is kind of closed communities that people may not be comfortable entering, so to

bring something that is usually from a closed community to the public is important, but it should be measured, it should be done with clear intention, it should be done with the audience in mind, how large is that audience? We don't have to tell all of the secrets to these one million people in the audience or for the hundreds of thousands of people in the audience, you know, but we can give a little taste from the feast – here's a grape ... It's going to be the most excellent grape you've ever experienced [laughter] ... but it's only one grape from the feast. And so I think it's important to do things in measured form, that being said you know, the opposite is also true [laughter].[19]

Exposing others to the poetry of Rumi has been significant to all aspects of Evanson's work. She offers her participants a taste (*dhawq*) of Sufism, but in "measured" ways, be it through Rumi, his poetry, or even *sama*. She is especially sensitive about these practices' utility for those who are located in racialized and Indigenous communities. She feels that Rumi and his legacy can offer much to such communities in terms of quenching their thirst. This view is shared by other poets and performers, like Sheniz Janmohamed and Zain Bandali, whom we encounter later. In Vancouver, another important group has been sharing the tradition of Rumi through his poetry in Farsi and English.

Zavieh Mystical Society, Vancouver

Zavieh Mystical Society is a not-for-profit group that is not religiously defined and that welcomes seekers to study Rumi's poetry. In its early days, this group held study sessions in a room at the YWCA. As its popularity grew, it purchased an office in downtown Vancouver, which is now their centre. Zavieh's website states its aims as follows:

> To create an environment where people [who] are interested in mysticism and the path to spiritual perfection can get together, learn and practice cultivating love. The general idea of ZAVIEH is to enrich the lives of every participant, to promote unity, provide a space for study and practice of mysticism while sharing the experience of the journey called LIFE. Through active interaction in Zavieh, we strive to learn, understand, practice and move on the path of perfection. Therefore, Zavieh could be viewed as a dynamic entity, which will change as members evolve. We derive our strength from appreciation of beauty and wish to draw some of that beauty to ourselves by attempting to be of benefit to others and wanting for others what we want for ourselves.[20]

Zavieh's mission statement does not explicitly indicate any links to Rumi or Sufism; rather, it rather ambiguously highlights "mysticism." It hosts various events, such as for the Persian New Year (*Nowruz*), as well as poetry sessions, in this way serving as a Persian cultural centre. A regular offering this organization has come to be known for, especially among Vancouver's many Sufi communities, is its courses on Rumi's *Mathnawi* (*Masnavi*) (both in English and Farsi), taught by Dr Parviz Sahabi. Sahabi, before his death in October 2022, was a scholar, architect, and city planner, born in Hamadan, Iran. Many students of Sufism in Vancouver have studied with him. Zavieh has attracted those who are interested in Sufism and Rumi, who come from as far away as Seattle. One student of Sahabi's first attended the Rumi Festival in 1998, where Sahabi invited those involved to study the *Mathnawi* with him in English and Farsi, as Brozak explained:

> He was teaching the Persian community here for, I don't know how many [years] ... probably well over a decade or more. I guess one of his students had been to the Rumi Festival so eventually she approached us and asked us if we would like to study the *Masnavi* with him in English. 'Cause there was the Nicholson translation, anyway, so we said sure, because he wanted to do two things. He wanted to try and reach out to young Persians, young Iranians who'd maybe grown up here ... 'cause the *Masnavi*, the Persian in the *Masnavi* is like trying to understand Shakespearian English, right, it's, you know, thirteenth-century Persian ... And you know, as he said, Nicholson would pick one word, right. And ... he would pick an accurate word but there were five other words as well ... Parvez [would] go and use the word *Haqq*, which always goes into English as truth, right. But ... I still have my hand notes in my *Masnavi* where he would list the other nine meanings of *Haqq* as well. So we started studying I think right in the year 2000, January of 2000, I think ... We started studying the *Masnavi* with Parvez and he finished it last July. The six books, yes. Now part of that was after about two and a half years, we stopped and went back to the beginning again because there was a whole new crop of people who were interested in studying it, ... he felt it was better to go back to the beginning because there was a fair number of people, rather than having them join halfway through book two. So anyway, so basically, we started in the year 2000 and finished whatever last July was I guess 2019, we finally got to the end of book six.[21]

Parvez set out to reconnect diasporic Persians to *Mathnawi* through the original language. But as Sufi communities in Vancouver organized, he also began to offer English classes of the *Mathnawi* so that it could be studied by non-Persian speakers as well. Shams al Haqq Farzad AttarJafari, the head of Rumi Canada and a *samazen*, was one of the students who took the *Mathnawi* course with Sahabi. He found it to be a formative moment for his path to Sufism:

> [When] I ended up in Vancouver, I came in touch with a very wonderful teacher [of] *Masnavi*, Ustad Sahabi, who still teaches at Zavieh Mystical Society in Vancouver. He takes you to through the whole six books of *Masnavi*, the whole thing

in Persian and English. And it will probably take you seven years to go through that whole study. And I sat with him, not the whole seven years, but maybe four or something like that and went through the first three or four books and then I really came to know Rumi, mysticism, and the way of thinking … That book is the whole human … psychology. He [Rumi] opens it, and puts it together … you'd think he was a mathematician when you read it. And then you think sometimes he's confused because he jumps from one story to another, okay, he lost track of what he was saying, but no, he's a master that knows what he's doing, exactly takes you back to the same spot. When you're supposed to hear the answer, he may wait even two books and leave a story there. So, you learn from this actually, that in our daily life some stuff we don't have to have answers right away, we let it [be]. So anyway, slowly I got cooked by the book.[22]

For interested seekers and initiated Sufis, not only in Vancouver but also in Seattle and across Canada, the Zavieh Mystical Society and Sahabi's work have been vital to the transmission of Rumi's teachings, both in Farsi and in English. Many Sufi leaders and students in Vancouver have studied with Sahabi and taken classes that have informed their relationship to Sufism and Rumi. Zavieh Mystical Society and the classes its offers address some of the misunderstandings and appropriations of Rumi in the spiritual marketplace by engaging directly with Rumi's works in both Farsi and English. The society was founded within a predominantly Persian diasporic community but has since opened itself to include classes in English where non-Persians can study the *Mathnawi*. At Zavieh, second- and third-generation diasporic Muslims are able to engage with Sufism as a spiritual tradition and reclaim their cultural identity and ancestral lineage.[23]

Sufi Poet Series in Toronto

On 8 February 2020, the East African Canadian poet and performer Sheniz Janmohamed reinaugurated the Sufi Poet Series in partnership with Small World Music. Small World Music Centre, in downtown Toronto, is a not-for-profit organization that focuses on "sharing cultural experience and ultimately, building bridges between cultures."[24] Many of those who perform there identify as part of the Iranian diaspora and use Sufi poetry (Rumi, Hafiz, Saadi, etc.) to locate their identity. This Sufi Poet Series, named *Panah* (پناه), aimed to raise funds for those who died in the crash on Flight 752 from Iran to Canada in 2020. Its original program included storytelling and spoken-word poetry as well as Persian music.[25] Close to eighty people attended. As advertised on Facebook: "The mandate of Sufi Poets Series is to invite performers and artists from a wide range of backgrounds to collaborate and breathe life into ancient and original poetry, while celebrating pluralism and practicing innovation." Since the first gathering, its events have included the poetry of Bulleh Shah (d. 1757), Rabia al-Adawiyya (d. 801), and "many other Sufi poets in previous incarnations of the series. We look to continue the tradition of reviving Sufi poets as we enter a new decade." The Sufi Poet Series had its beginnings with the poet and performer Sheniz Janmohamed.

Janmohamed studied English literature and comparative religion. She then earned an MA at the University of Guelph and studied with scholars like Kuldip Gill (d. 2009) at the University of British Columbia. Gill was one of the first South Asian Canadian women to write *ghazals* in English. Gill had published various anthologies of poems including *Dharma Rasa* (1999), which contains a section on *ghazals*:

> The Punjab plains, pink plumes of sugar cane stalk, the dust storm
> Crackles, razor grasses, whisks of white-bearded pampas.
> A nairee [duststorm]! They come, dervishes on the wind! Pillage the poorest village.
> Dreaded dacoit hidden in thickets.
> White-eyed horses, a bit-stretched mouths. Lightning legs, hooves, manes.
> Crops across wet flanks. Knotted white knuckles.
> Lock and bolt doors and gates; blow out dia. Hide, women! Hide!
> Vasanti says, Nairee aiee ha [a windstorm has come]! Dacoit thirst, red-eyes, for women. (95)

Gill uses her South Asian tradition as a rich landscape for her poetic repertoire, which includes imagery from Sikhism, Hinduism, Islam, and Sufism (via the "dervish" in the preceding extract). Her student Janmohamed follows a tradition of writing both in the *ghazal* form and in free form. She has authored three collections of Sufi-influenced poetry, *Bleeding Light* (2010), *Firesmoke* (2010), and *Reminders on the Path* (2021).[26] Though it draws from various traditions and practices, her poetry has often been understood as Sufi:

> I was always interested in Buddhism, I studied Buddhism in university. And even before that I had done my own kind of investigation and research, and reading the teachings of the Buddha. So I'd always been interested and I started studying, not formally, just to make that clear, Tibetan Buddhism with my teacher, who is trained to teach in the Gelugpa tradition. The way that he presents the practice is as a tool to investigate your mind, so I've never felt forced to choose one tradition over another tradition. I feel like they can, for me … live in the same place. But at the same time, I'm not claiming to be any of them, or attempting to make them "fit" into a world view that is convenient. So if I'm talking about Buddhism I say I practise, I don't say I am Buddhist. Or if I say I am Ismaili it's because I'm culturally Ismaili. Of course, I still adhere to some of the practices, but I would never call myself a Sufi, that's not something I would do unless I was formally part of a *tariqa*.[27]

Culturally and in religious and spiritual practice, Janmohamed is located between Ismaili, Sufi, and Buddhist traditions, the former being inherited identities and the latter being traditions she came to over the course of her own research and spiritual path. These different traditions have informed her practice and performance as a poet. She welcomes the diverse lens through which her work has been read, even while trying to avoid being labelled:

> I think it's more that I am trying to honour these traditions. In my poetry it's an honour but it's also questioning. In some poems, I refer to myself as a heretic as a means to check my own sense of "self," which may be limited by one fixed idea of my identity. So … I'm not projecting onto the world based on what I think Sufism should be. It's in relationship to my own practice and my own investigation of my life. If somebody were to ask me, I wouldn't be able to claim myself because I feel like that's also part of Sufism – you're shedding all of the labels, right? So maybe to someone I am a Sufi and maybe to someone else I am a Buddhist, maybe to my dad, I'm a heretic, or agnostic. I'm just joking [laughter]. But I'm just saying, what is identity? Identity is fluid, right?[28]

Janmohamed launched the Sufi Poet Series in 2012. One of the earliest events was held on 7 December 2013 (Sufi Poet Series III: American Sufi). She felt there was a real hunger for this tradition and culture of Sufi poetry, especially in cities like Toronto:

> There's such a hunger for it. I had this Sufi Poets Series for a couple of years and I purposefully chose poets based on their merit as poets not based on their traditions or beliefs. I chose poets because I felt they were grounded in their craft and creative practice, and open minded. So, we had poets that were atheists, Shia, Sunni, Christian – what mattered is they were unifying around the work of a long-gone Sufi poet, Bulleh Shah. So we had someone like Azalea Ray, who is versed and trained in those traditions, and then we had people who have never read Bulleh Shah before or never encountered his work before. So, protecting the integrity of the practices is a different thing altogether, but we need to share the poetry with the world, because there is a hunger for it.[29]

Beit Zatoun, a community space, cultural centre, and gallery, with a focus on Palestinian rights and justice, was located in the Annex neighbourhood in downtown Toronto. It hosted a number of Sufi-related events. It closed in 2016. Until then, the Sufi Poet Series was held at this venue. At those events, various local Canadian poets and performers participated, like Azalea Ray (mentioned earlier), a Bengali performer based in Toronto who specializes in Pakistani and Indian classical and traditional music. For Janmohamed, creating these spaces to experience South Asian poetic traditions that are not just Sufi but part of the broader culture of poetry has been a central aim of the Sufi Poet Series. This had been the intention of the Sufi Poet Series since it was first inaugurated, and continues to be so since it resumed in 2019:

> JANMOHAMED: Again, because these ... poets should be revived, they should be celebrated, and heard, and recited, and interpreted. So, I let people interpret the poetry however they chose to, whether that was contemporary expressions through music or collaborative pieces, whatever they [and] however they were drawn into the work, they could express themselves that way, but the poetry was the poetry of the poet that we were honoring. So, we had Rabia as the first poet, and the lineup was poets who identified as women, and then for the second show we had Bulleh Shah, and then for the third, we had a contemporary writer, Anand Mahadevan, who wrote *American Sufi*. He read from his book, and it was a soft launch as part of our series, and then we had to shut it down because the venue closed. But then I asked people on Facebook about reviving the series elsewhere.
>
> XAVIER: Yeah, I remember seeing that.
>
> JANMOHAMED: And I was like– okay, so I guess we're doing that again. So, I've already had people reaching out to me saying let's figure out a venue, get funding for it, we can help you. So, again, I think it's just a hunger because there aren't spaces like this and I've been working a lot with Farzad [AttarJafari], who is a Sufi of Persian descent, and I don't feel any barrier in that sense, but I think there's also a need for spaces to revive South Asian poetry, right? So that's something that's a challenge and a couple of people have expressed to me that they don't know where to go for that, especially the new generation because they don't always have access to the language. So, I mean they're not going to like a private *mehfil* [concert] that they wouldn't even know about ... so how do we bridge that gap when there is this desire to learn more and to participate, and be included in this lineage in some way, in the poetic lineage, but where do we do this? Where are the spaces for this? So that's really my question...[30]

In her reflections and her work, Janmohamed captures an important cultural, literary, and spiritual thread of Sufism in Canada, especially among many young second- and third-generation Muslims and non-Muslim racialized individuals, a trend also noted in Evanson's work as an arts director at the Banff Centre. Individuals are seeking an authentic experience of the poetic traditions of their inherited identities, such as South Asian poetic traditions, particularly in an era where young people are sensitive to decolonizing discourses in light of their relationship to the nation-state project of Canada. Some of what has been expressed by Janmohamed seems to counter some scholarship on generational approaches to musical traditions, and even poetic traditions, among the diasporic Muslim communities in Canada. For instance, Frishkopf (2011) notes that "among first-generation immigrants, reasoned rejection and fear of musical ritual may be accompanied by a pleasantly nostalgic emotional response deriving from memories of familiar practices of the homeland; however, the second generation, lacking such nostalgia, is more likely to respond with rejection, intellectual and emotional" (2011: 136).

For poets like Janmohamed, cultural and religious experiences remind them to look to the poetic traditions of South Asian Sufism as a means to reassert a diasporic Muslim and South Asian identity. The goal here is not to reject traditions, as Frishkopf suggests, but rather to engage and negotiate them in light of the Canadian social, cultural, religious and political landscape. In reflecting on Frishkopf's point, Janmohamed adds that "part of the artist's work is to question in relationship to tradition – so to question doesn't automatically equal rejection. There are many of us who question from within the tradition without negating it altogether."[31] We see this process in the social justice activism of queer East African–South Asian poet Zain Bandali, who, like Janmohamed, is also Ismaili and engages in Sufi practice:

> I think I came into my queerness very much knowing that I was an Ismaili Muslim, and that's the term I would use to describe myself, as an Ismaili Muslim. Although I am someone who is often in Sufi spaces I would maybe definitely use the term Sufi in terms of like a lower-case "s" because at the end of the day they're just labels but I think I've always felt comfortable with that label, being an Ismaili Muslim because of the fluidity that that identity has afforded to my ancestors and like the syncretic [nature] of Khojas and how did they come into being. But I think the reason why I'm mentioning this is because of having this sort of desire to uphold and celebrate a very politicized identity that's often at odds, not only like in general as a queer person, but just as a human being who is brown and living in Canada. Oftentimes it's very difficult for people to see the credibility that you have as someone who is LGBTQ and then also, at the same time, a person who is of faith. And so I would say organizing from my own sense, it's always been with those people in mind. Like understanding that ... if I'm this queer brown person who's Muslim and then trying to go into a LGBTQ centre that literally has no idea about my interests, the type of music I listen to, the fact that I am someone who has a religion that isn't Christianity or has the relationship with his parents that is not necessarily one of like outcast but one of acceptance. So, I think that because of the fact that I've never fit a narrative that maybe is homonormative, or heteronormative it's definitely been an area where I'm always considered that I am someone with faith and that I want to advocate for people who have been able to reconcile their faith with their sexuality, of their gender or any of those ... things.[32]

Bandali's intersectional identities as a queer Muslim East African–South Asian and his activism have together led to the formation of queer Muslim spaces on his university campus. These identities are also important to how he draws from Sufi poetry, as a poet himself:

> It's been really cool using *ghazal* as a framework and as a guiding sort of ... like a style that obviously has roots in the Islamicate world ... and being able to now use it for my own sort of leanings and it's something I'm still working on and I haven't perfected it by any means and it's something that I'm still pushing myself to do ... but I think *ghazal*, especially *ghazal* as a medium, there's a lot of queer or like silently queer folks throughout history like Aga Shahid Ali ... He was a very famous Kashmiri poet who, I think he's buried in the US and he's someone who like really took *ghazal* and in the English form and kind of brought it to a next level and he's very inspiring and he was someone who I think like silently was you know, homosexual, who lived a life that [way] and there's even Siraj Aurangabadi who was a Sufi saint, an *awliya* in the Chishti order, who lived in present-day Maharashtra but in the Deccan region India, so in the south, who was I think one of the first or second to write *ghazal* in Urdu, which until that point they were only ever written in Farsi. So, and he was a well-known queer, well queer again, a homosexual Sufi saint who today you might want to call queer, you know an individual who had a lot of like homoromantic motifs in his writing, who till this day sung in Qawwali and maybe those brown uncles don't know but they're singing you know, a man who was in love with another man. So ... I think ... there's very much this yearning that Sufism allows for and exudes constantly, is very much that same yearning that I think queer people have always felt throughout history and so I think that's why there's a very close ... symbiotic relationship and I think that's why maybe over time there's been a pull between, and we can talk about Rumi, we can talk about Shams, you can talk about Amir Khusrau and Nizam ud-Awliya and we can talk about Madhu Lal Hussein... and Madhu Lal Hussein, I don't know if you know Shah Hussein ... He was a Punjabi Lahori Sufi saint who's written many like *kalams* and his composite name is Madhu Lal Hussein cause Mahdu Lal was his Hindu lover and they're actually buried next to each other in Lahore. So, it's very beautiful, there's a lot of examples like that.[33]

Here, Bandali captures how historical Sufi poetry, especially South Asian Sufi literary traditions but also Rumi and Shams, and the form of the *ghazal*, have enabled him to engage with his varying identities, including those that do not fit the homo- or hetero-normative secular (Christian) Canadian context in which he exists. Sufi poetic registers and histories are tools of decolonization; they are also mechanisms for furthering social justice, especially for some young Muslims in Canada (a point I come back to in the epilogue). So, *contra* Frishkopf's (2011) assertation that "'ritual music' is most usefully invoked not to be performed, but to be denied, thus generating a productive marker of difference," among performers like Janmohamed and Bandali these Sufi artistic media serve as discursive tools for reasserting cultural and religious ties to lost homelands (136). They are utilized to reaffirm connections to Canadian spaces, be they secular or sacred.

The engagement with Sufi poetry and with the tradition of interpretation of the poetry of Rabia, Bulleh Shah, Rumi, Hafiz, Yunnus Emre, and many more, captures a trend in Sufism – toward approaching it as a literary and cultural experience, especially in cultural community spaces like Small World Music and the Aga Khan Museum (see below). Again, here the question of whether these experiences are sacred or secular – be they for the performer or for the audience – is entirely up for debate (though as a religious studies scholar, I envision such moments as intermingled). The point is to capture the ways in which Sufi literary traditions permeate the cultural and literary imagination in popular ways beyond how those traditions are portrayed in social media. These social media debates over real versus fake Rumi or Hafiz, which are based on critiques about dilution in the spiritual marketplace, have led poets to cultivate Sufi poetic spaces as sites for reasserting cultural expressions and identities; they have also generated requests for more such encounters, with the result that a new generation of young Muslims and racialized peoples now long for these traditions and for spaces where they can access Sufi poetry. All of this is often missed in the broader discussion about the consumption, commodification, and appropriation of Sufi poetry today. Still, poets are aware of the terrain on which their work is distributed and consumed. Janmohamed reflected on how readers' interpretations of her poetry have led her to rethink how the poetry of Sufi teachers, like Rumi, has resulted in a complex legacy of interpretations:

> I actually think Rumi would probably be amused and delighted by how many interpretations there are of his work. Now I'm not comparing myself in any sense to Rumi, but I find interpretation of one's work fascinating. I remember going into a class at U of T [University of Toronto] and the students were studying my book, which is such an out-of-body experience. I came in and one student was like, "This poem really symbolized to me colonial dominance over ..." I don't know what, it was some theory right? I don't even remember, I just wrote the poem because it felt right. So when I heard the interpretation, I was like, "Wow, I think I am going to use that from now on!" Obviously, you have an intention when you're writing, but if you want to hoard how it's interpreted then don't write or don't have it published or don't have it accessible to people, because the minute you write it and others receive it's not yours anymore. It's like a gift, a lesson in ... in letting go, impermanence.[34]

Thus poetry, as Janmohamed explains below, is not an "artefact." It *can* be that, but it is its embodied reality that gives it life for continued interpretation so that it lives beyond the author's intention:

It's also about how you're interpreting the poetry. Like, I mean if poetry is artefact, okay. But poetry is also living, so can you differentiate between the two? As a scholar you can speak of it as an artefact and limit your understanding and your interpretation and your study of it in its historical context, and then at the same time leave space and room for the living interpretation of it, because it contains both form and emptiness[35]

Poetry is not Rumi's only legacy in Canada.[36] Another tradition that has solidified on the cultural landscape is presentations of turning, which are associated especially with Toronto's Aga Khan Museum and Ismaili Centre.

Cultural Spaces and Musical Venues in Toronto

The Toronto region is home to thriving racial and ethnic communities, including their diverse cultural scenes. Community events that feature Sufi expressions of art and poetry have become common over the past two decades, especially in Muslim communities and spaces. The Noor Cultural Centre in North York has long been one important site (among others) for such gatherings and presentations. Its founders, Hassanali and Noorbanu Lakhani, built that space as a token of gratitude to Canada, which had allowed them to build a new life.[37] Their emphasis on Islamic education led them to establish the Noor Fellowship in Islamic Studies at York University, which eventually became a permanent chair. The centre has offered various programs, including lectures, weekly *jumah* (Friday) prayers, an Islamic school for children, and celebrations of Ramadan and Eid. The centre has also hosted book events, such as one that featured Dr Laury Silvers's Sufi novel *The Lover: A Sufi Mystery* (2019), and has participated in various social justice and interfaith workshops and lectures. The Noor Cultural Centre has hosted various ritual events, including presentations of *zikr* and *sama* to commemorate Rumi, in collaboration with Sufi communities in Toronto like the Rifai Sufi Order; these have involved the singing of *ilahi*s and presentations of *sama* by dervishes of Rumi Canada (in 2017). Sufi events have not always focused on ritual. In May 2015, Zia Inayat-Khan and the Sufi Order International held a two-day Sufi workshop titled *Awakening Your Mystic Heart*, and on 16 May 2019, the Noor Cultural Centre held the first ever "International Day of Living Together in Peace," an initiative of *shaykh* Khaled Bentounes of the International Association of the Sufi Alawiyya, who is based in Italy. The event was supported by Sufi communities in Toronto, including the Nimatullahi Sufi Order, the Sufi Order International, and the Canadian Institute of Sufi Studies (Rifai), as well as Emmanuel College of the University of Toronto.[38]

The Noor Cultural Centre has been a central cultural and educational hub for Sufi and Muslim events in Toronto. Other public venues, though, such as

Roy Thompson Hall and smaller musical venues (e.g., Small World Music and Beit Zatoun), have also presented various musical, cultural, and artistic expressions of Sufism and Islam for interested audiences. For example, Small World Music and the Aga Khan Museum together sponsored the world-renowned Qawwali singer Abida Parveen at Roy Thompson Hall and the Aga Khan Museum in May 2016. Small World Music (introduced earlier) has partnered with Janmohamed for her Sufi Poet Series. Overall, the centre has been a valuable collaborator in music events in Toronto.[39] Its programming has included South Asian (especially through its Asian Series), Persian, and world music (through its festival). The centre's executive director, Umair Jaffar, has served as a manager and curator at the Aga Khan Museum and the Harbourfront Centre.

Through its Sacred Step series, Harbourfront Centre has regularly hosted events, such as a turning meditation workshop (with AttarJafari, Evanson, and Burke), as well as workshops on Anishinaabe Pow-Wow, Indian dance of Kathakali, and Zimbabwean Mbira.[40] Harbourfront was also the first venue to host the Sufi Poet Series (see above). And in July 2017 it hosted the Tirgan Festival (Inner Journey II, "featuring Regard Persian and Rumi Canada Sufi Sacred Dancers"), which featured *samazen*s like Mira Burke, Raqib Burke, and AttarJafari. Overall, then, Sufi events, especially those led by Sufi practitioners involved in various Sufi communities, have been a significant thread of cultural and artistic expression at various Toronto venues, be it to promote Islam or cultural/heritage practices as part of multicultural programming. In recent years, however, one space in particular has solidified its Sufi-related programming.

Aga Khan Museum and Ismaili Center

The Aga Khan Museum is a cultural and religious centre that navigates between public and private, secular and religious dynamics in Canada. The museum is named after the current leader of the Ismailis. Ismailis are a Shia Muslim community that traces the lineage of the current Aga Khan back to Ali, the cousin and son-in-law of the Prophet Muhammad. The Aga Khan is believed to be the forty-ninth living Imam. The museum and its park occupy 6.8 hectares. The museum itself was designed by the award-winning Japanese architect Fumihiko Maki, the garden by the Lebanese architect Vladimir Djurovic. The Aga Khan Museum is today a major tourist attraction, serving as a museum of Islamic art and culture. Its theatre has drawn internationally renowned musicians and performers, such as Qawwali singers from Pakistan; it also hosts regular spoken-word poetry, Muslim comedy, film screenings, and much more. The space also hosts inter- and intra-Muslim and non-Muslim presentations of art and culture. Across from the museum and its park is the Ismaili Centre, which has a *jamatkhana* (prayer hall) used by Ismailis for their daily prayers. This magisterial glass-angled building was designed by the Indian architectural firm Charles

Correa.⁴¹ All of these venues, both sacred and secular (though these are complex dynamics), reflect the current Aga Khan's global investment in architecture and its relations with sacred realities, local environments, and Ismaili values of cosmopolitanism and pluralism (Dewji 2018).

At both the centre and the museum, Sufism has been a significant part of the programming. Ismailis have a proximate relationship to Sufism, especially in South and Central Asia, where the practices of various religious communities and the *batini* (inner) and esoteric spiritual approach of Ismaili theology have been inflected by Sufi praxis, theology, poetry, and institutions, and vice versa (Virani 2019; Khan 2003, 2004). This notable relationship is seen in the poetic practices of Janmohamed and Bandali. The Aga Khan is also known for celebrating and amplifying Islamic art, architecture, and cultural expressions, as evident in the preservation projects of the Aga Khan Development Network (AKDN) around the world; Sufi arts are pivotal to those global projects. Since it opened in 2014, the museum and the centre have engaged in Sufi programming. The museum, for example, offered "Sufism and the Mystic Poets of Islam," an eight-week course led by Reza Tabandeh, a postdoctoral fellow at the University of Toronto, who also delivered a six-session course on "Rumi and the Philosophy of Love and Ecstasy" and a lecture on "Rumi and the Religion of Love." Lectures are not the only way in which Sufi teachings are engaged; music and dance presentations have been another.

Aesthetic and Cultural Presentations of Sama

Shams al Haqq Farzad AttarJafari regularly collaborates with spaces like the Aga Khan Museum and the Ismaili Centre on large performance events that incorporate presentations of turning. An example is Rumi Canada: Sufi Whirling Meditation Session (March 2018). When helping produce events like these with the museum, AttarJafari often works with various Persian musicians, such as Shaho Andalibi and Amir Koushkani (who presented at the first Rumi Festival in Vancouver). Other regular events at the museum include Nuit Blanche activities, which have been held there annually for several years at the Ismaili Centre (and which I opened this book with), and the Hayiran Ensemble by Rumi Canada (February 2020). Film screenings – for example, of the documentary *Wajd: Songs of Separation* (by Syrian Canadian filmmaker Amar Chebib) – have included presentations of Sufi music and *sama*, with music from Koushkani, Nour Khedder, and Zohreh Shahbazy and turning from AttarJafari and Lindsey Ridgway (from Vancouver).⁴² These public *sama* events have heightened the popularity of turning as a performative dance (see figure 4.2).

AttarJafari has been presenting and producing these events since well before the existence of the Aga Khan Museum in Toronto. AttarJafari was often criticized (e.g., on Facebook), for being part of the "problem," that is, for

4.2. Nuit Blanche presentation September 2018 at the Ismaili Center. Photograph by author.

popularizing Sufism and Rumi for a western audience (by performing publicly). Some of his critics did not realize he was Muslim and/or Iranian or located in Sufi traditions, which suggests how identity politics can taint arguments over authenticity and cultural appropriation. Put another way, who should get to participate in public presentations of Sufi traditions at culturally Muslim spaces such as the Aga Khan Museum and the Ismaili Centre? I asked about these dynamics during our conversation:

> XAVIER: So, then, what do you think of people who critique and say Rumi's become too popular, too commodified, too distilled, like the essence of Rumi is lost because Americans, or westerners, are you know buying Rumi, selling Rumi?
>
> ATTARJAFARI: Yeah, I get that, sometimes they think I'm doing that ... Sometimes I ask myself why do I need to perform this Sufi whirling dance on a stage that sometimes is not sacred or mystical? But then, you know, anything with good intention is beautiful. It's all about intention. So, if your intention is to be a showman and be out there and show how much capability you have and you can bang ... your head and turn fast or slow and do this and that, but then loose

the essence of *sama* which is diving into stillness and bringing everybody in with you, then you have done unfairness to that practice. Any time we try that, whether we like it or not, we become channels to pass energy to the ones sitting there. There's a reason those three hundred people are there. And *alhamdulillah* [thank God], this one does it for that reason, and I've been in situations and I've come across yeah showmen and show women and things like that and you can tell. When you're a dervish and you practice this, the power of it is out of your control, it will manifest, you get out of the way and it manifests.[43]

For AttarJafari, it all goes back to ensuring that the message and the practice capture and share the legacy of Rumi for those who need it. Ultimately, though, his intention (*niyya*) is what matters most, and that is located in the heart (*qalb*). AttarJafari has recently been presenting large-scale collaborations between Canada's Indigenous musicians and the Canadian Arabic Orchestra in Vancouver (April 2019), along with Mira and Raqib Burke.[44] Still, when he produces these larger public events, such as at the Aga Khan Museum, he is very mindful of whom he is collaborating with so as to ensure there is a deep understanding of the practice, regardless of the non-formal context:

Anybody who's kind of involved with us, they may not announce it to you publicly, but they've kind of got their feet very rooted with a *pir* and with a master. And I see that [as] very important. And whenever we're putting projects or things together, we pay attention to that one might say, why? Because of the cooking process, that's why. And, there's a reason it's there and sure some like it, some don't like it, but I think it works. You need to give it time [for] anything ... to blossom ... So yeah it's a bit of a debate from both sides but you know we can't worry about that, we can't worry. I do what I do with the right intention and with attention to beauty and am I being fair to carry the name of this beloved and then representing them on his behalf? Is this what he would want to see? [Why] am I messing around with this? You can't lie to yourself, you can lie to others maybe but you can't lie to yourself. So, no everything we do is for that reason, for his [Rumi] message to come. So, I feel very blessed especially to share the knowledge of a man who is from the same land as I was born and spoke the language. And I always feel ... whenever I'm stuck I always ask *ya pir*, take me and help me. And he appears and helps, but it's all about intention. If you're connected to the right reason, to the right teacher, and the right source, you don't have to try hard, everything will happen in the most beautiful way. *Alhamdulillah*, whatever that has come up from Rumi Canada, you've witnessed a lot of it, but somehow whenever I look back and review something I'm like wow beautiful, look what manifested?[45]

I have known and worked with AttarJafari for more than ten years in various capacities around some of the events he referred to in our conversation. He has visited my students, who have taken classes on Sufism or Islam at institutions like Ithaca College and Queen's University, providing workshops to students on turning and Sufism. I am grateful for his time when he comes and spends it with my students and presents the tradition experientially to them. Still, he always responds that it is his service as a dervish and *samazen* to share the message through experience, for you never know how anyone in the room is going to respond to the encounter with the music or with the movements of turning. He is aware of some of the criticisms he faces for publicly presenting the practice of turning and offering it to those who are interested. Some feel it is further commodifying Rumi and Sufism, but he insists that is not his intention, which in fact is rooted in his deep practice of the tradition of Sufism, which goes back to Rumi, his *pir* and master. His intention defines the practice, whether it is presented in public or in private.

Evanson, too, regularly presents the tradition of turning with AttarJafari on Canadian and international stages. Since she began turning, she has presented *sama* around the world with the Vancouver Rumi Society and Rumi Canada and with artists like Mercan Dede and Niyaz, the Iranian Canadian music duo.[46] Many event organizers have approached her to "perform" whirling or "twirling," but she is very clear about whom she collaborates with:

> But it's very clear and now because it's been like almost twenty years of doing public presentations, it's very clear when a certain person asks and that person is known or we've worked together before, then it's a no-brainer, it's yes and, you know, tell me where to go and we'll go there, but when it's a person who is not known, then there's a conversation that has to happen, and it might start with an email then it will move to telephone. Certain … bases need to be cover[ed] and the context needs to be beautiful or else, you know … you don't need a whirling dervish to open your night club. It doesn't mean you can't have a certain quality of the performative in *sama*. Having a more performative quality to the *sama* is if it's done in beauty, if it's done in *haqq* [Truth], you know, if it's done with *ashq*, with love … then it is good and it will be useful for the people who are witnessing it. You just have to watch your ego or I have to watch my ego.[47]

Evanson, like AttarJafari, is very clear that the presentation of *sama*, if done with the right intentions of "haqq" and "ashq," can be beautiful, and the presentation will serve the audience in ways one cannot always imagine or know immediately. Thus, for them, it is the intention (*niyya*) more than the context or space that defines the essence of *sama*, even if it is presented in a performative manner. Still, Evanson is very clear that being a *samazen* is not a profession, even though she has performed globally:

> Being a *samazen* is not a profession. So the understanding is that you should always have a job in the community like have a service in the community, be an

accountant, be a, you know, I don't know, sell cars, be a teacher and then having this practice on this side, which informs in fact how you are in the community ... There might be money that comes in from that practice or those public presentations, but hopefully it keeps moving. Either it moves back into Sema Space [Montreal] or, you know, ... it has to keep moving. I mean I guess money only works when it's moving.[48]

Whatever critics might think, in the end, presenting the practice of *sama* in a public venue or to a paid audience need not diminish the sacred nature of the contemplative practice – at least, not for these *samazen*s. Mira Burke, the daughter of Brian Raqib Burke, has reflected on how the practice in public and sacred spaces has, for her, not easily been separable: "Over the years, I have had to reconcile what I see as the inner and outer qualities of whirling, the *batin* and *zahir*, the inner devotion and the outer performance. The form I practice on stage begins as service for the audience, and it is through my expressiveness that I communicate the power of whirling and bring the viewer with me" (qtd in Miller 2017: 266).

For AttarJafari, Evanson, and Mira, this practice goes back to Raqib Brian Burke, who first learned this approach from Feild. In their initial practice with Feild, they often presented the practice in small art galleries or large theatre spaces. Feild was a musician and a performer and enjoyed presenting the *sama* practice artistically. Burke remembers that this form was far more successful in front of public audiences than when whirling dervishes visited from Konya and presented the practice in Vancouver. This perception shifted Burke's understanding of the power of *sama* as an inner experience:

The patterns of the Mawlawi *sama* you could say, even if they were symbolic or spiritually ordained detail incorrect, that ... inner spiritual potency of the entire ceremony was ... perfect. Like the details could be wrong but it was absolutely a hundred percent clear that they didn't matter at all. Because the ... impact of the ceremony in its flow was ... unimpeded by any of it. And that ... I think anyone who, well ... For example, the first time the *sama* ... was actually produced ... I think two years before ... the dervishes from Konya had done a tour. And, you know, in a sense played Vancouver and they presented their impeccable ... you could say perfect ceremony. And it was presented by a dance impresario, ballet impresario, who would invite ballet companies from around the world to come and ... do a series in Vancouver ... And they didn't know what they were inviting or what it was about ... So ... I don't know how the evening went, but what I heard from a number of people was that by the time the ceremony got halfway through, people started to leave. It was so boring, man. It was, "I think they're still doing it. I think they're still gonna do this all day."... Then more people would get the message, like, "Okay, we've seen it." And ... okay, so you know, the spiritual energy ... didn't transmit, but for whatever reason, when it was our turn to do it, and it was at the same theatre ... just the smaller version of their one was a big one ... No one left and no one wanted to leave ... So obviously those dervishes in Konya were hoping that's what ... happened, but because it didn't get presented, it didn't get explained. It didn't get prepared. It ... wasn't understood. Whereas Reshad [Feild] set it up so beautifully as a theatre performance. Right. And got a cello player on stage. It was part of the group. And she started playing this beautiful solo in Yoyo Ma kind of cello inspiration. And then this single woman dervish comes out and there's this professional ... I don't know if he was an actor. I forget ... His voice starts cutting out and explaining what the meaning of all these movements is to this chilly music "and now she's raising her right hand. Now ... left hand," and it mesmerized everyone. So that when the ceremony started ... they could relate to it ... someone read ... [a] poem.[49]

Burke here is highlighting the thought that went into setting up public presentations by Feild and his students in order that it be "transmitted" properly to the audience. Such presentations of *sama* have continued to inform how Burke presents the practice, and what his students, AttarJafari, Evanson, and Mira, are also doing. It is also necessary to point out, as Burke does, that whirling dervishes from Konya were themselves participating in global tours, presenting the practice of turning in theatres around the world from Paris to Vancouver, creating what ethnomusicologists have termed "world music," under which rubric Sufi music and practice has become a highly popular commodity (Nikolaisen 2004; Shannon 2003; Jankowsky 2021). So these public presentations in Canada exist within a broader global scene of Sufi music and dance presentations: "It is linked to webs of consumerism where spirituality is one field, in the sense that the dervishes present a religious ritual, which is often adapted to an audience within the discourse of cultural heritage. The audience buys, consumes and enjoys the ritual. The dervishes also obtain larger degrees of visibility through their travelling, thereby spreading knowledge about mysticism" (Nikolaisen 2004: 94).

Public presentations of turning are not always understood as formal *sama* (see chapter 3), though they are tied to the practices of *samazen*s like Burke, AttarJafari, and Evanson. Venues like the Aga Khan Museum and many other venues across Toronto over the past decade have in many ways invested themselves in presenting these practices under the name of Rumi. This is sometimes a branding move on the part of the organizers. Regardless, the presentations are led by Sufis, who understand them through their particular lineage and, importantly, their own personal intention. For them, the aesthetics of Sufism are tied to the spiritual essence of the practice, from which the aesthetics cannot be severed. As Frishkopf (2011) writes: "Music, while frequently crucial to the symbolic and affective power of ritual performance, also challenges ritual boundaries of crossing back and forth into entertainment, and many of the critiques hurled against ritual musical practices throughout Islamic history can be understood as a reaction to what may be perceived as a dangerous blurring between ritual space-time and music's profane environment" (131).

This platform on which *sama* unfolds raises important questions, again, about the essence of *sama* as a practice (see the discussions by premodern scholars of Sufism in chapter 3). Scholars like Leonard Lewisohn (1997) highlight how *sama* developed in Muslim societies as a form of "intra-Islamic" "counter-concert," one that was "deliberately set in contrast to profane musical gatherings: the not so perceptible difference, in fact, between the sacred and the profane types of concert underlies the many disparaging remarks frequently made by both the nomocentric legalists and the more temperate mystics about the practice" (5). As such, *sama* is both an "art form" and a spiritual practice, and this has led to its diverse manifestations, as we saw in both the previous chapter and this one (6). There is no separation of art and performance from ritual practice, and this complicates efforts to separate sacred from profane moments, which some continue to try to do.

The debate over the role of Sufi music, and its existence in public and popular forms, has long been waged and still is. Such was the case with the popular Qawwali singer Nusrat Fateh Ali Khan (d. 1997) who collaborated with Coca-Cola for a commercial and later performed a musical score with Eddie Vedder for the Hollywood film *Dead Man Walking* (1995). He was sharply criticized for using sacred Sufi ritual music sung at Sufi shrines on Thursday evenings and commodifying it for Hollywood, but Khan did not see it that way. Rather, he felt it was important to share Qawwali music and its message with the world (Darlyrmple 2005). The whirling dervishes of Konya have toured globally, sharing this practice on world stages. Meanwhile, groups like Ensemble al-Kindi, a Syrian-based whirling dervish group, have at times received pushback for blurring the sacred and the secular (Shannon 2003). Yet other scholars have signalled to the ways in which Sufi music, be it Qawwali or Mawlawi Turkish music, exists in both sacred and profane contexts:

> Given that the form is only secondary to the actual performance, the Sufi sages advise us that the technique of *dhikr* [*zikr*], which involves mastering and directing inner psycho-spiritual energies, must be given inner illumination by purification of the heart's intent through surrender of the "imperious self" (*nafs al-ammāra*) and acquisition of noble virtues (*fādilat-i malaki*) if it is not to remain more than an empty and sterile technique. Such is the basic, the essential, condition of "Sufi music" according to both the Masters of the Path and the Sufi musical masters. The rest lies in the hands of God. Only He provides the musicians with talent, inspiration and grace; and only He provides the listener with the grace of the faculty of hearing. (During 2018: 287)

As discussed in the previous chapter, Rumi and his message of unity continue to manifest themselves in public sphere. Whether audiences understand what they are watching as *sama* or simply as a presentation of turning, they are as much a part of the ritual presentation of turning as are the *samazen*s themselves. This observation may be complicated in venues where hundreds are gathered, tickets are purchased, and a stage with fancy lighting and sound is involved, but it does not mean that the *samazen*s perceive any distinct difference – however elaborate the presentation, the audience may be moved by the "faculty of hearing." Much as with the reception of poetry and music, the presentation of meditative turning can be both spiritual and profane, both artistic and ritual. The aesthetic and sacred rituals and expressions of Sufism have often been difficult to separate and need not be mutually exclusive. Thus, for the *samazen*s, poets, performers, and artists whose voices are captured here, *sama* loses nothing immediately when presented to a public audience. At times, since the audience may not be ready, some simplification may be involved to ensure a safe exposure of the taste (*dhawq*) of the practice they are presenting. The presentation of the turning does not include the full ritual features (*salaam*s, recitations of the Quran, etc.; see chapter 3). But the features that *are* presented include components of the practice and offer an opportunity to "taste" the ritual. More than any other aspect, though, the presentation must depend on the intention of the *samazen*. Before I conclude this chapter's discussion of the popularization of Rumi in Canada, I turn to one final case study that further complicates our discussion of the popularization and commodification of Rumi: the Rumi Rose Garden in Vancouver.

Rumi Rose Garden and Café Vancouver

Rumi Rose Garden and Café in North Vancouver is a restaurant, grocery store, and Sufi meditation centre.[50] It is the home of the Naqshbandi Islamic Centre (of the Naqshbandi Haqqani Kabbani) and opened in 2011. It has a bookstore on the second floor and a grocery store that sells South Asian and Middle Eastern food items, along with locally popular Rumi teas and fragrances (oils). When I first walked in, in February 2020, the store was mostly empty. There was one white Muslim man sitting at a table with his Mac laptop doing some work. He welcomed me and asked if I needed anything. I told him I was just looking around. The lower floor functioned as a restaurant, with a grocery section at the back, with two small refrigerators and two aisles with various Indian spices and cooking condiments. The restaurant menu listed mostly kebabs and the like. The Rumi teas were in the front part of the store; bigger tins occupied the walls, smaller packaged bags to the right of the store's entrance. The stairs by the counter led upstairs to a library and prayer area, where the Naqshbandi Haqqani Kabbani order of Vancouver meets for prayers (*zikr*) on Thursday,

Friday, and Saturday nights. The space contained a bookshelf in the middle of the hall that divided the men's and women's sections. Many of the books were by *shaykh* Nurjan Mirahmadi or the head *shaykh* of the Kabbani order, and dealt with metaphysical topics. The chair where Mirahmadi, the leader of this community, sat was positioned so as to be visible to those sitting in both sections. In the women's section was a separate couch for his wife and women members of Mirahmadi's family.

Mirahmadi, the founder and president of Rumi Rose Garden, had come to Sufism through the Naqshbandi tradition during his time in Los Angeles. From there, to be close to his teacher, he went to Michigan, where the US headquarters of the Naqshbandi-Haqqani Sufi Centre is located (Dickson 2014, 2015). His teacher sent him to various places to teach and give public lectures. At one point, he visited Vancouver, where he felt at home: "Vancouver had a special energy here. There's a lot of diversity, you know, it wasn't just one type of people, because of the diversity there was so much interest in everything. And sort of … lent itself to a strong, a nice spiritual community."[51] During my interview with Mirahmadi, he explained that while Rumi teas might appear to be a western commodification of Rumi, this was not their intention; in fact, the selling of Rumi teas and oils was closely linked with the fundamental philosophy of the Naqshbandi-Haqqani Sufi Order.[52] Naqshbandi-Haqqani Sufi teaching focuses on energy and matter, especially as it relates to energy that can transform and alter one's spiritual states through bodily consumption – for example, through sounds:

> How do you bring in the energy … As negative is accessible to everyone, everyone's capable of achieving of negative energies without even thinking about it? So then there has to be you know, a God-given way on how to achieve positive energy, how to keep it, how to build it, and it's in the food, it's in the water, it's in everybody's environment that we keep. So, then what are all of the practices to sort of safe guard that? Then we go back to our own cultures and we'll understand why there were teachings, what you eat and drink is the saying you are what you eat. Yeah, of course, cause everything we eat has an energy. If you eat everything that has a negative energy, negative thought into it, the person who was using it had negative vibes, the creature was tortured in the process of eating it, has a negative in it, all of this negativity you put in your mouth, of course it's going to make the stomach sick. It just goes in like a bolt, you know, it shocks the body. So how then do you clean the energy while we only eat certain things and things that weren't tortured … You know I want only certain people to be sort of preparing those things and that they're not angry, they're not putting all of their…souls in it. And then when it comes to meals I want to be able to pray over it. And anything that was not perfect, people perfect this and make this to be a healing for me. So, there's a whole process on how to do [this] … it goes back to old teachings.[53]

The Rumi café is a community, religious, and restaurant space, and at the heart of its ritual practice is its transformative ability to change energy and thereby heal and provide blessings to those who ingest foods and teas that have absorbed this energy through the practice of *zikr*. The café and grocery store is located below the space where the community meets three times a week for *zikr*. Because of the alchemical transformations that unfold throughout *zikr*, these positive energies (i.e., as a result of reciting Allah's names) permeate the space and transform the people and objects in it. This understanding of *zikr* is also at the heart of *sama* practice, which is a form of *zikr* (see previous chapter). The objects transformed in this way include Rumi teas, which are then understood as detoxifying agents containing blessings (*karamat*):

> You know the tea was the traditional healing in our culture, the medicine was something that you ingested or in the perfume. So, we have the perfumes which are the anointing oils, the fragrances and aroma therapy was basically an angelic reality cause … The fragrances and smells are what heal you. So … the concept of the teas is that there would be healing in the different teas. These herbs, the ingredients, the camomile, all of the sort of ingredients within the tea had a tremendous healing to the body and now if you put on top of that all of the chanting that's done here on Thursday, Friday, Saturday is our dressing, our belief is that chanting dresses everything cause we believe it has an angelic energy … So this energy's continuously just dressing, dressing everything here. So, when we take this tea, you know, it wasn't in a store selling all sorts of crazy things, it was in a place of worship, so they take the tea and they make it at home and drink it as if they're taking a taste in a sip from this reality. The angels that accompany it and all of the blessings that are sort of accompanying it and it becomes a healing and takes away difficulties. What we call *baraka* and blessing that like excess positive lights and energies. What do we do to bring in extra *barakat* and extra lights in our life? And these can be from that eating and drinking from these types of fruit and these types of healing that bring blessings in our lives.[54]

When purchasing Rumi teas or fragrances, one can request that *shaykh* Mirahmadi complete a specific prayer (*dua*) over the items. This ties the selling of Rumi teas directly to the practice of *zikr* and the transformation that occurs in all matter through the recitation of the different names of God. The blessings of that transformation or *baraka* then infuse items such as Rumi teas and foods that are shared after *zikr* gatherings, as well as the teas that are purchased, taken home, and consumed. The Rumi Rose Garden and Café subverts what first appears to be a simple commodification of the name of Rumi. On closer analysis, these Rumi "commodities" point to the transformative and ritual significance of *zikr*. This is another variation of *sama* as a meditative practice that is transformative for the viewer (see above). But in this instance, it unfolds in another way: through the experience of ingestion. *Shaykh* Mirahmadi sees this as vital to the tradition of Sufism, adding that such practices, especially *zikr* and music, can help young people return to Sufism and Islam:

> So again, Sufism, traditional Sufism, you have to talk nice, good character, our recitations have a lot of drumming and very rhythmic, so when the young people come they say hey, this sounds so nice, we're competing with MTV, music, videos, YouTube, everything. So, you have to make it also presentable and enjoyable, at the same time they have to be able to see the teacher, they have to feel you know that they're on par with each other, equal with each other. It's just important and that's why Sufism is so successful. So, we go back to the way that you know, prophets had arranged ... and everything was based on tremendous amount of love and respect. But the cultures become dangerous because they inject their cultural beliefs and say that that's Islam, that's not correct.[55]

The selling of tea at the Rumi Rose Garden and Café is embedded in a belief in transformative experiences through embodiment as a way to return to traditions of the Prophet Muhammad. The Naqshbandi Haqqani Kabbani Order is not a Turkish Sufi community with a lineage leading back to Rumi, so using Rumi's name on their storefront may indeed be a branding move. Even so, the teas are "backed" by a particular philosophy – the name is not simply an exercise in commodification. Instead, the community understands the teas as remedies for those who need one. The teas have been transformed materially through *zikr*, just as the *samazen*s and the participants in *sama* are materially and spiritually transformed. This is understood as core to traditional Sufism and Islam. Similarly, the Rumi Restaurant in Montreal is run by students affiliated with the Naqshbandi-Haqqani Order.[56] It seems that storefront Sufism is a spatial and economic expression of some Sufi orders in Canada and that the distribution of Sufi commodities is a means to return to a central understanding of Islam. As such, purchasing and consuming these goods is viewed not as a diminishment of ritual, but as a reality of it. In this chapter we have seen that the voices of poets, *samazen*s, and Sufi teachers – many of whom are Muslim – utilize the legacy of Rumi, be it through poetry or ritual practice, in their work beyond Sufi communities and ritual spaces. Their audiences and consumers may be non-Muslims – they may not even be Sufis – but for my interlocutors, it is not the viewers' status or practice they are concerned with. Rather, their work and their commodities are informed by their own intention, practice, and philosophy. The rest, as they say, is up to Allah.

Consuming Rumi

As happens with most prophets and charismatic religious leaders (Buddha, Jesus, and many others), Rumi's legacy continues to transform and inherit new meanings even while remaining largely constant.[57] Such shifts were evident during Ataturk's secularization project when he was founding the Turkish Republic:

> In the case of Turkish intellectual history, orientalism and self-orientalism also operate together as forms of objectification defining the episteme of the time. As a consequence of the newly emerging and continuing discourses in the episteme of early Republican Turkey, allegedly one of the spiritual founders of the Ottoman Empire, Rumi was interpreted under the influence of new ideas, and once again, he became the myth of the new Turkish Republic, ultimately signifying the fact that historical myths and figures might be re-imagined, re-worked, and represented in novel ways, and re-framed with new discursive strategies within a new episteme conditioned by a novel configuration of power relations. (Saglam 2017: 426)

Mapping some of Rumi's ever-transforming legacies in Canada helps us understand what is attracting spiritual seekers, Sufis, and Muslims to Rumi. Doing so also tells us what consumers are consuming. This chapter has recentred the voices of Sufi practitioners as well as the producers of some of these expressions and commodities. Their personal, spiritual, and religious practices, whether they are Muslims or not, indicate that Rumi and his legacies are sustained in various ways, such as through poetry (*ghazal*) and meditative practice (*zikr* and *sama*). However, such practice is not restricted to private spiritual praxis; it permeates public, secular, and economic spaces so that Rumi and his legacy also effect the broader work of poets, performers, artists, teachers, and store owners. The private informs and defines the public, and the public presentation is a taste or a small reproduction of the sacred ritual. In some instances, it is mutually transforming. In the end, what do my Sufi interlocutors think about Rumi and his presence today? I asked AttarJafari this, and he replied:

> It's because you know Rumi as a historical person, was a person who was born 800 years ago and died 746 years ago. So that's not very important to us. But there is a message that he promoted that is timeless and universal. And that's what attracts hundreds and hundreds of people, followers and others. Why is he so popular? Because our society, this day and age, needs the messages that unites us instead of separating us. And he begins his book by complaining about separation. So, things like *Masnawi*, like Rumi, when you read him you know him ... but then you're a black, white, brown, Christian, Muslim it doesn't matter. You're like this is talking to me and you feel it and you relate to it. You don't have to be a Muslim, right, to affiliate with it; everybody affiliates with it because he's spoken a universal beautiful language of love, harmony, and beauty. And he was a linguistic master so he was capable of pouring out 65,000 lines of poetry ... First intellectuals caution, who is this Rumi? Oh, he is a poet, how many lines of poetry? Oh, 65,000, I need

to find out what he said. It's not twenty or one book, you're an academic and you know what has happened there. So, then you find out, oh, okay, and even Hafiz had five thousand *ghazals*, what you see here, seven or eight hundred of them ... This is where what happens in these things of *sama*, you become ... calm and your body becomes the body, your eyes become the eyes in which it sees and your ears become the ears in which it hears. This is in Quran also and we put it in practice. And that's why Rumi is very popular, because he gives you very basic methods to experience that and you relate to it.[58]

For AttarJafari, Rumi's popularity fills a spiritual lacuna in the present day, because he is accessible. His message of "universalism" and of "love, harmony, and beauty," which is the message of the Quran, informed his practice of Sufism, which manifested itself through the poetry that continues to resonate with so many today. This is the message that informs AttarJafari's practice as a Sufi and a *samazen*. He says it is a message that is available to everyone regardless of race, gender, or religious orientation.

Janmohamed also reflected on the significance of Rumi and his legacy in the present day, especially from her perspective as a poet:

I mean ... people [are] always going to be people. I'm sure he was co-opted even in his own time. That's the problem with language. I just think about so many, not just poets but figures in history and what they stood for and what they said, and then you have an interpretation of it and somehow it gets co-opted into a movement that may have been the antithesis of what they were speaking about. It's an expected reality but at the same time, if I'm going to see a Rumi quote and I know it's not Rumi, I'm going to call it out. I mean, I'm not going to be a vigilante and go to all of these people's Instagram accounts [laughter]. But it's interesting that even if it's an inaccurate quote of Rumi's ... there's still this desire and this hunger – so we're looking at the result but what's the symptom, why are people drawn to this? Maybe because something is lacking in our world and people need meaning, and this is an easy way to feel something meaningful. It doesn't end there, but for a lot of people it does. That's all they can hold, and so on one hand it really frustrates me, but on the other hand I have to keep humbling myself to understanding and holding compassion for that part of myself that was also searching for meaning. We all have lived experiences that inform how we arrive at our practice, and we all have limitations. If I'm really being compassionate, then maybe there's a better way than being dismissive. Maybe it's more like, "Hey, you know what, I think you'd really enjoy this collection of poetry translated by so and so," which would contain more accurate translations of Rumi or Hafiz, for example. Can we not approach it with some kindness so that we are actually encouraging people to learn more without deterring them or shaming them so that they just feel completely disengaged altogether? And isn't that the point of this work, to keep that door open?[59]

Even Janmohamed, as a poet, struggles with some of what she sees on social media and with the misquotations of Rumi's poetry. Like AttarJafari, however, she feels that it is more helpful to take a step back and ask, "What's the symptom, why are people drawn to this?" She feels that it is a spiritual thirst or longing that brings people to Rumi, even on social media. She does find mistranslations or misquotations of Rumi's poetry problematic. Even so, she tries to be more mindful of how she responds to what she justly feels are inaccurate translations of Rumi.

Ghazi, a leader of the Vancouver Rumi Society, also reflected on this process, especially in light of Barks's and his relationship to Bawa Muhaiyaddeen:

> And then so if we come to Rumi, you know obviously one of the major critiques that gets made is of Coleman Barks, and people say, "Oh yeah, well he watered down the Islam here or he took out the Muslim context there." First of all, I'd say when I read Coleman Barks, there's still so many Muslim words in there ... It's not as though it's all stripped away. And I think to be a really good translator you have to be so strong in the target language, which he is. He's like this really wonderful English poet. So, yeah, I think there's real transmission in what he does and people are receiving it and there is something really deep and genuine. I mean there are just too many people I speak [to] whose life paths are transformed or who have like real moments of realization in encountering his work. As you know, it was Bawa who came to him and said, I don't remember now if it was in like reality or in dream reality and super reality, but [he] said, "Do this, right." So, I have deep love and respect for him. I've met him and I think his work is ... a real treasure and I don't think he's claiming that it's a purely literal translation of Mawlana. That's not what he aimed to do, so you have to look at what he aimed to do and I think his intention was sincere ... that it's kind of become this industry ... I think it's like the power, the overflowing fountain energy power of Mawlana and his teaching, you know. Like first of all, how does something like the *Masnavi* pour out of you in the first place? ... But if it does, how can that not continue to have this energy? It's an ocean, it's like waves, it's a life force, and it's spread and I think it's emerging now in this powerful way because we're at certain points in globalization and communication and the world's become smaller and the needs become greater and who knows what ... We can analyse, like, globalization ... of everything ... language, culture, technology, economies that have made it possible. So, I wouldn't be so critical of that.[60]

Ghazi responds to some of the critiques that have been directed toward Barks, highlighting Barks's relationship with Bawa as well as reaffirming that Barks never claimed to be translating Rumi; rather, he rendered him in his own interpretations. Much like AttarJafari and Janmohamed, Ghazi reiterates that the message of Rumi resonates with people today. A Rumi "industry" has developed owing to the broader social, political, and capitalistic moment we exist in, but this does not diminish the "energy" and "force" of Rumi's words, which continue to spread after hundreds of years. Ghazi went on to address another issue – that of Muslims restrictively claiming Rumi:

> I also think that sometimes when I read Muslims who want to claim Rumi also, I just feel it's being done from this ego space ... like "he's ours!" You know? And so there's this verse in the Quran, it says Ibrahim was not a Jew and he was not a Christian but he was *muslim*, hanifa *muslim*. He was a hanif and a *muslim*. And there's some people who read it totally wrong, they read it like, well, he wasn't a Christian, he wasn't a Jew, he was a Muslim, like he belonged to us. And you can't really read it that way because if you look ... I mean, Ibrahim was before the Muhammadan dispensation which gave us the Islam that people recognize as, whatever, five daily pillars and a whole bunch of forms coming then out of whatever *hadith* and you know the *sharia* as it developed and all of the other disciplines that coalesced and made what we think about Islam as Islam now. So clearly *muslim* is being used in a different sense and the whole point of the verse is, like, Christians can't own him and Jews can't own him, he was one who was surrendered and he was beyond these labels, right. So, I feel ... this just kind of impetus to claim Rumi as Muslim is actually really denying that more universal strain that's in Rumi which is I also think such a deep outgrowth of the Quranic message and which is so important right now, which is so critical at this juncture because it's not just Muslims that need Mawlana, like the earth and the sky and the waters and humanity need Mawlana. And to expect that all of humanity is going to become Muslim in the particular orthodox form that you practise is actually not even something that God taught us. *We made you into nations and tribes that you might come to know and recognize one another* [quoting from the Quran]. So, recognizing one another doesn't mean everybody becomes Muslim. It's very clear that that's not divine intention, that's not reality.[61]

Ghazi is cognizant of how Barks is perceived and is sympathetic to his work, but she is also critical of some Muslims' claims to Rumi that restrict his "Muslimness." She draws from the Quranic tradition of prophets, such as Ibrahim (Abraham), who are read as *muslim*. She points out that *muslim*, in the literal sense and as it appears in Quranic tradition, means one who has "surrendered" – it does not necessarily mean Muslim in the traditional religious mode as we understand it today, as one who performs regular *salat* or fasts as a doctrine of Sunni Islam. This distinction is vital to her understanding of Rumi, so as not to restrict how we engage Rumi either. She speaks to how Rumi's poems help us better understand the Quran, just as AttarJafari has relayed. Yet Ghazi is aware that the relationship between Rumi and Islam is beginning to be erased in this an era of Islamophobia:

The Politics of Consuming Rumi   177

> I think absolutely there's Islamophobia that is present and a desire to strip away [Islam] ... it's really important to recognize that, yes, Mawlana has this beauty and it's a beauty that's emerged from the wellspring of the Islamic tradition. It's emerged from the Quran; it's emerged from the teaching of the prophet. The entire *Masnavi* is a *tasfir* [commentary] on the Quran. It's a Sufi *tawil* [inner meaning] of the Quran, which is why you have this whole volume called *ayat Masnavi*, which is just the verses of the Quran that are in the *Masnavi* in a dictionary of those verses.[62]

For Ghazi, then, Rumi's poetry and his legacy are essential for understanding Islam, and vice versa. For her, Rumi's poetry is a commentary on the Quran. We cannot comprehend his universalism unless we understand Islam through the Quran. Still, she is very clear that she is not making presumptions about how the teachings and transmissions of Rumi manifest themselves in real practice in the people she meets; experience has taught her that such judgments are inherently dubious. She is interested in deep connections to Sufism and to Rumi, and these may unfold in various configurations, so it is difficult to limit what Rumi and his legacy can and should look like today. Still, that does not mean that one should ignore issues of "appropriation" or avoid posing a "decolonial critique." She concludes:

> Mawlana is living authentically in so many spaces that we wouldn't know to look, you know? So I don't make a lot of presumptions. But you know the decolonial critique, I mean all of these kinds of things, this is really important ... We have to also make that critique and we also have to be aware of appropriation and these things. So I think when we're looking from that perspective, it's good, but I do get concerned about like looking at it from a narrow perspective on what Islam is, you know? And that's a mirror for the other thing because it's a narrow perspective of what Islam is that leads people also to be kind of like, well, "This is so beautiful, it really can't have much to do with Islam, let's just remove Islam from it." That's just like a catalyst to get rid of the essential teachings, it's deeply, deeply webbed together. It's like a content vessel, how do you separate them?[63]

Ghazi's comments, which I have quoted here at length, succinctly capture some of the complex issues of the contemporary legacy of Rumi and the nexus in which it operates. It is embedded in a contemporary postcolonial context in which systemic Islamophobia is rampant (especially in Canada), and thus the de-Islamicization of Rumi falls under a broader postcolonial critique of power and appropriation, a discussion with which I began this chapter. Just as these debates have been unfolding, a simultaneous argument has broken out about what constitutes being Islamic, especially in relation to Sufism (Ahmed 2015). Ghazi, like AttarJafari, Omid Safi, and Baraka Blue, contends that one cannot understand Rumi without understanding Islam and the Quran; at the same time, Rumi is necessary for understanding Islam. Furthermore, one cannot restrict Rumi, who cultivated a precise balance between Islam (particularism), Sufism, and universalism, a balance that my interlocutors understand as traditional Islam. This message, which defines the Islam and Sufism of Rumi, is a message of unity and love, one that reverberates today among non-Muslims. It is also a message that many Muslims, like Ghazi and AttarJafari, recognize as Islam. It is necessary to identify these various factors that are operating in the creation of the Rumi industry, for as Ghazi explains, they mutually inform one another.

Majid Buell, the *shaykh* who holds the post passed to him by Loras in Vancouver, reflected on Rumi and his legacy today:

Everyone and their mother has a version of what the whirling dervishes are, and the same with the poetry ... I'm on Facebook and I get a lot of quotes and I just wonder, who the heck actually said it? Because they don't quote the line and you know, they don't quote which volume, line, you know, whether it's the Persian version and this and that ... So there's been all of these things about Shams Tabriz, well, I'll quote him if I like the saying but I don't believe Shams said it. It's the same with Rumi, I don't know whether Rumi said that or not. It's in English, I can't tell. So the most popular poet, so called, in North America is American Rumi, I call him, he's not even real. You know, it's made up, which is great, because there are some good lines, but I mean people just quote things these days, it's like birthday cards ... And if it's profound enough, and deep enough, maybe somebody will take it and go to the bank with it, you know, and do something with it.[64]

For Buell, and for some of his fellow dervishes, the poems are meant to be an entry point to a deeper practice they can pursue if they are serious. Buell points to another essential reality, however. For him, the purpose of Rumi was less about bringing attention to Rumi or the practice of turning, and more about drawing attention to his teacher and master, Shams. A realization that came to him when he visited Shams's tomb, which some believe is in Konya near Rumi's tomb:

So I'm trying to visit Shams, I get about one third in and it was like somebody had plugged me into a hundred million volts. I was literally shaking, I was vibrating, I couldn't move, I was like this and I was trying to open my arms and I'm stuck. It went on for about two or three minutes, constant. Just whhhooom, whhhhooom, whhhooom, I don't know if it was an energy download or upload or whatever. But it almost burned out my circuits and I thought wow, that's him. So, I've always appreciated that contact and whenever I read, you know, about Shams, that's what I recognize, I don't recognize any of the kind of stories that are going around you know, well he's gay and that, you know. That doesn't mean anything, it's Shams made a connection. Shams gave the connection to Rumi, and then Rumi wrote it down. And that's the sequence I understand, 'cause if Rumi hadn't written it down, we would never have known Shams, and Shams was the connection and where Shams got it from, I have no idea.[65]

Conclusions

All that the critic can do for the reader or audience spectator is to focus his gaze or audition. Rightly or wrongly I think my blasts and essays have done their work, and that more people are now likely to go to the sources than are likely to read this book. (Ezra Pound 1918: 13)

The debates that persistently surround Rumi's life and legacy, and his poetry and its transmissions, revolve around the question of authenticity. These different claims about authenticity are broadly embedded in a contestation over the nature of Sufism as a tradition. There continue to be deep critiques regarding how Rumi is "translated." Many people contend that the renditions of Rumi's poetry by people like Barks have purged its Islamic legacies and Muslim cultural influences. Safi calls this process "spiritual colonialism," which in many ways is a continuation of the Orientalists' extraction of Sufism from Islam so as to claim it (Ali 2017). In this regard, some hold that there remains a disconnect between the historical Rumi, who was a Sufi scholar and a Muslim, and today's Rumi, who has become a New Age icon in the west. Yet even while Rumi's Islamic heritage is being erased in the west through the process of translation, his universal appeal is growing. People from various walks of life have developed an affinity for Rumi's poetry and philosophy. As understood by my interlocutors, that philosophy asks his readers to forgo any differences and walk on the path of love, a path that is accessible to everyone. It would seem, then, that there is a persistent tension in the legacies of Rumi that we experience today. That strain oscillates between a particularity that locates Rumi within Islam and a universalism that he espouses as his ethos and that is based on Islam while seeming to transcend it. Rumi cultivated this supposed tension. Of course, the fact that there is even a perceived tension is because of negative stereotypes of Islam in the public imagination, which finds it hard to reconcile that the admirable Rumi could be Muslim. In our scholarship, we continue to negotiate these frictions between the particular and the universal Rumi as the various expressions associated with him (and Sufism) place them in the worlds of contemporary Islam and Sufism, NRMs, New Age practices, popular spirituality, and the spiritual marketplace. This chapter has mapped some of these expressions, commodities, and praxes in the social, cultural, public, and capitalistic spheres, from poetry performances to public presentations of turning and the selling of Rumi teas.

This chapter has tried to disentangle some of these layers. In the process, further complexities have emerged – for example, with the figure of Barks himself, who catalysed the spread of Rumi's poetry in North America. Barks locates his own spiritual practice in Sufism – likely a non-Muslim universal form of Sufism – owing to his connections with Bawa Muhaiyaddeen. Barks's *Illuminated Rumi* (1997), which is a number one bestseller, involved a collaboration with Michael Green, also a student of Bawa Muhaiyaddeen and an American Sufi artist, who resides in Pennsylvania near Bawa's *mazar*, or burial spot. Those who have been at the centre of publishing and spreading various interpretations of Rumi to an English-speaking non-Muslim audience have been practising Sufis themselves, such as Barks and Michael Green (as well as Kabir and Camille Helminski, and *shakyka* Fariha al-Jerrahi of the Nur Ashki Jerrahi Order in New York City). They locate Rumi and Sufism within a universal ethos they recognize as a true reflection of Islam. The voices of Sufis in Canada captured in this chapter have followed a similar trend. Through their private and ritual spaces and communities, and in public-facing events and spaces, from Rumi festivals to poetry sessions and the Rumi Café, Sufis in Canada are presenting a form of Islam and Sufism that centres the poetic legacies of Rumi and at times other Sufi poets such as Hafiz as well as South Asian Sufi luminaries. They speak both to Muslims and to non-Muslims, but in many ways they exist in spheres of consumption and popular culture that include literary "translations" of Sufi poetry, Rumi consumption on social media, and the production of Rumi-based commodities. At times the thresholds of cultural appropriation are hard to discern, though they are quite entangled with NRMs and spiritual but not religious (SBNR) trends, communities, and practitioners. Still, to view all expressions of Rumi in popular culture or in the marketplace as inauthentic or weak expressions of Sufism is not productive, as this chapter has indicated. The dismissal of these Sufi artists and presenters would result in the erasure of the voices of many of my interlocutors in this chapter, who are firmly located in the practice of Sufism via Islam. These expressions of Sufism in various public and private spheres capture the complex lived realities of religious praxis and identities. As Lofton (2011) reminds us, we need to realize that commodification, consumption, or popularization does not equate to secularization or to erosion. Rather, these affinities are an invitation for us to rethink our notions of pieties and rituals in religious studies.

What is more, these issues of legitimacy and erosion were not the primary concerns for my interlocutors. For Sufis who centre their service and devotion to Rumi, what matters is their intention, service, and social activism, which hinges on an internal relationship with Rumi. They understand that those who are meant to come to the practice (i.e., turning or Sufism) will come. Suffice it to say, then, that the politics of Rumi's reception are not simple, because they point to broader contestations over the parameters of how to experience and practise Sufism, and Rumi is just one example of this broader discussion (see chapter 1). Therefore, we would err if we dismissed these historical, theological, political, and philosophical realities, ones that highlight deeply entangled cross-cultural expansions of Sufism across various spheres, be they sacred or secular, public or private, commodified or decommodified. Far better, then, for us to seriously consider the various registers of Sufism in the global west as highlighted in Canada in this chapter. The reception and translation of Rumi in Canada emphasizes one of the many shifting topographies of contemporary global Sufism, Islam, and popular spirituality and the overlapping spheres of various expressions and praxes they exist across and within. If we were to dismiss the legacies of Rumi today, even in popular culture and especially in the work, commodities, and productions created by Sufis themselves, as mapped in this chapter, we would miss elements of Sufism as it is unfolding before us and the historical processes that led to this moment. It would also further abstract Muslim expressions of Sufism and Islam and suggest that Muslims, such as some of those engaged with in this chapter, are not themselves seekers of spirituality or producers of Rumi-based commodities.

Chapter Five

Gender Dynamics in Sufi Rituals, Praxis, and Authority

The previous chapters focused on tracing *sama* through ritual, cultural, and aesthetic expressions in various spaces. This final chapter considers some broader gender dynamics in ritual contexts and also among some of the Sufi communities explored in this book. I first consider how gender norms, especially around the place of women's bodies, have informed Sufi experiences for women. Here, I draw on classical Sufi textual traditions and explore how gender appeared, for instance, in Rumi's poetry and how it later influenced institutional developments within the Mawlawi Order in Turkey. The second half of the chapter considers some of the gender dynamics I encountered during my fieldwork in ritual contexts. In my discussion of *sama* I focus on how the mixed-gender nature of the practice in Canada has led to various transformations and also complicated negotiations between Sufi communities. These Sufi communities include those that trace their lineage back to Feild in Vancouver, as well as others in Toronto, such as the Jerrahi and Rifai orders, that have had to negotiate gender norms and inclusion in their ritual practices. Another gender dynamic that is unfolding in Canada relates to the role of Sufi teachers who are women (*shaykha*). The last section of the chapter focuses on the religious and spiritual authority of two *shaykha*s who are actively leading Sufi communities in Canada: Seemi Ghazi, whose voice has been present throughout this study, for she is one of the institutional leaders of the Vancouver Rumi Society; and Ayeda Husain, a leader in the Inayati Order, based outside Toronto. I centre their voices and narratives to capture their lived experiences of Sufism and explore how they negotiate their gendered identities, be it on their own Sufi path or with other Sufi communities in Canada and around the world.

The presence of *shaykha*s is not unique to the Canadian milieu, and neither is mixed-gender turning; however, as this chapter will show, women Sufi leaders have played a precarious role in the development of Sufism and Islam. In the following discussion, note how gender – especially the presence of women's bodies in ritual contexts – is used to demarcate notions of authentic or real

Sufism in relation to New Age Sufism or Sufism that is deemed non-Islamic or unorthodox. The role of women in Sufi ritual and in authoritative contexts hinges on various other factors, such as endorsements from men leaders in the community and the age of the women leaders. So it behoves one to remember that gender dynamics within Sufi communities are complex and are continually unfolding through various embodied realities that are both individually and collectively negotiated. This line of analysis is also a response to early scholarship on Sufism in North America, which has often presented Sufism as a more gender-egalitarian expression of Islam, especially in the west. As I have suggested in my previous scholarship, this framing is rather pejorative and assumes that Islam defines women's roles in particular restrictive ways (Xavier 2018, 2021). Sufism's relations with women, gender, and the feminine ideal are intricate precisely because there are many configurations through which gender has been conveyed historically, be it at the social or cultural level (i.e., women more as biological entities) or at a metaphysical level that views the feminine (vs the female) as the highest cosmic principle. As such, gender in/and Sufism historically has been ambiguous; it follows that expressions of gendered Sufism in Canada will have retained some of these intricate contestations.

Gender and Sufism Historically

Gender dynamics in the context of Sufism are complex: one can approach gender and women in Sufi history down at least two analytical avenues, as summed up by Maria Massi Dakake:

> There are two aspects to the presence of the feminine in the Sufi tradition … First, there is the metaphysical aspect – that is, the role that the feminine principle plays in symbolic and mystical interpretations of the nature of God and the world. The second aspect of the role of the feminine in the Sufi tradition has to do with the historical role that female practitioners of the mystical path have played in the development and history of Sufism. (2006: 131–2)

The study of Sufism and gender historically can lead to the excavation of anthropological or social experiences of Sufi women, such as through stories of saints and hagiographies. In these texts, the idea of women or the feminine was used as a trope, especially in literary traditions (see below). At the same time, the notion of the feminine was at times tied to a cosmological or spiritual state of being rather than a social or biological identity. These various possibilities coexisted in the early textual traditions of Sufism, which were written when Sufism was being institutionalized in the classical and medieval eras by mostly literate elite men (Ayubi 2019). These sources and their frameworks of women and gender have continued to inform how women and gender are framed in contemporary Sufism. Thus, as Dakake (2006) adds, "a more feminine mystical view of God does not always entail an active role for human females in the worldly institution of mystical tradition" (132).

For instance, one can engage literary and historical sources, such as hagiographies, to understand the lives of early Sufi women. But in the process one soon finds that men were the authors of most if not all hagiographies or memorials of Sufis. So we learn more about their intentions and biases in their narrations of Sufi women than about the women themselves (Cornell 2019). A good example here is Rabia al-Adawiyya (d. 801) and her legacies, both as myth and as history. Though she predates the period when Sufism becomes institutionalized as a movement, she is often evoked as an early saint or a proto-Sufi. She captures the precursory traditions of asceticism and mysticism that would come to define Sufism's genesis. In her monumental study of the life and legacy of Rabia, Rkia Cornell (2019) writes that Muslim classical textual traditions of Rabia reflect the impressions and orientations of the authors of these hagiographies, more than the figures they presented:

> When medieval male writers of Islamic hagiography used gender-based stereotypes in their depictions of Rabi'a, she is often portrayed as emotional or even hysterical. For example, Ibn al-Jawzi depicts her as crying, weeping and fainting. Such images reinforce the long-held Muslim stereotype of women as deficient in intellect and emotional stability. Such portrayals undermine the image of Rabi'a al-'Adawiyya as a wise sage and cause the reader to treat her aphorisms skeptically. (251)

Yet other references to Rabia capture her as wise teacher. For example, Sufyan al-Thawri (d. 778) writes the following in reference to her: "Take me to the teacher (*mu'addiba*). For when I am apart from her, I can find no solace" (qtd in Cornell 2019: 33). Rabia then is portrayed contrarily in literary traditions, as an ascetic, lover, Sufi, and ultimately as a myth:[1]

> Despite the myth that was created, a "real" Rabi'a of Basra actually did teach, did practice asceticism, and did develop a mystical doctrine that was based (at least in part) on the love of God. This historical figure of Rabi'a is what emerges from the earliest accounts. In historiographical terms, to assume that Rabi'a was nothing but a myth would be to deny the very possibility of using tradition as a source for history. (qtd in 218–19)

In such entries, the inclusion of early mystic figures like Rabia in hagiographical traditions comes with qualifications so as to contend that Rabia's gender was not a hindrance to the ultimate goals of the path of Sufism. The most famous account of Rabia was written by Farid ud-Din Attar (d. 1221), the Persian biographer and a Sufi. Attar writes:

If anyone says, "Why have you included Rabeʿa [Rābiʿa] in the rank of men?" my answer is, that the Prophet himself said, "God does not regard your outward forms." The root of the matter is not form, but intention, as the Prophet said, "Mankind will be raised up according to the intentions." Moreover, if it is proper to derive two-thirds of our religion from Aʾesha [ʿAʾisha], surely it is permissible to take religious instruction from a handmaid of Aʾesha. When a woman becomes a "man" in the path of God, she is a man and one cannot any more call her a woman. (qtd in Küçük 2015: 107)

There are many hagiographies of early proto-Sufi and Sufi women; often, though, these sources' authors had to negotiate the stories of the women they included, sometimes by turning against their gender. This writing strategy or trope often entailed tethering them to a Sufi figure who was a man, such as a husband or father; other times, these women Sufis were presented as asexualized or non-gendered (male) in what Arezou Azad (2013) has framed as "reversed genderizations." Still, Cornell (2019) notes that "most Sufi women are depicted in hagiographical accounts as supporting the status quo, including gender distinctions, rather than opposing them" (253). Despite all this, historians have highlighted that "from the second/eighth century onwards, there were Sufi women who directed convents, that is, a *tekke* or *zāwiya*, or attended a *tekke* and succeeded to the position of spiritual director or shaykh after performing the duties of the shaykh of the *tekke*" (Küçük 2013: 112). One such female Sufi was Hafsa bint Sirin (d. 719 or 728); also, Ibn Arabi references Zawiyatu Aisha in Damascus and Dar al-Falak in Baghdad; both were spaces for Sufi women (Küçük 2015: 112, 114).

Another approach to understanding the role of gender in classical Sufi traditions is through the idea of the feminine principle. Metaphysical or cosmological traditions of Sufism have called attention to the ways in which the "feminine" represents a cosmic principle of Sophia or wisdom, which may have been perfected in figures like Maryam, the mother of Isa or Fatima, the Prophet Muhammad's daughter.[2] These instances point to traditions developed by classical Sufi thinkers like Ibn Arabi and Rumi (see below), who argued for the metaphysical necessity of Eve for Adam's capacity to truly know God. Adam was the first human to truly love God, but he needed Eve, without whom he would not have had the capacity to encounter the Divine, according to scholars like Saʿdiyya Shaikh (2012). In Sufism, then, a gender binary is cultivated, especially in metaphysical discussions of masculine and feminine principles, though these gender binaries are not necessarily defined in biological terms. William Chittick (1983) understands these complex portrayals of women in classical Sufi traditions of Rumi's poetry in this way:

> Like other traditional metaphysical and cosmological teachings, Sufism divides the realities of existence into active and passive, male and female, yang and yin.

Thus the Creator is masculine and active in relation to creation, which is female and receptive. Within the created order, the Universal Intellect or "Supreme Pen" (*al-qalam al-'alā*) is active, writing the objects of its knowledge in the Universal Soul or "Guarded Tablet" (*al-lawh al-mahfuz*), thereby bringing the individual creatures into existence. Likewise heaven or the spiritual world is active in relation to earth, the material world. (163)

The binary of masculine and feminine resulted in a tiered metaphysical and social gender hierarchy, wherein the feminine gender was elevated and praised as the ideal (Lover) or as the ideal spiritual state on the Sufi path that all must achieve (both men and women), while at the same time a social and biological female (i.e., socially constructed women) was disparaged. Women represented the lower *nafs*, or the lower soul.[3] Rumi, then, like many of his medieval colleagues, conformed at times to reductive tendencies as they related to women (for example, writing "First and last my fall was through woman"), while also subverting gender norms (Schimmel 1992: 96). One encounters these paradoxical trends in Rumi's poetry when he writes: "In the view of the intellect, heaven is the man and earth the woman: Whatever the one throws down the other nurtures" (qtd in Chittick 1983: 163). Chittick adds that "If man were to rejoin his primordial perfection, his intellect would once again play a masculine role, and his ego would live in harmony with it as its feminine mate" (164). Here, we see Rumi tether the ego to Eve and thus to a woman: "If duality were to leave our heart and spirit for a moment, our intellect would be Adam, our ego Eve" (qtd in 163). Chittick understands Rumi's logics this way: "Since the two sexes reflect these two universal principles of activity and passivity, men have a certain innate affinity with the intellect, while women are more directly coloured by the ego. Nevertheless, this does not mean that any given man is more dominated by the intellect than any given woman, since here it is primarily a question of form and not meaning" (163).

Often in Rumi's poems, one finds men described symbolically as "spiritual warriors," while women are "lackluster worldlings" (163). However, Chittick contends that the concept of men and women is not necessarily tied to sex or gender but rather to states of being: "Rūmī's verses often follow the symbolism of this cosmological scheme, so that 'men' are symbols of the saints and 'women' are symbols of the unbelievers. In other words, he (or she) who is dominated by the intellect is a 'man,' while he (or she) who is dominated by the ego is a 'woman.' Hence 'men' look at meanings, while 'women' are caught up in forms" (163).

Again, the gender binary of masculine and feminine is at times subverted, especially when referring to states of being, while at other times that binary reinforces a hierarchy wherein the woman is associated with an egoic (disparaged) state and the man is tied to rationality and "intellect." Chittick suggests that these tropes can be read in yet another way: "Although from this point of view femininity is negative because of its affinity with the ego and worldliness, from another point of view it is positive, since it reflects and displays God's beauty, Gentleness and Mercy" (163). Another poem by Rumi reads as follows:

> The woman always desires the necessities of the household – reputation, bread, food and position.
> Like a woman, the ego sometimes displays humility and sometimes seeks leadership to remedy its plight.
> The Intellect, indeed, knows nothing of these thoughts: its mind contains naught but longing for God.
> Know that your ego is indeed a woman – it is worse than a woman, for the woman is part of evil, your ego the whole. (qtd 165).

Rumi's concepts of masculine and feminine, and the symbolism of man and woman, often serve as literary tropes or tools in his poetry. They also reinforce important metaphysical and cosmological principles that are central to Sufi constructions of femininity. For Dakake (2006), then, "the feminine represents that which is deficient in man – his weakness and his desire for the world – with the world itself being symbolized as feminine temptress," and the feminine also comes to represent the *dhat* (Essence) (133). Thus,

> the *nafs* attracts men to the world with a false and fleeting, if manifest, beauty; while the *Dhāt* attracts with Its perfect, eternal, and infinitely unmanifest beauty. If the *nafs*, like a prostitute, is bold and quick to reveal ugliness that lies below here glided surface, the *Dhāt*, is silent and still, like a chaste woman, only revealing a glimpse of Its beauty to those who are patient and worthy. If the *nafs* hides its ugliness behind the veil of deceit, the *Dhāt* preserves its sacredness behind an existential veil. (134)

On the Sufi path, then, in order for one to access one's true essence (*dhat*), the lower self (*nafs*) must be annihilated. Only in this way can the tension be transcended between these spiritual processes, which often ascribe gendered norms in which women are the negative. Still, "given that both the passionate soul and the Divine Essence are connected with the feminine, human women could serve as symbols of both that which is lowest in man and that which is most sublime in God" (134–5). One encounters this tendency often, when certain holy female figures, such as Maryam, the mother of Jesus, are viewed as exemplars of the true metaphysical state of the feminine or even humanity: "Except rarely, when a Rustam is hidden within a woman's body, as in the case of Mary" (Rumi, qtd in 165).[4] In metaphysical terms, then, the state of the ideal woman is the ultimate goal of all humans. The state of negating the lower self (*nafs*) leads to the state of *insan al-kamil* or the perfected human being. Unlike *rajul* (men), *insan* refers to man in a universal human sense. It follows that, by some interpretations, this perfected spiritual state, which is the goal of Sufism, is accessible to all of humanity (Dakake 2006; Sharify-Funk et al. 2017; Schimmel 1992: 103). This is expressed by Rumi when he writes: "If one could become a 'man' by virtue of beard and testicles, Every buck would have sufficient hair and beard" (qtd in Schimmel 1992: 103).

In some Sufi frameworks, then, gender has not always been defined as a biological category; it has also been used to evoke metaphysical states of being.[5] These complex tendencies toward genderization in Sufism have led to an oscillation of gendered norms and praxis in both literary traditions and lived realities. So while women are disparaged and tied to the lower self, there are also occasions when women – or at least those women who represent the ideal feminine – are elevated and valued as exemplars on the Sufi path, as is obvious in the following extract from Rumi:

> The Prophet said that women totally dominate the men of intellect and
>   Possessors of Hearts,
> But ignorant men dominate women, for they are shackled by the
>   ferocity of animals.
> They have no kindness, gentleness, or love, since animality
>   dominates their nature.
> Love and kindness are human attributes, anger and sensuality
>   belong to the animals.
> She is the radiance of God, she is not your beloved. She is the
>   creator— you could say that she is not created. (qtd in Chittick
>   1983: 169)

So Dakake (2006) writes: "Thus from Rumi's perspective, woman could symbolize, on one level, the more negative qualities of humankind, and on the other level she could be seen as the 'radiance of God' even as the 'Creator' – perhaps alluding to the creative nature of the Divine *rahma*" (135). Other textual traditions capture further lived realities of Sufi women, through men's voices.

Ibn Arabi was known to have trained with various women teachers, including Fatima bt. Ibn al-Mutanna (d. 1198–99?) (in Seville, Al-Andalus) and Sams Umm al-Fuqara (Yasamin) (in al-Andalus). These two women were teachers with miraculous abilities (Küçük 2012b). He also references his family members, including his mother (Nur al-Ansariyya) and his two sisters (elder sister Umm Ala and Umm Sad) (489). Ibn Arabi was inspired by the figure of Nizam (Ayb al-Sams wa-l-Baha), who was the muse for his poetry *The Translator of Desires* (Sells 2021). Of Nizam he wrote that she was "a sun among the scholars," "a garden among the literary man," and "a distinguished woman from among the worshippers, scholars, and ascetic" (qtd in Küçük 2012: 703). Ibn Arabi explains in his *Diwan* that he invested fifteen people with initiation, of whom fourteen were women, and also suggests that one of his women students, a daughter of Zaki l-Din, was given permission to initiate other students, including men and *jinns* (spirits). This has led some scholars to hold that Ibn Arabi appointed her as his successor, adding: "Follow my way and style. My way is the Prophet's way" (Küçük 2012:707). Küçük writes the following of Ibn Arabi's teachings:

> According to Ibn al-'Arabi, women and men are equal to each other in everything varying from being the substitutes of God on earth to being the *Qutb*, the chief-saint at the top of the saints' pantheon. In fact, according to him, since woman is created from the costal bone of man, a woman is primarily a man and then a woman. And his love towards her can be deemed as "love of the whole world (*al-kull*) towards its part (*guz'*)." To him, a woman is the complementary half of man's gnosis of God. That is, without her, he cannot know of God completely, since half of God's attributes are located in the woman. (688)

These writings by Ibn Arabi on gender have driven much academic study on gender in relation to Ibn Arabi, with varying opinions among scholars (Murata 1992; Shaikh 2012). Of course, such examples of the elevation of Sufi women, even if it is by men, must be considered in light of other notable discussions about the place of women from that era, such as this statement from al-Ghazali in the twelfth century: "Consider the state of the God-fearing women and say (to your soul), 'O my soul, be not content to be less than a woman, for a man is contemptible if he comes short of a woman, in respect to her religion and (her relation) to this world'" (qtd in Formichi 2020: 23). Also, Al-Ghazali writes in his *Ihya*: "If your lower self finds it difficult to follow the example of these great male Sufis, now I will offer you some account of female Sufis. You should blame your lower self if it falls below a woman in religious and worldly attainments" (qtd in Küçük 2015: 110). Some scholars have argued that it was the institutionalization of Sufism during the medieval period that led to gender segregation and, in turn, to the less visible presence of women Sufi authority:

> After centuries of practicing asceticism, being disciples of great masters, and participating (sometimes leading) community gatherings of *dhikr* ("remembrance" of God), by the twelfth century women disciples and their male masters were compelled to explore new ways to properly and "legally" pursue initiation ceremonies in their tariqas without any direct touching. But by the fourteenth century social norms of segregation had taken over in the institutionalized mystic orders. (Formichi 2020: 24)

The institutionalization of Sufi orders, especially spatially in the medieval period, and the development of particular ritual and spiritual practices, such as seclusion (for retreats or *chilla*), may have led to the marginalization of women's involvement in these emerging Sufi practices:

> In early centuries ascetic Islam had privileged the "ethical vision" of the Qur'ān (to embrace Leila Ahmed's analysis), thus allowing women to thrive in their circles, but the institutionalization of Sufi orders, with the secluded life of the isolated *khanaqa*s and the paramount importance assigned to the relationship between teacher and pupil, women were pushed out of this world. (84)

As such, gender norms were implicated by other sociological factors that demarcated women as mothers, wives, and daughters, and it is within these gendered identities that Sufi women asserted their practices and roles (Silvers 2014: 29; Buturović 2001: 148). Amila Buturović (2001) explains that "Sufi women's participation in the mystical path was never simple: rather ... it was predicated on their ability to navigate ... social constructions – Sufi and non-Sufi alike – of gender and public/private space" (135). These opportunities for women's participation, even informally and in private domains, have been documented within the development of Sufism. The above shift in the role of Sufi women and in the authority they held was noted as a trend also in the institutionalization of the Mawlawi Order of Rumi.[6]

Women, Authority, and the Mawlawi Order

It seems that Shams, Rumi's spiritual master, felt that women were unqualified for the position of spiritual authority. In a conversation with Rumi, he reputedly said: "You mean that it would be better if a man becomes a shaykh. No, I mean much more than that. I mean this is definitely not for women. Either in place or out of place, I would change my faith in the Prophet Muhammad, had Hadrat Fatima [d.11/632] and 'A'isha become shaykhs. Thank God, they did no such a thing" (qtd in Küçük 2015: 125).

It would also seem, however, that Shams's opinion of women holding positions of authority (if this is indeed an accurate account), and even achieving sainthood, did not deter Rumi, and the Mawlawi Order that developed posthumously from investing women with spiritual and institutional authority. According to Küçük (2015), that order was "woman-friendly" because of Rumi's own position on women: "Rumi sees women as superior beings compared to men, citing the following verse from the Qur'ān: 'Fair in the eyes of men is the love of things they covet. Women and sons, heaped-up hoards of gold and silver'" (116). Notwithstanding his complicated and at times contradictory tropes of women in his poetry, Rumi had numerous women disciples, such as Nizam Khatun and Gumaj Khatun; he also seemed to have actively trained some of his daughters-in-law (117–18). Records indicate that "women in Konya used to gather at their homes and ... invite Rumi to their meetings because he was very well disposed towards them" (118). Sultan Walad, the son and a successor of the Mawlawi Order, had men and women students (Küçük 2012: 44). By the fifteenth century, "Sufism experienced much repression at the hands of the exoteric scholars ('ulamā'), partially as a consequence of urbanization" (Küçük 2015: 115). Women's public authority often depended on men (husbands, brothers, or fathers), though a few orders, such as the Mawlawi and the Bektashi, did continue to appoint *shaykha*s, even if only as ancillary leaders (Küçük 2015: 115). There were also women descendants or *inath chalabi*s/*chelebi*s, who are significant for the Mawlawi lineage (*silsila*) (118). Arifa-yi Khwush-liqa-yi Qunawi was the "first officially appointed female Mawlawi substitute" for the son of Sultan Walad, Ulu Arif Chalabi (d. 1319) in Tokat (119).

Also, the Mawlawi tradition includes stories of women substitutes who were appointed as *shaykha*s in instances when sons were too young to take over, as in the case of Dastina Khatun (d. 1630), or when husbands had retreated from their tasks as *shaykh*s, as in the case of Gunash Khan in the seventeenth century (120–1). There are also occurrences of *shaykha*s: Kamila Khanim became one after the death of Sultan Mehmed III, as did her daughter, Khwaja Fatima Khanim (d. 1710). Both were *shaykha*s of the Mawlawi *khana* of Kutahya (121). In her reading of Gölpinarli, one of the writers of the Mawlawi history, Küçük summarizes the overall position of women in the Mawlawi tradition:

> It seems that during the early years when the Mawlawī Sufi tradition had first spread to the villages, women were not excluded from society and were not considered inferior to men, at least in villages where the Mawlawī Sufis flourished. Nevertheless, due to the Mawlawī Order's direct relation with the state in the social context of the institution of charitable endowments (*waqf*) and its consequent connect with the position of Shaykh al-Islam, the Mawlawīs had to restrict women's positions in the order. After the seventeenth century, we no longer encounter any female Mawlawī *shaykh*s, just as we do not encounter any village *Mawlawikhanas* [centres]. In spite of everything, Mawlawī women obtained a fairly high position in the Mawlawiyya, at least in comparison with other Orders. Mawlawī women could wear special costumes and could perform the Mawlawī whirling ritual (*samā'*), sometimes even together with elderly Mawlawī Dadas [men] accompanied by the *nay* and *qudum*. But this was allowed only as a form of consolation: Mawlawī etiquette rituals had taken their final shape with men all leading positions, leaving no room for women to initiate others into the order, perform seclusion, or even enter Mawlawī ritual square. (126)

According to this understanding, then, much of the transition toward restricting women's authority and involvement in Mawlawi institutional and ritual life came during a time of contestation between religious authorities and Sufi teachers regarding the role of Sufism and the validity and theological appropriateness of ritual practices such as *sama*. Women's marginalization was a response to these broader theological and legal issues, a trend that is notable in Canada today (see below) (126). Still, occasional voices of Sufi women in the Mawlawi tradition can be found. Writing in the eighteenth century, Fatima Hanum, a student of Rumi and the mother-in-law of Sahik Dede, wrote the following *ghazal*:

> We have friendship with God and we are the Mevlevi!
> We are intoxicated by the mystical secrets revealed in the *Mathnawi*!
> Like the reed flute, we journey through *maqams* [spiritual stations]
> into spiritual awakening,
> Ecstatic longing leads us, bliss and love fill us!
> We follow the way of our Pir not as strangers,
> We are intimate companions on the caravan of True Reality!
> Without falling or rising, we transcend space into the unseen world.
> We are born travelers, and our camels are rays of light.
> O Fatima, be like the sun set on its solitary path!
> We have friendship with God, and we are the Mevlevi!
> (qtd in Reinhertz 2001: ix)

Also, miracles were associated with women in the Mawlawi Order:

> One of Rumi's chief disciples was Fakhr an-Nisa, known as "the Rabi'a of her age." One day, seven centuries after her death, it was decided to reconstruct her tomb. Shaikh Suleyman Hayati Dede, who was then the acting spiritual head of the Mawlevi Order, was asked to be present when she was exhumed. He later described that, when her body was uncovered, it was totally intact and the fragrance of roses filled the air. (Sultanova 2011: 46)

The challenge entailed in archival excavations of Sufi women and studies of Sufi textual traditions is that even in secondary literature (of the sort what I have cited above), scholars assert their own lines of inquiry, consciously or otherwise, the result being normative or "straight" (as opposed to queer) readings of gendered histories of Sufism (Kasmani 2022). More simply, modern-day studies of Sufism and gender sometimes say much more about scholars' orientations than about the topic being studied. My own scholarship is not absolved from this. It is useful, then, to foreground that we all bring our training and disciplinary subjectivities into our analyses of gender and Sufism (or any field of study, for that matter). Despite all the shifts in women's positionality in medieval and premodern Sufism and the varied approaches to studying these dynamics, contemporary studies of Sufi women continue to be shaped by gendered authority and ritual practices, albeit with some negotiation.

Living Traditions of Sufi Women

Women's authority has been formative for ritual contexts. It is often tied to sacred spaces or patriarchal familial connections. For instance, studies such as those by Razia Sultanova illustrate the cross-fertilization between Sufi ritual practices – especially of music and poetry – and Indigenous traditions of shamanism and Zoroastrianism in Central Asia. In her ethnographic research, Sultanova found that in Central Asian countries like Uzbekistan, women were at the forefront of these traditions, leading rituals, teaching, and training Sufi students while preserving oral traditions (Sultanova 2011). One notes similar ritual presence and authoritative roles for women in various other Sufi communities across the Muslim world, such as among the Bektashis, "an order in which women have always been integrated with men in ceremonies, many women have continued the tradition of composing sacred songs [*illahis*]" (Sultanova 2011: 45). And in Turkey, the Mawlawi tradition has a rich and complex history of women's presence, as noted earlier. Scholars have suggested that Rumi initiated women disciples and that some women practised *sama*.[7] The turning ceremonies were often separate for men and women, though according to some scholars there were rare instances when men and women turned together (Sultanova 2011). Women have been involved in various capacities in South Asia, especially in proximity to Sufi shrines, which have immense social, religious, and economic weight in South Asia. In her discussion of South Asian Sufism, Annemarie Schimmel writes that "in India, the lower Indus Valley and the Punjab are dotted with minor sanctuaries of women saints, either single individuals or whole groups (preferably 'Seven Chaste Ladies' or so) who are said to have performed acts of unusual piety. Some are venerated for their chastity, some were blessed with performing miracles and others are noted for their healing properties" (qtd in Formichi 2020: 251).

One often encounters women and non-gender-confirming people at Sufi saints' (*awliya*) shrines, for such sites have always tended to be more gender-inclusive than *masjid*s in regions such as South Asia (Kasmani 2022).[8] These expressions of piety by women and non-binary people may manifest themselves through *sama* performances but may also draw authoritative figures, such as women healers and spiritual leaders (Flueckiger 2006; Pemberton 2004; Abbas 2002; Kasmani 2022).[9] In other instances, women's authority in Sufism is relative to a familial man's authority who endorses their capacity to lead. Various past and present-day examples can be found of women's leadership that relies on patriarchal familial connection and authorization, be it through a father, a husband, or a brother, who provides an opening through association for Sufi women to maintain authority. One such example is the life of Nana Asmau (d. 1864), the daughter of Usman dan Fodio (d. 1817), a Qadiri Sufi *shaykh*, in what is modern-day Nigeria. Asmau was educated in Islamic traditions and texts. She trained her numerous students, especially students who were girls and women, in similar textual traditions. Her importance and fame travelled to the Americas with the slave ships, and her legacy is still alive among African Americans, especially in Pittsburgh (Boyd and Mack 2000).

Similarly, Joseph Hill's many publications explore the role of *muqaddama* (feminine of *muqaddam*, which means spiritual guide of the Tijani Sufi order) (2010, 2014, 2018). These women Sufi leaders are able to maintain authority because of their relationships to men family members (i.e., husband or father) who are *muqaddam*s. These women develop leadership roles, gather disciples, and even lead rituals, such as *zikr*, even though such roles were often limited to men in this cultural context. Hill (2010) highlights how women in today's Senegal, by oscillating between "domesticity" and "publicity," act as leaders, albeit at the discretion or with the approval of a Sufi *shaykh* who are men in the order (383). Similar studies have noted the importance of women Sufi leaders in Somalia (Declich 2000) and Indonesia (Birchok 2016). Turkey is another place where Sufi women's authority is prominent today. One sees this in popular Turkish *shaykha*s such as Nur Artiran of the Mawlawi Sufi Order, who succeeded her teacher Sefik Can (d. 2005), and Cemalnur Sargut Hoca, a teacher of the Rifai-Jerrahi order (see below) (Sharify-Funk et al. 2017).[10] In Canada, the two Sufi *shaykha*s profiled at the end of this chapter do not rely on familial patriarchal relationships to solidify their authority as teachers and leaders of public rituals and to mentor their students. This broader shift reflects some of the ways in which women's authority in Sufism is emerging in the North American milieu, where it is the discretion of a Sufi *shaykh* (usually a man) that enables women to take on authoritative roles, be it in ritual contexts or in leadership. That said, Sufi women's authority is not entirely dependent on them, as some other studies have indicated.

Contemporary Sufi Women in Canada

Some scholars and adherents of Sufism have suggested that Sufism in western Europe and North America is more gender-egalitarian as a result of westernization and not because of any of Sufism's inherent tendencies. The prevailing view that Sufi women in the west enjoy more access to their faith than women in Islam- or Muslim-majority contexts is far too reductive, in that it ignores the traditions of Islam and Sufism, as well as the experiences of Muslims and Sufis, especially women and gender-diverse people. The American milieu has seen a unique trend in women's religious authority, such as the formation of women-only mosque spaces, though these are not unique to the modern-day west.[11] Gendered religious authority has also emerged, with women and queer imams leading ritual prayers. Perhaps most famous here is the social justice activism of amina wadud, who led mixed-gender prayer in 2005 in America, having previously done so in South Africa.[12] Juliane Hammer (2012) posits that

> It is in the North American context that some women have risen to the ranks of prominent Muslim intellectuals. This development can in part be explained through different economic, social, and political opportunities for women, even though gender equality is an ideal more than a reality. It may also be explained by an Orientalist obsession with supporting purportedly oppressed Muslim women in their quest for "liberation" though this liberation may more often take the form of expecting women to shed their religious convictions altogether (103–4).

Sufi women's authority in North America sometimes arises within the ambit of broader Muslim authority and leadership, though only if the Sufi community is perceived as a Muslim one. In Canada, Muslim women's bodies continue to be viewed through an "oppressive" lens. Baljit Nagra (2018) has captured how "Muslim women are constructed as romantic heroines who are being oppressed by cruel fathers and trapped in backward cultures" (264). In Canada, as in much of the west, there is still an obsession with Orientalist and Islamophobic portrayals of Muslim women that links them especially to narratives of honour killings or to the global war on terror (264). In response to these global stereotypes, many nations have developed programs and policies to police minoritized racialized communities, including Muslims. The height of these racist interventionist policies in Canada was, perhaps, Bill 21 in Quebec, which was passed in 2019. That bill banned the wearing of religious symbols in various workplaces. This bill disproportionately targeted Muslim women and Sikh men.

A 2001 census survey of Muslims in Canada found that "only about one quarter of Canadian Muslim women were born in Canada, while three times as many were born abroad"; thus, immigrant Muslim women in Canada are also informed by their "socio-cultural and religious understandings of Islam, be it a Bengali, an Egyptian, a Somali, an Iranian, a Pakistani, or an Indonesian understanding of Islam" (Marcotte 2010: 357). The experiences of Muslim women in Canada, of course, are immensely diverse (religiously and culturally), and various organizations have been founded – such as the Canadian Council of Muslim Women (CCMW) – that focus on social justice and provide resources for Canadian Muslim women (358). Canadian Muslim women are politically and socially active. The nature of Muslim women's piety in Canada has yet to be closely examined. Some studies suggest that in some Sunni Muslim mosques, a trend is developing toward more restrictive gender norms. For instance, "in 1994, 52% of Canadian mosques had partitions between men and women, but by 2000 that number had climbed to 66%, maintaining an upward trend that does not appear to be declining" (359). Mosques are playing new roles in the diaspora. for they are sites that can help "develop and strengthen ... ties [to] religious and ethnic communities. The mosque often serves as a social and cultural center" (359).[13] In these discussions of Muslim women and their experiences in Canada, we only sometimes find representations of Muslim women's Sufi experiences, especially in ritual contexts. These discussions largely avoid acknowledging any sectarian diversity (for instance, that Ismaili prayer spaces have long maintained women's presence and authority). This chapter is a step toward addressing that lacuna. Of course, the dearth of discussion of Sufism in these particular discourses reminds us that Sufism is not viewed as representing Muslim women's experiences in Canada and in Islam more generally. People, including members of other Muslim communities, often examine the dynamics of gender regulation in Sufi communities to ascertain those groups' relationship to Islam – that is, as a means to measure a group's authenticity in relation to Islam. Sufi communities that are categorized as New Age or non-Muslim universal are often not seen as legitimate Muslim communities, which means that women's roles and authority in them are viewed as less problematic because they are not "really" Islamic spaces anyway. At this point one begins to notice how, within Sufi and broadly Muslim communities, women's bodies are used to bolster broader theological and religious arguments regarding the orthodoxy and legitimacy of Sufism itself.

Despite these external pressures, today as in the past we continue to find Sufi women active in various public and private roles. They work with other Sufi teachers (men), they travel, and they cater to their communities both locally and globally, publicly and privately. They have blog pages, Facebook groups, Twitter handles, and Instagram accounts. No longer are they simply being written about; now they are speaking for themselves, and those who are interested can access them directly rather than through mediators (usually). None of this is necessarily new; instead, it can be seen as a continuation of classical and premodern trends, as noted earlier. Some modes of leadership are innovative, largely due to new technologies. These tools have influenced how authority is dispersed and experienced, such as through social media. Turning to Canada, two overarching modes of women's role in Sufism can be seen, first of ritual involvement (namely during *sama*) and then of formal authority. The second half of this chapter considers some of these issues. They were alluded to in earlier chapters, but here I engage them directly and consider how various members of Sufi communities are negotiating these dynamics. I begin with ritual practices, especially of *zikr* and *sama*, and women's role in them.

Gender Norms and Ritual Practices

There are diverse ways to study gender in Sufism in Canada. One way is to reflect on gendered expressions during ritual performances. Sufi communities, such as the Naqshbandi Haqqani Kabbani in Vancouver and the Jerrahi Order in Toronto, maintain gender-segregated spaces, especially during community gatherings and in ritual contexts (i.e., *zikr*). *Shaykh* Nurjan Mirahmadi of the Naqshbandi Haqqani Kabbani discusses women's inclusion and access in his community, comparing it to that of other Muslim communities:

> We were talking about the traditional Islamic centres ... the Afghani Centre, the Pakistani Centre, and they eat and there's food and a lot of their programs are based on their cultural background and how they run the mosque is all cultural and women are in the corner or in the closet and men are *here* ... But that's not the traditional way and it's not the traditional teaching [of] Sufism. Its miraculous nature is diversity, and we have every type of background, so you have to first teach people good manners, so when guests are coming be good to them because they're all coming in new and they can see how we teach. The women are here and you get to see the teacher, they get to experience the teacher, and at a lot of Islamic centres they sort of block them away and that's not working very well, especially because this generation of ... girls are going to school.[14]

Mirahmadi explains that many of the issues of gender inaccessibility for women in Muslim communities in Vancouver are largely cultural in nature and do not reflect Muslim or Sufi gender practices. He views gender inclusion as a return to traditional practices of Islam and Sufism. Other communities, such as the Inayati Order across Canada and the Nimatullahi Order in Toronto, do not practise gender segregation during rituals or gatherings. The role of women in ritual and community life was one factor that led to a split between the Jerrahi and Rifai communities in Toronto.[15] *Shaykh* Murat Coskun has cultivated a gender-inclusive Sufi community. For him, neither gender nor sexual orientation has any bearing on one's journey on the Sufi path: "To me, *ruh* is sexless, *ruh* is colourless. So, every human being is a gift from Allah."[16] This egalitarian approach has drawn criticism from other Sufi communities in Toronto, specifically from the Jerrahi Order, a community with which the Rifais share some history: I asked Coskun about push-back from other Sufi communities with regard to gender-egalitarianism:

> They're not happy because ... we are changing ... The first ones always get the stones, you see? So, if we were a bit diluted, I call it like New Age group, nobody would bother us. But I follow the Sufi traditions strictly, the *zikr*, the prayers, the

fasting, the *shariat* [law], and I'm introducing women into the stage and it's our other half. So, the Jerrahis ... are always criticizing us since we left them because of this reason and there are other groups who say it is wrong ... I didn't come here to fight for women either. I took on the work ... that Kenan Rifai started a hundred years ago and I'm continuing it still and as you see, there is still a lot of work to be done for women to be accepted. But ... most recent criticism [is from] a professor in Turkey, and they had a big *shaykh*, that we are getting away from Islam by doing this, by taking women into our *zikr* and into our prayers. I sent a message back; I said tell them to strengthen their *iman* [faith] so when they see a woman they don't lose their relationship with Allah. I don't know how they took it [laughing]. I didn't hear from him. But it's that, at the end it comes to that, really, like, if your *iman* is so loose and if you see a woman and start thinking of those things instead of your connection to Allah, you'd better strengthen that because you cannot forever keep your temptations hidden. Do you understand?[17]

Coskun's biweekly gatherings include *zikr* and *meskh* (sacred concerts). At times, the gathering also includes *samazen*s, either those who are dervishes initiated with Coskun, such as his son, or those from Rumi Canada (like Farzad AttarJafari). During *zikr*, men and women sit in one circle together, with no separation of gender. This is different from what one sees in the weekly *zikr* gatherings of Jerrahi Sufi Order, where women sit in a separate balcony area and men sit in the main gathering space of the *dargah* in a circle with *shaykh* Tevfik Aydöner. Still, Coskun is clear that his Sufi order follows Islamic law and that if they were a "New Age" group they would likely not have faced criticism from other Muslim Sufi groups. Even Sufi communities in Turkey have reproached Coskun for his gender-egalitarian practices in Toronto. Coskun's wife (Talar), who often sits next to or near Coskun at the head of the circle, usually begins *zikr* with her soft singing; the group's singers are a mix of women, men, and non-gender-conforming dervishes. Interestingly, then, it is the following of Islamic practices, such as praying five times a day and fasting for Ramadan, that has brought this community's legitimacy into question. If they framed themselves as a New Age or non-Muslim Sufi order, they would not face pushback, because they would not technically be seen as real Sufis, at least by other Muslim Sufis. In this instance, women's bodies and gender norms serve as a litmus test for ascertaining the legitimacy of Sufi communities. This is even more the case in North America, where Sufi communities are judged by their degree of *Islamicness*. As Marcia Hermansen writes:

> To the degree that Islamic shari'a-based rituals are incorporated by hybrid or Islamic Sufi Orders, gender distinctions may become visibly operative [in] America. In the more strictly Islamic Sufi movements such as the Naqshbandi-Haqqani Order led in the United States by Shaykh Hisham Kabbani women participate in the gender segregated rituals but are not accorded formal leadership roles. Female

members of the leaders' families are viewed as the role models for women disciples. In the case of many American Sufi women, gender segregation and other restrictions on female participation are likely to provoke some discomfort. It is noteworthy that when Western women visit Sufi teachers in the Muslim world they are often accorded privileges of the shaykh's company and occupying male spaces denied to local females. The symbolic masculinization of Sufi women in American Orders may include adopting symbols of affiliation and authority that had been traditionally unique to men such as wearing special caps or robes. (Hermansen 2006: paras. 8 and 9).

Especially in Sufi communities in North America, women's role, presence, and embodiment in ritual contexts has become one means to ascertain a Sufi community's Islamic legitimacy, as Hermansen explains. So it would seem that where Islamic law and precepts are practised, gender segregation must follow. Sufi communities like Coskun's frame their understanding of gender norms within metaphysical Sufi traditions to support their practice. As Coskun explains, the essential soul or *ruh* is not gendered, and therefore the outward form should not matter. He traces his gender-egalitarian practices back to Kenan Rifai, a Sufi teacher who lived during a transitional period between the end of the Ottoman Empire and the beginning of the Turkish secular republic. Rifai's mother, Hatice Cenan, influenced his spiritual path in Sufism and introduced him to his spiritual teacher *shaykh* Edhem Efendi. Rifai's understanding of women was foundational for the inclusion of women in his community. He writes:

> For centuries so many things were told and written, and so many bloody adventures were attempted for the sake of women. Sometimes her name was used as a means of unbonded ambitions and was sometimes delivered as a flag to the hands of virtue. But none of the mentalities, or the philosophies have been able to appreciate her and to determine her actual place as much as Islamic mysticism. No matter how much the way is regarded by Islam is distorted due to personal benefits through the centuries, the value given to women can not be doubted. The greatest evidence of this is in the Kuran [Qur'ān]. In the Book all the addressing is given without any discrimination as "muminin and müminat, [believer] salhin and salihat" [pious] Mumine and saliha women are not separated from mumin and salih men. In the early periods of Islam, women accompanied men in every phase of social life. She even actively joined gazas (war of Islam) (in "His Understanding of Woman").[18]

Referring back to Rumi's poem (cited earlier) that places woman as a "creator," Rifai asks, "Where does the significance that Islam gives to women come from?" His answer is that it arises from her creative capacity, which is divinely endowed; he adds that "love (muhabbet) for woman is because of being able to witness God in mirror-like existence of woman" ("His Understanding of Woman").[19] As Coskun explained earlier, this is dependent on one's faith (*iman*), or, according to Rifai, on one's spiritual knowledge (*irfan*) ("His Understanding of Woman"). Rifai's mother, and Semiha Cemal as well, were formative teachers in his understanding of the role of women not only for the Sufi path but for all of creation. Today, this authority of women is seen in his successor Cemalnur Sargut, who was also a student of Samiha Ayverdi (d. 1993) and was taught by her mother Meskure Sargut.[20] In an interview, Cemalnur Sargut explained the role of gender in Sufi authority:

> I think the guide can be neither a woman nor a man. They must be someone who has surpassed the gender ... Of course, the woman will not lose their femininity and the man won't lose from their masculinity, but ... the guide can only be the one who does not bring their gender to the fore, the one who doesn't remember it. The one who knows their student as their child ... even if they are of the same age, the one who knows the student as a child and struggles for them ... in truth, I believe that a guide is one who serves their children. (qtd in Sharify-Funk et al. 2017: 237)[21]

Scholars have noted how Turkish Sufism, both in Turkey and in North America, has had flexible gender norms, as evident in Kenan Rifai's community, which includes successors who are women. A similar trend toward gender inclusion, in both ritual contexts and leadership positions, is evident in some lineages of the Mawlawi Order, as seen with the inclusion of mixed whirling by Suleyman Loras (and the Vancouver Rumi Society) and the Halveti-Jerrahi of Muzaffer Ozak, especially the Nur Ashki Jerrahi Order.[22]

Ozak came to the United States in the 1970s and established three separate branches: those of Nur al-Jerrahi (Lex Hixon) and Tosun Bayrak in upstate New York, and that of Ragib (Robert) Frager in the San Francisco area. Hixon's group (Nur Ashki Jerrahis) developed into a lineage that now has *shaykha* Fariha Fatima al-Jerrahi as its head in New York City; Aydöner's Jerrahi Order in Toronto traces its lineage back to Bayrak in upstate New York. So it is noteworthy that even within a predominantly Turkish lineage, the communities led by Coskun and Aydöner – one located in the Rifai tradition (but with early linkages to the Jerrahis) and the other located in the Jerrahi tradition – have developed different ritual approaches to women. Aydöner's community, which follows *sharia* practices and is rooted in Turkish Sufism, has a predominantly immigrant Turkish and eastern European Muslim membership. This ethnic and cultural composition of the Sufi community in Toronto may have led to more gender separation in ritual practices, as seen in public presentations of *sama* in chapter 3; the opposite happened with Coskun's community.

I want to add that though women may have a segregated presence and ritual involvement and no formal leadership opportunities in this particular Jerrahi community, it does not follow that the women who belong to this Sufi group do not find agency there. For them, to be included (even if segregated) is itself agentic, when considered in light of other Muslim spaces (be they Sufi or non-Sufi) where they are not readily welcomed or spatially privileged (a point made earlier by Mirahmadi). I do not want to dismiss these experiences, given that they are personally defined. In the end, according to Coskun, the metaphysical realities of spiritual states require one to look beyond social or biological notions of gender. He explained that the masculine and feminine qualities of Allah (*esma* in Turkish) need to be refined for everyone, not just for women:

> Since we accepted Allah contains everything that he created, he has masculine and feminine qualities. But on this planet for our survival we have to have the sexes so some of the *esma*s [names or qualities of Allah] are polarized in male and female, do you understand? Let's say the strength went to the men; the motherhood went to the women ... I'd give examples, a mother's love to a kid is unconditional. A father may not be like that ... But a mother, even if I go out and kill a hundred people, my mother would still love me. So, this is a quality of Allah that has given it as a present to females. And not only in human beings ... even in most mammals we see these qualities. So, it's an *esma* of Allah, obviously ... It completes the human being, male and female. So ... with our part in this we become one, a whole. So how can I deny my mother, my sister, my wife, my daughter from what I am enjoying the most in this life, or put them on a balcony and say you are not allowed here, just watch it? So, I added to the letter [sent to a Turkish critic], I said what kind of unity they are talking about that they cannot come together with their own other half. So, if I'm an alien coming to a *zikr*, I will only think that ... only male exists in these species, women are non-existent, and unfortunately, this is true in a mosque, this is also true in most *dargah*s. But it will change, *inshallah*, in your lifetime and your kids' lifetime it will change.[23]

Coskun follows metaphysical principles of masculinity and femininity as qualities that are the attributes or names (*asma* or *esma* in Turkish) of Allah that need to be balanced. This informs how he leads his community and ensures not only gender-egalitarian practices but also the inclusion of those with various gender and sexual identities. Coskun's Rifai Sufi order with its gender- and LGBTQIA+-inclusive space does not reflect the trend found in most Canadian Sufi communities, though groups like the Vancouver Rumi Society and the Inayati Order (see below) also confirm the inclusion of everyone, regardless of gender or sexual orientation. Coskun's community is rare in this way; even so, it is an important thread of Turkish Canadian Sufism as it is developing in the Toronto milieu. For him, it amounts to a return to truly *Islamic* (via Sufi) metaphysics, or a return to tradition, one that ensures these practices are sustained. Another ritual practice that has received some attention, and at times resistance, is the practice of *sama* and its gender-egalitarian development in Canada.

Gender Dynamics and the Tradition of Turning

Another thread of Turkish Sufi practice in Canada that this book has highlighted is the ritual of turning or *sama*, which is linked with the Mawlawi Order. In her discussion of this practice in North America, Hermansen wrote that "among these disciples are American women who are set on breaking the barrier to female participation in the *dhikr*. Traditional *shaykhs* from Turkey may be pleased that Americans are becoming dervishes but unsettled to be asked to give permission for females to whirl, at least publicly" (2006: para. 11). Feild and Loras introduced the latter practice to the west and let men and women turn together. Speaking of her time with Loras, Shakina Reinhertz (2001) reflected on her experience of this mixed-gendered turning. She understands the tradition as located within Rumi (in the stories of how he taught his daughter-in-law and granddaughters to turn) and highlights the role of women in the Mawlawi *tekke* (xxii). She also traces the genesis of this meditative practice in North America to Sufi Sam and the Dances of Universal Peace (xxii). Lewis was a student of Inayat Khan. Though Khan was a musician, he did not formalize the practice of meditative movement in his communities. Today, however, we see the emergence of *sama* as a practice in the Inayati Order as *samazens* have taken hand (*baya*) with Zia Inayat-Khan. Through Jelaleddin Loras, the son of Suleyman, the practice of mixed-gender turning continued to develop in North America. In Canada, the presence of the *shaykh* Majid Buell, appointed by Loras, and the presence of the *samazanbashi* or *sama* master Raqib Brian Burke meant that the practice would continue through a separate lineage. Burke trained his daughter Mira and students like Tawhida Tanya Evanson and Farzad AttarJafari, who now train men and women in the practice.

In the early stages of this mixed-gender turning, some Sufi leaders in the community were displeased. AttarJafari spoke to me about these dynamics:

> Yeah, cause we're very progressive and sometimes we break some rules but we excuse ourselves and we say may Allah help us understand and learn better. Dervish is dervish, there's no female or male in this school, I learned this. And yes, there is a little bit of controversial saying about this ... At the end of the day, that comes into play, and I get it, when you put it in an eastern culture and the context where men hardly get to hang out with women and once in a while you see them, sure, we want to keep them separate, here is irrelevant and there needs to be respect in a safe place and whoever I learn with we always have a boundary to respect it and so people feel safe and come and go. But then, yeah, there was a bit of resistance.[24]

For AttarJafari, in his understanding of Rumi's teachings he sees no duality, just unity (oneness), which pushes him forward in his gender-egalitarian practice of *sama*. He adds that gender segregation cannot work in Canada, where cultural and social gender segregation is not the norm, though it would perhaps work in some Muslim-majority ("eastern") countries. After years of practising mixed-gender turning, AttarJafari says that some Sufi leaders have slowly become more open to mixed-gender turning while others still have not. Some Sufi teachers do not publicly endorse mixed-gender turning but offer silent support.

Tawhida Tanya Evanson, a Black woman *samazen* in Canada, has encountered fascinating responses to her gender identity as a *samazen* in Canada and in Turkey. She holds that her experience of turning has been defined mostly by Turkish Sufism, which has made space for her presence. Of course, this does not mean there have never been moments of resistance to her presence as a woman *samazen*:

> Lots of stories there because I also lived in Istanbul for four years, so, yeah. Within the Rifai Marufi *tariqat* there are no restrictions and in fact *shaykh* Sharif Baba is known as the feminist *shaykh* in Turkey because ... the genders are not separated. Dervish is dervish, you know, it's already post-gendered. So, I think there was a great *kismet* and kind of meeting this group right away because in the encounters with other groups there's been really bizarre resistance and the feeling that how can you say *la illaha illallah* and separate and then name genders and separate them. So, for this one [me] there's just quite a lot of confusion there ... and it's also based on, you know, some rules that were meant for another time period and a lot of people want to hold those traditions so as to not lose anything, but in fact [in] holding on to those traditions much is being lost because there are traditions of separation....[25]

Evanson highlights that in the Rifai Marufi tradition, Sherif Baba Çatalkaya, whom she is initiated with, has been formative for her experience of a largely "post-gendered" experience of Sufism. Çatalkaya, who is based in Turkey and has a group in Seattle and many students in Vancouver (especially among the Rumi Society), has similarly cultivated a gender-egalitarian practice of Sufism, like that of Coskun, adding that this post-gendered experience is a return to traditional Sufism.[26] Both Coskun and Çatalkaya locate their communities within a Rifai lineage by way of Turkey. Evanson's experiences of turning as woman and as a Sufi are captured in her poetry collection *Bothism* (2017). The narratives relayed in this collection oscillate between "post-gendered" experiences of Sufism, especially in ritual contexts, and the reinforcement of gender segregation. The latter is the focus of one story in her collection *Bothism* (2017) titled "The Silent Dervish," in which the protagonist meets *shaykh* (Emre) in Istanbul and is invited to *zikr*:

So she went with him by car. They left Istanbul. Left the city. They drove and drove. One hour later they arrived at a suburban home. Nothing she knew before applied here. The front door of the house swung open and they were welcomed. She covered her head with her red shawl just as they were invited into a large living room. She sat down and waited. The room was full of Turkish-speaking strangers. They tried communicating with her but she could not speak the language and Sheikh Emre had disappeared. Dervishes are always doing that.

[...]

After the food and tea they invited everyone into the basement. She was ushered into a room full of women, covered, silent. Once all the women had been gathered there, the lights were turned off and the door locked. In the darkness and quiet the opening sounds of the *zikruallh* could be heard next door. *Bismillah ir-Rahman ir-Rahim. La ilaha illallah, la ilaha illallah, la ilaha illallah, la ilaha illallah* ... [In the Name of Allah, the most compassionate, most merciful, there is no god but Allah]. The chanting of the dervishes. A chorus of voices in worship pulsating through the building. Sonics bubbling up through the floors. Ceilings bursting. Mad male frequencies. Ecstatic frames of *daf* drums, clapping hands, headbanging, whirlings. The air alive, only half. In the room, the women sat without saying a word. Some were in personal prayer, swaying quietly back and forth, thumbing the *tesbih* [prayer beads]. But not allowed to be in the room with the men. Not allowed to witness the ceremony. Not allowed to drum. Not allowed to dance. Yin removed from yang. The circle and dot separate. The opposite of tawhid—unity. The red shawl fell from her head onto the floor. Her mouth opened but no sound came. Sheikh Emre was never seen again. (27–8)

Evanson indicates that there have also been clear traditions of gender-egalitarian practice in Sufism, adding that "dervish is dervish." AttarJafari and Evanson both express that at the end of the day, any outward form is a limitation, one that denies the unity in the practice of Sufism. Still, Evanson goes on to note that she has experienced similar gender segregation in some Sufi communities in Toronto as well. So it should be evident that even among the various Turkish-based Sufi communities in cities like Toronto, there is no uniform implementation of gender dynamics during Sufi ritual praxis. But the Rifai lineage as reflected in two Rifai orders in Canada – one through Kenan Rifai among the Rifai in Toronto, the other through Sherif Baba Çatalkaya – has cultivated a gender-egalitarian ritual milieu in Sufi communities in Canada and Turkey. Part of this points to the Rifai tradition of Sufism, which has historically maintained a countercultural and subversive antinomian Sufi praxis (Kuehn 2018). In North America and elsewhere, women's role, especially in Sufi ritual praxis, continues to be negotiated within some Sufi communities, just as it was in the past. In many of the Sufi communities discussed in this book, women are present and involved in ritual spaces and practices to various degrees.

There is another approach to examining gendered norms and practices in Canadian Sufi communities today, especially those that link their practices and communities to Rumi, and that is with regard to the presence of *shaykha*s, or women Sufi leaders. In this final section, then, I shift to the voices of two South Asian Muslim Sufi *shaykha*s in Canada, one in Vancouver and the other outside Toronto. By centring their voices and their narratives, I locate how the authority of the *shaykha* is another formative thread of Sufism in Canada, one that draws from traditional Sufi paradigms while situating them in a new setting.

Sufi *Shayhkas* of Canada[27]

As part of Nuit Blanche in Toronto in September 2019, a public presentation of *sama* was held at the Ismaili Centre to commemorate Rumi's birthday. Ayeda Husain, a teacher in the Inayati Order, sat at the head of the *zikr* circle and led *zikr* while the *samazen*s bowed to her (as the *shaykha*) and the musicians sat behind her. This gathering brought together members of various Sufi communities in Toronto, including the Nimatullahi *shaykh* and several Sufi members from other groups, including the Rifai Order. It is noteworthy that a woman Sufi teacher was leading *zikr* while joined in the circle by men Sufi teachers, live musicians, and *samazen*s (who were mixed-gender). In my decade of involvement with and study of Sufi communities in Toronto, this was the first time I had seen a *shaykha* lead *zikr* in a large public gathering. In Vancouver, Seemi Ghazi had held public Sufi gatherings; now Husain has formalized this same praxis and authority as a teacher of the Inayati Order in Toronto. Though led by Zia Inayat-Khan, the Inayati Order has many leadership and official positions held by women. Zia Inayat-Khan initiates women leaders to positions of authority and understands this as a continuation of his grandfather's and father's legacy. Of course, there are Sufi orders in the west, such as the Nur Ashki Jerrahi Order and the Threshold Society, that are helmed by *shaykha*s (Fariha al Jerrahi and Camille Helminski). However, Camille has not been officially appointed as a *shaykha*; instead she serves as the co-director of the Threshold Society. Her husband Kabir was appointed by Celaleddin Celebi (d. 1996), a descendent of Rumi who resided in Istanbul (Küçük 2015: 127). It is to Ghazi and Husain's stories that I turn next.

Seemi Ghazi and the Vancouver Rumi Society

I introduced Seemi Bushra Ghazi in chapter 2 while discussing the founding of the Vancouver Rumi Society. So here I avoid repeating her biographical details too much. As already noted, she is a student of the Rifai Marufi Sufi tradition (of Sherif Baba Çatalkaya), but she also draws her lineage from her inherited familial understanding of Sufism in South Asia as well as from her own academic and intellectual journey. All of this has informed her understanding of the traditions of Sufism, which include engagement with "Quakerism" from her time studying the Quran with Professor Michael Sells, as well as with Ibn Arabi, Cemalnur Sargut, M.R. Bawa Muhaiyaddeen, and Meister Eckhardt (c. 1328). Ghazi is also a renowned Quran reciter.[28] With John Brozak, Raqib Brian Burke, and Majid Buell, she is a founding member of the Vancouver Rumi Society, where she hosts and leads monthly unity *zikr* on the last Fridays of each month (see chapter 2).

Since COVID-19, these gatherings have moved to Zoom. The small community gatherings (fifteen or so) begin with invocations from Majid Buell and Ghazi's recitation of passages of the Quran; she then leads *zikr*. Ghazi has led in larger public presentations of *zikr*, such as those that are held during *Shab-i arus* (see chapter 3), where she has also turned in *sama*. The community she leads is religiously and racially diverse, and is a mix of various genders, though like Ayeda Husain's community in Toronto (below), it tends to attract more women, likely because a *shaykha* is at its helm. Ghazi is also involved in various Muslim women's spiritual organizations, such as the Women's Islamic Initiative in Spirituality and Equality. Overall, as with Sufi *shayhka*s in Turkey, who have maintained academic, pastoral, and spiritual roles, Ghazi holds various roles as a Muslim Sufi woman who also happens to be an academic and spiritual leader in Muslim and non-Muslim spaces. We spoke about all of this when we sat down for a conversation at her home in Vancouver. I quote our conversation here at length because it highlights some of her ongoing work in these various arenas and how she has navigated the complexities that have come with it:

> GHAZI: I am quiet about what I do, you know?
> XAVIER: Yeah. Is it because, I mean is it the path or is it ...
> GHAZI: It's many things. Yeah, one thing is that the real path is hidden, right? The real teaching is hidden, the real centres are hidden, and many of the real teachers are hidden. You know, so much of the work that we do happens in this very safe, it's the womb, it's this nexus, if you open it up to the light, then the process stops. You know what's happening inside the rose when it's closed and you don't want to force that open, right, and that [a] fetus can't be exposed to the world till it's ready to be born in a certain form ... I'm probably aware as a woman who traverses many worlds. So I have a really strong clear relationship with say the *masjid*, the Sunni mosques ... Well, I come from a very mixed family actually but we're Sunni, very traditional Sunnis. Like ... the heart of the heart of Sunnidon, Sunni *ulama*. That's what I come from and I really have this relationship that's very respectful and beautiful that I love with the kind of mainstream Muslim community. The Shia mosque will invite me to come and recite an entire *milad* [celebration of the birthday of the Prophet Muhammad].

So I have this relationship with them and then I'm also very much involved in universal Sufism and in that context, things are really different, the gender roles are different, you know. I work with Muslims who are LGBTQ. I really love doing spiritual work, healing work, and particularly through the Quran, talking about the Quran in those communities. So, a lot of this is probably you know there's definitely like some mutual non-compatibility in terms of the perspectives of people in these communities and so one of the ways I navigate that is just like quietly doing my thing, right. So jeopardizing that is, something. And then I'm in the academy and I'm not at the school of theology, I'm in religious studies and there's a secular, whatever distinction. So, for example, I have students there [University of British Columbia] and I'm teaching them classical Arabic language and literature and I'm teaching them the Quran and I'm teaching them how to step aside and put a parenthesis around their own belief system and let's take a look at this as literature, let's analyse the grammar, let's look at this historically, that's my role there. But then there's another context in which what I'm doing is really like pastoral work and so probably being low-key and under the radar temperamentally suits me but it also strategically suits me and it also protects that work ... We're supposed to be ... very, very humble about this and really be conscious that we're vessels. So, it's a challenge. And I'd say you've arrived at a moment where ... I'm thinking about legacy. So personally I've given so many talks, I give so many *sohbet*s [discourses], I lead so many *zikr*s, but there's this kind of, well, when I'm not there in the room, I'm really aware that media or a book like yours or YouTube videos are a way that you reach out and you also, if you have some light to share and you've been offered something, whatever we all have you can reach so many people and you can reach people in perpetuity and so that's an offering and one shouldn't shy away from that either, you know? That can be like a false humility or stinginess but to be strategic in how you do that is really important. And then many of the great teachers who are here among us, they wouldn't want their names or their faces or their persons to be revealed at all, but actually they're the heart of the heart of the work.[29]

In her reflections on her role and authority as a Muslim woman and a Sufi *shaykha*, Ghazi highlights some of the complex intersections within which her authority and life are delicately located. Some of these are particular to her personal social locations; others are informed more by her understanding of Sufi and spiritual work. For instance, her role as an academic (an educator of Arabic at the university) in a secular context and her active involvement as a Muslim in Sunni and Shia circles coexist with her leadership in universal Sufi groups, such as the Vancouver Rumi Society. She understands that her roles, especially as a woman, are not "mutually compatible" across these spaces; instead, they vary, which requires some deft strategic balance on her part. That is, she must negotiate how to exist and work in these diverse private and public domains that constitute her life. All of this locates her at the nexus of various expressions of academia, Islam, Sufism, and spirituality. Given that she is a South Asian Muslim woman, these roles are further complicated by her many identities, which all hinge on one another and can undermine relationships she has formed and, more importantly, the work she does as a pastoral and spiritual leader for her various communities. So, much of her early work in these capacities was done quietly, sometimes in order to protect herself, and this led to the compartmentalization of her activities.

At the same time, Sufism, like most mystical and spiritual practices, is a tradition. As with most mystical and spiritual traditions in a multitude of cultural and social contexts, there is a sense that one should not openly and publicly speak about spiritual "work" or practice. For example, to even identify oneself as a Sufi may be understood as oxymoronic, for a Sufi is one who is *not*. In this vein, a Sufi is often encouraged to hide aspects of their practice – such as prayer, devotion, and healing – and leave them unspoken. Many Sufis remain concealed and nameless in the work they do; they may even choose not to identify themselves, and as Ghazi explains, some of these hidden masters are at the "heart of the heart" of Sufism. During the research for this project, many Sufis in various communities, even other women teachers, declined to partake in this project for this very reason. They were supportive of my work, but they told me that their spiritual work was not something they wanted to speak about publicly. Even so, they encouraged me to continue what I was doing, viewing it it as a service to their tradition. Ghazi alluded to this earlier as she reflected on her legacy.

The first-generation Sufi leaders are growing old, and a new generation of them are leading the work in Canada. Ghazi contends that books such as this one, as well as social media, are valuable sites of institutional memory as well as a means to make teachings accessible to a broader and perhaps new audience. This sort of "memory work" is important especially when it comes to Sufi women's stories and voices, and it is especially important today, at a time when many historical details about Sufi women have been lost or are being purged for theological and political reasons. Ghazi in our conversation was alert to all this and was strategically navigating these metaphysical, social, cultural, religious, and gendered norms, as many early Sufi women have done in the past.

What ties together all the traditions and spheres in which Ghazi exists is the path of Sufism. She is located in a universal Sufi path represented by the Vancouver Rumi Society and the lineages of Rifai Marufi and the Inayati Order, both Turkish and South Asian American-Canadian expressions of Sufism. Ghazi talked to me about what it meant to be a Sufi teacher who is a woman, focusing especially on what drew her to Turkish Sufism and on her own unique location as a South Asian Canadian Muslim woman:

GHAZI: I think that one of the reasons that Turkish Sufism has been very powerful for me is that there's just so much space for women's leadership, and women's voices and just women's embodiment and also I am very intellectual and I live in my head a lot and I think that actually I was meant to be in a *tariqa* where there is this kind of like wild dervish sort of antinomian energy out on the margins and where people are playing big drums and doing these fierce, you know … *Ya Hayy Ya Hayy* [the Ever-living] kind of thing. That's because I come from this very refined Lucknow North Indian Mughal South Asian eldest daughter … an academic … my parents are both academics. My dad is like a *ghazal* poet, so there's all of this kind of refinement and elevation, but also, you know, we weren't supposed to dance … This whole way of holding your body, that was very controlled as well, right … So I think that being in this kind of path actually has released so many things for me. I mean it's allowed a certain kind of energy to flow and not just live in my cerebellum, or even not just in my heart … but to spread that if you think about *chi* or something, through my body in allowing me to actually go out in the world, and be more expansive and expressive. I think that's been really, really powerful … I know traditional Chishti South Asian Sufism, women, you have like stories of these amazing *bibi*s and *hajjah*s and women who did incredible things or had spiritual experiences, but there's just not the same space, I think, you know, for leadership. I mean you have amazing women, you have Abida Parveen … but some of it's just a function of the South Asian kind of class that I come from, or family … But I don't know if part of what's going on with Turkey [is that] it sits at this boundary of what we call east and what we call west. And so I think as a Muslim who has grown up in North America and who is herself, always living between these boundaries, it also makes sense that Turkish Sufism is something that has really spoken to me. But you know these *shaykha*s that we have, these people like Cemalnur and, I mean, and her teacher Samiha Ayverdi was also a woman … and she's just one. I think it's really powerful … that it's just like there's a space for me to be the one who gives the *sohbet*s and the teaching. There's a space for me to be the one who leads the *zikr*. I mean I've led prayer in my community for decades actually, but I just never talk about this because people won't understand, this is for the dervishes, this is for your dervish community, your sisters and brothers, you don't need to publicize this because look at what happened to Aisha, the wife of the prophet, if you know the story … where she was falsely accused of being unfaithful … the story where she lost her necklace and the story of the *ifk* [Quran]…

XAVIER: It's fascinating that that's the story that they bring up, yeah.

GHAZI: So that was the story, so just remember Aisha and the *ifk* and this is how people are. So, I talk about it now because first of all, I'm on the other side of fifty so you know I'm not vulnerable in the way that I was twenty years ago. And also society's moved a long way, like Muslim culture, and it's amazing, we've had amina wadud and now there's been studies of studies of studies of amina wadud in that moment and all of that. You have the women's mosque but I was leading the *namaz* in our dervish community and giving *khutbah* in our dervish community. A long time, at that time thirty years ago there was no kind of South Asian space that I knew of or this kind of thing was possible, you know.[30]

Ghazi draws from various Sufi ritual and historical contexts in her practice and leadership. Much of her work in the Sufi community in Vancouver draws from the Turkish tradition, for she has been initiated into the Rifai Marufi Sufi Order with the post-gendered Sufi framework utilized by Çatalkaya. Her experience of Turkish Sufism exposed her to *shaykha*s like Cemalnur Sargut (introduced earlier), who are active religious authorities in Turkey. Additionally, though she comes from South Asia, where women's presence has also been documented, even popularly with figures like Abida Parveen, the famous Qawwali singer, Ghazi's class and regional ancestry in north India likely further influenced how she experienced Sufism, which was in a sober or "refined" manner. Her encounter with Turkish Sufism, such as through the musical tradition of the Rifais and Mawlawis, in which the drum (*daf*) and the turning are prominent, was transformative for her new understanding of Sufism and her embodiment of it.

It is telling that in Ghazi's reflections on her own journey and on what has informed her particular orientation to South Asian and Turkish Sufism, she raises the story of Aisha, a wife of the Prophet Muhammad who was accused of adultery (known as the story of *ifk*), when she draws parallels to what she is doing as Sufi leader and the theme of shame evoked by this Quranic narrative. This highlights what Ghazi and other Muslim Sufi women face as figures of authority. Despite these societal challenges, she has been leading *namaz* and *zikr* for more than three decades in Vancouver and in various other dervish spaces, though until now she has been inclined to be more private about these aspects of her practice. Now, however, she has come to see that religiously and socially, North American Muslim society has changed, as a consequence of people like the social justice activist and retired professor amina wadud as well as the diversification of Muslim communities in Vancouver and Canada. Ghazi recounts that when she first came to North America from South Asia, American *masjid*s did not allow for encounters with Sufism. She found that many of the *masjid*s were far more influenced by the teachings of Abu Ala Maududi (d. 1979) or the Muslim Brotherhood, which were not the traditions to which she had been exposed during her unbringing.[31] Women-only mosques are active in cities like Toronto and Los Angeles, and figures like wadud have led public mixed-gender prayers. The landscape of Muslim practice in relation to gender is slowly changing, and this has left Ghazi feeling less vulnerable in terms of speaking about her role in these movements. Nevertheless, she notes carefully that it is her age that gives her the most security at this moment in her life: being a mother and "on the other side of fifty" has protected her – a sentiment that will be shared by Husain below.

The Sufism that Ghazi has come to understand and practise – that is, universal Sufism – reflects the Quran. Ghazi also has deep academic experience of Sufism that has been defined by some of the leading English-speaking academics in the United States, such as Michael Sells, Bruce Lawrence, miriam cooke, Vincent Cornell, and Rkia Cornell. During her graduate studies, she was part of a cohort of leading North American scholars of Islam, such as Siraj Scott Kugle, Omid Safi, Kecia Ali, Robert Rozehnal, and Rick Colby. She draws on these communities of scholars, often welcoming figures like Safi to Vancouver to lead in Sufi or spiritual retreats. Her encounter with her Sufi teacher Sherif Baba Çatalkaya has further solidified her understanding of the Quran, and in this, she does not separate her academic and religious studies. These collective realities inform her Sufism as well as her practice, leadership, and much more.

Ghazi added that the relationship between Sufism and Islam has long been complex, and even more so now that it is unfolding in the social and political milieu of Canada and America. During our conversation she raised the example of the Inayati Order and its South Asian lineage in the Chishti tradition:

> I always say that the Inayati Chishtis, what they're doing, it's not just this is some New Age, New World invention that we can be deeply Sufi and not Muslims. This is something that has been present in the Chishti lineage for a long, long time. So it's authentic to that Chishti heritage, you know. If someone, you know, wants a historical precedent, right ... that's why that's different than the other types of Sufism, where they might insist, well, you become Muslim and then you could be somebody's *murid* or their disciple, you know? And then Bawa ... he shows up as a Hindu guru, right ... So I do think that one thing one has to be careful about in the universal Sufism is that the ways in which it can erase Islam and the ways in which people can be Sufi and still have quite explicit or unexamined Islamophobia ... and that's kind of a painful thing to experience. I think I have a lot of patience with that, because of my commitment to the path, you know? So in that realm, I'll have patience ... try to do the quiet work of releasing that without calling out culture or whatever ... And that's been an interesting thing even just to see Pir Zia because he's brought much more of the Islamic... in his own personal practice and life and family and all of that. That's much more present than it was for his father, right? So that's a direction he's gone in and how that's impacted their communities is interesting.[32]

Being located as Sufi Muslim and leading a universal Sufi community that at times may be suspected of being "New Age," Ghazi is sensitive about tracing back some of the universal tendencies noted in contemporary Sufi communities, such as the Inayati Order and the Bawa Muhaiyaddeen Fellowship, to their historical precedents and traditions. She draws from the traditions of Chishti Sufism in South Asia, where there is historical precedent for pluralism, especially in the religiously and culturally diverse landscape of India, where Hindus, Muslims, Sikhs, and Christians have been drawn to Sufi teachers (Ernst and Lawrence 2022). She sees this as the legacy of Zia, who, unlike his father, practises Islam but also understands that the Inayati Order is embedded in and defined by the intersection of universalism and Islam. These elements of Sufism are complementary, not contradictory. These trends and tensions between the particularism of Sufism *in* Islam and the universalism of Sufism *through* Islam have been negotiated by various Sufi teachers, including, for example, Bawa Muhaiyaddeen, who had a predominantly Tamil Hindu following in northern Sri Lanka but a religiously eclectic following in America (Xavier 2018). The legacies and teachings of these *shaykh*s continue to be contested and negotiated through the institutionalization of their charismatic authority, often after their death, as we see in the case of the Bawa Muhaiyaddeen Fellowship. What Ghazi critically highlights is that at times, arguments over Sufism's universal tendency have been marred by explicit or implicit Islamophobia, which results in the desire or need to separate Sufism from Islam. This tendency was a consequence of European Orientalists' approaches to Sufism, which set one of the trajectories of universal Sufism in western Europe and North America (see chapter 1). In reflecting on these dynamics, especially in light of her own authority across these diverse spheres of Sufi expressions, Ghazi drew from a lesson given by Vincent Cornell, her former professor:

> I think about it through one of my marvellous teachers Vincent Cornell, he used to use Venn diagrams all the time for everything and I remember [him] having us do this exercise of "Well, what's the relationship of Islam to Sufism?" Right, and you've got like a Venn diagram where there's Islam and Sufism and there's areas of overlap and there's areas of not overlap, right. And then there's the Venn diagram where you have Islam is the big circle and then Sufism is the circle inside it. It's like, well, Sufism is the heart of Islam. And then you've got like the big Sufism one and then Islam's in the middle and Islam's the heart of Sufism, right [see figure 5.1]. I mean, and you know, my response to this is yes and yes and yes, like these are all legitimate ways of exploring this really complex relationship, you know? We're not going to pin it down to one thing and so much of it actually you do have to look at lands of origin. So if you look at a place like Morocco, I mean I've spent time there and if you talk to Muslims there and I could say somebody could be a Sufi and not a Muslim ... They were just uncomprehending ... that's nothing they've seen. They're like, well, it goes back to Muhammad, like how do you have Sufism without Muhammad, just like *salawat* [praise of Muhammad] is so important. So for them it's incomprehensible, you know. And while you had rich Jewish communities ... in Morocco and you've had Christians in Morocco, and it's been a

5.1. Visual of Ghazi's Venn diagram as discussed in her interview. Left to right, Sufism and Islam as overlapping, Sufism as the heart of Islam, and Islam as the heart of Sufism.

pluralistic society in that way, up until very recently ... But then you go to India and it's totally different. All of the shrines are like Muslims, Sikhs, Hindus, you know, the Sufi shrines all kinds of people from different faiths are there. I mean first of all, just talking about faith and religion itself, as a term, is so problematic, that itself is not probably a term that actually applies very well to Hinduism, you know, which never was an ism or to Islam.[33]

For Ghazi, much of Sufism's development has been defined by the localized cultural contexts in which it has been institutionalized. Here, she draws our attention to two examples of Sufism in Morocco in comparison to Sufism in South Asia. In the former region, the idea of Sufism without Islam may seem impossible to many local Muslims, while in the latter they would not find it so jarring, for Sufism has existed beyond Islamic contexts, especially in devotional culture at shrines. As such, for Ghazi, as explained by her teacher Cornell's exercise, all of these aspects, Sufism and Islam's shared practices, Sufism as the heart of Islam, and Islam as the heart of Sufism, are all ways in which Sufism unfolds today, particularly in the west. Defining Sufism in one singular way is not productive, she explains. Still, in the west – in Canada, for example – Sufi communities that are framed as universal are often also understood as (or accused of being) "New Age," as a means to signal to their lack of Islamic-ness (Xavier and Dickson 2020; Piraino 2020). It is precisely these narrow categorizations of Sufism that lead to approaching Islam restrictively and thus deem it unable to contain such diversity. Furthermore, the label of New Age, and the framing of a Sufi community as non-Islamic, are then tied to gender roles and praxis in a Sufi community, as was highlighted by Murat Coskun's experiences (see above). For Ghazi, her authority within and outside of Muslim, Sufi, and academic communities is informed by her understanding of Islam, Sufism (Turkish, South Asian, and North American), and her academic study of these traditions. These understandings of Islam and Sufism are mutually compatible. Another *shaykha* who who has found herself at similar crossroads is Ayeda Husain, a *shaykha* in the Inayati Order.

Ayeda Husain and the Inayati Order

After one of her biweekly Tuesday night *zikr* gatherings at her home outside of Toronto, Husain and I sat down for a conversation about her journey with Sufism and her experiences as a *shaykha*. She relayed that she began the journey to Sufism as a student in New York City in 1988. She was inspired to study and practise Sufism by her mother, who is a Sufi. She was initially connected with the Chishti-Sabri Sufi Order, a community she spent fifteen years with – a lineage shared by Ghazi. When she was ready to pursue Sufism more seriously, her teacher, who lived in Pakistan, passed away. Around that time, she learned about Vilayat Inayat Khan:

> I had a dream in which an old, distinguished man with a white beard was telling me to come to the mountains. I wasn't sure what it meant. Then a friend of mine told me about a Sufi retreat in the Swiss Alps. When I Googled the name of the Sufi group, I saw the same man I had seen in my dream. So I said okay, let's go. I booked my ticket. It was non-refundable. A month before I was supposed to be there he passed away [2004]. I was quite flustered. The ticket was non-refundable. I figured I'll just take a book, I'll hang out alone in the Alps and read. That is when I realized he had a son and his son was to be my *murshid*. When I saw him I knew ... this, I recognized that purity which my teacher had, which I had not seen after him. So ... again that was fifteen years ago and I have not looked back.[34]

Husain's dream led her to the Zenith Institute in the Swiss Alps, where Vilayat Khan hosted Sufi summer school seminars (some students in Vancouver spoke about these in chapter 2.) Husain's attendance led her to meet his son Zia, who had been named the *pir* of the Sufi Order International. Since this encounter, Husain has been on the path of the Inayati Order. She has hosted *zikr* gatherings in Lahore and Dubai, where she has lived and worked for nearly eighteen years. Her relocation to Toronto led her to host *zikr* gatherings in her home, where on a biweekly basis ten to fifteen students gather to partake in the teachings and poems of Rumi, Hafiz, and Inayat Khan, as well as *zikr* and meditation as taught by Inayat, Vilayat, and Zia Inayat-Khan. These gatherings at times include live music and singing, and they are usually followed by some food, such as soup. Though many of Husain's students are South Asian Muslim women whom Husain has known over her time in Pakistan and the Gulf States, she has also attracted new students who may have been initiated into other Sufi communities, such as the Rifai Sufi Order and Rumi Canada. There is no gender segregation during *zikr* – everyone sits together in a circle while Husain leads. Within the Inayati Order, Husain is a *shaykha* and also a *cheraga* or a minister, which gives her authority to lead in the Inayati Order's ritual of Universal Worship. That ritual tradition was instituted by Inayat Khan and has been central to the Inayati Order's praxis, as Amir O'Loughlin noted in chapter 2:

> As a *shaykha* I'm, well you know what a *shaykha* is, but as a *cheraga* you undertake a study for a couple of years in which you study the different religions of the world before you are authorized to conduct the Universal Worship service. It's something very unique to our order; in which you honour every religion of the world on the same altar. We have candles representing different religions and as we light them, we share readings from those scriptures and also present … either … a chant or a hymn from the tradition. So, it requires a fair amount of study. I am a *shaykha* because my *murshid* believes I have it in me to teach. I am a *cheraga* however because of intensive learning and research that have to be undertaken to gain a deeper understanding of the world's religions. It is a beautiful balance – as a *shaykha*, one is grounded in one's own tradition, teaching classic Sufism. As a *cheraga*, one is connected with all of the other traditions of the world. This is the philosophy of the whirling dervish, you know, you have one foot that does not move. It stays on the ground and the other foot moves. That means you are grounded in your own religion while being one with other religions of the world at the same time. In the Inayati order, this is something I can do, remain grounded in my own tradition while being open to all other traditions which other orders would not be, perhaps, open to.[35]

Like Ghazi, Husain is located within a South Asian Muslim milieu and has come to the universal Sufi tradition of Inayat Khan and his successors. In her role as *cheraga* and in her practice of leading Universal Worship, she understands the practice as that of the dervish, one who is rooted in one's own tradition (in her case in Islam) and gleans from all traditions of the world. This approach defines her understanding of Sufism and its accessibility to those who seek the path. Though Husain spoke at length about the significance of being a *cheraga*, who has a unique role in the Inyati Order, she found that the title of *shaykha* was not as dramatically important as many make it seem:

> XAVIER: Did you imagine that you would become a *shaykha* when you first began?
> HUSAIN: Never.
> XAVIER: On this journey?
> HUSAIN: Never.
> XAVIER: Okay.
> HUSAIN: I've been an academic my whole life. I was writing about Sufism, about others, yet always in an academic context … My teacher saw something and encouraged me to come out of the role of a student and become a teacher. I was sceptical initially because my style is casual and conversational and the excessive outer signs of piety that many eastern cultures place so much value on simply are

not a part of who I am. I was not sure I had the right personality. But I guess once again, my *murshid* saw something which I didn't ...

XAVIER: What does that mean to you to be a *shaykha*, especially in our contemporary contexts?

HUSAIN: You know, honestly, it's not a big deal; it just means you are a female teacher. I mean I was a teacher of literature ... I didn't have a name; they just called me Miss, whatever I was. So in Sufism I guess, it's so unique to have women teachers that you actually have your own name, but whatever another male can teach his *murid* [student] is what I'm teaching [my] *murid*. I don't think it makes me exotic or amazing or different, it just means that I'm a female teacher, that's all it means.[36]

Husain does not see her role as *shaykha* as exemplary in any way. A *shaykh* is simply someone who can teach students on the path of Sufism. She was hesitant when Zia encouraged this path for her, especially since she was an academic, much like Ghazi, and had been a journalist for more than two decades, having lived in New York, Lahore, and Dubai. Even so, she accepted the task. Since then, Husain has been a member of the Inayatiyya Advisory Council and has held numerous Sufi retreats within the Inayati Order and in Tokyo (with Buddhist monks) and also as part of a UN international delegation of spiritual leaders. She is the author of *The Sufi Tarot: A 78-Card Deck and Guidebook* (2022).[37] Like Ghazi, Husain maintains both public and private forms of spiritual and authoritative practice. She is firmly rooted in the Inayati Order and during our conversation spoke less about her involvement in Muslim or Islamic communities.

Husain recounted that while living in Dubai and leading *zikr*, she encountered resistance from many who attended her gatherings. She found that the anxiety over her authority was often tied to her age or to the fact that she was not over seventy-five. It seems that for both Ghazi and Husain, age long worked against their early practice of their Sufi authority, and that for Ghazi today, age is now working to her advantage. The issue of age seems to be tied to sexuality and beauty, which, as Coskun relayed earlier, is a limitation for those on the path as well as a reflection of their spiritual state. Using age as a vector for accessing space or enacting authority is not a modern practice, but rather a theological variable employed in the past by jurists in *fiqh* (Islamic law). This has its parallels in debates over women's access to mosques, in which age has been applied as a barrier to access (Katz 2014). This negotiation of age is also encountered in hagiographies written by Muslim chroniclers: women who had reached old age were no longer marriageable and were sexually unavailable, and apparently this signalled that they were now wise and sagacious – and, of course, that they were no longer restricted by the social norms surrounding domestic responsibilities. Even today, for some Muslims who are concerned about women's role as spiritual leaders, age seems to remain a mitigating factor in vetting women's Sufi authority.[38]

Husain had a Sufi centre in Lahore, Pakistan, for six years and also held meetings in Dubai while living there. In Dubai, another criticism she encountered was tied to her ethnic and linguistic identity. The latter was less about her South Asian identity and more about her lack of fluency in Arabic. She is an Urdu-speaking Muslim, and this was often seen as insufficient in Dubai. At times, age, gender, and linguistic identity collectively was used to delegitimize her authority while she led in Dubai.[39] Since then she has moved to Toronto (in 2018), where she has been holding gatherings. These gatherings are a parallel to the meetings of the Sufi Order International that Hafiz holds in his home in Toronto (chapter 2). In her years leading Sufi gatherings in Dubai and other centres, she attracted a mix of men and women students who were drawn to her authority. In her Dubai gatherings, she sometimes attracted slightly more men. In Toronto, where she has fifty or so regular members, her gatherings tend to attract more women. She feels that this is probably because people attend her Tuesday *zikr* through word of mouth. Her home is not in downtown Toronto (like the Rifais and the Jerrahis, and like Sema Space in Montreal). As a result, her gatherings attract an older, more suburban middle-class demographic. Still, she has established connections with various Sufi communities in Toronto, regularly attending their *zikr*s and community events. So her suburban location means that those who attend her biweekly gatherings must make a concerted effort to participate:

> You know, if I lived in downtown Toronto in a convenient location that people could walk to, things would be different. But I live [outside Toronto]. Coming to me is not easy so people are driving from Waterloo and Kitchener and some people from ... farther out ... more north, like North York, it can take them an hour and a half to get here. So I assume that they are serious. But there are also those who come for curiosity's sake, to see what's happening so they can go and tell people they have been to a *zikr* led by a *shaykha*, so on and so forth. It is the people who are regular and keep coming back that I believe are serious because it takes an effort to make it here.[40]

In the end, then, Husain's understanding of Sufism is universal – that is, based on a universal approach to Islam, much like that of Ghazi:

> Sufism is the heart of Islam as far as I'm concerned. The order which I belong to is universal ... There are no forced conversions as we believe that Sufism, which was formalized in Islam, has pre-existed in all formal religions. We believe that Adam was the first Sufi. The essence of Sufism, the sound of Hu [Him/Allah] which we believe existed [in] pre-eternity, has always been there. So to restrict it to Islam

would be to say that it didn't exist until fourteen hundred years ago which is not really accurate. It has always been there. I identify as being a Muslim and a Sufi and I believe that Sufism is at the heart of Islam. It's also the heart of every other world religion, it is the essence, it's the core of what every religion teaches which is your connection with the Divine. It is about understanding the essence of the message without getting obsessed with the form.[41]

Husain frames Sufism as a twofold process: it is located within the teachings of Islam, as the form, but also has an essence that transcends any religious traditions. Drawing from the teachings of Inayat, Vilayat, and Zia Inayat-Khan, the Inayati Order holds that the first Sufi was the prophet and patriarch Adam. Accordingly, as Ghazi expressed in chapter 4, the "dispensation" of Islam as a specific religious and cultural form cannot contain the essence of Sufism as a spiritual tradition that has always existed. In this sense, Sufi teachings are the essence of all religious traditions. It is this universalism that is captured in the practice of the Universal Worship that was first implemented by Inayat Khan and that continues to be practised by the Inayati Order. That is the practice that Husain leads. When I asked her about her experience of Sufism, especially as she has led Sufi communities and spaces in South Asia and the Gulf States, she told me:

HUSAIN: Sufism is definitely attracting people ... Rumi has become a Facebook meme and events with the word Rumi or Sufi are often packed. However, not everyone is there because they want to commit to serious or long-term learning; many are there to be able to say that they went and saw whirling dervishes, or took part in a Sufi meditation, or did *zikr* without really wanting to get into it any deeper. How deep one goes, or not, that is up to the individual.
XAVIER: Right, so it doesn't really matter what your background is, it's kind of your intentionality, your commitment to this path?
HUSAIN: Yes, yes, I mean you can be an orthodox Muslim who has grown up in an ancient, historical city with Sufi roots and have no potential or interest in going deep into the teachings. Or you can be a Caucasian Canadian from a small town for whom Sufism is so new and yet take to it like you have been thirsting for it your whole life, without even knowing what it was called. Again, it varies from individual to individual.[42]

In Husain's experience, then, the cultural container or identity of a Sufi practitioner cannot be a determining factor in ascertaining the legitimacy of Sufism, especially if one considers racial, cultural, or religious identity. She has had white Canadian students who have taken up the practice far more seriously than some Muslims who had been exposed to it growing up. In light of this, I asked whether she thought a unique form of Sufism was developing in Canada:

Sufism doesn't change, it is Sufism. It is the people, their receptivity and openness, that determines how it will be received. In Ontario, and Toronto especially, there is so much cultural diversity that even if you are coming from a different demographic, chances are you will have been exposed to enough, you know, eastern cultures to be open to it. This way it is not something you have never heard of or seen before ... When people live so close together in big cities, such close contact makes it harder to dehumanize each other. I feel very embraced as a female Sufi teacher in Canada. In fact I have been surprised at some of the events we've done, with four hundred, four hundred fifty people, with nothing but positive feedback.[43]

Since her arrival in Toronto, Husain has been welcomed and accepted into the Sufi scene there. Moreover, those who study and meditate with her are from across the spectrum, both Muslim and non-Muslim, and have diverse racial identities. She does note the general trend toward the popularization of Rumi, especially in a city like Toronto, where attending a Rumi event or seeing a *sama* presentation earns one social media capital. Nevertheless, these events sometimes can serve as a catalyst for those who are truly interested in seeking out Sufism and finding a Sufi teacher. Many of my interlocutors noted the same (see chapter 4). For Husain, then, the individual seeker must take the first step, regardless of one's religious or gendered identity, especially with a community like the Inayati Order, which practises a universal understanding of Sufism. Based on her understanding and experiences, Husain feels that Sufism remains the same at its core, be it in Pakistan or in Toronto. In Canada, the students she has encountered are of diverse ethnic, religious, and cultural backgrounds. However, their dedication to the practice has not necessarily changed. An attraction to Sufism can be catalysed by Rumi's presence in the spiritual and popular landscape; those who are spiritually interested may seriously pursue Rumi and his teachings, leading them to teachers like Husain or Ghazi. *Samazen*s like Farzad AttarJafari and Tawhida Tanya Evanson, and teachers like Murat Coskun, Seemi Ghazi, and Ayeda Husain, told me that exposure to Rumi, wherever it occurred, served as a starting point on the path of Sufism. According to these various Sufi leaders, Sufism does not discriminate against gender, religious, cultural, and/or racial identity. Some communities, like the Rifai, practise Islam; for other Sufi communities, like the Vancouver Rumi Society and Inayati Order, the practice of Islam is not a requirement. All of these variations have existed in historical and classical periods, and they continue to exist in Canada.

Conclusions

This final chapter mapped how gender norms around women are unfolding in Canada. The first half of the chapter described the patterns found in historical and textual Sufi sources and how women were portrayed in early and medieval writings of Sufism. This discussion was not meant to be comprehensive in any way; rather, it was meant to engage Canadian trends, especially moments of continuities and fissures in Sufi gender norms. Narratives of Sufi women in classical periods were complex, primarily because they were authored by elite literate men, with the result that we learn more about these men's biases than we do about the Sufi women they were writing about. At the same time, the metaphysical elevation of the feminine, as an ideal spiritual state and perhaps the only true spiritual state that one must actualize on the Sufi path, provided women with some social, ritual, and religious capital for negotiating some societal gender norms within premodern Sufism and Islam. Figures like Ibn Arabi were known to have studied with *shaykha*s, while others, including Rumi, wrote about women in contradictory ways. Notwithstanding these variegated representations, Rumi's Mawlawi Order, which developed after his death, included women as substitute leaders and allowed for some ritual access for women, especially if they had familial connections with a Mawlawi Sufi teacher. In lived practice then, especially in studies of ethnographies on Sufi women's presence in South Asia, North Africa, and the Middle East, various scholars have documented the negotiated ways in which Sufi women have maintained their presence during ritual praxis, such as at Sufi shrines, or religious authority, which often depended on a familial patriarch who endorsed such authority. The point here is that these roles have always existed, albeit informed by various factors such as class, age, family status, culture, and social location. This is the backdrop against which I have considered the development of Sufism and gender dynamics in Canada.

In the development of Sufism in North America and western Europe, it was at the discretion of a Sufi teacher who arrived in the west that gender norms and authority were implemented. Some Sufi teachers reinforced gender segregation in ritual practice and only appointed men as leaders, while others broke with some of these established gender norms and cultivated egalitarian gender practices. We saw some of the legacies of these shifts in this chapter, particularly with the practice of *sama* as it was first introduced by Reshad Feild and solidified under the Mawlawi Sufi teacher of Konya, Suleyman Loras. His students, including Raqib Brian Burke, continued this legacy of teaching men and women to turn in *sama* together, which has been taken up by his daughter Mira Burke and further institutionalized in new Sufi communities formed by Shams al Haqq Farzad AttarJafari (Rumi Canada) and Tawhida Tanya Evanson (Sema Space). Evanson's experience as a Black woman *samazen* was insightful: she pointed out moments of exclusion and inclusion she experienced in Turkey and in Canada. Murat Coskun, the Sufi *shaykh* of the Rifai order in Toronto, was adamant about the gender-egalitarian practices in his community, for which he has attracted criticism, including from Sufi teachers in Turkey. He reminds his detractors about classical metaphysical teachings in Sufism that the soul knows no gender or race. Sufi teachers like Coskun and Çatalkaya, and *samazens* like Evanson and AttarJafari, justify Sufi women's involvement in ritual practices by drawing from classical Sufism, especially metaphysical teachings about the essence of the soul. In evoking these Sufi teachings, they explain that gender-egalitarian rituals are ultimately a return to the essential traditions of Sufism and not necessarily a western (here, Canadian) innovation.

The second half of the chapter turned to the voices of two *shaykhas* I encountered over the course of my fieldwork on *sama* and Rumi-based communities and practices in Vancouver and Toronto. My documentation of their stories is an attempt to recentre the role of Sufi women (in Canada) and to further nuance how we think about gender, Sufism, and Islam in Canada. I quoted extensively from our conversations in this chapter in that hope that books like this one will serve as archives of women's stories in Sufism, in light of historical lacunae regarding such narratives. Also, the discussion has helped trace their particular experiences of gendered Sufi authority in light of their respective lineages, especially as South Asian Muslim women who lead universal Sufi communities. Ghazi and Husain pointed to the ways in which external variables such as age were a factor in the reception of their authority and leadership in various Sufi ritual and Muslim spaces. For instance, Ghazi highlighted that she found that age was used less often than before to challenge her authority. Like Husain, Ghazi has an international experience of Sufism, one that is defined by encounters with Sufism in Saudi Arabia, India, and Pakistan; both women continue to draw from those encounters as they teach Sufism in Canada. It is worthwhile to reflect on the ways in which these two prominent South Asian Sufi Muslim *shaykhas* in Canada are involved in actively cultivating Sufi communities and institutions with significant ties to the Inayati Order and the Rumi Society while drawing from South Asian and Turkish (Rifai Marufi for Ghazi) traditions of Sufism. Their communities include Muslim and non-Muslim seekers and Sufis alike. Both of them locate their authority in their Islamic South Asian roots while working within dynamic spaces that attract various members to their circles. Ghazi's authority is malleable, in that it exists both in Muslim and academic spaces and in inter- and intra-religious and spiritual communities, as well as in explicitly Sufi spheres, where she leads in prayers (*namaz*), *zikr*, and songs and gives discourses or *sohbets*. Husain's authority is more firmly located in the Inayati Order. They both lead universal Sufi communities and find that the essential teachings relayed in these communities are the crux of Islam.

One reality that has emerged throughout this chapter's discussion is that women's location in ritual practice and in authoritative positions is often used as a means to declare whether a Sufi community is Muslim or not, and whether its version of Sufism is real or not (i.e., New Age). Historically, discussions around the practice of Sufism have encountered this dilemma: women's prominence at Sufi shrines, for instance, often resulted in theologians or jurists condemning Sufi shrines as adulterated and, it follows, as heretical or innovative (*bida*). Notably, Ghazi and Husain both locate their Sufi communities as universal, as informed by their relationship with Islam and the Quran. As such, they have had to delicately balance their authority. Coskun's Rifai Sufi community is not framed as a universal order, though it is inclusive. It is a Muslim Sufi order that maintains gender-egalitarian practices. Earlier, he explained that his decision to uphold gender-egalitarian practices would have been better received if his group had indeed been a New Age one. Here, then, I return to the term evoked earlier by Evanson: "post-gender," which is conceptually a productive expression to think through and with. Metaphysically (and technically), Sufi teachings can allow for post-gendered expressions of Sufism, but Sufism, Canadian or not, is not always post-gendered in embodied realities, for it is coloured by social, cultural, religious, and political elements. There are Sufi communities that sustain gender-equal praxis, and others, like the Inayati Order and the Rifai Marufi community, that allow women leadership authority; these latter communities might be framed as post-gender. However, Sufi communities that are framed as post-gender are further scrutinized because their post-gendered practices are deemed part of New Age (or western) trends and thus non-Islamic. Yet as captured in the voices above, for many Sufi leaders and practitioners, post-gendered Sufism, be it in terms of ritual practice or of gendered authority, is a return to the essence of Sufism as found in metaphysical teachings of Rumi and other Sufi masters. According to their understanding, this form of gender-inclusive Sufism is inherently Islamic. From their perspective, these gender dynamics are neither a western innovation nor a result of popular spirituality. Nevertheless, many of my interlocuters in Canada have had to navigate these realities between notions of traditional Islamic and New Age (universal) frameworks in their praxis.

Epilogue

On 30 May 2020, many American cities were engulfed in flames as crowds took to the streets to protest the murder of George Floyd by the police. At the same time, various protesters took to the streets in Toronto in response to the suspicious death of Regis Korchinski-Paquet, who fell twenty-four floors from her apartment during an encounter with the police. In light of these two deaths, protesters across the United States and Canada called for an end to systemic violence and institutional racism against Black, Indigenous, and racialized people. Even during a pandemic, these protests and riots brought to the forefront an even more prominent and implicit/explicit virus that has existed since colonial times and has continued to rage in the form of the settler-colonial and carceral state. One day around that time, I logged onto the weekly *sama* that was being hosted by the Inayati Order, a *sama* I have been joining every week since the start of the pandemic, during which many Sufi communities' ritual and communal activities had shifted to Zoom and Skype platforms. Unlike previous sessions, the heaviness of this *sama* was felt, as close to a hundred people from around the globe (including Turkey, Cyprus, Germany, Canada, and the United States) logged in with me. The host of the *sama* and the moderators dedicated the gathering to George Floyd and all African-descended people who continue to suffer injustice. This point was echoed and affirmed by Zia Inayat-Khan, who joined the session. The *sama* went on to include the recitation of Allah's name of justice (*ya Adil*) and love (*ya Wadud*), in dedication to the BlackLivesMatter movement. The session concluded with a prayer of peace by Inayat Khan:

> Send us Thy peace, O Lord,
> which is perfect and everlasting, that our souls may radiate peace.
>
> Send us Thy peace, O Lord,
> that we may think, act, and speak harmoniously.

Send us Thy peace, O Lord,
that we may be contented and thankful for Thy bountiful gifts.

Send us Thy peace, O Lord,
that amidst our worldly strife we may enjoy Thy bliss.

Send us Thy peace, O Lord,
that we may endure all and tolerate all in the thought of Thy grace and mercy.

Send us Thy peace, O Lord,
that our lives may become a divine vision, and in Thy light all darkness may vanish.

Send us Thy peace, O Lord,
our Father and Mother, that we, Thy children on earth may all unite in one family.

Amen

The next day, 31 May 2020, a town hall was held on "Race, Justice and Love." The Zoom forum drew more than six hundred people. Participants dialled in from a multitude of global centres, including Norway, the United States, and Canada. The Inayati Order and many institutional leaders served as facilitators, some of whom were African Americans and/or Muslims.[1] Zia posted to his Facebook page the following statement: "George Floyd's invocation of Mama is a message, a door opening out onto a vast space suffused with love and justice" (29 May 2020 on Facebook). In his opening remarks to the forum, Zia connected George Floyd's last words of "mama" with his Aunt Noor's words of "liberté" before she was assassinated. Noor Inayat Khan (d. 1927), the daughter of Inayat Khan, had involved herself in the resistance against Nazi Germany by joining the British Special Operations Executive and was eventually murdered while in captivity. In Canada, Sufi communities like the Vancouver Rumi Society were reflecting on and praying for the soul of Ejaz Ahmed Choudry, a sixty-two-year-old man and father of four young children who had been shot and killed by the police on 20 June 2020. Choudry had schizophrenia. Many Muslim organizations had mobilized protests across cities, including Toronto. These difficult social moments and various Sufi communities' responses raise important questions about the role of Sufism today in Canada and throughout North America.

Spiritual practices such as Sufism are often viewed as a retreat from the world, but how do spiritual and Sufi communities step into the world and wed their spiritual and esoteric practices with activism while remaining not of the world, as the Prophet Muhammad taught? From the start, a formative thread of Sufism was its dervishes and wandering mendicants. These early ascetics lives were "a form of religious and social protest" (Kuehn 2018: 255). "Those who chose this particular anti-nomian ('against the law') mode of life and the associated bodily, social and spiritual disciplines, were often distinguished by bare feet, garments of animal skins, even dirt-caked nakedness, features which serve as symbols of wild social transcendence" (257). Kuehn continues that

> over one hundred years later a larger number of such wandering antinomians emerged as the extreme end of a spectrum of anti-conventional "mystical" behavior, often carrying paraphernalia such as a gnarled staff (*manteshā* or *'asā*), an alms-cup (*kashkūl*), trumpet made from the horn of an ibex or deer (*nafīr* or *būg*) and an animal skin (*pūst*). They emerged as a distinct movement concerned with denunciatory piety in the Muslim world which developed as a reaction against the gradual institutionalization of Sūfism. (258)

Traditions of rebellion and social deviance are also associated with the Qalandar Sufis, especially in their literary and poetic compositions, which evoke taverns and brothels to unsettle hegemonic societal norms. Some Qalandar Sufis even engaged in radical sexual practices, while others adopted celibacy. In the far extreme, they even engaged in bestiality (264; Karamustafa 1994). In thinking about the relationship between queer and religious/Islamic studies (Sufism specifically), anthropologist Omar Kasmani (2022) theorizes about notions of "unstraight" lineages, traditions, and practices, such as at Sufi shrines, to unsettle our normative approaches to the study of Sufism.

Sufis are often perceived as reclusive and pacifist, yet the history of Muslim societies highlights clear examples of how Sufism offered a template within which discussions of justice, peace, and love unfolded. Here we encounter anticolonial resistance, telling examples of which are the activities of Sufi orders like the Tijaniyya in North Africa and North America (Wright 2020; Miller 2020b). The Algerian military leader Abdelkader al-Jazairi (d. 1883) fought the French colonial occupation of Algeria in the nineteenth century. Of course, in the broad context of Islam and Muslim societies, resorting to Islam as a means to raise discourses of human rights (including feminist discourses) has been formative, as evident from groups like the Sisters of Islam in Malaysia and figures like Zainah Anwar and amina wadud. These dynamics signal the ways in which Islamic discourses and texts have been essential to social and political activism. Figures like Malcolm X (d. 1965), whose relationship with Sufism remains ambiguous, remind us that Islam and racial justice are deeply intertwined (Curtis 2019). These figures' social activism was informed by their understanding of Islamic teachings. Sufism has been central to many African American Muslim communities, as indicated by Rasul Miller in his history of African American Sufism (Miller 2020b), especially during the civil rights era.

There was a tendency in Bawa Muhaiyaddeen to work toward peace and justice through engagement in his immediate surroundings; this promoted non-violence and dialogue as means to foster mutual respect. This approach by Bawa has led scholar-activists like Saʿdiyya Shaikh and Scott Kugle (2006) to associate the tradition of "engaged Sufism" with Bawa, whose teachings are utilized in peace and conflict studies within Islam (Said, Funk, et al. 2001).[2] Vilayat Inayat Khan is another engaged Sufi whom Kugle and Shaikh discuss. Vilayat began the Hope Project in 1975 as part of his outreach program in the *basti* or neighbourhood where his father and Nizamuddin Awliya are both buried.[3] This initiative started off serving milk and food to children and women in the *basti*; in its present iteration, it also offers health and education networks, training, and mentorship programs for youth, as well as a kitchen staffed by hired locals who cook regular meals – a service they continued during the COVID-19 pandemic.

History also showcases how Sufi women have long been active in public and civic spaces. An important modern example is that of Noor Inayat Khan, mentioned earlier. Contemporary examples of such activism in public spheres include Dr Nahid Angha, the daughter of Moulana Shah Maghsoud, a twentieth-century century Persian Sufi of the Uwaiysi School of Sufism, who established a centre in Novato, California. Angha, from Tehran, helped found and lead the International Association of Sufism (IAS) and the international Sufi Women Organization (SWO) (Buehler 2016: 200). She engages in peacebuilding by speaking at various forums and conferences, such as the UN. Many Sufi women are active beyond formal Sufi communities and spaces; they include academics as well as translators of Sufi and Islamic texts, such as Laleh Bakhtiar (d. 2020), Gray (Aisha) Henry (of Fons Vitae), and Daisy Khan, the Executive Director of the American Society for Muslim Advancement (ASMA). Civic engagement, both local and national, and social justice activities have been deeply tied to some Sufi communities and practices, including the ones discussed in this book. Sufism is, then, a platform that enables Muslim and non-Muslim Sufis to advocate for social justice. An *engaged* Sufism informs both their spiritual and religious practice and thus their social and civic activism.

The Jerrahi Order of Canada led by *shaykh* Tevfik Aydöner placed service at the heart of many of its activities; indeed, Aydöner started the group in Toronto as a means to give back to Canada, a country that he felt had given him so much (see chapter 2). One section on this group's website is titled "Community Work" and features causes they have supported in the past, such as "relief work in west Africa":

> Jerrahi Sufis have a long tradition of community work and service to help humankind. From supporting fundraisers at IDRF (International Development and Relief Foundation), to raising money locally for Angela's Place, to helping internationally for community sponsored in the village of Irim in Burkina Faso. Jerrahis continue to help the village of Irum in Burkina Faso annually during Eid and throughout

the year. Jerrahis have raised money to help build water wells so they have clean water to drink. At Eid ul Adha, the village is provided with fresh meat to eat.[4]

Members of the Jerrahi Order can donate $150 (the price of one sheep) or $120 (the price of a share of a cow) to purchase meat for the people of Irim, Burkina Faso, as they did for Eid ul-Adha in August 2019. They have also supported the unhoused as volunteers and donors, providing food and winter clothes in Hamilton, just outside Toronto. The order has also been active in various interfaith activities throughout Toronto, such as the International Peace Day in 2014, where it provided *sama* as well as music from the Lachan Choir and the Metropolitan United Church Choir.[5] It participates in various other similar ecumenical gatherings, such as the Interfaith Fest and the Prayer Breakfasts, gatherings that focus on dialogue. As noted on its website, in reference to its involvement in the Prayer Breakfast, "the Canadian Sufi Cultural Centre is proud to support interfaith initiatives to build bridges with members of the community. Our message is one of love, peace, and harmony for all."[6] Often central to these gatherings is the tradition of Rumi, be it through his poems and teachings or through the presentation of *sama*. On such occasions, Rumi serves as a facilitator of activism, especially interfaith dialogue.[7] Rumi also serves as a cultural broker and translator among those of other faith traditions, or no faith traditions. He is an ambassador for Islam and Sufism. The Jerrahi Order is also one of the few Sufi orders in Toronto that are politically active. Aydöner is often photographed with Conservative politicians, and he regularly hosts them and other politicians, such as Mississauga mayor Bonnie Crombie, at the Jerrahi centre.

Moreover, Sufism and queer identities have been central to many grassroots movements that emphasize social justice (Abdou 2022). The Tanzanian-born Canadian refugee and immigration lawyer and activist El-Farouki Khaki orients his activism and human rights discourse within the framework of Sufi Islam. In 1991, Khaki started Salaam in Toronto, a support group for gay, lesbian, and trans Muslims. It was the first Canadian group of this kind. The organization functioned for about two years. Khaki's activism came to the fore in the early 1990s as he became known for his legal advocacy for queer refugees in Canada. In May 2009, along with Laury Silvers, a Muslim Canadian gender and LGBTIQ activist and academic, and Khaki's partner Troy Jackson, they started El-Tawhid Juma Circle, or Unity Masjid. In a documentary on his life and work, Khaki expressed that his goal is "global transformation and global oneness" (*Accidental Activist*, 2020).[8] At the centre of the weekly gatherings is an inclusive approach to Islam broadly defined. Their mosque is affirming of all gender and sexual orientations, religions, and ways of being. It is inclusive of Sunni, Shia, and Sufi approaches to God. The weekly *khutbah*s are delivered by various members of the community, and the regular *juma* prayers often conclude with the *salawat* (blessings) to the Prophet Muhammad, and the prayer of *nur* (light) associated with Muhammad, while drawing from the *wird* (litany) of the Threshold Society, the Sufi community of Kabir and Camille Helminski. Many members are affiliated with other Sufi communities in Toronto. Even before COVID-19, the weekly *juma* gatherings were streamed via Facebook live, so this community truly has a global attendance. Khaki's mobilization has led to the formation of many other similar spaces and communities globally. It has also captured the rise of a new generation of young queer Muslim activists, such as Zain Bandali, whose story and understandings of poetry located within Sufism and Ismaili identities was discussed in chapter 4. Clearly, then, an intersection of Sufism with social justice has emerged, especially in Toronto, among a young generation of Muslims, who are building upon the work of earlier generation of Muslims. Many from Muslim-inherited identities (i.e., second- or third-generation diasporic Muslims) have found that the universalism of Sufism (which they understand as Islamic) serves as a platform for translating gender and sexual equality as well as anti-racist discourse in the contemporary Canadian social moment. The examples of Khaki and Bandali are significant in terms of the nexus of Sufism and social justice advocacy. Khaki is a queer Muslim Sufi. Khaki explains that these identities inform his work as an immigration lawyer and social activist in various Toronto communities.

For many contemporary Muslims and non-Muslims in the LGBTIQ community, Rumi has even been hailed as a torchbearer "of homoeroticism and spirituality" (Darlymple 2005). Aside from speculations about the nature of Rumi and Shams's relationship, the rich cultural and ritual lives of *hijras* (third-gender) in places such as India, Pakistan, Bangladesh, Indonesia, and Iran continue to be central to this discourse on Sufism and queer identity (Najmabadi 2005; Kasmani 2022). This was evident in the outpouring of responses when homosexuality was legalized in India in September 2018. Many on social media platforms highlighted that laws against homosexuality were the result of colonial and imperial legal discourses impacting cultures where non-binary genders and sexualities had long existed, pointing to Sufi traditions to support their argument. Of course, these discussions around sexuality and Sufism historically need to be further nuanced, but it is helpful to underscore how Rumi and Sufi queer identities have been utilized in the discourse of LGBTIQ rights today by Muslims and non-Muslims, especially in popular culture and social media.

Conversations about intersectionality, decoloniality, and social justice among practitioners of Sufism in Canada, and in the United States, are a critical indicator of the continuity of Sufi tradition in a new milieu, at least according to my interlocutors. The study of Sufism in Canada, then, cannot be untethered from questions of race, social justice, gender, and intersectionality. Sufism has always been both about the inner dimension and cultivation of the heart (*qalb*) and about an esoteric path; but there is another vital feature of Sufism in Canada, especially among a younger demographic who rely on Sufi teachings for their social justice mobilization and civic engagement. It is essential to note this trend precisely because the transmission of Sufism to Canada, United States, and western Europe was mobilized by white seekers. Many among this older generation of seekers are now encountering young people, both Muslims and non-Muslims, who are racialized and who are coming to Sufism from a social justice milieu. They have infused Sufism in Canada with social justice that does not call for a completely reclusive approach of the sort that some seekers in the earlier generation may have cultivated. So we need to be incisive regarding how we talk about Sufism in Canada, especially when we frame it solely as a white and New Age practice. Of course, some threads of Sufism consist of these trends, which this book has highlighted (see chapters 1, 2, and 3), but there are other dimensions that call for more focused studies of Sufism in Canada, and broadly in North America; these include stories about racialized, gendered, LGBTIQ, and activist Sufis. When we dismiss Sufism in Canada as New Age or as diluted, we silence these voices. These narratives emphasize dynamic links among social justice, faith, spirituality, Sufism, and Islam and how these inform Sufi institutions, praxis, and community life.

Sufism in North America and western Europe has influenced popular spirituality as well as Islamic diasporic communities' expressions of faith. Scholarship on this topic has not engaged in any serious way with Canada, and this book has been a small first step in beginning to point to this dynamic as well as an invitation for scholars and students interested in Islam and popular spirituality in Canada, and more broadly in religions in Canada, to think seriously about how Sufism and Islam have been affecting popular spirituality for decades. This study has traced some of the popular and religious legacies of Rumi in Canada. From literary and poetic expressions of Rumi and Sufism to *sama* presentations, Rumi's presence is deeply tied to Sufism, popular spirituality, and consumption, but for the Sufis' voices captured in this study, these practices also exist beyond these public and commodified spaces. For them, Rumi is formative for the practice of Sufism, especially among communities that take part in regular *sama* and *zikr*. Here, we encountered how the practice of *sama* has become a central legacy of Rumi in Canada, one that is tied to Reshad Feild and Suleyman Loras in the 1970s and has been affirmed through other Turkish Sufi communities that formed in the late 1990s. Today, *sama* is publicly presented at concert halls and other venues, such as the Aga Khan Museum, as well as at universities for cultural and educational purposes, but these presentations may not include all the elements of *sama* that often unfold in private ritual contexts (see chapter 3). Regardless, these presentations are no less sacred for the *sama-zen*s who present the tradition to a public audience. Criticism has arisen that *sama* and Rumi have been popularized and commodified as New Age "badges," yet for many of my interlocutors, participation in these spaces was at the core of their service in spreading the teachings of Rumi for those who need it. Their practice was defined by their intention (*niyya*).

For the many who worry that the essence of the historical Rumi is being lost or tempered through these popular transmissions unfolding in Canada and the west today, it is helpful to remember that religious or historical figures are never fixed for all time. For instance, in her study of Rabia, Rkia Cornell (2019) concludes that "in light of the undeniable importance of her figural image, we must conclude that the history of Rabi'a that is most significant is not her empirical history (although this is still important) but the history of her literary representation from narrative to myth" (373). Cornell (2019) quotes from Roland Barthes (1957):

> "Myth is a *value*, truth is no guarantee for it; nothing prevents it from being a perpetual alibi: it is enough that its signifier has two sides for it always to have an 'elsewhere' at its disposal. The meaning is always there to *present* the form; the form is always there to *outdistance* the meaning. And there never is any contradiction, conflict or split between the meaning and form." (376–7)

Cornell speaks about Rabia's "mythological legacy" as applicable to other Muslim figures. This same framework, then, can be productively applied to help us process the current state of Rumi, whose iconic and mythological status this book has engaged with. I have contended in this book that while it is imperative to keep asking who the historical Rumi was, one should also consider asking *who Rumi has become*. In reformulating our line of inquiry, we summon the social and religious factors that amplify broader questions, issues, and concerns. Sufism in Canada has shown that Rumi remains an influential teacher and guide for many students, *samazen*s, poets, and leaders. Many of my interlocutors recognize that the current popularization and consumption of Rumi is at times problematic, but they are also aware it may lead to serious interest among seekers, who will then make efforts to access the path of Sufism. Most of my interlocutors were not so quick to dismiss this possibility. Still, they reaffirmed that Rumi was a Muslim who was located deep within Islamic practice, which informed his approach to Sufism. Many of my interlocutors engaged Rumi to (re)affirm what they recognized as traditional Islam. Accordingly for them, traditional Islam, as defined by the Quran, is universal and inclusive and not a product of New Age or NRM inflections of westernization or modernization (see chapter 1). The latter framework brought to the forefront a central question that informed many of the chapter discussions, that is, of Sufism and its relationship to Islam.

This question of Sufism and its relationship to Islam also pointed to concerns regarding the legitimacy or authenticity of Sufism itself. In my discussion about the institutionalization of various Sufi communities in Canada, this question was a central point of contention. Some universal Sufi communities were criticized by Muslim-based Sufi communities for their lack of *Islamic-ness*, and this at times revolved around the position of women in ritual praxis or around gendered authority, as chapter 5 highlighted. Sufi communities like the Chishtis of South Asia have a long tradition of religious pluralism, which their *shaykhs* have actively cultivated. These examples then serve as necessary precedent for (and/or rejoinder to) some of the practices noted in the Inayati Order today. Given the universalism that was noted in some Sufi communities, be it the Vancouver Rumi Society or the Inayati Order, teachers like Husain and Ghazi were quick to explain that these examples of universal Sufism are set within a classical tradition of Islam and thus *are examples of being Islamic*. Ghazi reminded us that this universalism does not mean that there are no Sufis who are not Islamophobic, explicitly or implicitly.[9] Popular expressions and practices of Sufism are unfolding just as Islamophobia is on the rise around the world. These tendencies at times seep into some communities' aversion to the Islamic roots of Sufism, especially in Canada, where the practice of turning is at times tokenized as a cultural commodity.

Several patterns are discernible between the two fields of studies from which this book draws: namely, Islam and popular spirituality. Some of these patterns revolve around demographics. For instance, early studies on Buddhism in Canada were located between two demographic groups: white Buddhists, and Buddhists who were diasporic/Asian Buddhists and/or newcomers to North America.[10] The ethnic composition of newly emerging religious and spiritual communities has been wielded to theorize how culture and ethnicity inform NRMs. The literature about Muslim communities in Canada, for instance, locates various sectarian and cultural dynamics between South Asian Muslim communities and North African Muslim communities as these national, ethnic, cultural, and racial identities implicate religiosity and praxis. At the same time, observations about the composition of various groups have been used to label spiritual communities, such as Buddhist and Hindu communities that are mainly white, as a means to locate their own religiosity *vis-à-vis* ethnicity and race, in particular, whiteness. These ethnic and racial fault lines are significant and were critical to consider during the genesis of many religious and spiritual communities in Canada, but an analysis of Sufi communities in Canada also captures how there are no easy correlations between white Sufis and non-white Sufis, especially in the present day, when these various Sufi communities bleed into one another. Moreover, Canadian Muslims are also active seekers and are gravitating toward universal Sufi communities, challenging the idea that spiritual seekers, consumers, producers, and distributors are only white middle- and upper-middle-class people. Some seekers in Canada are Muslims, and some easily gravitate toward far more universal Sufi Islamic communities as a reaction to the insular or restrictive Islam in which they may have been raised. Even so, they recognize universal Sufism as an expression of true Islam. In fact, the two *shaykha*s featured in chapter 5 are South Asian Muslim women who lead universal Sufi communities. Most of the Sufis who come from non-Muslim backgrounds tend to be white, but this is by no means always the case. The dynamics vary from one Sufi community to the next. This study has added breadth to how we think about Muslims and Islam in Canada and underscored the need to analyse individual Sufi communities in future studies.

Additionally, where Sufis have tended to be white and initially non-Muslim, many have converted to Islam in order to participate fully in a particular Sufi community. For example, the Jerrahi community in Toronto tends not to attract non-Muslims, for it is located within a Turkish cultural expression of Sufism that includes other eastern Europeans such as Albanians, whereas the group that split from this movement, the Rifais, tend to attract far more white Sufis, many of whom have converted to Islam at the direction of Murat Coskun, the *shaykh,* who himself was an Armenian Christian. This community also attracts an urban and younger generation of Muslims, some of whom are located in LGBTIQ, queer, and non-gender-conforming communities. Generally, this book has moved away from easy and binary categorizations in its discussion of lived Sufism in Canada. These identities are far more complicated in embodied realities and require regular negotiation by adherents who are Sufis. Ideas of race and ethnic identity remain at the forefront for many young activists and artists in Toronto, who take a decolonial approach to their social justice work, of which Sufism is one thread; for others, such as Sufi teachers in Toronto, this is not the case. When I asked Tawhida Tanya Evanson what Sufism is, she quoted from Rumi: "Sufism is the sudden feeling of joy when disappointment comes."[11] She added that though there are many intellectual definitions one can find about Sufism, really, "if you fall into the ocean, the *ashq* [love], don't try to get out ... keep swimming deeper into it and that's also *tasawwuf.*"[12] The latter definition does not use words like Islam or even mysticism; instead it gestures to an abstract experience that resonates with Muslims and non-Muslims today who are seekers.

Finally, this study has aimed to unsettle the field of religious studies in Canada. Throughout my review of the literature on Islam and popular spirituality, as well as religions in Canada, it became evident that religious studies in Canada still privileges a Christian-centric or post-Christian-centric, European (white), heteronormative approach to religion. My hope in beginning to ask questions about Sufism in Canada, and mapping how it is unfolding among Rumi-based Sufi communities in cities like Toronto, Montreal, and Vancouver, is to invite critical reflection about the ways in which religion in Canada must account for race, ethnicity, gender, sexuality, and, most importantly, non-Christian influences. Such a story cannot render Islam as a foreign vector that has suddenly altered the climate for Canadian diasporic religions; indeed, Islam, including notions of Sufism in various universal and particular capacities, was visible in print culture and literature and among early enslaved peoples well before the arrival of some of the first Arab Muslims in Canada in the twentieth century. Not highlighting these various genealogies only marginalizes Islam further in the story of religion and popular spirituality in Canada, framing it as existing in pure and pristine form in the faraway east. It also discounts the experiences of Muslims in Canada and keeps them tied to discourses of terrorism, violence, and racism. As Chiara Formichi (2020) writes in her book about Islam in Asia, "physical geography becomes irrelevant to discourses of hierarchy and authenticity," and technology is "ultimately only an enabler of transformations induced by socio-economic changes" (262). Islam is often treated as a "derivative reality" compared to what many may think are authentic geographies of Islam, such as Arab-speaking countries or what is broadly conceived as the Middle East, whereas regions such as North Africa, South East Asia, western Europe, the United States, and Canada are treated as peripheral to these geographies of "authentic" Islam (266).

Many scholars have highlighted that Islamic studies still favours the Middle East, even in university departments, while privileging the study of Arabic texts. This sort of reductive focus neglects the stories of Black Muslims in the Atlantic world, for example. I hope this book will encourage scholars, especially a younger generation interested in religions in Canada, to ask new questions, to bring their experiences to the field and seek new creative lines of inquiry that will take them into the archives to tell new qualitative and quantitative stories about religions in Canada. These narratives will hopefully include journeys into the field and dialogues with interlocutors that challenge easy categorizations of religion and popular spirituality and the people who practise them. To that end, they must start with the reality that the study of religion is inherently a study of race, for religion is raced. So there must be a move away from notions of minority religions or orthodoxy, so as to centre marginalized voices instead of developing binaries of centre and peripheries. Concerted efforts need to be made to capture processes and dynamisms of translations, transmissions, and transformations, as we encountered in this book when we pursued Rumi and *sama* and how these praxes have defined and are continuing to define the making of Sufism in Canada.

Notes

Introduction

1 The Aga Khan Museum, which opened in 2014, has been the centre of numerous Islamic exhibitions and music and dance concerts, as well as special talks on Muslim cultures and societies; across from the museum is the Ismaili Center, with the *jamatkhana* (prayer hall).
2 I note here that our SSHRC applications proposing research on Sufism in Canada were not funded simply as a response to Aaron W. Hughes' chapter "Research Funding and the Production of Knowledge about Islam: The Case of SSHRC" in Barras et al., eds., *Producing Islam(s) in Canada*. Hughes importantly highlighted in his chapter the political realities regarding which projects on Islam in Canada receive federal funding.
3 For more discussion of positionality in fieldwork, see the excellent chapters in Section 3, "Positioning Selves," of Barras, Selby, and Adrian, eds., *Producing Islam(s) in Canada*.

1 Situating the Study of Sufism in Canada

1 A famous example is the Moroccan Estevanico of the Narváes expedition (1527–36), whom we know about from Álvar Núñez Cabeza de Vaca's 1542 account (Khan 2020: 36).
2 Khan's *Far from Mecca* (2020) offers an excellent account of how the Sufi aesthetic was important for the literary productions of enslaved peoples in the Afro-Caribbean, especially in British Guiana (Guyana), and of how Sufi traditions influenced figures like Muhammad Kaba Saghanughu and Abu Bakr al-Siddiq. Both were West Africans who were enslaved in Jamaica in the early nineteenth century (35).
3 All of these archival materials have been digitalized thanks to the Documenting the American South Project. Many of these archives make reference to Canada and are waiting for scholars to engage with them. These materials are also great

resources for those who teach about Islam in Canada and the United States. They can be accessed at https://docsouth.unc.edu/index.html.

4 For access to this study, visit https://www.pewresearch.org/fact-tank/2019/07/01/5-facts-about-religion-in-canada.

5 Siobhan Chandler's 2011 dissertation discusses the limitations of 1960s and 1970s New Age Movement and how contemporary manifestations of SBNR and religious nones capture a long history of seekers in Canada.

6 For more about the history of Theosophy in Canada, visit https://www.theosophycanada.com/history-of-theosophy-in-canada.php.

7 The 3HO was founded in 1969 in the United States by Yogi Bhajan. It focused on the practice of Kundalini yoga. For more about this community, visit its website, https://www.3ho.org. Bhajan has since been faced with civil lawsuits regarding various counts of sexual abuse against women and minors.

8 Personal blog by rdnhansen, "The World Symposium on Humanity, Vancouver, 1976" (17 Mins). On *To Say Nothing*, visit https://tosaynothing.wordpress.com/2018/08/09/the-world-symposium-on-humanity-vancouver-1976-17-min.

9 Interview with Zainb Paula Ford via Zoom, 7 September 2020.

10 Since his death, several accusations of sexual abuse have been made against Carlebach. For more on these claims, visit Sarah Blustain's "Rabbi Shlomo Carlebach's Shadow Side" in *Lilith: Independent, Jewish & Frankly Feminist* (9 March 1998), https://lilith.org/articles/rabbi-shlomo-carlebachs-shadow-side.

11 In her study of Amma's transnational movement, Lucia uses the terms "inheritors" and "adopters" from Jan Nattiers's study of Buddhists in America. Here, inheritors are those who grew up with Hinduism and are South Asian, whereas adopters are those who have come to Amma and are white, African American, or Latinx (2014: 149).

12 In "Neo-Sufism," his contribution to *The Cambridge Companion to New Religious Movements* (2012), Mark Sedgwick frames Sufism in the west as "Neo-Sufism," adding that "the term 'Neo-Sufism' was first used by scholars to describe an unusually fertile wave of new orders and sub-orders in the eighteenth-century Muslim world. The term is now increasingly used, however, to describe various forms of Sufism found in the West since the nineteenth century. The main difference between these and Sufism as found in the Muslim world is that the limits within which Sufism operates in the West are much looser, and the influence of the local is much greater" (199). Here the local is contrasted with the global. Though I understand the complex origins of Sufism in the west, I prefer to phrase this reality as Sufism in the (global) west, and not as neo-Sufism, for it is precisely this debate over "newness" insinuated by the prefix "neo" that I wish to decentre in my own scholarship on Sufism in the west.

13 Not all Orientalists who first encountered Sufi literary traditions and Sufis were involved in colonial projects. That said, the Christian lens through which these people encountered Islam and Sufism was strongly Protestant, and this sharply

influenced some of the criticism directed at the Sufis. An important example here is Martin Luther (d. 1546), the famed reformer. For more, please see Sharify-Funk et al. (2017).

14 Ayeda Husain speaks about this practice in chapter 4.
15 In his extensive research, Geaves found that Sufism in Britain was "tightly bound up with ethnic identity, as a means of maintaining traditions and customs closely linked with localities in the place of origin" (2009: 98). Some of the prominent *tariqa*s in Britain include Naqshbandiya, Qadiriya, Chishtiya, Alawiya, and Tijaniya.
16 Vaughan-Lee has published numerous books, such as *The Face Before I Was Born: A Spiritual Autobiography* (1997), *Sufism: Transformations of the Heart* (1995), *The Signs of God* (2000), and *Love Is a Fire: The Sufi's Mystical Journey Home* (2009).
17 More information about this group and its centres can be found on their website, http://www.nimatullahi.org/our-order/history/dr-javad-nurbakhsh.php.
18 Some of these titles include *Jesus in the Eyes of the Sufis* (1983), *The Path: Sufi Practices* (2003), and *The Psychology of Sufism* (1992).
19 Further important work on Aguéli is now being done by scholars. This includes the new edited volume *Anarchist, Artist, Sufi: The Politics, Painting, and Esotericism of Ivan Aguéli* (2021) edited by Mark Sedgwick. Also, Gregory Vandamme has been researching fascinating aspects of Aguéli's Italian letters, which are archived at the Cini Foundation in San Giorgio in Venice, Italy.
20 Keller resides in Amman, Jordan, and publishes widely on Sufism and Islam. His book titles include *Sufism and Islam* (2002) and *Sea without Shore: A Manual of the Sufi Path* (2011). Allegations of spiritual abuse have recently been tied to this community. For more, visit https://muslimmatters.org/2022/06/06/spiritual-abuse-sufi-nuh-keller.
21 The position and approach I take in this book differs, for instance, from how Sophia Rose Arjana thinks about the commodification of Sufism and Rumi in *Buying Buddha, Selling Rumi* (2020).

2 Early Sufi Communities in Canada

1 For more on Gurdjieff, see the book John G. Bennett *Is There "Life" on Earth? An Introduction to Gurdjieff* (1973) or Gurdjieff's writings such as *Beelzebub's Tales to His Grandson: An Objectively Impartial Criticism of the Life of Man* (1950). See Mark Sedgwick's *Western Sufism: From the Abbasids to the New Age* (2016).
2 For more information on the Gurdjieff Foundation: Society for Traditional Studies, visit http://gurdjieff-foundation-toronto.org/whoWeAre.html. The foundation maintains the Traditional Studies Press.
3 For more information about the Gurdjieff Society of Atlantic Canada, including a brief history, visit http://www.gurdjieffatlanticcanada.com/aboutus.htm.

4 For a poster on a public talk, visit http://gurdjieff-foundation-toronto.org/images/PathsToFreedom_Talk.pdf.
5 For a post about this music presentation, visit http://gurdjieff-foundation-toronto.org/images/CharlesKetchamConcertNov21.pdf.
6 For more information about the Sufi Circle Study Group and Dr Baig, visit http://muslimcanada.org/sufi/whoarewe.htm.
7 Interview with author via Zoom, 31 July 2020.
8 For more on the Lucis Trust Library in New York City, visit https://www.lucistrust.org/arcane_school/library/new_york_headquarters_library.
9 Carol Sill's archive project on Shamcher can be found at http://www.shamcher.org.
10 The Sufi Circle Canada has a well-structured online presence. In particular, their website provides much of this oral history along with more information about the community. Visit https://www.sufimovementincanada.ca/ABOUT/about-sufi-circle-canada.
11 Nizamuddin Awliya (d. 1325), who is buried in New Delhi, was one of the foremost Chishti Sufi teachers and saints. His *dargah* or shrine is a popular site of pilgrimage and is in the same neighbourhood (*basti*) where Inayat and Vilayat Khan are buried.
12 Music sheets with lyrics were passed around, so that everyone could sing together.
13 Interview with author, 21 February 2020, Vancouver.
14 Interview with author, 21 February 2020, Vancouver.
15 Celia Genn has studied the Inayati Order in Australia through a sociological lens, not as a Sufi tradition but as an "Asian-derived" New Religious Movement. She has explored the institutionalization of the community and how its non-Muslim followers have propelled Khan's philosophy of "universalism" to the forefront of the Inayati Movement, which for Genn is the reason why it has succeeded (Genn 2007:2004). Differing categorizations still persist in the study of Inayat Khan's movement among various scholars who study its complex institution and affiliates.
16 Interview with author, 16 August 2018, Toronto.
17 Wali Ali Meyers is a student of Samuel Lewis, who initiated him in 1970 to become a teacher (*shaykh*) of Sufism. Meyers continues to hold retreats and teachings, while remaining the director of the Esoteric School of the Ruhaniat International. More about him can be found at https://www.ruhaniat.org/index.php/explore/leaders/2012-06-15-13-40-56.
18 Interview with author, 16 August 2018, Toronto.
19 Interview with author, 16 August 2018, Toronto.
20 Interview with author, 16 August 2018, Toronto.
21 For more on Jewish Sufi traditions, see Emily Sigalow's *American JewBu: Jews, Buddhists, and Religious Change* (2019). Sigalow engages figures like Samuel Lewis as examples of universal and Jewish Buddhists. Presumably, the first American Jew who became a Sufi was none other than Inayat Khan's first student, Rabia Martin (aka Ada Ginsberg [d. 1947]).

22 "Rabbi Zalman Schachter-Shalomi Extended Interview," in *Religion and Ethics News Weekly*, 30 September 2005. Visit https://www.pbs.org/wnet/religionandethics/2005/09/30/september-30-2005-rabbi-zalman-schachter-shalomi-extended-interview/9753.
23 Kestenbaum 2016. "5 Jewish Sufis You Should Know."
24 There has also been research on the Mawlawi Order in western Europe, for example, by Gritt Klinkhammer in Germany (2009).
25 For more on the history of this space, visit https://scalar.usc.edu/works/the-house-of-love-and-prayer/the-house-of-love-and-prayer.
26 Interview with author via Skype, 8 June 2020, Vancouver and Kingston.
27 Gold and his spiritual teachings and movements elide easy categorization. Petsche writes that the "central message that binds Gold's work is that people need to be shaken out of their mechanical, sleep-like condition in order to transform spiritually and become conscious" (347). Gold is the author of several books, including *Autobiography of a Sufi* (1977) and *Secret Talks with Mr. G* (1978). Petsche has indicated that much of his self-narration of his life seems to parallel the life of G.J. Gurdjieff, so it is difficult to determine how much of it is real. He is also known for the Institute of the Development of Harmonious Human Being (IDHHB).
28 For an important study on the Beshara community in the United Kingdom, see Taji-Farouki (2007).
29 Interview with author via Skype, 8 June 2020, Vancouver and Kingston.
30 Interview with author via Skype, 8 June 2020, Vancouver and Kingston.
31 For more on the Mawlawi Order of America, see Simon Sorgenfrei's dissertation, *American Dervish: Making Mevlevism in the United States of America* (University of Gothenburg, 2013).
32 In his autobiography, Murat Yagan writes that he thinks that the Canadian Turkish Society did not ask him to act as the translator because he was not a "proper Moslem." See Johnston and McIntyre 1984: 146.
33 Interview with author via Zoom, 21 August 2020. Vaughan-Lee's Golden Sufi Center is in Northern California. However, a small group was organized by Dale Genge after Vaughan-Lee visited Vancouver in 1992; he had gone there to give a talk about Sufism and dreams at the Vancouver Jung Society. The group meets on Salt Spring Island and has around nine people. None of the Canadian students are Muslims, though some of Vaughan-Lee's students in California are Muslim (i.e., Iranian). One member of the Canadian group is Indigenous.
34 Interview with Raqib Brian Burke, 17 May 2022, Vancouver.
35 Burke interview, 17 May 2022, Vancouver.
36 Burke interview, 17 May 2022, Vancouver.
37 Burke interview, 17 May 2022, Vancouver.
38 Burke interview, 17 May 2022, Vancouver.
39 Interview with author via Skype, 8 June 2020, Vancouver and Kingston.
40 I profile Ghazi in chapter 5.

Notes to pages 68–76

41 For more about Seemi Ghazi and the Women's Islamic Initiative in Spirituality and Equality, visit http://wisemuslimwomen.org/muslim-woman/seemi-bushra-ghazi-2.
42 Visit the Vancouver Rumi Society, https://sites.google.com/site/rumisocietybc/home.
43 For more about Muzaffer Ozak's teachings, see *Love Is the Wine: Talks of a Sufi Master in America* (2009), compiled and edited by one of his students and successors, Ragiq Frager al Jerrahi al Halveti. For more biographical information about Ozak and his time in America, see Gregory Blann's *Lifting the Boundaries: Muzaffer Efendi and the Transmission of Sufism to the West* (2015).
44 I am grateful to Cem Aydogdu, the translator and *murid* of Sherif Baba, who took the time to speak with me from Turkey on 11 August 2020 and replied to my regular messages. All of this helped me map the history of Sherif Baba in Turkey, the United States, and Canada, as well as some of his teachings.
45 Interview with author, 20 February 2020, Vancouver.
46 Interview with author, 20 February 2020, Vancouver.
47 Interview with author, 20 February 2020, Vancouver.
48 For a study of *sama* in the Nimatullahi Sufi Community in Toronto, see Ghani 2018.
49 For more on Dr Ahmet Fuad Sahin, visit http://iqra.ca/2017/dr-ahmet-fuad-sahin-appointed-to-order-of-canada.
50 The Jerrahi Order has an expansive transnational network and various sub-branches. Its main headquarters, in Chestnut Ridge, New York, is led by *shaykh* Yurdaer Doganata al-Jerrahi; other centres are in California (led by Ragib Frager al-Jerrahi), Chicago, Los Angeles, and Philadelphia. There are also centres in Argentina, Chile, Spain, Italy, Brazil, and Australia. The only Canadian branch is in Toronto.
51 Interview with author, 26 October 2019, Toronto.
52 Interview with author, 26 October 2019, Toronto.
53 Interview with author, 26 October 2019, Toronto.
54 Interview with author, 26 October 2019, Toronto.
55 For more on the community, visit their website at http://www.jerrahi.ca/aboutus.html.
56 Interview with author, 3 January 2018, Toronto.
57 For more on Kenan Rifai and the Rifai in Turkey, see chapter 5.
58 Interview with author, 3 January 2018, Toronto.
59 Accessed via the Canadian Institute of Sufi Studies website, which also offers a short documentary titled *Islamic Mysticism- The Sufi Path*, which captures the early story of Coskun. Visit https://www.rifaisufi.org/about-us.
60 Interview with author, 3 January 2018, Toronto.
61 Interview with author, 3 January 2018, Toronto.

62 For more on Nurbakhsh and his order, visit their website, https://www.nimatullahi.org.
63 For more on the Toronto centre of the Nimatullahi Order, visit http://torontosufihouse.com.
64 Interview with author, 15 December 2019, Toronto.
65 Interview with author, 15 December 2019, Toronto.
66 Interview with author, 15 December 2019, Toronto.
67 Interview with author via Skype, 17 May 2019, Kingston and Montreal.
68 Interview with author via Skype, 17 May 2019, Kingston and Montreal.
69 Interview with author via Skype, 17 May 2019, Kingston and Montreal.
70 Interview with author via Skype, 17 May 2019, Kingston and Montreal.
71 Interview with author via Skype, 17 May 2019, Kingston and Montreal.
72 Interview with author via Skype, 17 May 2019, Kingston and Montreal.
73 One particular political reality in the Turkish diaspora is the presence of both Sufi and Muslim communities and their differing opinions about the Gülen Movement led by Fethullah Gülen, a Turkish scholar. His movement has reached into more than a hundred countries around the world. One focus of the movement is education, and it has established schools across Turkey. His movement blends together various facets of Turkish identity, Islam, Sufism, and activism based on service. Since his falling out with the current president of Turkey, Recep Tayyip Erdoğan, he has been in political exile in Pennsylvania. The military coup that took place in 2016 in Turkey was allegedly organized by Gülen's followers. Political tensions between Gülen and Erdoğan have carried over into the diaspora. For more on this movement, see J.D. Hendrick's *Gülen: The Ambiguous Politics of Market Islam in Turkey and the World* (2013).
74 Interview with author via Skype, 17 May 2019, Kingston and Montreal. Some hold that all of Sufism is *adab*. Sufi masters over the centuries have written on this and trained their *murid*s in various aspects of *adab*. You can see this in the writings of the Ahmed Tijani (d. 1815), the Algerian *shaykh* and founder of the Tijani Sufi Order, which is prominent in North Africa and in the global west: "Etiquette (*adab*) among the jurists is an expression of righteous deeds (*qiyām*) following what is legally obligatory and the example of the Prophet. These include deeds of excellence and those strongly encouraged pertaining to the (external) states of people, whether while sleeping, awake, eating or drinking, in remembrance and in supplication, and things like this. Among the Sufis, etiquette is an expression of all acquired virtue and piety. It is the description of all noble attributes and praiseworthy character traits related to the divine adoration and the exaltation of divinity. Whoever gathers such traits in himself becomes refined and well-mannered in the presence of God the Exalted, and in the presence of His messenger, God's peace and blessing upon him. The first (juristic) meaning of etiquette is thus contained within the second" (qtd in Wright 2020: 80).

3 *Sama, Shab-i arus*, and Rituals of Remembrance

1. This community has centres in Canada, Mexico, and the United Kingdom.
2. The use of sound in Islamic traditions is very common. One can easily note the sonic expressions of Quranic recitation (*tilawa*) to the call of the *adhan*. Still the place of music, dance, and sounds generally are quite complex within the development of Islam. For instance, music has been a point of tension for some reformist communities, which has even continued to influence diasporic Muslim communities in Canada. For more see Michael Frishkopf studies of music amongst Canadian Muslim communities (2011).
3. Jean-Louis Michon (2006) categorizes Muslim philosophers such as the Brethren of Purity, Ya'qub al-Kindi (d. 873), and Ibn Sina (d. 1037) as representing a school of thought that was interested in the science of music. The other school, or tendency, was found among the Sufis. The Sufis were interested in music, but their focus was on refining the *qalb* (heart) and soul in order to achieve union with the Divine (158–9).
4. We see this ritual practice especially in Mughal India. There, the sharing of *sama* among non-Muslims was one influential way in which Sufism spread in the Indian context Lewisohn 1997: 10; During 2018.
5. Some *hadith* traditions claim that the Prophet Muhammad permitted dance. For example, the *musnad* of Ahmad Hanbal (d. 855) related that Abyssinians were in the presence of Muhammad where they danced and played the tambourine, and he listened to them. Lewisohn 1997: 25.
6. For more on this discussion, please see Küçük 2010.
7. It seems that both the Ghazali brothers, Ahmed and Hamid, forbade the use of stringed instruments in *sama*, associating their use with other forms of social gatherings seen as antithetical to God. Clearly, though, not everyone takes this stance, given that the use of stringed instruments is common in the Canadian *sama*. Michon 2006: 168.
8. Interview with author, 19 February 2020, Vancouver.
9. Interview with author, 17 May 2022, Vancouver.
10. Interview with author, 17 May 2022, Vancouver.
11. Interview with author, 17 May 2022, Vancouver.
12. Interview with author, 20 February 2020, Vancouver.
13. Interview with author, 20 February 2020, Vancouver.
14. Interview with author, 20 February 2020, Vancouver.
15. Interview with author, 15 December 2019, Toronto.
16. I use the term anti-Sufis here to broadly refer to the diverse groups of Muslims who find Sufism and/or its expressions theologically problematic. I borrow that term from Sirriyeh's book *Sufis and Anti-Sufism* (1999). In that book she maps "some of the ways in which Sufism has been challenged over the last two centuries by the forces of anti-Sufism, understood at times as opposition to Sufism in all its aspect,

at times as criticism of certain Sufi beliefs and practices regarded as unacceptable innovations with no authentic basis in the Qur'ān and Sunna, no laudable purpose" (xi). An example of such a practice critiqued by some anti-Sufis is the *sama*.

17 Interview with author, 15 December 2019, Toronto.
18 Interview with author via Skype, 17 May 2019, Kingston and Montreal.
19 Interview with author via Skype, 17 May 2019, Kingston and Montreal.
20 Interview with author via Skype, 17 May 2019, Kingston and Montreal.
21 Interview with author via Skype, 17 May 2019, Kingston and Montreal.
22 Interview with author via Skype, 17 May 2019, Kingston and Montreal.
23 Interview with author via Skype, 17 May 2019, Kingston and Montreal.
24 Interview with author via Skype, 17 May 2019, Kingston and Montreal.
25 Interview with author via Skype, 17 May 2019, Kingston and Montreal.
26 Interview with author via Skype, 17 May 2019, Kingston and Montreal.
27 In May 2020, Evanson, who heads the Sema Space in Montreal, held an online *sama* or "Infinite Sema" via Zoom. Unlike her regular monthly gatherings in Montreal, which include live music, *zikr,* and *sama*, this online gathering included the singing of *ilahi*s and *zikr*, and those who wanted could turn. The gathering was focused on sacred audition. The small gathering about fourteen people included participants from Vancouver, Montreal, and beyond. It started with the reading of poetry by Rumi, which discussed al-Hallaj.
28 Interview with author, 20 February 2020, Vancouver.
29 The *ilahi*s were from the booklet titled *Tasavvuf Iahiler: Ilahi Lyrics in Turkish and English*, edited by Cem Williford April 2008.
30 For more information about this organization, https://csaturkishstudies.wordpress.com/#:~:text=The%20Canadian%20Society%20for%20the,Ottoman%2C%20Turkic%20and%20Ancient%20Anatolian.
31 I discuss these dynamics further in chapter 5.
32 Interview with author, 20 February 2020, Vancouver.

4 The Politics of Consuming Rumi

1 The Facebook post has since been removed; however, its content became part of a longer blog piece, found here: https://muslimmamas.com/where-is-islam-in-rumi-by-baraka-blue.
2 For more on Safi's critique of the erasure of Islam in Hafiz's poetry, see "Fake Hafez: How a Supreme Persian Poet of Love Was Erased," in *Al-Jazeera*, 14 June 2020, at https://www.aljazeera.com/indepth/opinion/fake-hafez-supreme-persian-poet-love-erased-200601073431603.html.
3 William Jones played a key role in transmitting the history and literature of the east to the west while he served in government in Bengal and Calcutta from 1783 to 1794.
4 This race-centred approach to philology would inform the development of religious studies in Europe. For more on this, see Masuzawa 2005.

5 Chris Martin has spoken publicly about how important Rumi, and later Sufism, was for him while he was divorcing the American actress Gwyneth Paltrow; see Doyle 2015.
6 Many in the scholarly and non-scholarly worlds are expressing concerns about literal translations of Rumi. An even more fascinating trend is now unfolding: the popularity of Rumi's poems has led to a new (unintentional) trend of outright misquoting Rumi, especially on various social media platforms, such as Facebook and Instagram. An example of this was when Tiffany Trump, a daughter of Donald Trump, posted a (supposed) Rumi quote on Instagram. In addition to a photograph of herself dressed in a silver and beige skating outfit for the television show *Dancing with the Stars*, she wrote: "'Raise your words, not your voice. It is rain that grows flowers, not thunder.' – Rumi #rumi #rumiquotes." https://jezebel.com/did-tiffany-trump-post-a-fake-rumi-quote-on-instagram-1834511565.
7 This question of how to process the various new spheres of popular culture, especially in this era of new media technology, has long been a field of inquiry among cultural and communication studies scholars, such as Neil Postman (d. 2003), Umberto Eco (d. 2016), and Paul Gilroy.
8 For more on the global reception and success of the Turkish series *Resurrection Ertugrul*, visit https://www.theguardian.com/tv-and-radio/2020/aug/12/ertugrul-how-an-epic-tv-series-became-the-muslim-game-of-thrones?fbclid=IwAR03riLBOeEbm9Eq8gy0CcHqNzzW6hbSCbgHyjeDPGdFXMGUcF6LJaZpi9Y.
9 For more, visit https://www.muslimfuturism.com.
10 Thanks to my colleague Ashwini Vasanthakumar for recommending this helpful article to me.
11 Schimmel (1992) explains that the *ghazal* is "the traditional form of love lyric, consists generally of five to twelve lines and employs one single rhyme throughout the whole poem. The rhyme often grows into a *radif*, an overrhyme that consists of a word, several words, or even a full sentence" (38).
12 Interview with author, 20 February 2020, Vancouver.
13 Interview with author, 17 May 2022, Vancouver.
14 For more about Zuleikha, who is currently working in India and offers various movement-based classes, visit her website: https://zuleikha.com/about-zuleikha.
15 For more on Mercan Dede, visit his website http://www.mercandede.com.
16 Interview with author, 20 February 2020, Vancouver.
17 Interview with author, 20 February 2020, Vancouver.
18 For more about Tanya Tawhida Evanson, visit http://www.mothertonguemedia.com/info_bio.html.
19 Interview with author via Skype, 17 May 2019. Kingston and Montreal.
20 Visit http://zavieh.org/en/about.
21 Interview with author via Skype, 8 June 2020, Vancouver and Kingston.
22 Interview with author, 15 December 2019, Toronto.
23 Furthermore, universities, including the University of British Columbia, with which Ghazi is affiliated, have served as important institutional spaces for

organizing collaborative events. For instance, when Omid Safi was invited to deliver a public lecture sponsored by UBC, he also spent time working with Sufi communities in Vancouver through partnership with Ghazi. Post-secondary insitutions from Toronto to Vancouver have played a vital role in offering spaces where speakers on Sufism or whirling can give public talks and share in classroom presentations.

24 For more on Small World Music, visit https://smallworldmusic.com/about/#historySection.

25 Featured poets and performers included Sahar Golshan, Khashayar Mohammadi, Bänoo Zan, and storyteller Ariel Balevi, as well as An Ensemble, comprised of Bamdad Fotouhi (percussion), Nima Safaei (*santour*) and Kouhyar Babaeian (*tar*), Zohreh Shahbazy (percussion), Kianoush Khalilian (*ney*) and Shahin Fayaz (*tar*, *setar*).

26 You can learn more about the author on her website: https://shenizjanmohamed.com.

27 Interview with author, December 2018. Toronto.
28 Interview with author, December 2018, Toronto.
29 Interview with author, December 2018, Toronto.
30 Interview with author, December 2018. Toronto.
31 Email correspondence with author, 14 July 2022.
32 Interview with author, 24 June 2020, via Skype.
33 Interview with author, 24 June 2020 via Skype.
34 Interview with author, December 2018, Toronto.
35 Interview with author, December 2018, Toronto.
36 The next Sufi Poet Series was scheduled for the end of April 2020, but because of the COVID-19 pandemic, it was cancelled. The theme of this second series was to be the poetry of Shah Abdul Latif.
37 For more, visit the homepage of the Noor Cultural Center, https://noorculturalcentre.ca/about-2/the-founders.
38 The Noor Center has since closed permanently due to financial pressures.
39 For more on Small World Music, visit https://smallworldmusic.com/about/#historySection.
40 For more about this workshop, visit http://www.harbourfrontcentre.com/whatson/learning.cfm?id=7227&festival_id=204.
41 Ismaili prayer structure differs from that of Sunni and other Shia Muslims. For instance, Ismailis tend to pray three times a day and often gather to pray on Friday evenings as a congregation. Their prayer does not include *salat* (or *namaz*), where they prostrate themselves. Instead, Ismaili prayer includes various recitations of the shorter *surah*s of the Quran, as well as a recitation of the lineage of some of the Imams going back to Ali. Men and women pray side by side and are led in prayer by one man and one-woman prayer leader, who are appointed by the Aga Khan.

246 Notes to pages 162–84

42 For more details about the screening of *Wajd: Songs of Separation* (2018) at the Aga Khan Museum, visit https://agakhanmuseum.org/programs/wajd-songs-of-separation-with-performance-by-rumi-canada.
43 Interview with author, 15 December 2019, Toronto.
44 For more on the charity Canadian Arabic Orchestra, visit https://canadianarabicorchestra.ca/home.
45 Interview with author, 15 December 2019, Toronto.
46 For more about Niyaz, visit https://www.niyazmusic.com.
47 Interview with author via Skype, 17 May 2019, Kingston and Montreal.
48 Interview with author via Skype, 17 May 2019, Kingston and Montreal.
49 Interview with author, 17 May 2022, Vancouver.
50 More about the Meditation Center can be found on its website, https://www.sufimeditationcenter.com. The community has a robust online and social media presence that includes Facebook and YouTube and their homepage. It livestreams its events on Facebook.
51 Interview with author, 18 February 2020, Vancouver.
52 For some historical context regarding the Naqshbandi, specifically in the Ottoman context, see Dina Le Gall's *A Culture of Sufism: Naqshbandīs in the Ottoman World* (2005).
53 Interview with author, 18 February 2020, Vancouver.
54 Interview with author, 18 February 2020, Vancouver.
55 Interview with author, 18 February 2020, Vancouver.
56 You can learn more about Rumi restaurant at https://www.restaurantrumi.com/?lang=en. For more on the Naqshbandi-Haqqani in Montreal, see Mercier-Dalphond 2021.
57 Various scholars, such as Vaziri (2015), have underscored Rumi's humanism, perennialism, Islamic-ness, and much more.
58 Interview with author, 15 December 2019, Toronto.
59 Interview with author, December 2018, Toronto.
60 Interview with author, 20 February 2020, Vancouver.
61 Interview with author, 20 February 2020, Vancouver.
62 Interview with author, 20 February 2020, Vancouver.
63 Interview with author, 20 February 2020, Vancouver.
64 Interview with author, 19 February 2020, Vancouver.
65 Interview with author, 19 February 2020, Vancouver.

5 Gender Dynamics in Sufi Rituals, Praxis, and Authority

1 Cornell (2019) points to parallels between Rabia and Plato's Diotima as another possible example of the influence of Neo-Platonism on the development of Sufism, especially as the "Lover" (188–96).

2 For more about the tradition that developed around Fatima, and its linkages to Maryam, see Alyssa Gabbay, *Gender and Succession in Medieval and Early Modern Islam: Bilateral Descent and the Legacy of Fatima* (2020) by.
3 The Arabic language, which is gendered, also informed these metaphysical approaches. As Schimmel (1992) explains, "for the Muslims this view – which stands in stark contrast to the Prophet's own words and practice – was facilitated by the fact that Arabic word *nafs*, which was usually understood as the *nafs ammāra*, "the soul inciting evil" (Sura 12/53), is grammatically feminine and thus could be associated with any number of images and metaphors. This negative attitude was strengthened by another grammatically feminine word, *dunyā*, 'this world,' 'the world of matter' (as contrasted with *al-ākhira*, the "other world"). Representations of the material world as dangerous woman occur in Islamic literature as they do in Christian texts as well as in Manichaean and gnostic writings" (96–7).
4 Many contemporary Sufi communities continue to evoke expressions of gender, especially of the feminine, through cosmological orientations. An example is the Maryamiyya's focus on Mary, which developed from the mystical vision of the Virgin Mary by Frithjof Schuon (d. 1998) in 1965. This experience altered the course of his Alawiyya branch and led to the group being renamed the Maryamiyya (see Sedgwick 2004; 2016). However, despite taking a metaphysical approach to gender that privileges the feminine, which in turn influences the theological and philosophical discourse of the movement, the social and institutional structures of some Traditionalist-oriented Sufi movements, like the Maryamiyya, still tend to reinforce a gender hierarchy, especially of a patriarchal nature.
5 *Mukhannath*, which Schimmel (1992) translates as "hermaphrodite," is another reoccurring figure in the poetry of Rumi. In Rumi's tales, this figure is "a model of those unreliable, hypocritical ones who belong neither to this world nor to the other, and he cannot help telling of such a person who met a shepherd and then complained that the buck in his herd had given him a funny look and laughed at him" (103).
6 There are few Sufi sources written by women. One is by the fifteenth-century Damascene Aishah al-Bauniyyah and is titled *The Principles of Sufism*, which has been translated by Emil Homerin (2016). This is a Sufi manual on comportment and practice.
7 Catherina Raudvere (2002) also captures how Sufi women had to negotiate various public and private spaces in contemporary Istanbul during ritual participation, such as during *zikr*.
8 There is a rich corpus of studies on Sufi shrines and women's devotion in South Asia. Examples include Bellamy (2012), Fluekiger (2006), Pemberton (2004), Anand Vivek Taneja, *Jinnealogy: Time, Islam, and Ecological Thought in the Medieval Ruins of Delhi* (2017), and Omar Kasmani, *Queer Companions: Religion, Public Intimacy, and Saintly Affects in Pakistan* (2022).

9 Abbas (2002) explores Sufi shrines, such as to Bulleh Shah in Kasur, Bibi Pak Daman, Data Ganj Bakhsh Hujwiri, Shah Hussain, and Mian Mir in Lahore, Lal Shahbaz Qalandar and Shah Abdul Latif in Sind, and Bahauddin Zakariya and Rukunuddin Shah Alam in Multan. At these various shrines, Abbas found women leading rituals such as *sama*. She highlights how the feminine trope or voice of Sufi women has been maintained in poetic traditions that are sung, such as Qawwali music.
10 For more on these figures, see "Gendering Sufism" in Sharify-Funk et al. (2017).
11 For an excellent study of women's mosques, please see Jacqueline H. Fewkes, *Locating Maldivian Women's Mosques in Global Discourses* (2019).
12 For more on this activism and wadud's legacy, see Kecia Ali, Juliane Hammer, and Laury Silver, eds., *A Jihad for Justice: Honoring the Work and Life of Amina Wadud* (2012).
13 For more perspectives on immigrant Muslim experiences, see Parin Dossa, *Racialized Bodies, Disabling Worlds: Storied Lives of Immigrant Muslim Women* (2009).
14 Interview with author, 18 February 2020, Vancouver.
15 Sufi women have a varying presence in the Persian tradition of Sufism, an important thread that has not been properly captured by my study due to this book's limited scope. I hope that future scholarship on Sufism in Canada will consider this important dimension. Javad Nurbakhsh, the Sufi *shaykh* of the Nimatullahi Order, which has a branch in Toronto, has published a hagiography of Sufi women titled *Sufi Women* (1983), which is available in English.
16 Interview with author, 3 January 2018, Toronto.
17 Interview with author, 3 January 2018, Toronto.
18 Visit Cemalnur Sargut, http://cemalnur.org/contents/detail/his-understanding-of-woman/664.
19 Visit Cemalnur Sargut, http://cemalnur.org/contents/detail/his-understanding-of-woman/664.
20 Cemalnur's global presence can be seen in her Twitter following, which has almost 100,000 followers. She has also established Islamic studies academic positions, named after Kenan Rifai, at the University of North Carolina and Kyoto University. Visit her website http://cemalnur.org/contents/detail/cemalnur-sargut-kimdir/12. Samiha Ayverdi, a Turkish writer and Sufi, succeeded Kenan Rifai. For more on Cemalnur, please see Sharify-Funk et al. (2017).
21 For more on Cemalnur Sargut's teachings in English, see Thaver (2017). See also Feyza Burak-Adli, "Trajectories of Modern Sufism: An Ethnohistorical Study of the Rifai Order and Social Change in Turkey" (PhD diss., Boston University, 2020).
22 Muzaffer Ozak al-Jerrahi has published many books in English for a western audience, such as *Blessed Virgin Mary* (1991), which captures again a classical trend of the veneration of the creative feminine principle in the figure of Mary.
23 Interview with author, 3 January 2018, Toronto.
24 Interview with author, 15 December 2019, Toronto.

25 Interview with author via Skype, 17 May 2019, Kingston and Montreal.
26 This comment was relayed to me during my conversation with Cem Aydogdu, the translator and *murid* of Sherif Baba Çatalkaya, on 11 August 2020.
27 There are other Sufi women leaders in Canada; however, for this book I have looked specifically at communities that are broadly affiliated with Rumi and his legacy. So I have had to exclude other voices. Again, I hope future scholars on Sufism in Canada will develop these threads further. For instance, the Canadian branch of the Azeemia Spiritual and Healing Center Canada, whose current leader is Khwaja Shamsuddin Azeemi, regularly meets in Mississauga in the Greater Toronto Region. That centre organizes an annual Adam's Day ("Unity in Diversity") to honour the origins of humanity in the patriarch. That day, initiated by Khawja Shamsuddin Azeemi, is celebrated in America, the United Kingdom, and Canada. The same event celebrates the anniversary of the order's patron saint Qalandar Baba Auliya, who founded the *silsila-e-azeemia* in Karachi, Pakistan. The community has centres across Europe, the UK, Thailand, the United Arab Emirates, the United States, and Canada. It is oriented toward Islam and Sufism but also utilizes colour therapy, meditation (*muraqba* or mental concentration), and parapsychology while stressing scientific thought. Its website streams events live and provides access to audio and video archives; also, *duas* can be requested online. The community also commemorates a *mehfil e meelad* for the Prophet Muhammad and an *urs* for its *shaykh*, Qalandar Baba Auliya. The Mississauga branch is led by a Pakistani woman, and much of the organizing of the events involves women and men students. This *shaykha* holds regular gatherings in her home and has also led *zikr* and prayers in public gatherings, such as during Adam's Day.
28 Her recitations are included in Michael Sells's *Approaching the Qur'ān: The Early Revelations* (1999) as well as the PBS documentary *Islam, Empire of Faith* (2000).
29 Interview with author, 20 February 2020, Vancouver.
30 Interview with author, 20 February 2020, Vancouver.
31 Maududi founded Jamaat-e Islami, a religio-political party in Pakistan. He was a scholar, activist, journalist, and jurist. He died in Buffalo, New York. The Muslim Brotherhood, an anti-colonial social justice movement founded in Egypt by Hassan al-Banna (d. 1949), has become one of the world's most influential Islamist political movements.
32 Interview with author, 20 February 2020, Vancouver.
33 Interview with the author, 20 February 2020, Vancouver.
34 Interview with author, 18 December 2018, Oakville.
35 Interview with author, 18 December 2018, Oakville.
36 Interview with author, 18 December 2018, Oakville.
37 A link to the tarot cards is https://www.penguinrandomhouse.com/books/712682/the-sufi-tarot-by-ayeda-husain.
38 For more, see Katz (2014).
39 Interview with author, 18 December 2018, Oakville.

40 Interview with author, 18 December 2018, Oakville.
41 Interview with author, 18 December 2018, Oakville.
42 Interview with author, 18 December 2018, Oakville.
43 Interview with author, 18 December 2018, Oakville.

Epilogue

1 These individuals have been members of the movement for decades (and thus when labelling this group, a white Sufi community, it erases their presence).
2 See the special issue of *Journal of Islamic Studies* on "Engaged Sufism" edited by Kugle and Shaikh; see also Said, Funk, et al. (2001). Sri Lanka was plagued by civil war for nearly three decades, and this informed Bawa's approach to non-violence. During his ministry in northern Sri Lanka, he often tried to dissuade his Tamil students from engaging in violence. He arrived in Philadelphia at a time when race-based Muslim organizations like the Nation of Islam (NOI) and the Moorish Science Temple (MST) were forming in America. During his initial ministry there, he attracted many African American students from these organizations. Bawa was himself a racialized man, and this resonated with racialized Americans.
3 Rozehnal (2019) in his study of the Inayati Order and its cyber-presence highlights some of the ways in which Zia Inayat-Khan and his community's online presence include social justice and activism work.
4 https://www.jerrahi.ca/relief-work.
5 For pictures and more details, visit http://iqra.ca/2014/bridges-beyond-faith-an-event-dedicated-to-peace.
6 https://www.jerrahi.ca/gallery.
7 See other such events on their homepage, https://www.jerrahi.ca/events.
8 For a documentary on the life and activism of El-Farouk Khaki, visit https://vimeo.com/395012143?fbclid=IwAR2HKopRibk4Gym1xifzQIQNt3vcuMAsPnbDBvF_fOaCP8IPNp36A6MgRy0.
9 Interview with author, 20 February 2020, Vancouver.
10 Whiteness is also not a stable category and never has been. For more on this discussion, see Neda Maghbouleh, *The Limits of Whiteness: Iranian Americans and the Everyday Politics of Race*.
11 Interview with author via Skype, 17 May 2019, Kingston and Montreal.
12 Interview with author via Skype, 17 May 2019, Kingston and Montreal.

Bibliography

Abbas, Shemeen Burney. 2002. *The Female Voice in Sufi Ritual: Devotional Practices of Pakistan and India*. Austin: University of Texas Press.

Abdou, Mohamed. 2022. *Islam and Anarchism: Relationships and Resonances*. London: Pluto Press.

Ahmed, Sahab. 2016. *What Is Islam? The Importance of Being Islamic*. Princeton: Princeton University Press.

Aidi, Hisham D. 2014. *Rebel Music: Race, Empire, and the New Muslim Youth Culture*. New York: Vintage Books.

Albanese, Catherine. 2008. *The Republic of Mind and Spirit: A Cultural History of American Metaphysical Religion*. New Haven: Yale University Press.

Aldred, Lisa. 2000. "Plastic Shamans and Astroturf Sun Dances: New Age Commercialization of Native American Spirituality." *American Indian Quarterly* 24, no. 3: 329–52.

Ali, Rozina. 2017. "The Erasure of Islam from the Poetry of Rumi." *The New Yorker*, 5 January 2017.

Ali, Kecia, Juliane Hammer, and Laury Silvers, eds. 2012. *A Jihad for Justice: Honoring the Work and Life of Amina Wadud*. 48hourbooks. https://www.bu.edu/religion/files/2010/03/A-Jihad-for-Justice-for-Amina-Wadud-2012-1.pdf.

Alvi, Sajida, Homa Hoodfar, and Sheila McDonough, eds. 2003. *The Muslim Veil in North America: Issues and Debates*. Toronto: Women's Press.

Aminrazavi, Mehdi, eds. 2014. *Sufism and American Literary Masters*. Albany: SUNY Press.

Arjana, Sophia Rose. 2017. *Pilgrimage in Islam: Traditional and Modern Practices*. London: Oneworld.

– 2020. *Buying Buddha, Selling Rumi: Orientalism and the Mystical Marketplace*. London: OneWorld.

Arjana, Sophia Rose, and Kim Fox. 2018. *Veiled Superheroes: Islam, Feminism, and Popular Culture*. Lanham: Lexington Books.

Aslan, Rose. 2014. "The Museumification of Rumi's Tomb: Deconstructing Sacred Space at the Mevlana Museum." *International Journal of Religious Tourism and Pilgrimage* 2, no. 2: 1–16.

Atwood, Margaret. 1985. *The Handmaid's Tale*. Toronto: McClelland and Stewart.

Austin, Allan D. 1984. *African Muslims in Antebellum America: Transatlantic Stories and Spiritual Struggles*. New York: Garland.

Avery, Kenneth S. 2004. *The Psychology of Early Sufi Samaʿ*. Abingdon: Routledge.

Ayubi, Zahra. 2019. *Classical Islamic Ethics of the Self, Family, and Society*. New York: Columbia University Press.

Azad, Arezou. 2013. "Female Mystics in Medieval Islam: The Quiet Legacy." *Journal of Economic and Social History of the Orient* 56, no. 1: 53–88.

Bakht, Natasha. Eds. 2008. *Belonging and Banishment: Being Muslim in Canada*. Toronto: TSAR.

Baquaqua, Mahommah Gardo. 1854. *Biography of Mahommah G. Baquaqua, A Native of Zoogoo, in the Interior of Africa*. Geo. E. Pomeroy & Co., Tribune Office.

Baquaqua, Mahommah Gardo. *The Biography of Mahommah Gardo Baquaqua: His Passage from Slavery to Freedom in Africa and America*, edited by Robin Law and Paul E. Lovejoy. Princeton: Wiener, 2007.

Barber, Theodore, 1986. "Four Interpretations of Mevlevi Dervish Dance, 1920-1929." *Dance Chronicle* 9, no. 3: 328–55.

Barks, Coleman. 1995. *The Essential Rumi*. San Francisco. Harper.

Barks, Coleman, and Michael Green. 1997. *The Illuminated Rumi*. New York: Broadway Books.

Barras, Amélie, Jennifer A. Selby, and Melanie Adrian, eds. 2021. *Producing Islam(s) in Canada: On Knowledge, Positionality and Politics*. Toronto. University of Toronto Press.

Bainbridge, William Sims, and Rodney Stark. 1982. "Church and Cult in Canada." *Canadian Journal of Sociology/Cahiers canadien de sociologie* 7, no. 4: 351–66.

Bazzano, Elliott, and Marcia Hermansen, eds. 2020. *Varieties of American Sufism: Islam, Sufi Orders, and Authority in a Time of Transition*. New York: SUNY Press.

Bellamy, Carla. 2011. *The Powerful Ephemeral*. Berkeley: University of California Press.

Bennett, John G. 1973. *Is There Life on Earth?: An Introduction to Gurdjieff*. New York: Stonehill.

Birchok, Daniel Andrew. 2016. "Women, Genealogical Inheritance and Sufi Authority: The Female Saints of Seunagan, Indonesia." *Asian Studies Review* 40, no. 4: 583–99.

Blann, Gregory. 2015. *Lifting the Boundaries: Muzaffer Efendi and the Transmission of Sufism to the West*. New York: Pir Press.

Bodian, Stephan, eds. *Yoga Journal*. January–February 1992, 1–122.

Bram, Chen, and Meir Hatina. 2014. "From Sufism to Universal Vision: Murat Yagan and the Teaching of Kebzeh." *Journal of Sufi Studies* 3: 67–92.

Bramadat, Paul, and David Seljak, eds. 2009. *Religion and Ethnicity in Canada*. Toronto: University of Toronto Press.

Bibliography

Bramadat, Paul, Patricia O'Connell Killen, and Sarah Wilkins-Laflamme, eds. 2022. *Religion at the Edge: Nature, Spirituality, and Secularity in the Pacific Northwest*. Vancouver: UBC Press.

Bucar, Elizabeth. 2017. *Pious Fashion: How Muslim Women Dress*. Cambridge, MA: Harvard University Press.

– 2022. *Stealing My Religion: Not Just Any Cultural Appropriation*. Cambridge, MA: Harvard University Press.

Buehler, Arthur F. 2016. *Recognizing Sufism: Contemplation in the Islamic Tradition*. London and New York: I.B. Tauris.

Burak-Adli, Feyza. 2020. "Trajectories of Modern Sufism: An Ethnohistorical Study of the Rifai Order and Social Change in Turkey." PhD diss., Boston University.

Buturović, Amila. 2001. "Between the Tariqa and Shari'a: The Making of the Female Self." In *Feminist Poetics of the Sacred: Creative Suspicions*, edited by F. Devlin-Glass and L. Mcredden, 135–60. Oxford: Oxford University Press.

Cannon, Garland, ed. 1970. *The Letters of Sir William Jones*, vol. 1. Oxford: Clarendon Press.

Chandler, Siobhan. 2011. *The Social Ethic of Religiously Unaffiliated Spirituality*. PhD diss., Wilfrid Laurier University.

Chittick, William. 1983. *The Sufi Path of Love: The Spiritual Teachings of Rumi*. Albany: SUNY Press.

Chitwood, Ken. 2021. *The Muslims of Latin America and the Caribbean*. Boulder: Lynne Rienner.

Choquette, Robert. 2004. *Canada's Religions*. Ottawa: University of Ottawa Press.

Ciabattari, Jane. 2014. "Why Is Rumi the Best-Selling Poet in the US?" *BBC*, 21 October.

Cirianni-Salazar, Lucía. 2021. "Sufism in Mexico: A Transformed or Trans-Formal Tradition?" *Bloomsbury Religion in North America*, 1–17. London: Bloomsbury Academic.

Cornell, Rkia E. 2019. *The Many Faces of Islam's Most Famous Woman Saint, Rabi'a Al-'Adawiyya*. London: Oneworld.

Curtis IV, Edward E. 2019. *Muslim American Politics and the Future of US Democracy*. New York: NYU Press.

Dakake, Maria Massi. 2006. "'Walking upon the Path of God Like Men?' Women and the Feminine in the Islamic Mystical Tradition" in *Sufism Love and Wisdom*, edited by Jean-Louis Michon and Roger Gaetani, 131–51. Bloomington: World Wisdom.

Darlyrmple, William. 2005. *Sufi Soul: The Mystic Music of Islam*. Brighton: Electric Sky. http://www.aspresolver.com/aspresolver.asp?ANTH;1869249.

Dass, Ram. 1971. *Be Here Now*. San Cristobal: Lama Foundation.

Daulatzai, Sohail and Junaid Rana, eds. 2018. *With Stones in Our Hands: Writings on Muslims, Racism, and Empire*. Minneapolis: University of Minnesota Press.

Dawson, Lorne L. 1998. "The Cultural Significance of New Religious Movements and Globalization: A Theoretical Prolegomenon." *Journal for the Scientific Study of Religion* 37, no. 4: 580–95.

Declich, Francesca. 2000. "Sufi Experience in Rural Somali: A Focus on Women." *Social Anthropology* 8, no. 3: 295–318.

Dewji, Sahir. 2018. *Beyond Muslim Xenophobia and Contemporary Parochialism: Aga Khan IV, the Isma'ilis, and the Making of a Cosmopolitan Ethic*. PhD diss., Wilfrid Laurier University.

Dickson, William Rory. 2012. "Living Sufism in North America: Between Tradition and Transformation." PhD diss., Wilfrid Laurier University.

– 2014. "An American Sufism: The Naqshbandi-Haqqani Order as a Public Religion." In *Studies in Religion* 43, no. 3: 411–24.

– 2015. *Living Sufism in North America: Between Tradition and Transformation*. New York: SUNY Press.

– 2020. "The Golden Sufi Center: A Non-Islamic Branch of the Naqshbandiyya-Mujaddidiyya." In *Varieties of Sufism: Islam, Sufi Orders, and Authority in a Time of Transition*, edited by Elliot Bazzano and Marcia Hermansen, 27–54. New York: SUNY Press.

– 2022. "Sufism and *Shari'a*: Contextualizing Contemporary Sufi Expressions." *Religions* 13, no. 5: 449. https://doi.org/10.3390/rel13050449.

Dickson, William Rory, and Meena Sharify-Funk. 2017. *Unveiling Sufism: From Manhattan to Mecca*. Sheffield: Equinox.

Dickson, William Rory, and Merin Shobhana Xavier. 2019. "Disordering and Reordering Sufism: North American Sufi Teachers and the Tariqa Model." In *Global Sufism: Boundaries, Narratives, and Practices*, edited by Mark Sedgwick and Francesco Piraino, 137–56. London: Hurst.

Diouf, Sylviane A. 2013. *Servants of Allah: African Muslims Enslaved in the Americas*, 15th anniversary edition. New York: NYU Press.

Domínguez Díaz, Marta. 2022. "Gender Reconfigurations and Family Ideology in Abdul Rauf Felpete's Latin American Haqqaniyya." *Religions* 13: 1–23. Special Issue: Female Mystics and the Divine Feminine in Global Sufi Experience.

Dosa, Parin Aziz. 2009. *Racialized Bodies, Disabling Worlds: Storied Lives of Immigrant Muslim Women*. Toronto: University of Toronto Press.

Doyle, Patrick. 2015. "Chris Martin on Post-Divorce Depression, Coldplay's New 'Hippie Album.'" *Rolling Stone*, 19 November. https://www.rollingstone.com/music/music-news/chris-martin-on-post-divorce-depression-coldplays-new-hippie-album-38145.

Drew, Benjamin, 1856. *A North-Side View of Slavery. The Refugee: or the Narratives of Fugitive Slaves in Canada. Related by Themselves, with an Account of the History and Condition of the Coloured Population of Upper Canada*. Boston: John P. Jewett and Company.

During, Jean. 1992. "What Is Sufi Music?" In *The Legacy of Medieval Persian Sufism*, edited by Leonard Lewisohn, 277–87. London: Khaniqahi-Nimatullahi.

– 2018. "What Is Sufi Music?" In *The Heritage of Sufism: The Legacy of Medieval Persian Sufism (1150–1500)*, vol. 2, edited by Leonard Lewisohn, 227–87. Oxford: Oneworld.

Einboden, Jeffrey. 2014. *Islam and Romanticism: Muslim Currents from Goethe to Emerson*. London: Oneworld.

Emerson, Ralph Waldo. 1858. *The Atlantic Monthly: A Magazine of Literature Art, and Politics*. Boston: Phillips, Sampson and Company.

Ernst, Carl. 1997. *Sufism: An Introduction to the Mystical Tradition of Islam*. Boulder. Shambhala.

– 2005. "Situating Sufism and Yoga." *Journal of the Royal Asiatic Society*, 3rd series, 15, no. 1: 15–43.

Ernst, Carl W, and Bruce B. Lawrence. 2002. *Sufi Martyrs of Love: The Chishti Order in South Asia and Beyond*. New York: Palgrave Macmillan.

Evanson, Tanya. 2017. *Bothism*. Victoria: Ekstasis Editions Canada.

– 2018. *Nouveau Griot*. Okotoks: Frontenac House.

– 2020. *Book of Wings*. Montreal: Véhicule Press.

Fansi, Muhsin, David Shea, and Anthony Troyer. 1901. *The Dabistan or School of Manners: The Religious beliefs, observances, Philosophic Opinions and Social Customs of the nations of the East*. London and Toronto: L.B. Tetens.

Fayez, Ghulam M. 1980. "Images of the Divine in Rumi and Whitman." *Comparative Literature Studies* 17, no. 1: 33–43.

Feild, Reshad, 2002. *The Last Barrier: A Journey into the Essence of Sufi Teachings* [1976]. Great Barrington: Lindisfarne Books.

Fewkes, Jacqueline H. 2019. *Locating Maldivian Women's Mosques in Global Discourses*. Cham: Palgrave Macmillan.

Flueckiger, Joyce Burkhalter. 2006. *In Amma's Healing Room: Gender and Vernacular Islam in South Asia*. Bloomington: Indiana University Press.

Ford, Arthur L. 1987. "The Rose Garden of the World: Near East Imagery in the Poetry of Walt Whitman." *Quarterly Review* 5, no. 1: 12–20.

Formichi, Chiara. 2020. *Islam and Asia*. Cambridge: Cambridge University Press.

Frager, Ragip, ed. 2009. *Love Is the Wine*. Chino Valley: Hohm.

Friedlander, Shems. 2003. *Rumi and the Whirling Dervishes*. New York: Parabola Books.

Frishkopf, Michael. 2009. "Globalizing the Soundworld: Islam and Sufi Music in the West." In *Sufis in Western Society: Global Networking and Locality*, edited by Markus Dressler, Ron Geaves, and Gritt Klinkhammer, 46–76. London: Routledge.

– 2011. "Ritual as Strategic Action: The Social Logic of Musical Silence in Canadian Islam." In *Muslim Rap, Halal Soaps, and Revolutionary Theatre: Artistic Developments in the Muslim World*, edited by Karim van Nieuwkerk, 115–48. Austin: University of Texas Press.

Gabbay, Alyssa. 2020. *Gender and Succession in Medieval and Early Modern Islam: Bilateral Descent and the Legacy of Fatima*. London: Bloomsbury Press.

Gallardo, M.V. Romero. 2016. "Sufism in Mexico." *Encyclopedia of Latin American Religions*, edited by Henri Gooren, 1–3. New York: Springer.

Le Gall, Dina. 2005. *A Culture of Sufism: Naqshbandīs in the Ottoman World 1450-1700*. New York: SUNY Press.

Gardner, Robert H. 2000. *Islam Empire of Faith*. PBS.
Geaves, Ron. 2000. *The Sufis of Britain: An Exploration of Muslim Identity*. London: Cardiff Academic Press.
– 2009. "A Case of Cultural Binary Fission or Transglobal Sufism? The Transmigration of Sufism to Britain." In *Sufis in Western Society: Global Networking and Locality*, edited by Ron Geaves, Markus Dressler, and Gritt Klinkhammer, 97–112. Abingdon: Routledge.
Geaves, Ron and Theodore Gabriel, eds. 2013. *Sufism in Britain*. London: Bloomsbury.
Geertz, Clifford. 1998. "Deep Hanging Out." *New York Review of Books*. 45, no. 16: 69–72.
Genn, Celia. 2007. "The Development of a Modern Western Sufism." In *Sufism and the "Modern" in Islam*, 257–78. London: I.B Tauris.
– 2004. "Exploration and Analysis of the Origins, Nature and Development of the Sufi Movement in Australia." PhD diss., University of Queensland.
Ghani, Katayoun, 2018. *The Sound of Silence: An Ethnography of the Samaʿ Ritual in the Nematallohi Kaneqah in Toronto*. MA thesis, York University, Toronto.
Gill, Kuldip. 1999. *Dharma Rasa*. Roberts Creek: Nightwood Editions.
Gilroy, Paul. 1995. *The Black Atlantic: Modernity and Double Consciousness*. Cambridge, MA: Harvard University Press.
Gray, Biko Mandela. 2015. "Show and Prove: Fiver Percenters and the Study of African American Esotericism." In *Esotericism in African American Religious Experience*, edited by Stephen Finley, Margarita Simon Guillory, and Hugh R. Page, Jr, 177–97. Leiden and Boston: E.J. Brill.
Grewal, Zareena. 2013. *Islam is a Foreign Country. American Muslims and the Global Crisis of Authority*. New York: NYU Press.
Gurdjieff, G.I. 1950. *Beelzebub's Tales to His Grandson: An Objectively Impartial Criticism of the Life of Man*. Victoria: Rare Treasures.
Haddad, Mouloud. 2008. "Zawiya réelle, zawiya virtuelle. Soufisme, francophonie et nouvelles technologies au Québec." In *Globe, Revue international d'études québécoises Érudit*, 197–208.
Hammer, Julianne. 2012. *American Muslim Women, Religious Authority, and Activism: More Than a Prayer*. Austin: University of Texas Press.
Harding, John S., Victor Sōgen Hori, and Alexander Soucy, eds. 2010. *Wild Geese: Buddhism in Canada*. Montreal and Kingston: McGill-Queen's University Press.
Hazen, Juliane. 2017. *The Alami Tariqa of Waterport, New York*. Lanham: Lexington Books.
Hermansen, Marcia. 1997. "In the Garden of American Sufi Movements: Hybrids and Perennials." In *New Trends and Developments in the World of Islam*, edited by Peter B. Clarke, 155–78. London: Luzac Oriental Press.
– 2006. "Sufism and American Women." *World History Connected* 4, no. 1. https://worldhistoryconnected.press.uillinois.edu/4.1/hermansen.html.
Hendrick, Joshua D. 2013. *Gülen: The Ambiguous Politics of Market Islam in Turkey and the World*. New York: NYU Press.

Hill, Joseph. 2010. "'All Women are Guides': Sufi Leadership and Womanhood among Taalibe Baay in Senegal." *Journal of Religion in Africa* 40, no. 4: 375–412.
- 2014. "Picturing Islamic Authority: Gender Metaphors and Sufi Leadership in Senegal." *Islamic Africa* 5, no. 2: 275–315.
- 2018. *Wrapping Authority: Women Islamic Leaders in a Sufi Movement in Dakar, Senegal*. Toronto: University of Toronto Press.

Hodgson, M.G. 1974. *The Venture of Islam: Conscience and History in a World Civilization*. 3 vols. Chicago: University of Chicago Press.

Hoffman, Valerie. 2009. *Sufism, Mystics, and Saints in Modern Egypt*. Columbia: University of South Carolina Press.

Hogben, Murray. 2021. *Minarets on the Horizon: Muslim Pioneers in Canada*. Toronto: Mawenzi House.

Holub-Moorman, Grant, and Frank Stasio. 2020. "'Impossible Documents' – How an Enslaved Muslim Scholar Illuminates Southern Identity." WUNC 91.5, North Carolina Public Radio. https://www.wunc.org/post/impossible-documents-how-enslaved-muslim-scholar-illuminates-southern-identity?fbclid=IwAR28AXhsLYI_PkTEBnsqairTEsOf8SW5zW50bV5VNM4VT_FeL1jiTbTYreo.

Homerin, Emil. 2016. *Aisha al-Ba'uniyya: A Life in Parise of Love*. London: Oneworld.

Hussain, Amir. 2001. *The Canadian Face of Islam: Muslim Communities in Toronto*. PhD diss., University of Toronto.

Hussain, Amir, and Jamie S. Scott. 2012. "Muslims." In *The Religions of Canadians*, edited by Jamie S. Scott, 161–218. Toronto: University of Toronto Press.

Inayat-Khan, Zia. 2006. *A Hybrid Sufi Order at the Crossroads of Modernity: The Sufi Order and Sufi Movement of Pir-o-Murshid Inayat Khan*. PhD diss., Duke University.

Ingram, Brannon. 2018. *Revival from Below: The Deoband Movement and Global Islam*. Berkeley: University of California Press.

Irwin, Robert. 2019. "Global Rumi." In *Global Sufism: Boundaries, Structures, and Politics*, edited by Francesco Piranio and Mark Sedgwick, 15–34. London: Hurst.

Jackson-Best, Fatimah. 2019. "Black Muslims in Canada: Challenging Narratives of Belonging and Rootedness." *Maydan*. https://themaydan.com/2019/03/black-muslims-in-canada-challenging-narratives-of-belonging-and-rootedness.

Jain, Andrea R. 2015. *Selling Yoga: From Counterculture to Pop Culture*. Oxford: Oxford University Press.

Jankowsky, Richard C. 2021. *Ambient Sufism: Ritual Niches and the Social Work of Musical Form*. Chicago: University of Chicago Press.

Janmohamed, Sheniz. 2010. *Bleeding Light*. Toronto: Mawenzi House.
- 2014. *Firesmoke*. Toronto: Mawenzi House.
- 2021. *Reminders on the Path*. Toronto: Mawenzi House.

Jerrahi Order of Canada. https://www.jerrahi.ca.

Al-Jerrahi, Muzaffer Ozak. 1991. *Blessed Virgin Mary*. Westport: Pir Press.

Jironet, Karin. 2009. *The Life, Times, and Leadership of Hazrat Inayat Khan Brothers, 1927–1967*. Leuven: Peeters.

Johnston, Patricia, and Joan McIntyre, eds. 1997. *I Come from Behind Kaf Mountain: The Spiritual Autobiography of Murat Yagan* [1984]. Vernon: Kebzeh.

Karamustafa, Ahmet T. 1994. *God's Unruly Friends: Dervish Groups in the Islamic Later Middle Period, 1200–1550.* Salt Lake City: University of Utah Press.

Kasmani, Omar. 2022. *Queer Companions Religion, Public Intimacy, and Saintly Affects in Pakistan.* Durham: Duke University Press.

Katz, Marion Holmes. 2014. *Women in the Mosque: A History of Legal Thought and Social Practice.* New York: Columbia University Press.

Kazemipur, Abdolmohammad. 2014. *The Muslim Question in Canada: A Story of Segmented Integration.* Vancouver: UBC Press.

Kazi, Nazia. 2018. *Islamophobia, Race, and Global Politics.* Lanham: Rowman and Littlefield.

Keller, Nuh Ha Mim. 2002. *Sufism and Islam.* Amman: Wakeel Books.

– 2011. *Sea without Shore: A Manual of the Sufi Path.* Beltsville: Amana.

Kestenbaum, Sam. 2016. "5 Jewish Sufis You Should Know" in *Forward*. https://forward.com/news/352213/5-jewish-sufis-you-should-know.

Khabeer, Su'ad Abdul. 2016. *Muslim Cool: Race, Religion, and Hip Hop in the United States.* New York: NYU Press.

Khan, Aliyah. 2020. *Far from Mecca: Globalizing the Muslim Caribbean.* New Brunswick: Rutgers University Press.

Khan, Dominique-Sila. 2003. *Conversions and Shifting Identities: Ramdev Pir and the Ismailis in Rajasthan.* New Delhi: Manohar.

– 2004. *Crossing the Threshold: Understanding Religious Identities in South Asia.* London and New York: I.B. Tauris.

Khan, Hidayat Inayat. 1994. *Sufi Teachings: Lectures from Lake O'Hara.* Victoria: Ekstasis Editions Canada.

Khan, Vilayat Inayat. 1974. *Toward the One.* New York: Harper and Row.

Knight, Michael Muhammad. 2020. *Metaphysical Africa: Truth and Blackness in the Ansaru Allah Community.* University Park: Penn State University Press.

Knysh, Alexander. 1999. *Ibn 'Arabi in the Later Islamic Tradition: The Making of a Polemical Image in Medieval Islam.* New York: SUNY Press.

– 2017. *Sufism: A New History of Islamic Mysticism.* Princeton: Princeton University Press.

– 2019. "Definitions of Sufism as a Meeting Place of Eastern and Western 'Creative Imaginations.'" In *Sufism East and West: Reorientation and Dynamism of Mystical Islam in the Modern World*, edited by Jamal Malik and Saeed Zarrabi-Zadeh, 53–75. Leiden and Boston, E.J. Brill.

Küçük, Hülya. 2008. "A Brief History of Western Sufism." *Asian Journal of Social Science* 36, no. 2: 292–320.

– 2010. "Sultān Walad's Understanding of Sufism: Between Populism and Theosophy." *Asian Journal of Social Science* 38, no. 1: 60–8.

– 2012a. "Sultān Walad's Role in the Foundation of the Mevlevi Sufi Order" in *Mawlana Rumi Review* 3: 22–50.

- 2012b. "From His Mother Nūr al-Ansāriyya to his šayh Fātime bt. Ibn al-Mutannā: Important Female Figures around Muhyī l-Dīn b. al-'Arabi (d. 638/1240)." *Arabica* 59: 685–708.
- 2015. "Female Substitutes and Shaykhs in the History of Sufism: The Case of the Mawlawiyya Sufi Order from Its Early Phase to the Eighteenth Century." *Mawlana Rumi Review* 4: 106–31.

Kuehn, Sara, 2018. "Wild Social Transcendence and the Antinomian Dervish." In *Moralities of Warfare and Religion. Interdisciplinary Journal for Religion and Transformation in Contemporary Society* 4, no. 1: 254–85, https://doi.org/10.14220/23642807-00401014.

Law, Robin, and Paul E. Lovejoy. 2007. "Introduction: The Interesting Narrative of Mahommah Gardo Baquaqua." In *The Biography of Mahommah Gardo Baquaqua: His Passage from Slavery to Freedom in Africa and America* [1818]. Princeton: Markus Wiener.

Lawrence, Bruce. 2021. *Islamicate Cosmopolitan Spirit*. New Jersey: John Wiley and Sons.

LeBlanc, Marie Nathalie. 2013. "Sufi Muslims in Montréal: Tensions between Cosmopolitanism and the Cultural Economy of Difference." *Anthropologica* 55, no. 2: 425–40.

Lenard, Patti Tamara, and Peter Balint. 2020. "What Is (the Wrong of) Cultural Appropriation?" *Ethnicities* 20, no. 2: 331–52. Special Issue: Diversity in an Anti-Immigration Era.

Lewis, Franklin D. 2000. *Rumi: Past and Present, East and West: The Life, Teachings and Poetry of Jalâl al-Din Rumi*. London: Oneworld.

Lewis, Samuel L. 1973. *This Is the New Age, in Person*. San Francisco: Sufi Ruhaniat International.

Lewisohn, Leonard. 1997. "The Sacred Music of Islam: Samāʿ in the Persian Sufi Tradition." *British Journal of Ethnomusicology* 6: 1–33.

Lings, Martin. 1961. *A Sufi Saint of the Twentieth Century: Shaikh Ahmad Al-ʿAlawi, His Spiritual Heritage and Legacy*. Crows Nest: Allen and Unwin.

Lipka, Michael. 2019. "5 Facts about Religion in Canada." *Pew Research Center*. https://www.pewresearch.org/fact-tank/2019/07/01/5-facts-about-religion-in-canada.

Lofton, Kathryn. 2011. *Oprah: The Gospel of an Icon*. Berkeley: University of California Press.
- 2017. *Consuming Religion*. Chicago: University of Chicago Press.

Lucia, Amanda. 2014. *Reflections of Amma: Devotees in a Global Embrace*. Berkeley: University of California Press.
- 2020. *White Utopias: The Religious Exoticism of Transformational Festivals*. Berkeley: University of California Press.

Mack, Beverly B., and Jean Boyd. 2000. *One Woman's Jihad: Nana Asma'u Scholar and Scribe*. Bloomington: Indiana University Press.

Maghbouleh, Neda. 2017. *The Limits of Whiteness: Iranian Americans and the Everyday Politics of Race*. Stanford: Stanford University Press.

Marcotte, Roxanne D. 2010. "Muslim Women in Canada: Autonomy and Empowerment." *Journal of Muslim Minority Affairs* 30, no. 3: 357–73.

Marcus-Sells, Ariela. 2022. *Sorcery or Science? Contesting Knowledge and Practice in West African Sufi Texts*. University Park: Penn State University Press.

Markoff, Irene, 1995. "Introduction to Sufi Music and Ritual in Turkey." *Middle East Studies Association Bulletin* 29, no. 2: 157–60.

Masuzawa, Tomoko. 2005. *The Invention of World Religions Or, How European Universalism Was Preserved in the Language of Pluralism*. Chicago: University of Chicago Press.

McDonough, Sheila. 2000. "The Muslims of Canada." In *The South Asian Religious Diaspora in Britain, Canada, and the United States*, edited by Harold Coward, John R. Hinnells, and Raymond Brady Williams. Albany: SUNY Press, 174–90.

– 2005. "Muslims in Canada: From Ethnic Groups to Religious Community." In *Religion and Ethnicity in Canada*, edited by Paul Bramadat and David Seljak, 133–54. Toronto. Pearson Longman.

McKittrick, Katherine. 2006. *Demonic Grounds: Black Women and the Cartographies of Struggle*. Minneapolis: University of Minnesota Press.

– 2020. *Dear Science and Other Stories*. Durham: Duke University Press.

Mercier-Dalphond, Geneviève. 2021. "Local Tales of Sufism in Quebec: Secular Politics of Moderation and the Production of Charismatic Muslims." *ReOrient* 6, no. 2: 129–50.

Michon, Jean-Louis. 2006. "Sacred Music and Dance in Islam." In *Sufism Love and Wisdom*, edited by Jean-Louis Michon and Roger Gaetani, 153–77. Bloomington: World Wisdom.

Milani Milad, Adam Possamai, Firdaus Wajdi F. 2017. "Branding of Spiritual Authenticity and Nationalism in Transnational Sufism." In *Religions, Nations, and Transnationalism in Multiple Modernities*, ed. Patrick Michel, Adam Possamai A., and Bryan S. Turner, 197–220. New York: Palgrave Macmillan.

Miller, Bruce. 2018. *Rumi Comes to America: How the Poet of Mystic Arrived on our Shores*. Decatur: Miller eMedia.

Miller, Rasul. 2020a. "The Black American Sufi: A History." in *Sapelo*. https://sapelosquare.com/2020/03/18/the-black-american-sufi-a-history.

– 2020b. "When the Divine Flood Reached New York: The Tijani Sufi Order among Black American Muslims in New York." In *Varieties of American Sufism: Islam, Sufi Orders, and Authority in a Time of Transition*, edited by Marcia Hermansen and Elliott Bazzano, 209–36. Albany: SUNY Press.

Mosurinjohn, Sharday, and Emma Funnell-Kononuk. 2017. "Free the Children as a 'New Secular Spiritual Movement': A Case Study on the Conceptual Boundaries between 'spirituality,' 'the Sacred,' and "New Religious Movements."' *Journal for the Study of Spirituality* 7, no. 2: 114–27.

Murata, Sachiko. 1992. *The Tao of Islam: A Sourcebook on Gender Relationships in Islamic Thought*. Albany: SUNY Press.

Nagra, Baljit. 2018. "Cultural Explanations of Patriarchy, Race, and Everyday Lives: Marginalizing and 'Othering' Muslim Women in Canada." *Journal of Muslim Minority Affairs* 38, no. 2: 263–79.

Najmabadi, Afsaneh. 2005. *Women with Mustaches and Men without Beards: Gender and Sexual Anxieties of Iranian Modernity*. Berkeley: University of California Press.

Nasir, Kamaludeen Mohamed. 2016. *Globalized Muslim Youth in the Asia Pacific: Popular Culture in Singapore and Sydney*. Hampshire: Palgrave Macmillan.

Newbolt, Henry. 1902. *The Sailing of the Long-Ships and Other Poems*. Toronto: George N. Morang & Company.

Nieuwkerk, Karin Van, ed. 2011. "Introduction: Artistic Developments in the Muslim Cultural Sphere: Ethics, Aesthetics, and the Performing Arts." In *Muslim Rap, Halal Soaps, and Revolutionary Theatre: Artistic Developments in the Muslim World*, 1–26. Austin: University of Texas Press.

Nieuwkerk, Karin Van, Mark Levine, and Martin Stokes, eds. 2016. *Islam and Popular Culture*. Austin: University of Texas Press.

Nikolaisen, Bente. 2004. "Embedded Motion: Sacred Travel among Mevlevi Dervishes." In *Reframing Pilgrimage: Cultures in Motion*, edited by Simon Coleman and John Eade, 91–103. London and New York: Routledge.

Nimer, Mohamed. 2002. *The North American Muslim Resource Guide: Muslim Community Life in the United States and Canada*. New York: Routledge.

Nurbakhsh, Javad. 1983a. *Jesus in the Eyes of the Sufis*. New York and London: Khaniqahi-Nimatullahi.

– 1983b. *Sufi Women*. New York and London: Khaniqahi-Nimatuallahi.

– 1992. *The Psychology of Sufism*. New York and London: Khaniqahi-Nimatullahi.

– 2003. *The Path: Sufi Practices*. New York and London: Khaniqahi-Nimatullahi.

Pardoe, Julia. 1837. *The City of the Sultan and the Domestic Manners of the Turks, in 1836*. London: Henry Colburn. http://www.gutenberg.org/files/51878/51878-h/51878-h.htm#Page_40.

Pemberton, Kelly. 2004. "Muslim Women Mystics and Female Spiritual Authority in South Asian Sufism." *Journal of Ritual Studies*, 11: 1–23.

Petsche, Johanna. 2014. "The Value of E.J. Hold: Unearthing the Real Mr. G." *Journal for the Academic Study of Religion* 27, no. 3: 346–66.

Piraino, Francesco. 2016. "Between Real and Virtual Communities: Sufism in Western Societies and the Naqshbandi Haqqani Case." *Social Compass* 63, no. 1: 93–108.

– 2020. "Sufism Meets the New Age Discourse: Part 1: A Theoretical Discourse." *International Journal for the Study of New Religions* 11, no. 1: 1–22. Online.

Pound, Ezra. 1918. *Literary Essays of Ezra Pound*. New York: New Directions.

Qureshi, Regula. 2003. "Lineage, Shrine, Qawwali, and Study Circle: Spiritual Kinship in Transnational Sufism." *Religious Studies and Theology* 22, no. 1: 63–84.

Qureshi, Regula B., and Qureshi Saleem M.M. 1983. "Pakistani Canadians: The Making of a Muslims Community" in *The Muslim Community in North America*, edited by Earle H. Waugh, Baha Abu-Laban, and Regula Qureshi, 127–48. Edmonton: University of Alberta Press.

"Rabbi Zalman Schachter-Shalomi Extended Interview." 2005. *Religion and Ethics News Weekly*, 30 September. https://www.pbs.org/wnet/religionandethics/2005/09/30/september-30-2005-rabbi-zalman-schachter-shalomi-extended-interview/9753.

Raudvere, Catherina. 2002. *The Book and Roses: Sufi Women, Visibility, and Zikr in Contemporary Istanbul*. Sweden: Bjärnums Tyrckeri.

Reinhertz, Shakina. 2001. *Women Called to the Path of Rumi: The Way of the Whirling Dervish*. Prescott: Homn Press.

Rozehnal, Robert. 2019. *Cyber Sufis: Virtual Expressions of the American Muslim Experience*. London: Oneworld.

Rozehnal, Robert, ed. 2019. *Piety, Politics, and Everyday Ethics in Southeast Asian Islam*. London: Bloomsbury Press.

Roof, Wade Clark. 1999. *Spiritual Marketplace: Baby Boomers and the Remaking of American Religion*. Princeton: Princeton University Press.

Safi, Omid. 2020. "Fake Hafez: How a Supreme Persian Poet of Love was Erased." *Al Jazeera*, https://www.aljazeera.com/indepth/opinion/fake-hafez-supreme-persian-poet-love-erased-200601073431603.html?fbclid=IwAR1IfA4N5Ef-hfCZsxGbSn1sxPFrl322cO6VugSNpMsg5EnWA-506seF3C8.

Saglam, Burcu. 2017. "A Discussion on the Myth of Mevlânâ in Modern Turkey." *Journal of Intercultural Studies* 38, no. 4: 412–28.

Said, Abdul Aziz, and Nathan C. Funk, et al., eds. 2001. *Peace and Conflict Resolution in Islam: Precept and Practice*. Lanham: University Press of America.

Said, Nicolas. 1873. *The Autobiography of Nicolas Said, A Native of Bournou, Eastern Soudan, Central Africa*. Memphis: Shotwell & Co.

Saif, Liana. 2019. "Introduction: What Is Islamic Esotericism?" In *Correspondences* 7.1: 1–59.

Schimmel, Annemarie. 1975. *Mystical Dimensions of Islam*. Chapel Hill: University of North Carolina Press.

– 1992. *Rumi's World: The Life and Work of the Great Sufi Poet*. Boston: Shambhala.

Sedarat, Roger. 2019. *Emerson in Iran: The American Appropriation of Persian Poetry*. Albany: SUNY Press.

Sedgwick, Mark 2004. *Against the Modern World. Traditionalism and the Secret Intellectual History of the Twentieth Century*. Oxford: Oxford University Press.

– 2012. "Neo-Sufism." In *The Cambridge Companion to New Religious Movements*, edited by Olav Hammer and Mikael Rothstein, 198–214. Cambridge: Cambridge University Press.

– 2016. *Western Sufism: From the Abbasids to the New Age*. Oxford: Oxford University Press.

– 2018. *Sufism in Latin America: A Preliminary Survey*. Melancolia, 4–34.

Sedgwick, Mark, ed. 2021. *Anarchist, Artist, Sufi: The Politics, Painting, and Esotericism of Ivan Aguéli*. London and New York: Bloomsbury Press.

Selby, Jennifer A., Amélie Barras, and Lori G. Beaman. 2018. *Beyond Accommodation: Everyday Narratives of Muslim Canadians*. Vancouver: UBC Press.
Sells, Michael, ed. 2007. *Approaching the Qurʼān: The Early Revelations*. Ashland, Oregon: White Cloud Press.
– 2021. *The Translator of Desires* by Muhiyiddin Ibn ʻArabi. Princeton: Princeton University Press.
Shah, Idries, 1964. *The Sufis*. London, United Kingdom: Doubleday.
Shaikh, Saʻdiyya. 2012. *Sufi Narratives of Intimacy: Ibn ʻArabi, Gender and Sexuality*. Chapel Hill, NC: University of North Carolina Press.
Shaikh, Saʻdiyya, and Scott Kugle. 2006. "To Love Every Life as Your Own: An Introduction to Engaged Sufism". *Journal for Islamic Studies* 26: 1–11.
Shannon, Jonathan H. 2003. "Sultans of Spin: Syrian Sacred Music on the World Stage." *American Anthropologist* 105, no. 2: 266–77.
Sharify-Funk, Meena, William Rory Dickson, and Merin Shobhana Xavier. 2017. *Contemporary Sufism: Piety, Politics, and Popular Culture*. New York: Routledge.
Sharify-Funk, Meena, and Jason Idriss Sparkes. 2021. "Expressions of Sufism in Canada." In *Producing Islam(s) in Canada: On Knowledge, Positionality, and Politics*, edited by Amélie Barras, Jennifer A. Selby, and Melanie Adrian, 154–74. Toronto: University of Toronto. Press.
Shirazi, Faegheh. 2016. *Brand Islam: The Marketing and Commodification of Piety*. Austin: University of Texas at Austin.
Sigalow, Emily. 2019. *American JewBu: Jews, Buddhists and Religious Change*. Princeton: Princeton University Press.
Sijapati, Megan Adamson. 2019. "Sufi Remembrance Practices in the Meditation Marketplace of a Mobile App." In *Anthropological Perspectives on the Religious Uses of Mobile Apps*, 19–41. Cham: Palgrave Macmillan.
Silvers, Laury. 2014. "Early Pious, Mystic Sufi Women." In *The Cambridge Companion to Sufism*, edited by Lloyd Ridgeon, 24–52. Cambridge: Cambridge University Press.
– 2019. *The Lover: The Sufi Mysteries Quartet. Book One*. Laury Silvers.
Sirriyeh, Elizabeth. 1999. *Sufis and Anti-Sufism: The Defense, Rethinking, and Rejection in the Modern World*. London: Routledge Curzon.
Sorgenfrei, Simon. 2013. American Dervish: Making Mevlevism in the United States of America. PhD Thesis., Göteborgs Universitet.
– 2020. "The Mevlevi Order of America." In *Varieties of American Sufism: Islam, Sufi Orders, and Authority in a Time of Transition*, edited by Elliott Bazzano and Marcia Hermansen, 121–50. New York: SUNY Press.
Starling, Marion Wilson. 1988. *The Slave Narrative: Its Place in American History*, 2nd ed. Washington, DC: Howard University Press.
Steel, Flora Annie. 1918. *The Mistress of Men*. Toronto: S.B. Gundy.
Sultanova, Razia. 2011. *From Shamanism to Sufism: Women, Islam, and Culture in Central Asia*. New York: I.B. Tauris.

"Swami Vivekananda chronology." *Vedanta.org*. Archived from the original (PDF) on 4 November 2013.
Taji-Farouki, Suha. 2007. *Beshara and Ibn 'Arabi: A Movement of Sufi Spirituality in the Modern World*. Oxford: Anqa.
Talbot, Émile, J. 2006. "Serge Patrice Thibodeau and the Sufi Encounter." *Studies in Canadian Literature* 31, no. 2: 160–72.
Taneja, Anand Vivek. 2017. *Jinnealogy: Time, Islam and Ecological Thought in Medieval Ruins of Delhi*. Stanford: Stanford University Press.
Thaver, Tehseen, ed. 2017. *Beauty and Light: Mystical Discourses by a Contemporary Female Sufi Teacher, Cemalnur Sargut*. Louisville: Fons Vitae.
"Theosophy Canada." https://www.theosophycanada.com.
Thiessen, Joel, and Sarah Wilkins-Laflamme. 2020. *None of the Above: Nonreligious Identity in the US and Canada*. New York: NYU Press.
Thompson, John, with Rob Winger. 2019. *Stilt Jack* [1978] Toronto: House of Anansi.
Tweed, Thomas. 2006. *Crossing and Dwelling: A Theory of Religion*. Cambridge, MA: Harvard University Press.
Tweedie, Irina. 1979. *Chasm of Fire: A Woman's Experience of Liberation Through the Teachings of a Sufi Master*.
Uždavinys, Algis. 2005. "Sufism in the Light of Orientalism." *Acta Orientalia Vilnensia* 6, no. 2: 114–25.
Vaughan-Lee, Llewellyn. 1995. *Sufism: Transformations of the Heart*. Point Reyes: Golden Sufi Center.
– 1997. *The Face Before I Was Born: A Spiritual Autobiography*. Point Reyes: Golden Sufi Center.
– 2000. *Love Is a Fire: The Sufi's Mystical Journey Home*. Point Reyes: Golden Sufi Center.
– 2001. *The Signs of God*. Point Reyes: Golden Sufi Center.
Vaziri, Mostafa. 2015. *Rumi and Shams' Silent Rebellion: Parallels with Vedanta. Buddhism, and Shaivism*. New York: Palgrave Macmillan.
Virani, S. 2019. "Persian Poetry, Sufism, and Ismailism: The Testimony of Khwājah Qāsim Tushtarī's Recognizing God." *Journal of the Royal Asiatic Society* 29, no. 1: 17–49.
Waugh, Earl. 2018. *Al Rashid Mosque: Building Canadian Muslim Communities*. Edmonton.
Weitbrecht, H.U. 1915. "Turkey and Islam." *Canadian Churchman*, 11 March 1915, 151.
Wheeler, Kayla. 2018. "The Ethics of Conducting Virtual Ethnography on Visual Platforms." *Fieldwork in Religion* 12, no. 2: 163–78.
Whitfield, Harvey Amani. 2022. *Biographical Dictionary of Enslaved Black People in the Maritimes*. Toronto: University of Toronto Press.
Wigmore, Gregory. 2011. "Before the Railroad: From Slavery to Freedom in the Canadian-American Borderland." In *Journal of American History* 98, no. 2: 437–54.

Wilkins-Laflamme, Sarah. 2017. "Religious-Secular Polarization Compared: The Cases of Quebec and British Columbia." *Studies in Religion* 46, no. 2: 166–85.

Williford, Cem, ed. 2008. *Tasavvuf Iahiler: Ilahi Lyrics in Turkish and English*. Self-published.

Wilson, Jeff. 2014. *Mindful America: Meditation and the Mutual Transformation: Buddhist Meditation and American Culture*. Oxford: Oxford University Press.

Winger, Robert Sean. 2009. *John Thompson, Phyllis Webb, and the Roots of the Free-Verse Ghazal in Canada*. PhD diss., Carleton University.

– 2019. "Introduction by Rob Winger." In John Thompson, *Stilt Jack*. Toronto: House of Anansi Press Inc.

Workman, Nancy V. 1989. "Sufi Mysticism in Margaret Atwood's *The Handmaid's Tale*." *Studies in Canadian Literature* 14, no. 2: 10. https://journals.lib.unb.ca/index.php/scl/article/view/8103/9160.

Wright, Zachary. 2020. *Realizing Islam*: Chapel Hill: University of North Carolina Press.

Xavier, Merin Shobhana, and William Rory Dickson. 2020. "Between Islam and the New Age: The Jerrahi Order and Categorial Ambiguity in the Study of Sufism in North America." in *Religion Compass.*, 1–10.

Xavier, Merin Shobhana. 2018. *Sacred Spaces and Transnational Networks in American Sufism: Bawa Muhaiyaddeen and Contemporary Shrine Cultures*. London: Bloomsbury Press.

– 2021. "Gendering the Divine: Women, Femininity, and Queer Identities on the Sufi Path." In *the Routledge Handbook of Islam and Gender*, edited by Justine Howe, 163–79. New York: Routledge.

Yagan, Murat. 1984. *I Come from Behind Kaf Mountain*. Vernon: Kebzeh.

Zine, Jasmin. 2022. *Under Siege: Islamophobia and the 9/11 Generation*. Montreal and Kingston: McGill–Queen's University Press.

Zine, Jasmin, ed. 2012. *Islam in the Hinterlands: Exploring Muslim Cultural Politics in Canada*. Vancouver: UBC Press.

Index

Abbas, Shemeen Burney, 248n9
activism, 17, 223–4, 225–7. *See also* social justice
adab (etiquette), 38, 82–3, 84, 241n74
Al-Adawiyya, Rabia, 154, 184–5, 230
African Americans. *See* Black Muslims
Aga Khan, 161, 162
Aga Khan Museum, 3, 77, 161, 162, 167, 235n1
age, 210, 216–17
Aguéli, Ivan, 37, 237n19
Ahmad, Aijaz: *Ghazals of Ghalib*, 145
Ahmed, Shahab, 19; *What Is Islam?*, 43
Aisha (wife of Prophet Muhammad), 209, 210
Akram, Al-Hajj Wali, 34
Aksoy, Cemil, 75
Alami *tariqa* (Waterport, NY), 35
Al' Alawi, Ahmed, 34, 37
Albanese, Catherine, 26
Aldred, Lisa, 29–30, 139
Ali, Agha Shahid, 145–6, 158
Ali, Kecia, 211
Ali, Syed Mumtaz, 40, 49
Andalibi, Shaho, 162
An Ensemble (music group), 245n25
Angha, Nahid, 226
Anjuman Islam, 33
anti-Sufism, 32–3, 99, 108, 242n16
Anwar, Zainah, 225

Arabic language, 247n3
Arberry, A.J., 137
Arjana, Sophia Rose, 7, 237n21
Artiran, Nur, 57, 194
Asmau, Nana, 194
Atatürk, Mustafa Kemal, 98, 99, 173
Attar, Farid ud-Din, 184–5
AttarJafari, Shams al Haqq Farzad, 106–10; author's relationship with, 9; background and lineage, 65, 78, 82, 103, 106, 129; gender-egalitarian practices, 202–3, 220; public *sama* events, 108–9, 162–5; on Rumi, 109, 173–4, 177–8, 219; Rumi Canada and, 78–9, 106–7, 129; on Sahabi's *Mathnawi* course, 152–3; on *sama*, 107–8, 112, 113, 129–30; SamaKhaneh retreat and, 7; at *shab-i arus* celebrations, 121, 124, 126; at Tirgan Festival, 4, 161; virtual *sama* during COVID-19 pandemic, 131. *See also* Rumi Canada
Atwood, Margaret, *The Handmaid's Tale*, 146
Aurangabadi, Siraj, 158
Avery, Kenneth S., 94
Awliya, Nizamuddin, 51, 145, 158, 238n11
Aydogdu, Cem, 69

Index

Aydöner, Tevfik, 71–4, 84, 127, 198, 200, 226–7. *See also* Jerrahi Order of Canada
Ayverdi, Samiha, 200, 248n20
Azad, Arezou, 185
Azeemi, Khwaja Shamsuddin, 249n27
Azeemia Spiritual and Healing Center Canada, 249n27

Baig, M. Qadeer Shah, 40, 48–9, 54, 85
Bainbridge, William, 29
Baker, Ora Ray (Ameena Begum), 33
Baker, Peter, 19
Bakhtiar, Laleh, 226
Balevi, Ariel, 245n25
Balint, Peter, 141, 143
Bandali, Zain, 151, 157–8, 162, 228
Baquaqua, Mahommah Gardo, *Biography of Mahommah G. Baquaqua*, 21–2
Barks, Coleman, 59, 62, 68, 133–4, 137–8, 175–6, 179, 180
Barthes, Roland, 230
Al-Bauniyyah, Aishah: *The Principles of Sufism*, 247n6
Bawa Muhaiyaddeen, M.R., 137, 175, 180, 206, 211, 212, 225–6, 250n2
Bawa Muhaiyaddeen Fellowship (BMF), 9, 34, 137, 211
Bayrak, Tosun, 72–3, 75, 200
Bektashi Order, 66, 89, 96, 191, 193
Bentounes, Khaled, 160
Beorse, Shamcher Bryn, 50
Berenji, Farima, 4
Beshara Centre, 58, 60
Bhajan, Yogi, 27, 236n7
bint Sirin, Hafsa, 185
Black Lives Matter movement, 17, 223–4
Black Muslims: among African Americans, 34, 38, 194, 225, 250n2; among Afro-Caribbeans, 235n2; in early Canada, 18, 19–23, 38–9, 43, 47

Blake, William, 135
Blavatsky, Helena, 26
Blue, Baraka, 133–4, 177
Bly, Robert, 137
Bolat, Latif, 104
Bramadat, Paul, 25
Brautlacht, Atiya (Charlotte), 58
Brethren of Purity (Ikhwan as-Safa), 88, 242n3
British Columbia, 25
Brozak, John: background and lineage, 57–8, 62; on Rumi, 147; Rumi Festival and, 68, 147; on Sahabi, 152; Schachter-Shalomi and, 56, 57; Unity *Zikr* and, 104, 106; Vancouver Rumi Society and, 59, 60–1, 62, 68, 206; Yagan and, 62, 66, 67
Buddhism, 28–9, 154–5, 231
Buell, Majid: background and lineage, 65–6, 68, 69–70; gender-egalitarian practices, 202; on Rumi, 147, 178–9; *sama* and, 87, 101–2, 103; *shab-i arus* and, 119, 125; Unity *Zikr* and, 104, 106; Vancouver Rumi Society and, 67–8, 206
Al-Bukhari, Jalal al-Din Husayn, 94
Burke, Mira Hunter: background and lineage, 65, 103, 104–5, 129; gender-egalitarian practices, 202, 220; public *sama* events, 164, 166; at Tirgan Festival, 4, 161
Burke, Raqib Brian: background and lineage, 63–5, 82, 87; gender-egalitarian practices, 202, 220; on public *sama* events, 166–7; Rumi Festival and, 147; *sama* and, 13, 63–5, 102–3; as *samazenbashi*, 65, 129; at Sema Space's *shab-i arus*, 121–3, 125; students of, 65, 78, 79, 106, 129; at Tirgan Festival, 4, 161; Unity *Zikr* and, 69, 104, 106; Vancouver Rumi Society and, 206
Buturović, Amila, 190

Canada: diasporic Muslim communities, 23–4, 39, 71; early Black Muslims, 18, 19–23, 38–9, 43, 47; Islam in, 19–24; multiculturalism, 4, 6, 13, 28, 87, 132; popular spirituality, 25–31; religious affiliations, 24–5. *See also* Sufism, in Canada

Canadian Arabic Orchestra, 164

Canadian Churchman, The, 100

Canadian Council of Muslim Women (CCMW), 195

Canadian Institute of Sufi Studies (Rifai): background and lineage, 74–6, 128; collaboration with Inayati Order, 55; gender-egalitarian practices, 197–8, 201, 203, 204; inclusiveness of, 76, 120, 125, 201, 222, 232; initiatic allegiance within, 53; "International Day of Living Together in Peace" and, 160; at Nuit Blanche, 3, 205; *shab-i arus* celebration, 76, 124–6. *See also* Coskun, Murat

Canadian Society for the Advancement of Turkish Studies (CSATS), 126

Carlebach, Shlomo, 27, 57, 66, 236n10

Çatalkaya, Sherif Baba: background and lineage, 69–70, 203; Buell and, 69–70; Burke and, 65; Evanson and, 79, 111, 150; gender-egalitarian practices, 16, 203, 204, 221; Ghazi and, 68, 205, 210, 211; Rumi Festival and, 149; Unity *Zikr* and, 104. *See also* Rifai Order

Celebi, Adil, 95

Celebi, Celaleddin Bakir, 62, 205

Celebi, Ulu Arif, 95

Cemal, Semiha, 200

Cenan, Hatice, 199, 200

Chandler, Siobhan, 236n5

Chebib, Amar: *Wajd: Songs of Separation* (documentary), 162

Chishti Order: African Americans and, 34; dance and music meditations, 94; diasporic communities in Canada, 71; Ghazi and, 68, 211–12; Husain and, 214; Inayati Order and, 54, 85, 211; Nizamuddin Awliya, 51, 145, 158, 238n11; religious pluralism of, 231; Sufi Study Circle and, 48, 85; women in, 209

Chittick, William, 96, 185–7

Chopra, Deepak, 137

Choudry, Ejaz Ahmed, 224

Church Guardian of Montreal, 143–4

Cirianni-Salazar, Lucícia, 37

clothes, ritual, 61, 64

Colby, Rick, 211

Coldplay, "Guest House," 138

commodification. *See* consumption

consumption: approach to, 14, 134, 179–81; cultural appropriation, 139, 141–3, 180; *ghazal* poetry, 145–7, 154, 244n11; Islamic consumption and popular culture, 140–1; public *sama* events, 162–9, *163*; religion and, 138–9, 180; Rumi café's storefront Sufism, 169–72; Rumi's contemporary legacy and, 172–9; Sufi Poet Series, 153–4, 155–6, 161, 245n25, 245n36

cooke, miriam, 211

Cornell, Rkia, 184, 185, 211, 230, 246n1

Cornell, Vincent, 211, 212–13

Coskun, David, 76, 126

Coskun, Murat: on age, 216; background and lineage, 74–6; gender-egalitarian practices, 16, 73, 197–8, 199–200, 201–2, 203, 220–1, 222; at Nuit Blanche, 3; on Rumi, 219; at *shab-i arus*, 125. *See also* Canadian Institute of Sufi Studies

Coskun, Talar, 3, 198

counterculturalism, 26–8, 34, 57–8, 84

COVID-19 pandemic, 8, 9–10, 69, 131, 206, 223, 226
cultural appropriation, 139, 141–3, 180. *See also* consumption
cyber-Sufism, 10

Dagestani, Abd Allah, 36
Dakake, Maria Massi, 183, 184, 187
Dances of Universal Peace, 50, 52, 58, 202
Danner, Victor, 37
Dass, Ram (Richard Alphert), *Be Here Now*, 27–8, 65
death anniversaries, 119
Dede, Mercan, 79, 104, 124, 149, 165
Deobandi movement, 32
Desert Fellowship of the Message, 56
Dhu'l Nun the Egyptian, 88
Dickson, William Rory, 5, 31, 42
Diouf, Sylviane, *Servants of Allah*, 38
Documenting the American South Project, 235n3
Domínguez Díaz, Marta, 37
Drew, Benjamin: *A North-Side View of Slavery*, 22
Durakovic, Asaf, 35
During, Jean, 90

ecstasy (*wajd*), 94
Efendi, Edhem, 199
Eliot, T.S., 136
Emerson, Ralph Waldo, 32, 136, 137
Emre, Yunnus, 72, 159
Ensemble al-Kindi, 168
Ernst, Carl, 41, 57
etiquette (*adab*), 38, 82–3, 84, 241n74
Evanson, Tawhida Tanya, 110–17; appeal of, 124; background and lineage, 65, 79–80, 103, 110, 113, 129, 150; gender-egalitarian and post-gender practices, 202, 203–4, 220, 222; inclusiveness of, 121; publications, 150, 203–4; public *sama* events, 165–6; Rumi's poetic legacy and, 150–1, 219; *sama* and, *81*, 110–12, 115–16, 129–30; Sema Space and, 80–2, 111–13, 129; *shab-i arus* celebration, 120, 121–3; on shamanic practices and *sama*, 113–15; on Sufism, 82–3, 84, 232; virtual *sama* during COVID-19 pandemic, 243n27

Faisal, Daoud, 34
Feild, Reshad (Richard Timothy): background and lineage, 58–9; gender-egalitarian practices, 202, 220; public *sama* presentations, 166–7; *sama* taught by in Vancouver, 13, 59–61, *60*, 62, 63–5, 68, 84, 86, 101, 102–3; split with Loras, 62–3
feminine principle, 183–4, 185–8, 220, 247nn3–4
Fitzgerald, F. Scott, 136
Ford, Zainb Paula, 26–7, 50, 51, 52
Formichi, Chiara, 41–2, 140, 233
Frager, Ragib (Robert), 200, 240n43, 240n50
Friedlander, Shems, *Rumi and the Whirling Dervishes*, 64, 99–100, 121, 122
Frishkopf, Michael, 39, 100, 156–7, 158, 167–8
al-Fuqara, Sams Umm (Yasamin), 188

Ganam, Saleem, 39
Ganam, Sied (Sied Ameen Ganam Kadri), 39
Geaves, Ron, 35, 237n15
gender: approach to, 15–17, 182–3, 219–22; activism and, 226; age and, 210, 216–17; contemporary Muslim and Sufi women in North America, 194–6; egalitarian practices, 101, 129, 131, 197–8, 199–200, 201–2, 202–4,

220–1; feminine principle, 183–4, 185–8, 220, 247nn3–4; hagiographic accounts of women, 184–5; historic Sufi understandings, 183–90, 220; Ibn Arabi on, 188–9; institutionalization of Sufism and, 189–90; as litmus test for Sufi legitimacy, 198–9, 221–2; living traditions of Sufi women, 193–4, 248n9, 248n15; Mawlawi Order and, 190–2, 193, 200, 220; post-gender, 203, 210, 222; ritual practice and, 197–202; Rumi and, 186, 190–1, 193; *sama* and, 202–4; scholarship on, 192–3; *shaykha*s in Canada, 205–19, 221, 249n27; Sufi sources written by women, 247n6. *See also* Burke, Mira Hunter; Evanson, Tawhida Tanya; Ghazi, Seemi Bushra; Husain, Ayeda

Genge, Dale, 35, 239n33

Genn, Celia, 238n15

Georgius de Hungaria, 86

Gérôme, Jean-Léon: "The Whirling Dervish," 98

Ghazali, Ahmad, 93, 242n7

Al-Ghazali, Abu Hamid, 13, 90, 91–2, 93, 108, 127, 189, 242n7

ghazal poetry, 145–7, 154, 244n11

Ghazi, Seemi Bushra, 205–13; approach to, 16, 182, 221; academic experience, 211; age and, 210, 216; background and lineage, 68, 69, 205–6; positionality of, 206–8; Quran recitations, 206, 249n28; on Rumi, 175–8, 219; Rumi Festival and, 147, 149; on *sama*, 113, 128; on *shab-i arus*, 119, 120; as *shaykha*, 205, 208–10; Unity *Zikr* and, 104, 105–6; on universal Sufism and Islam–Sufism relationship, 211–13, *213*, 222, 231

Gill, Kuldip, 154

globalization, 34–7, 46

Goethe, Johann Wolfgang von, 31, 135

Gold, E.J., 58, 239n27

Golden Sufi Center, 35

Golshan, Sahar, 245n25

Green, Michael, 180

Guénon, René, 37

Gülen Movement, 241n73

Gurdjieff, Georges Ivanovich, 47

Gurdjieff Foundation: Society for Traditional Studies, 47

Gurdjieff societies, 58, 75, 84, 87

Gurdjieff Society of Atlantic Canada, 47–8

Hafiz (Inayati Order leader in Toronto), 55, 71, 85, 217

Hafiz (poet), 7, 31, 109, 134, 135, 136–7, 144

Halveti Order, 89, 96. *See also* Jerrahi Order

Hammer, Juliane, 195

Hanbal, Ahmad, 242n5

Hanum, Fatima, 192

Al-Haqqani, Muhammad Nazim, 35, 36

Harawi, Mir Husayn, 91

Harbourfront Centre (Toronto), 161

Harding, John S., *Wild Geese* (with Hori and Soucy), 28

Harris, Rabia Terri, 72

Harvey, Andrew, 137

healing, 116–17

Helminski, Camille, 86, 129, 137, 180, 205, 228

Helminski, Kabir, 62, 78, 82, 86, 106, 129, 137, 180, 205, 228

Henry, Gray (Aisha), 226

Hermansen, Marcia, 198–9, 202

Hill, Joseph, 194

Hodgson, Marshall, *The Venture of Islam*, 42–3

Hogben, Murray, *Minarets on the Horizon*, 39

Hori, Victory Sōgen, *Wild Geese* (with Harding and Soucy), 28
House of Love and Prayer, 57
Hughes, Aaron W., 235n2
Humboldt, Wilhelm von, 135
Husain, Ayeda (Nizam un-Nisa), 214–19; approach to, 16, 182, 221; background, 214; resistance against, 216–17; Rumi and, 57; as *shaykha* and *cheraga*, 55, 205, 214–16, 217; on Sufism in Canada, 218–19; on universal Sufism, 217–18, 222, 231
Hussain, Amir, 47
Hussein, Madhu Lal, 158
Hussen, Ahmed, 4

Ibn Abi l-Khayr, Abu Said, 91
Ibn Arabi, Muhiyddin, 16, 58, 95–6, 185, 188–9, 206, 220
Ibn Battuta, 89
Ibn al-Jawzi, 88, 184
Ibn al-Mutanna, Fatima bt., 188
Ibn Said, Omar, 19, 23, 39
Ibn Sina, 242n3
Ibn Taymiyyah, Taqi al-Din, 32
ilahis (ritual songs), 106, 111, 125
Inayati-Maimuni Order, 56
Inayati Order (formerly Sufi Order International), 49–57; activism by, 223–4, 250n3; background and lineage, 27, 45, 49–50, 84; Cenn on, 238n15; gender-egalitarian practices, 197, 202, 205, 222; Ghazi and, 68, 211; inclusiveness of, 201; Jewish Sufis and, 56; Noor Cultural Centre and, 160; rebranding as Inayati Order, 54; Rumi and, 56–7; in Toronto, 55, 85; universal Sufism and, 57, 71; Universal Worship Service, 33–4, 214–15, 218; in Vancouver, 51–4; virtual *sama* during COVID-19 pandemic, 131, 223. *See also* Husain, Ayeda; O'Loughlin, Amir Peter
Inayat-Khan, Zia (Sarafil Bawa): activism and, 223, 224, 250n3; AttarJafari and, 106; gender-egalitarian practices, 205; Ghazi and, 68; Husain and, 214, 216; as Inayati Order leader, 50, 54, 56; Noor Cultural Centre and, 160; on Rumi, 133; *sama* and, 202; universal Sufism and, 212; virtual *sama* during COVID-19 pandemic, 131
India, 119, 144–5, 193, 212, 228, 242n4
Indigenous Peoples, 111, 113–14, 115
Indonesia, 194
Ingram, Brannon, 32
Institute for Conscious Life, 62, 68
intention (*niyya*), 15, 163–6, 169, 230
International Association of Sufism (IAS), 226
International Association of the Sufi Alawiyya, 160
"International Day of Living Together in Peace," 160
International Sufi Movement, 57
Islam: in Canada, 19–24; consumption and, 140–1; diasporic communities in Canada, 23–4, 39, 71; early Black Muslims in Canada, 18, 19–23, 38–9, 43, 47; relationship with Sufism, 24, 32–3, 211–13, *213*, 230. *See also* Sufism
Islam, Empire of Faith (documentary), 68, 249n28
Islamic Mission of America, 34
Islamophobia, 6, 36, 87, 101, 132, 143, 176–7, 212
Ismaili Centre, 3, 9, 107, 127, 161–2, *163*, 205, 235n1
Ismailis, 3, 23, 71, 161, 162, 196, 245n41

Jackson, Troy, 227
Jaffar, Umair, 161

Index

Jalalis, 94
Janmohamed, Sheniz, 151, 153–7, 159–60, 161, 162, 174–5
Al-Jazairi, Abdelkader, 225
Al-Jerrahi, Fariha Fatima, 57, 86, 129, 180, 200, 205
Al-Jerrahi, Muzaffer Ozak, 34, 69, 72, 86, 129, 200, 248n22
Al-Jerrahi, Nur (Lex Hixon), 69, 200
Jerrahi Order, 34, 72, 240n50. *See also* Halveti Order; Jerrahi Order of Canada; Nur Ashki Jerrahi Order
Jerrahi Order of Canada, 71–4; background and lineage, 71–3, 128, 200; Canadian context, 74; community demographics, 73, 120, 232; community engagement, 73, 226–7; gender practices, 73, 127, 129, 197, 198, 200–1; Rumi Canada and, 107; *shab-i arus* celebration, 126–7, 128. *See also* Aydöner, Tevfik
Jewish Sufis, 56, 57, 238n21
Jones, William, 31, 135, 243n3

Kabbani, Hisham, 36
Karamustafa, Ahmet T., 85
Kasmani, Omar, 8, 225
Keller, Nuh Ha Mim, 38, 237n20
Khaki, El-Farouki, 227–8
Khan, Aliyah: *Far from Mecca*, 235n2
Khan, Daisy, 226
Khan, Gunash, 191
Khan, Hidayat Inayat, 50, 57, 71, 84; *Sufi Teachings: Lectures from Lake O'Hara*, 50. *See also* Inayati Order
Khan, Inayat: Brozak and, 58; music tradition of, 52, 131; *sama* and, 202; Sufism introduced to west, 33–4, 45, 50, 84; Universal Worship Service, 214–15. *See also* Inayati Order
Khan, Noor Inayat, 224, 226
Khan, Nusrat Fateh Ali, 168

Khan, Vilayat Inayat: activism by, 226; Brozak and, 59; in Canada (Vancouver), 50, 51, 57, 71, 84; comparison to Zia Inayat-Khan, 54; Ford and, 26–7, 50; Husain and, 214; Jelaleddin Loras and, 63; Jewish Sufis and, 56; *Toward the One*, 28. *See also* Inayati Order
Khanim, Kamila, 191
Khanim, Khwaja Fatima, 191
Khatun, Dastina, 191
Khatun, Gumaj, 191
Khatun, Nizam, 191
Khayyam, Omar, 136–7, 145; *Rubaiyyat*, 135
Khedder, Nour, 162
Khusrau, Amir, 145, 158
Al-Kindi, Ya'qub, 242n3
Klinkhammer, Gritt, 239n24
Knight, Michael Muhammad: *Metaphysical Africa*, 34
Knysh, Alexander, 19, 43
Konya (Turkey), 68, 99, 103, 118
Koushkani, Amir, 103–4, 162
Küçük, Hülya, 95, 189, 190, 191
Kuehn, Sara, 224–5
Kugle, Siraj Scott, 211, 226

Ladinsky, Daniel, 137
Lakhani, Hassanali and Noorbanu, 160
Lal, Radha Mohan, 35
Lama Foundation, 28
Lanes, Edward, 89
Latin America, 36–7
Lawrence, Bruce, 43, 211
Lenard, Patti Tamara, 141, 143
Less, Shahabuddin David, 51
Lewis, Franklin, 7, 109
Lewis, Samuel L. (Sufi Ahmed Murad Chishti, Sufi Sam), 50, 51, 57, 63, 84, 87, 202, 238n17
Lewisohn, Leonard, 92, 93, 168

LGBTQIA+. *See* queer Muslims
Lings, Martin: *A Sufi Saint of the Twentieth Century*, 37
Lofton, Kathryn, 29, 138–9, 180
Loras, Jelaleddin, 62, 63, 65, 103, 119, 131, 202. *See also* Mawlawi Order
Loras, Suleyman: background and lineage, 61–2; Buell and, 65, 68; death, 65; Feild and, 62–3, 101; gender-egalitarian practices, 200, 202, 220; *sama* and Sufism taught by, 84, 86, 87, 100, 101, 103; scholarship on, 57; Yagan and, 11–12, 66–7. *See also* Mawlawi Order
Lucia, Amanda J., 9, 26, 28–9, 139, 142, 236n11
Lucis Trust Library, 50
Luther, Martin, 236n13

Maghribi, 92–3
Mahadevan, Anand, 156
Maimonides, Abraham, 56
Malaysia, 225
Malcolm X, 225
Marcus-Sells, Ariela: *Sorcery or Science?*, 22–3
Markoff, Irene, 96
Martin, Chris, 244n5
Martin, Rabia, 238n21
Mary (Virgin Mary), 37, 187, 247n4, 248n22
Maryamiyya Order, 37–8, 247n4
Masjid al-Iman (Montreal), 80
Mathews, George, 57
Maududi, Abu Ala, 210, 249n31
Mawlawi Order: Evanson and, 82; influence in Vancouver, 103; ritual tendencies within, 85; *sama* and, 95, 96–8, 99–100; *sama* at Rumi's tomb, 118; women and authority in, 190–2, 193, 200, 220. *See also* Loras, Jelaleddin; Loras, Suleyman; Mevlevi Order of America

mazar (shrine), 118–19
McDonough, Sheila, 39, 40
McKittrick, Katherine, 39
Mevlevi Order of America, 57, 61, 63, 65, 119. *See also* Mawlawi Order
Meyer, Wali Ali, 55, 238n17
Michon, Jean-Louis, 115, 242n3
Milani, Milad, 36
Miles-Yépez, Netanel, 56
Miller, Bruce, *Rumi Comes to America*, 62–3
Miller, Joe, 51
Miller, Rasul, 34, 225
Mir, Mir Taqi, 145
Mirahmadi, Nurjan, 15, 170, 171–2, 197, 201. *See also* Naqshbandi-Haqqani Order
Mohammadi, Khashayar, 245n25
Montreal, 46, 80, 112. *See also* Sema Space
Moorish Science Temple (MST), 34, 250n2
Moriscos, 19, 235n1
Mouridiyya Order, 57
Moyne, John, 137
Muhammad, Prophet, 31, 116, 119, 224, 242n5
multiculturalism, 4, 6, 13, 28, 87, 132
Muridi Sufi Brotherhood, 34, 80
music: as conduit to Sufism, 124; debates over, 88–9, 168, 242nn2–3; Qawwali, 48, 94, 168, 248n9; *sama* and, 92–3, 103–4, 242n7
Muslim Brotherhood, 210, 249n31

Nagra, Baljit, 195
Naqshbandi-Haqqani Order: background, 36; branches and membership, 77, 112; gender practices, 197, 198–9; Rumi café and storefront, 15, 30, 134, 169–72. *See also* Mirahmadi, Nurjan
Naqshbandi Order, 80, 96, 108

Naqshbandiyya-Mujaddidiyya, 35, 62
Narváes expedition (1527–36), 235n1
Nasr, Seyyed Hossein, 37–8
Nation of Gods and Earths, 141
Nation of Islam (NOI), 34, 141
Nattiers, Jan, 236n11
Neoplatonism, 56, 88, 246n1
Neo-Sufism, 236n12
New Age: about, 29–30, 42; cultural appropriation and, 139; framing Sufi communities as, 30–1, 196, 197–8, 211, 213, 221–2, 229; Lewis and, 50; limitations of, 26; Yagan and, 66
Newbolt, Henry, "The Sufi in the City," 144–5
Nicholson, Reynold, 137
Nigeria, 194
Nimatullahi Order: AttarJafari and, 82; background, 36; in Canada, 71, 76–7, 80, 85; gender-egalitarian practices, 77, 197; Noor Cultural Centre and, 160; at Nuit Blanche, 3, 205. *See also* Nurbakhsh, Javad
Nimer, Muhamed, *The North American Resource Guide*, 40
Niyaz (music group), 80, *81*, 165
niyya (intention), 15, 163–6, 169, 230
non-binary-gender people, 193, 228. *See also* queer Muslims
Noor Cultural Centre (Toronto), 124, 160, 245n38
Nova Scotia, 19
Nuit Blanche festival, 3, 162, 205
Nur Ashki Jerrahi Order, 57, 72, 200, 205
Nurbakhsh, Alireza, 36, 76, 77
Nurbakhsh, Javad, 35–6, 76, 77, 237n18; *Sufi Women*, 248n15. *See also* Nimatullahi Order

Olcott, Henry Steele, 26
O'Loughlin, Amir Peter, 51–4, 57, 80, 120, 131, 215
Ontario, 23–4, 25

Orsi, Robert, 9
Ozak, Muzaffer, 34, 69, 72, 86, 129, 200, 248n22

Pardoe, Julia, 97–8
Parveen, Abida, 161, 209, 210
Petsche, Johanna, 239n27
Piraino, Francesco, 19, 42
popular culture, 140–1, 180, 244n7
Postman, Neil, 244n7
Pound, Ezra, 179

Qalandar Sufis, 225
Qawwali music, 48, 94, 168, 248n9
Quebec, 23, 25, 195
queer Muslims, 157–8, 195, 225, 227–8, 232
Qunawi, Arifa-yi Khwush-liqa-yi, 191
Qureshi, Regula, 40, 48, 49

race, 135, 233, 243n4
Al Rashid Mosque (Edmonton), 23, 47
Raudvere, Catharina, 247n7
Rauf, Bülent, 58, 59, 62, 84, 102
Ravindra, Ravi, 48
Ray, Azalea, 155
Regard Persian (musical group), 4, 161
Reinhertz, Shakina, 202
religious studies, 11, 232–3, 243n4
remembrance, 115–17. *See also zikr* (prayer of remembrance)
Rich, Adrienne, 145
Ridgway, Lindsey, 162
Rifai, Kenan, 75, 199–200, 204
Rifai Order (Rifai Marufi), 51, 68, 69, 89, 203, 210, 222. *See also* Canadian Institute of Sufi Studies; Çatalkaya, Sherif Baba; Coskun, Murat
Romanticism, 31, 135
Roy Thompson Hall (Toronto), 161
Rozehnal, Robert, 10, 211, 250n3

Ruhaniat International (formerly Sufi Islamia Ruhaniat Society), 50, 51, 55, 57, 63, 84

Rumi: approach to, 4–5, 7, 14, 133–5, 179–81, 230; AttarJafari on, 109, 173–4, 177–8, 219; authenticity concerns and, 179; Barks's renditions and popularization of, 137–8; Buell on, 147, 178–9; Canadian festivals honouring, 3–4; consumption of, 139, 172–9, 246n57; cultural appropriation and, 142–3; death, 117–18; Evanson and poetic legacy of, 150–1; and feminine principle and women, 186–8, 190–1, 193, 220; as gateway to Sufism, 219; Ghazi on, 175–8, 219; Inayati Order and, 56–7; Janmohamed on, 174–5; Jerrahi Order and, 227; mausoleum, 99; misquotations of, 175, 244n6; *mukhannath* figure, 247n5; queer identities and, 228; restrictive claiming by Muslims, 176; *sama* and, 13, 91, 95–6, 114, 117; universalism of, 109; Whitman and, 136; Zavieh Mystical Society's classes on, 151–3. See also *shab-i arus* (Rumi's death anniversary)

Rumi Canada, 3, 13, 78–9, 106–7, 129, 160. See also AttarJafari, Shams al Haqq Farzad

Rumi Festival (Vancouver), 68, 69, 147–50, *148*

Rumi Restaurant (Montreal), 172

Rumi Rose Garden and Café (Vancouver), 15, 30, 134, 169–72

Saadi Shirazi, 135, 136

Safi, Omid, 7, 68, 133, 134, 137, 147, 177, 179, 211, 244n23

Saghanughu, Muhammad Kaba, 235n2

Saglam, Burcu, 99

Sahabi, Parviz, 14, 106, 152–3

Sahin, Ahmet Fuad, 72

Said, Nicolas, *Autobiography of Nicolas Said*, 22

Salaam (queer support group), 227

sama (sacred audition): approach to, 13–14, 15, 85, 86–7, 131–2, 229–30; by AttarJafari and Rumi Canada, 107–8, 112, 113, 129–30; author's experience at SamaKhaneh retreat, 7–8; criticisms of, 108, 109–10; cultivating a safe space for, 113; definition, 87–8; early Canadian mentions, 100; early development, 89–90, 95, 168; Evanson and, *81*, 110–12, 115–16, 129–30; gender dynamics and, 101–2, 129, 202–4; lineage and transmission in Canada, 129; Mawlawi Order and, 95, 96–8, 99–100; as meditative movement, 93–4; Mira Burke on, 104–5; music and poetic recitations, 88–9, 91–3, 103–4, 168, 242n7; at Nuit Blanche, 3; public events, 108–9, 162–9, *163*; purpose of, 94, 110, 115–17; research methodology and, 9; Rumi on, 13, 91, 95–6, 117; shamanic practices and, 113–15; significance in Canadian Sufism, 70–1, 127–30; Sufi Study Circle and, 48–9; taught by Feild and Loras in Vancouver, 13, 59–61, *60*, 62, 63–5, 68, 84, 86, 87, 101–3; time, place, and participant considerations, 90–1; in Turkey, 99–100; virtual *sama* during COVID-19 pandemic, 131, 223, 243n27. See also *shab-i arus* (Rumi's death anniversary); *zikr* (prayer of remembrance)

SamaKhaneh (retreat), 7–8

samazenbashi, 65, 129

Sargut, Cemalnur, 194, 200, 206, 210, 248n20

Sargut, Meskure, 200

Index

Schachter-Shalomi, Zalman, 56, 57
Schafer, R. Murray, 40
Schimmel, Annemarie: on female Sufis, 193; on feminine principle in Arabic, 247n3; on *ghazal* poetry, 244n11; on meditative movement, 115; on *mukhannath* figures, 247n5; on music, 88; Rumi translations by, 137; on *sama*, 95, 96–7, 118, 121
Schuon, Frithjof (Isa Nur al-Din), 37–8, 247n4
Sedgwick, Mark, 36, 47–8, 56, 236n12
Sells, Michael, 206, 211; *Approaching the Qur'an*, 68, 249n28
Sema Space, 80–2, 111–13, 120–4, *123*, 129. *See also* Evanson, Tawhida Tanya
Senegal, 28, 34, 46, 57, 71, 194
Shahbazy, Zohreh, 162
shab-i arus (Rumi's death anniversary): approach to, 13–14, 120; by Canadian Institute of Sufi Studies (Rifai), 76, 124–6; by Jerrahi Order, 126–7, *128*; at Rumi's tomb, 99, 118; at Sema Space, 120–4, *123*; by Vancouver Rumi Society, 119–20
Shabistari, Mahmud, 92
Shadhili Order, 34, 37, 38, 71
Shah, Bulleh, 154
Shah, Ikbal Ali, 33
Shaikh, Sa'diyya, 226
shamanism, 89, 113–15
Shams of Tabriz, 70, 95, 178–9, 190
Sharify-Funk, Meena, 40
Shea, David, *The Dabistàn* (with Troyer), 144
Shelley, Percy Bysshe, 135
Shibli, 94
shrine (*mazar*), 118–19
Al-Siddiq, Abu Bakr, 235n2
Siddiqui, Maulana Muhammad Abdul Aleem, 47
Sigalow, Emily, 238n21

Sill, Carol, 50
Silvers, Laury, 227
Sirriyeh, Elizabeth, 242n16
Sisters of Islam, 225
Small World Music Centre (Toronto), 153, 159, 161
snake handling, ritual, 89
social justice, 17, 157–9, 226, 228–9, 232. *See also* activism
social media, 17, 80, 123, 159, 175, 208, 219, 244n6
Somalia, 194
Sorgenfrei, Simon, 61, 65; *American Dervish*, 57
Soucy, Alexander Duncan, *Wild Geese* (with Harding and Hori), 28
South America, 36–7
Sparkes, Jason Idries, 40
spiritual but not religious (SBNR), 24–5, 139, 180
spiritual colonialism, 179
Spiritualism, 26
spirituality, popular, 25–31, 42
Sri Lanka, 28, 119, 250n2
Stark, Rodney, 29
Starling, Marion Wilson, *The Slave Narrative*, 39
Steel, Flora Annie, *The Mistress of Men*, 145
Sufi (journal), 36, 77
Sufi Circle Canada, 238n10
Sufi Islamia Ruhaniat Society (now Ruhaniat International), 50, 51, 55, 57, 63, 84
Sufi Order International. *See* Inayati Order
Sufi Poet Series, 153–4, 155–6, 161, 245n25, 245n36
Sufism: activism and community work, 17, 223–4, 225–7; *adab* (etiquette), 38, 82–3, 84, 241n74; anti-Sufism, 32–3, 99, 108, 242n16; banned in Turkey, 98–9;

Sufism (*cont.*)
  Black Muslims and, 22–3, 34; counterculturalism and, 26–8, 34, 57–8; cultural appropriation and, 142–3; cyber-Sufism, 10; death anniversaries, 119; dervishes and mendicants, 224–5; diffusion through transcultural literary networks, 135; establishment in west, 33–4, 38; European colonial encounters with, 31–2, 236n13; globalization and, 34–7, 46; hiddenness, 208; Ismailis and, 162; Jewish Sufis, 56, 57, 238n21; legitimacy debate, 31, 44, 49, 53–4, 71, 85, 230–1; literary transmission to US, 135–7; *mazar* (shrine), 118–19; Neo-Sufism, 236n12; queer identities and, 157–8, 227–8; relationship with Islam, 24, 32–3, 211–13, *213*, 230; in South America, 36–7; traditionalism and, 37–8; in UK, 35–6, 237n15. *See also* music; Rumi; *sama*; *shab-i arus*; universalism and universal Sufism; *zikr*
Sufism, in Canada: approach to, 5–7, 10–17, 18–19, 40–3, 43–4, 229–30, 235n2, 237n21; collaboration between communities, 53, 55; comparison to US, 82; COVID-19 pandemic and, 9–10; as cultural experience and identity, 156–60; demographics, 231–2; early Black Muslims and, 18, 19–23, 38–9, 43, 47; early literary transmission, 143–5; *ghazal* poetry and, 145–7, 154; history and development, 38–40, 45–6, 46–7, 71, 77–8, 84–5; Husain on, 218–19; in Montreal, 80; music, 103–4; popular spirituality and, 25–31, 42; religious studies and, 11, 232–3; research methodology, 7–10; significance of *sama* and *zikr* in, 70–1, 127–30; social justice and, 157–8, 228–9. *See also* consumption; gender; *sama*; *shab-i arus*; *zikr*; specific communities

Sufi Soul (documentary), 104
Sufi Study Circle, 40, 48–9, 54, 85
Sufi Women Organization (SWO), 226
Suhrawardi, Abu Hafs Umar, 93–4
Sultanova, Razia, 193
Suzuki, D.T., 28
syncretism, 41

Tabandeh, Reza, 162
Talbot, Émile, J., 146
El-Tawhid Juma Circle (Unity Masjid), 227–8
teas, Rumi, 15, 30, 134, 170–2
Al-Thawri, Sufyan, 184
Theosophical Society, 26, 32, 135
Thibodeau, Serge Patrice, 40, 146
Thiessen, Joel, 25
Thompson, John, 145–6
3HO Society, 26–7, 66, 236n7
Threshold Society, 55, 86, 129, 205, 228, 242n1
Tijani, Ahmed, 241n74
Tijani Order, 34, 194, 225, 237n15, 241n74
time, 90–1
Tirgan Festival, 4, 161
Toronto, 46, 160–1
traditionalism, 37–8
Transcendentalism, 32, 135
transmission, 116
Tremoureux, Fattah, 59–60
Troyer, Anthony: *The Dabistàn* (with Shea), 144
Turkey, 98–9, 173, 194
turning. See *sama*
Al-Tusi, Muhammad, 90, 92, 94, 108, 116–17, 127
Tuzon, Selman, 100
Twain, Mark, 136
Tweed, Thomas, 9
Tweedie, Irina, 35, 62

United Kingdom, 35–6, 237n15
United States of America, 28, 34–5, 82, 84, 135–7
Unity Masjid (El-Tawhid Juma Circle), 227–8
Unity *Zikr*, 69, 80, 104, 105–6
universalism and universal Sufism: development in Canada, 84; Ghazi and Husain on, 211–13, *213*, 217–18, 221–2; Islam and, 211–13, *213*, 217–18, 231–2; queer identities and, 227–8; Rumi and, 109, 174, 177
Universal Peace, Dances of, 50, 52, 58, 202
Universal Worship Service, 33–4, 214–15, 218
universities, as public venues, 244n23

Vancouver, 46, 49
Vancouver Rumi Society (formerly Vancouver Turning Society), 57–71; about, 13, 57; activism and, 224; background and lineage, 11–12, 57–61, *60*, 62, 63–5, 66, 68, 69–70; inclusiveness of, 201; *sama* practice, 61, 63–5, 101–3, 104; self-description, 68–9; *shab-i arus* celebration, 119–20; Unity *Zikr*, 69, 80, 104, 105–6; universalism and, 71. *See also* Brozak, John; Buell, Majid; Burke, Raqib Brian; Ghazi, Seemi Bushra
Vandamme, Gregory, 237n19
Vaughan-Lee, Emmanuel, 35
Vaughan-Lee, Llewellyn, 35, 62, 237n16, 239n33
Vaziri, Mostafa, 246n57
Vivekananda, Swami, 26

wadud, amina, 195, 209, 210, 225
wajd (ecstasy), 94

Wajd: Songs of Separation (documentary), 162
Walad (Velad), Sultan, 95, 191
Watts, Alan, 28
Webb, Phyllis, 145
Weitbrecht, H.U., 100
Welch, Louise and William, 47
whirling. See *sama*
whiteness, 43, 143, 231, 250n10
Whitfield, Harvey Amani: *Biographical Dictionary of Enslaved Black People in the Maritimes*, 20–1
Whitman, Walt, 136
Wilkins-Laflamme, Sarah, 25
Winfrey, Oprah, 138
Winger, Robert Sean, 145–6
women. *See* gender
Women's Islamic Initiative in Spirituality and Equality, 68, 206
World Symposium on Humanity (Vancouver), 27
Wright, Donald, 20

Yagan, Murat, 11–12, 62, 66–7, 239n32
Yalçınkaya, Şerife, 126
Yeats, W.B., 145
Yoga Journal, 27
Yoga Vedanta (Vancouver bookstore), 58
Yusuf, Hamza, 38

Zan, Bänoo, 245n25
Zavieh Mystical Society, 14, 78, 151–3
Zenith Institute, 214
zikr (prayer of remembrance): about, 90, 94, 110; by AttarJafari and Rumi Canada, 107; by Nimatullahi Order, 77; at Nuit Blanche event, 3; Rumi teas and, 171; significance in Canadian Sufism, 127–8; Unity *Zikr*, 69, 80, 104, 105–6. See also *sama*
Zuleikha (story dancer), 149, 244n14